Kashrus Halacha
הלכות כשרות – אמרי דוד

Bitul & B'lios

Select applications of
הלכות תערובות **and** הלכות בשר בחלב
as they apply at home and in commercial food establishments

Written by:
Rabbi Dovid Cohen
Administrative Rabbinic Coordinator
cRc Kosher

The contents of this series were first presented as *shiurim* for the cRc *Kashrus* staff, and that is reflected in the title, אמרי דוד / *Dovid's spoken words*. It also hints at the dedicated commitment and endless energy which our parents – אברהם יהושע בדרך us מחנך being in invested – Ely מאיר דוד וסימא חיה and ,Cohen ומרים רחל דורות ישרים ומבורכים see and ברכה והצלחה have to continue they may ;ישראל סבא.

Thank you to ק"ק קהל חסידים, under the leadership of Rav Efraim A. Twerski, for providing a מקום תורה ותפילה where much of this *sefer* was written.

Also by this author, available at
www.kashrushalacha.com:

© 2024

Dovid Cohen
6646 N Sacramento Ave.
Chicago, Illinois 60645
dcohen@cRcKosher.org
773-491-0084

This *sefer* is dedicated לזכר נשמת

הרב שרגא פייוול ב"ר אליעזר הכהן כהן זצ"ל
Rav Feivel Cohen zt"l

כ"ו חשון תשפ"ג

מחבר ספרי בדי השולחן על
הלכות נדה, טבילה, בשר בחלב, תערובות, אבילות,
צדקה, השבת אבידה, נדרים ושבועות

He asked that no דברי הספד be written or spoken about him. Therefore, we will only cite from the הסכמה that Rav Hutner זצ"ל wrote for him in תשכ"ז/1967, which was printed in early editions of בדי השולחן:

הלא אלף נכנסים למקרא ואחד יוצא להוראה. ועליך אני מעיד כי גם בשעה שנכנסת בין האלף, כבר היית ה"אחד", אשר כל רואיך הכירוך כי לגדלות של הוראה נוצרת.

ובשעה שזכיתי לראותך יוצא להוראה, ידעתי ברורות, כי כבושים גדולים במלחמתה של תורה נכונים לך, וברבות השנים תרבה מקנתך באוצרות תורה בש"ס ופוסקים, חריפות ובקיאות, ורבים יתבשמו מריח תורתך.

In addition to learning from his ספרים, this author was privileged to learn under his tutelage, and that relationship was built on the lifetime friendship of דבר ה' זו הלכה that he shared with my father. This dedication is a small expression of gratitude for the direction and knowledge that he shared.

תהא נשמתו צרורה בצרור החיים

TABLE OF CONTENTS

BOOK ONE

Introduction 1
    Scope ◆ Concepts

Part A
סימן פ"ז

1. דבר המעמיד 5
   Exceptions ◆ Examples ◆ Kashering afterwards ◆ חמץ שעבר עליו הפסח
   Bishul akum and kitnios ◆ Whey ◆ Three ha'amados ◆ Tevillas keilim

2. זה וזה גורם 13
   Principle ◆ Flavors ◆ Different contributions ◆ פסח ◆ יש בזה כדי לחמץ
   Sherry casks and blenders ◆ Simultaneous or consecutive ◆ Emulsifiers

Part B
סימן צ"ב

3. חתיכה נעשית נבילה 31
   Basis Halacha: יבש and לח ◆ שאר איסורים and בשר בחלב
       Safek issur / steam system ◆ ידיעת התערובת
   Exceptions: היתר ◆ Chametz ◆ חלב סתם / איסור דרבנן ◆ Not batel b'shishim
       כלים ◆ סופו להתפשט ◆ Cold

4. טיפת חלב / Steam Systems 51
   Introduction: Cooking with steam ◆ Questions
   B'lios: Halacha ◆ Observable phenomena ◆ 10% rule
       Preventing cross-contamination
   Pegimah: Davar hapogem ◆ Chavos Da'as ◆ Reversibility
       Nosein ta'am lifgam ◆ Three approaches ◆ Pegimah candidates

5. אש שורף דבר מועט 71
   Stovetop and oven
   Freeze Dryer: Operations ◆ Hashgachah ◆ Segregation

6. זיעה 77
   Basic halacha ◆ Stovetop ◆ Oven ◆ Microwave oven
   Hookah and e-cigarettes ◆ זיעה בעלמא ◆ Media

7. אין הבלוע יוצא מכלי לכלי בלא רוטב 85
   כלי לכלי and אוכל לאוכל ◆ Industrial examples Stovetop grates ◆ Induction cooktop

Part C
סימנים צ"ג-צ"ד

8 Pot Cover 97

9 Dripping 99
    Basic halachos ◆ Steam vacuuming

10 Ta'am Travelling and Transferring 103
    חם מקצתו חם כולו ◆ Kovush ◆ Distance ◆ Connections ◆ Speed

Part D
סימנים צ"ה-צ"ז

11 נ"ט בר נ"ט 115
    Basic halachos ◆ Certified items ◆ "DE" foods ◆ Keurig ◆ Steam table

12 Meat and Fish 127
    Danger ◆ Separation ◆ Bitul ◆ B'lios

13 Washing Dishes 137
    General halachos: נ"ט בר נ"ט ◆ Pegimah
    Washing dishes in one sink: עירוי כלי ראשון ◆ נ"ט בר נ"ט ◆
      Proper practice ◆ Pesach and non-kosher
    Residential dishwasher: Operations ◆ Considerations
      Kashering ◆ Double drawer dishwasher
    Commercial dishwasher: Operations ◆ Meat and dairy
      Kashering ◆ Dish sanitizer

14 דבר חריף 167
    Gemaros ◆ Other halachos ◆ What is charif ◆ Vegetable names

15 דוחקא דסכינא 179
    Levels of absorption ◆ Knives nowadays ◆ Pressing
    Multiple steps / אבן העוזר ◆ Six hours

16 מחליא ליה לשבח 199
    How it operates ◆ Halacha / בית מאיר ◆ Vinegar ◆ מחליא for foods
    Knife of unknown status ◆ Wine and whisky ◆ Common examples

17 Dairy Bread 217
    Basics ◆ Kashering ◆ Bitul ◆ Which foods ◆ כעין תורא ◆ Timing

Part E
סימן צ"ח

18 Tasting 233
    טעימת קפילא ◆ טעימת ישראל ◆ Pesach production
    What is "tasting" ◆ Fast days ◆ 6 hours

19 טעימת ספק איסור 243
    Tasting issur ◆ Tasting safek issur ◆ Boiler condensate
    Toothpaste and mouthwash ◆ e-Cigarette juice

20 Bitul Calculations 253
    Volume vs. weight ◆ How much issur is there
    Estimations ◆ Modern pots ◆ Formulas

21 מין במינו בתר שמא או בתר טעמא /
Bourbon from a Jewish Owned Company 269
בתר שמא או בתר טעמא ◆ חמץ שעבר עליו הפסח
Bourbon ◆ Distilled alcohol (מנחת ברוך)

22 סלק את מינו ואת שאינו מינו רבה עליו ומבטלו 275

23 ספק חסרון ידיעה 279

24 אפשר להסירו 283
דאורייתא או דרבנן? ◆ Fat and fat ◆ Orange juice
Enriched rice for Pesach ◆ Hopelessly lost

25 B'lios Passing Through Eggshell 293

26 עבידא לטעמא 297
Basic halachos ◆ Kitnios ◆ זה וזה גורם ◆ מלח הבלוע מדם

BOOK TWO

Part F
סימנים צ"ט-ק"ב

27 Bone Products 309
Gelatin ◆ Glucosamine ◆ Calcium ◆ In a mixture ◆ Bone char ◆ Other halachos

28 אין מבטלין איסור לכתחלה 317
Which foods ◆ Non-food issues ◆ Which people ◆ אין כוונתו לבטל

29 כלי העשוי להשתמש בשפע 327
Rashba ◆ Logic ◆ First source ◆ פגם ◆ Second source ◆ Halacha ◆ Questions

30 בריה 339
מלקות ◆ Four criteria ◆ Other details ◆ Berachos

31 חתיכה הראויה להתכבד 347
Basic halachos ◆ Defining ראויה להתכבד ◆ Raw meat ◆ Blends

32 Comparing Fish Fillets 357
Background ◆ Fish fillets ◆ Skin tags

33 דבר שיש לו מתירין 361
Basics ◆ מין במינו ◆ Chodosh malt ◆ ספק ספיקא
Yoshon flour milling and barley pearling ◆ תרי משהו
Meat without melichah

34 ספק איסור משהו 377
נתבקעו ◆ Questions ◆ Infant rice cereal

35 חזותא 385
Sources and opinions ◆ Other details

36 Bitul of Keilim 391
Non-automatic heter ◆ Kashering ◆ Tevillas keilim

Part G
סימנים ק"ג-ק"ד

37 נותן טעם לפגם 405
    Rashba and Ran ◆ Details and examples

38 הגדיל האיסור מדתו 411
    Nutramigen ◆ Carmine manufacturer

39 Not לפגם and Not לשבח 419
    Bee legs ◆ אין בו טעם כלל ◆ Applications

40 בשר פוגם את השמן 427

41 אינו בן יומו 429
    General halacha ◆ Calculation ◆ Not effective b'dieved ◆ Rely on l'chatchilah

42 סתם כלים אינם בני יומן 437
    Basic halacha ◆ Kashering ◆ Pesach ◆ Factories

43 Coatings 443
    Pots and pans ◆ Pre-seasoned cast iron pans
    Styrofoam cups ◆ Fruits and vegetables ◆ Medicine

44 עכבר 457

45 Mitzvah Items 459

46 Bugs are נותן טעם לפגם 461
    בריה ◆ Cricket powder ◆ נפשו של אדם קצה מהם

Part H
סימן ק"ה

47 B'liah Without Heat 471

48 כבוש 473
    Standard kovush ◆ Fast kovush

49 יד סולדת בו 481
    Heat vs. temperature ◆ Shiurim from Poskim

50 כלי ראשון וכלי שני 491
    Basic halacha ◆ Exceptions ◆ דפנות מקררות ◆ עירוי כלי ראשון
    Tunnel pasteurizer and cooling tunnel

51 דבר גוש 501
    What ◆ Mixture ◆ Bishul ◆ Kashering

52 תתאה גבר 505
    Basics ◆ Tumbler ◆ Heat sealer ◆ Shrink tunnel

53 ניצוק חיבור 513

54 מלח 519
    מלח הבלוע מדם ◆ מליח כרותח

Part I
סימנים ק"ו-ק"ט

55 Surface Propagations 525
  Inherent status: נתפטמה כל ימיה ◆ יוצא ◆ גידולים
  Separation: חנ"נ ◆ לח בלח ◆ No ta'am left ◆ אפשר לסוחטו

56 Keilim Used for Safek Issur 537

57 ריחא 541
  Different types of vapor ◆ ריחא details ◆ Large vs. small oven

58 Meat and Milk Cooking Side by Side 549

59 מרדה 555

60 Cigtrus and Air Up 557
  Vapors ◆ Cigtrus ◆ Suitability for hashgachah ◆ Air Up water bottle

61 יבש ביבש 563
  ביטול ברוב ◆ Pesach ◆ B'lios

Part J
סימן ק"י

62 דבר שבמנין 573
  What qualifies ◆ Meat ◆ Sefer Torah

63 כל קבוע, כל דפריש 581
  כל דפריש ◆ קבוע דרבנן ◆ קבוע דאורייתא ◆ What is considered פריש ◆ Pesach

64 Kashrus Scandals 593
  Assumptions ◆ Issues ◆ Raw meat in the store
  Prepared food in the store ◆ Food taken home ◆ Kashering

65 נתגלגל 603

66 Papain 605
  Papaya ◆ Papain ◆ Peel ◆ Papaya revisited ◆ Eggplant plus

Epilogue 615

Index 617

הסכמות printed on the coming pages
were written for the first volume of this series

Rabbi Alfred Cohen
5 Fox Lane
Spring Valley, N.Y. 10977

Study: 914-425-5540

אלול תשע"ז

On the occasion of our son, Dovid,
publishing a *sefer* about *Pas Yisrael* and *Bishul Yisrael*:

One of the intriguing questions which arise in Jewish thought is the *beracha shehecheyanu*—what are the circumstances which trigger the requirement to recite this *beracha*, and what is its essential message. In *Gemara Sukkah* 46a, *Tosafot* speculate as to the criteria for recitation of this beracha: מאי שנא דיש מצות שתקינו לברך שהחיינו ויש מצות שלא תקינו-- how come the Rabbis instituted saying *shehecheyanu* for the performance of some *mitzvot*, but not for others? For example, upon construction of a *sukkah*, the *Gemara* says one recites *shehecheyanu*, but not for making *tefillin*; for a *pidyon haben*, the father recites *shehecheyanu*, why not for a *bris*?

Over the centuries, our Rabbis have continued to probe this issue, trying to determine clear guidelines for when to thank *Hashem* for an exceptional experience, but there is no consensus on the matter. Thus, the *Rema* writes that the first time someone performs a *mitzvah*, he/she should make this *beracha*; nevertheless, Rav Ovadia Yosef rules that the first time a woman lights candles for *Shabbos* she should not recite *shehecheyanu*. There is much discussion about reciting *shehecheyanu* at *Kiddush* on the second night of *Rosh Hashanah*, or upon blowing *shofar* the second day of *Rosh Hashanah*.

But while there is lack of consensus about the occasions requiring *shehecheyanu*, there is no discussion whatsoever about the nature of the *beracha* – it is universally recognized as the expression of gratitude by a human being to the *Ribono Shel Olam* for the goodness He has bestowed in letting us experience a singular event.

It is with this feeling of overwhelming gratitude to *Hashem* that your mother and I regard the auspicious occasion of your publishing a *sefer* about *Pas Yisrael* and *Bishul Yisrael*. No doubt, it will be of great help in disseminating knowledge of these *halachot* and lead to enhanced observance of several *mitzvot*. We are overjoyed at your accomplishment, not just of this undertaking, but even more so that you have dedicated your life to learning *Torah*, becoming a *talmid chacham*, and spreading *Torah* knowledge. We know that in writing this *sefer* you have taken exceptional care to fully understand not only all the technicalities of the halacha, but also all the factual realities which determine how the halacha is to be applied. We feel blessed that we have been able to witness and participate in your growth as a *ben Torah* and as an exemplary human being. Truly, the emotion of gratitude *shehecheyanu vekiyimanu vehigiyanu* fills out hearts. This occasion calls for us to be aware how fortunate we are in having such a son and in being able to witness his achievements.

As you launch this labor of love to which you have devoted so much time and effort, we ask *Hashem* to reward your efforts with much *beracha*. Our particular *beracha* to you can best be expressed in the well-known incident recorded in *Gemara Taanis* 5b:

A wayfarer once came to rest in the course of his wandering. Tired, hungry, thirsty, he laid his weary body down under a tree; sitting in its welcome shade, he ate from its delicious fruits and drank water from the stream at its foot. As he arose, refreshed, he wanted to 'thank' the tree for the benefits it had afforded him.

"*Ilan ilan, bema avarechecha...*"

O, tree, he said, how can I bless you?

Should I wish for you to have sweet fruits – behold, your fruits are already sweet.

If I were to say, let your shade be pleasant – behold, your shade is already pleasant.

Were I to say, let there be water flowing beneath you – indeed, the water is already flowing.

Rather, אלא יהי רצון שכל נטיעות שנוטעין ממך יהיו כמוך

May all the plantings that are planted from you be like you!

Our *beracha* to you, dear son, is that we wish *Hashem* will give you and your dear wife the opportunity to continue in all the good things that you do, and may your precious children continue in the noble path you have set. And may we have the *zechut* to see it.

CHICAGO RABBINICAL COUNCIL

2701 W. Howard Street · Chicago, IL 60645-1303 · (773) 465-3900
www.crcweb.org   Fax · (773) 465-6632

בס"ד

19 Iyar 5777

It is my privilege to recommend this groundbreaking volume on the halachos of kashrus authored by Rabbi Dovid Cohen א"שליט, our illustrious colleague at the Chicago Rabbinical Council. Rabbi Cohen, who is renowned as an expert in areas of Kashrus and Practical Halacha, has performed a tremendous service to the Jewish community by compiling his voluminous notes on contemporary halakhic issues in kashrus for publication. A master teacher, his ability to present דבר דבור על אפניו is nonpareil.

אשר תשים לפניהם - אמר לו הקדוש ברוך הוא למשה לא תעלה על דעתך לומר אשנה להם הפרק וההלכה ב' או ג' פעמים עד שתהא סדורה בפיהם כמשנתה, ואיני מטריח עצמי להבינם טעמי הדבר ופירושו, לכך נאמר אשר תשים לפניהם, כשלחן הערוך ומוכן לאכול לפני האדם (רש"י שמות כא:א)

Rabbi Cohen's combination of analytical depth and breathtaking clarity enables him to "set the table" and convey complicated ideas and nuanced concepts in a digestible and satisfying fashion. He has a rare ability to explain kashrus topics in terms of both the basic building blocks as well as the advanced discussions among the Rishonim, Acharonim and Poskim that emerge from the core ideas.

Very often in halacha, there is a tendency to focus upon the minutiae of the law without a sufficient appreciation of the original sources, concepts and underpinnings. By unraveling basic principles and rigorously examining their contemporary applications, Rabbi Cohen carefully and adroitly guides the reader into the realm of halacha l'ma'aseh when it comes to modern day kashrus issues, whether in terms of kashering retorts, tithing Israeli produce with a perutah chamurah, using modern technology to create bishul yisroel, understanding why shellac may be kosher but not carmine, establishing parameters for greenhouses to grow shemita produce, or determining when it is or is not permissible to puree fruits and vegetables to remove possible bugs.

This is a book that can be appreciated on many levels. Those who are looking to gain an understanding of contemporary kashrus practices will appreciate Rabbi Cohen's lucid and accessible style, and his numerous illustrations and diagrams. At the same time, even accomplished rabbinic scholars will be able to elevate their understanding of the subject matter through the enormous scholarship, insight and practical knowledge that Rabbi Cohen brings to each chapter.

Perhaps most significantly, this book is also a primer in יראת שמים. In each page of this book, the author's humility and his reverence for Hashem and His Torah shine through inspirationally and unmistakably. This is a book that teaches not only practical halacha, but also a proper halakhic and hashkafic perspective towards life. The Mesilas Yesharim (Chapter 11) writes about how avoidance of non-kosher must be viewed as equivalent to the avoidance of the consumption of actual poison. This volume, like its author, is permeated with a sacred desire to do what is right in the eyes of Hashem in terms of what we eat, how we prepare our food, and how to ensure, through proper kashrus standards, that we furnish impeccably kosher food to our families and our communities.

With Torah blessings,

Yona Reiss
Rabbi Yona Reiss, Av Beth Din

President
RABBI DR. ZVI ENGEL
Vice-Presidents
RABBI ELISHA PRERO
RABBI SHAANAN GELMAN

Secretary
RABBI WES KALMAR
Treasurer
RABBI YOSEF POSNER
Executive Director
RABBI LEVI MOSTOFSKY

Rosh Beth Din
RABBI GEDALIA DOV SCHWARTZ א"שליט
Av Beth Din
RABBI YONA REISS א"שליט
Kashruth Administrator
RABBI SHOLEM FISHBANE

בס"ד

Rabbi Ephraim Friedman
6521 North Sacramento Avenue
Chicago, Illinois 60645

ב' אלול תשפ"ג

הנה ידידנו הרב דוד בן כהן שליט"א הודיעני שאת אחת שוב אשר אינה שלום בית ויש לו ידיעות רחבות בעניני גלוח, והגדיל לאת שליחי לשרות הגאולים וגם המצאה. וראיתי אצלו בקי נפלא בין אופני הגילוח לאחת הסכנה של ספרים שנתנו ע"י תלמידי חכמים אוחזקים, ובכן ע"י הרי לידינו יחד אם גדרים הנכונים בתוך הספר הנוכחי, ופועל י שהמחבר שליט"א הצליח הרבה מאות לברר העניני גלוח, הן ע"י לאסף וליבור סוגיות וגם ודברי הפוסקים, הן ע"י בירור המציאות בעצת לברר הדין.

לכן הנני אומרים שיבנה לעולם הדרוש לאור גדולה ולהאמשיך לעזור להרבים שלא יכשל פתע לפאוחז בע"י לעבור כל אג אנינן לבה, נקי שיהי אלא יכן לבורים ותעיירים לעוץ ולהבין דברי הגמרא הקדושה ולעבת להורות הלכה למעשה, כי ד' יתן חכמה מפיו דעת ותבונה.

ולקיים דברינו בעים לכתוב,
אפרים פרידמן

תרה ג׳ כסלו

רב יעקב ודוד הי"ו
ישיבת רבינו יצחק אלחנן

מכתב ברכה

עברתי על כמה פרקים מספרו של ידידי-יקירי הר"ר דוד כהן, שיחי׳, ממנהלי מחלקת הכשרות של ועד הרבנים דשיקאגו, על עניני בשול עכו"ס ופת עכו"ס, וראיתי שהדברים נכתבו בטוטו"ד, בבהירות ובסגנון שכזה שהכל יכולים להבין את כל הענינים בעומקם, ומוחזקני לו בר' דוד, שיחי׳, שאינו מוציא מתחת ידו דבר שאינו מתוקן, ואברכהו שימלא ספרו זה חן בעיני הקוראים, ותרבה הדעת בישראל, ויזכה המחבר להוציא עוד ספרים בהלכה.

בכבוד,

צבי שכטר

ב"ה

אבא יקר, רציתי לומר לך תודה על כל מה שאתה
עושה בשבילי. יש הרבה דברים שלא הצלחתי
להגיד לך בעל פה, ולכן החלטתי
לכתוב לך את זה במכתב. תודה ואני
מעריך אותך מאוד שתמיד, גם אחרי
יום ארוך,
אתה מוצא זמן לשחק איתי במשחק
הכדורגל שלנו. אתה איש מצחיק
ויש לך לב טוב וכל הזמן אתה רוצה
לשמח אותי. תודה רבה על הכל.
אוהב אותך המון המון ותמיד,
שיהיה לך רק בטוב,
מ- אורי שלך

RABBI MOSHE HEINEMANN
6109 Gist Avenue
Baltimore, MD 21215
Tel. (410) 358-9828
Fax. (410) 358-9838

משה היינעמאן
אב"ד ק"ק אגודת ישראל
באלטימאר
טל. (410) 764-7778
פקס (410) 764-8878

בס"ד

כבוד ידידי הרב החשוב מזה"ר ונעלה הרב ר' דוד כהן שליט"א.

ראיתי קטעים מספרו הבהיר "אמרי דוד" על הלכות פת וכישולי עכו"ם, ששלח לי כבודו
והנני רואה את קדושתו הרחבה ופירות חכמתו של הרב המחבר וידיעותיו בש"ס ומפרשיו
ודברי רבותינו הראשונים והאחרונים, ואסף הכל בסידור נכון ובהבנה עמוקה.
אני מכיר אישית את הרב המחבר שליט"א שהוא תלמיד חכם גדול ובקי בפוסקים וגם
בהלכה למעשה, ואמרו חז"ל בסוף פ"ק דקידושין תלמוד גדול שהתלמוד מביא לידי
מעשה.

לכן דבר טוב עשה המחבר בעמלו, להפיץ תעניתיו חוצה, ויהי רצון מלפני אבינו שבשמים
שיתקבל ספרו זה בין הלומדים, ובין הדרושים לעצות רצונו יתברך איך לנהוג למעשה, ויהי'
בו ברכה.

ובזה הנני חותם לכבוד המחבר ולכבוד תורתו בברכת כט"ס בחמישי בשבת לסדר
ויקהב לנו וישמענו אותה, שלשה ועשרים יום לחדש אלול, שנת חמשת אלפים ושבע מאות וששים
ושבע לבריאת עולם.

משה בהרה"ר ברוך גד-ליב ז"ל לומשפחת היינעמאן החונה פעה"ק באלטימאר

בס"ד

יהושע העשיל אייכענשטיין

בהרה"צ מוהרר"א זצ"ל

מזידיטשוב ~ שיקאגו

Rabbi Yehoshua H. Eichenstein
6342 N. Troy St.
Chicago, IL 60659
(773) 973-5161

בעזהשי"ת

ימי ענפי יו"כ שנת תשע"ח

יום שמחה הוא לנו לראות פרי עמלו הכתבים שנכתבו בלשון ברור וצח שבו נתלבנו הלכות הנחוצות ביו"ד הלכות פת ובישול ע"י קרבינו וידידינו, מחשובי קהילנו ומחשובי רבני עיר שיקגו, הלן בעומקו של הלכה למעשה, מו"צ בבי"ד cRc, חריף ובקי, הרה"ג רבי דוד כהן שליט"א, וראיתי להעתיר כאן דבר בעיתו ובמקומו את דברי פוסק הדור הגאון רבי שלמה זלמן אויערבאך זצוק"ל, הובא בספר הליכות שלמה הלכות עשי"ת, וז"ל שם:

וכאן המקום להעתיק רשימת חכ"א שליט"א העוסק בעייני הכשרות בארה"ב, והיא תוכן שיחתו של רבמ בביקור הנ"ל אצלו בחדשי חייו האחרונים, וז"ל: הצעתי לפני הגאון זצוק"ל שאלות וספיקות רבים בנוגע לעייני בישול עכו"ם, ולאחר שראה שאיני חותר אחר קולא דקא הסכים לענות לשאלותי באופן כללי, וכה היו דבריו אלי, שנאמרו בכאב לב גדול ובהתרגשות עצומה:

אומר לך שיטתי בכללות ענין בישולי עכו"ם בזמננו. הנה בדורותינו נתרבו נשואי התערובת ר"ל, בפרט בארה"ב, באופן שלא היה מעולם בכלל ישראל, ובודאי שומה עלינו לחתור ולפשפש איכה נהייתה הרעה הגדולה הזאת. אכן כבר גילו לנו חכמינו ז"ל להדיא שורש הדבר, ואמרו שהגורם לנשואין עם גויים ר"ל הוא אכילת פיתם וייננם, כמבואר בגמ' ע"ז ל"ה ע"ב וטוש"ע סי' קי"ג, והנה תחת שישמרו בכל עוז גזירות חז"ל הללו הורגלו בדורותינו לחתור ולחפש אחר כל מיני קולות בזה, אשר הם ודאי נגד רצון חז"ל, וגברה המכשלה כאשר נמשכו איזה מן המורים במדינות חו"ל להקל קולות גדולות ביותר. סוף דבר אין אנו נזהרים לדאבוננו כראוי באלו העניינים, וראיה ברורה לזה הוא עצם המצב המחריד וה"טראגעדיע" הלזו של נשואי התערובת, שהורו לנו חז"ל בבירור שהגורם לזה הוא בישולי עכו"ם ויין נסך כנ"ל.

והנה בכל פזורות ישראל קמו אנשים נכבדים יראי ד' ורבים בפעולות גדולות ועצומות למניעת נשואי תערובת, אבל עדיין לא נושענו מן הצרה הגדולה הזאת, ויש לדעת כי הסיבה לכך היא כי בו בזמן שמתנמצאים להציל הנפשות מלהטמע בין הגויים ר"ל, עדיין ממשיכים לאחוז בכל אותן קולות שהן היפך הגמור מרצון חז"ל בתקנותיהם.

ולכן העצה היחידה לכך היא לילך מן הקצה אל הקצה, ולהחמיר עד מקום שידינו מגעת, ואע"פ שאנו בני אשכנז יוצאים ביד רמ"א ואיננו חזים מהוראותיו, עכ"ז בדאית היא הצלת ישראל שנדחוק בשבילה בכל האפשר במה שהקיל הרמ"א, ונחמיר בכל ענייני בישול עכו"ם כמעט כשיטת הב"י.

ובאמת אם יתן אחיינו בני ישראל אל לבם ויבינו גודל הסכנה שיש בהקולות הללו, יתאמצו להעמיד ממונים ומשגיחים בכל מפעל ומפעל, שהיא התקנה הטובה ביותר, ואם התקנה הזאת קשה, יש באפשרי יעשו עכ"פ במדת האפשר.

וסיים הגאון זצוק"ל ואמר לי, אשריכם אם תצליחו לקיים העצה והגדרים הנכונים ברוח כוונתם האמיתית של חז"ל, ואם תמנעו בישולי עכו"ם בין אחב"י היראים והחרדים לדבר ד', תציילו עי"ז את זרע ישראל הרחוקים משמירת התורה מלהטמע בין הגויים רח"ל, וגדול יהיה שכרכם מן השמים, ע"כ רשימת הדברים הנ"ל.

וברכתינו הוא שיצליח מאוד בכל מקצועות התורה אשר תפנה להאיר באור תורתנו לזכות ולהרבים ללמוד וללמד לשמור ולעשות ושלא יצא תקלה מתחת ידינו בעניני כשרות, ונזכה לסייעתא דשמיא ולראות בישועתם של ישראל ובביאת גו"צ בב"א.

כ"ד ידידו המוקירו כערכו הרם
יהושע העשיל אייכענשטיין
בהרה"ג אב"ד דק"ק מגדיל דוד שיקאגו

Rabbi Shmuel Fuerst
6100 North Drake Avenue
Chicago, Illinois 60659
(773) 539-4241
Fax (773) 539-1208

בס"ד

הרב שמואל פירסט
דיין ומו"ץ אגודת ישראל
שיקאגא, אילינאי

אודות מכונת גילוח

הנה ידידי הבה"ח הרב דוד כהן שליט"א רצה להדפיס
ספר על הלכת גילוח והיה רצונו ורצוני, והנה ידוע דתחודר
הוא לא גרוע והבה רצוני שרות, ודוח אשר עמק
המשפט איש הגדולים דפחה על עיוני הבעיא יחדש הלכ'
והפוסקים. וגם זה הם חזון המוגר בני אדם יעיין ועיון.
ויה' רצון שאקה"ק הפר הגדולות ישא"ל לעשא ברכה
וארכת כקוב שמים על ידו ויבנה להגדיל עורת ולהבדירה
ולקדשה ע"פ אמת.

הכלום לכבוד הגורה לומדי
שמואל פירסט

Part F

סימנים צ"ט-ק"ב

- Chapter 27 ....Bone Products
- Chapter 28 ....אין מבטלין איסור לכתחלה
- Chapter 29 ....כלי העשוי להשתמש בשפע
- Chapter 30 ....בריה
- Chapter 31 ....חתיכה הראויה להתכבד
- Chapter 32 ....Comparing Fish Fillets
- Chapter 33 ....דבר שיש לו מתירין
- Chapter 34 ....ספק איסור משהו
- Chapter 35 ....חזותא
- Chapter 36 ....Bitul of Utensils

Chapter 27

Bone Products

שולחן ערוך סימן צ"ט סעיף א
חתיכת נבלה שיש בה בשר ועצמות שנפלה לקדירת היתר עצמות האיסור מצטרפים עם ההיתר לבטל האיסור, ואצ"ל שעצמות ההיתר מצטרפין עם ההיתר, אבל המוח שבעצמות איסור מצטרף עם האיסור, וגוף הקדירה אינה מצטרפת לא עם האיסור ולא עם ההיתר. הגה: ויש מחמירים שלא לצרף עצמות האיסור עם ההיתר לבטל ובמקום הפסד יש לסמוך אמקילין ומתירין כי כן עיקר.

The current halacha[1] teaches that when calculating whether non-kosher meat is *batel b'shishim*, one is only required to consider the meat/muscle portion and there is no need to be *mevatel* the bones that are in the meat. In this chapter, we will see a *Gemara* that directly speaks to this point, consider several applications, and then note some other *kashrus*-related halachos that relate to bones.

Gelatin

There is a *korban* (איל נזיר) where one part of it (the זרוע) can only be eaten by *kohanim*, while the rest is permitted to all Jews. The *Torah*[2] describes how the entire animal is cooked together, and the *Gemara*[3] says that this indicates that the animal is so large that any *ta'am* coming from the זרוע [which cannot be eaten by non-*kohanim*] is *batel* in the rest of the animal [which can be eaten by non-*kohanim*]. Not only that, but the ratio of "animal" to זרוע will teach us how much is generally required when some forbidden food gets cooked with kosher food. What is that ratio? The *Gemara* brings one opinion that it is a 60:1 ratio, because the entire זרוע exudes forbidden *ta'am* which must become nullified, and another opinion that it is a 100:1 ratio, because only the meat/muscle portion of the זרוע

---

[1] *Shulchan Aruch* 99:1.
[2] *Bamidbar* 7:19.
[3] *Gemara, Chullin* 98b.

Bone Products

must become *batel*, but not the bones. Thus, the *machlokes* whether bones are forbidden translates into a *machlokes* whether *bitul* requires 100:1 (bones are permitted) or 60:1 (bones are forbidden).

Tur cites some *Rishonim* who say that since the halacha is well known that a 60:1 ratio (i.e., *bitul b'shishim*) is enough to dilute *issur*, it follows that *ta'am* coming from the bones of forbidden animals must also be *assur*. But other *Rishonim* disagree, and their opinion is the one cited in our halacha. *Shach* and *Beis Yosef* offer different suggestions of what this lenient opinion holds. *Shach*[4] says, based on *Ran*,[5] that the bones that the *Gemara* was discussing were <u>soft</u> bones (e.g., cartilage) and those, in fact, are forbidden, but standard <u>hard</u> bones are permitted. *Beis Yosef*[6] says that although the *Gemara* seems to say that the 60:1 ratio is derived from the aforementioned *posuk*, that is not the true source. Rather, the 60:1 ratio is something which *Chazal* calculated on their own, and they found an allusion to that concept (אסמכתא) in the *posuk*. Thus, although the *Gemara* says that the 60:1 rule is intertwined with bones being forbidden, those two halachos are not truly connected. Accordingly, it is possible to rule that the *ta'am* coming from bones is permitted, and simultaneously say that *bitul b'shishim* suffices.

Both explanations for the lenient opinion regarding bones are consistent with *Toras Kohanim*[7] which says that when the *Torah* forbids eating the בשר of non-kosher food (מבשרם לא תאכלו), it teaches that only בשר/meat is forbidden, but bones, hooves, etc. of non-kosher species are permitted.

Turning to *Rambam*, we see two relevant points. Firstly, *Rambam*[8] appears to have understood the *Gemara* in the same manner as noted above from *Beis Yosef*, because he says that איל נזיר is just an אסמכתא (ומנין סמכו חכמים על שיעור ששים...). Secondly, when *Rambam*[9] cites *Toras Kohanim*, he records that although one is not held liable for eating bones, etc., it is nonetheless forbidden (אף על פי שהוא אסור הרי זה פטור). The meaning of this second *Rambam* was one of the main points of contention in a halachic

---

[4] *Shach* 99:1.
[5] *Ran*, *Chullin* 35a.
[6] *Beis Yosef* to 99:1, based on *Rash*, *Terumos* 5:9.
[7] *Toras Kohanim* to *Vayikra* 11:8.
[8] *Rambam*, *Hil. Ma'acholos Assuros* 15:21.
[9] *Rambam*, ibid. 4:18.

dispute in the middle of the 1900s regarding the kosher status of gelatin made from the bones of animals which did not have שחיטה.[10]

Achiezer[11] said that *Rambam* is referring to <u>soft</u> bones (as per *Ran/Shach*), but standard hard bones are completely permitted. Therefore, *Achiezer* ruled that gelatin made from hard bones (or from beef hides), which have no meat attached to them, are permitted even if the animals did not have שחיטה. [Nowadays, the vast majority of gelatin is made from pigskins which the *Gemara* and *Rambam*[12] specifically note as being forbidden just like meat. Thus, *Achiezer's* position, which is based on the permissibility (and inedibility) of bones, does not apply].

Many *Poskim* disagreed, and there were two main reasons for their strict positions. Rav Aharon Kotler[13] said that the permissibility of bones is based on their being inedible, but if something is done to convert the bone into something that can be eaten or can be used as a food ingredient, then it "reverts" to its natural state of being forbidden. That is exactly what happens when gelatin is created. Gelatin is naturally found in bones, and the processing done to the bones essentially strips away all other parts of the bone, leaving behind just the gelatin.[14] Once those other parts are removed, the gelatin is now a usable food ingredient; therefore, according to Rav Kotler, it is forbidden just like an edible piece of meat.

Iggeros Moshe[15] understands *Rambam* as referring to all bones (hard and soft) and saying that although bones are permitted *mid'oraisah* (as per

---

[10] The points noted below are just one element of the discussion regarding the kosher status of gelatin made from animal bones.
[11] *Achiezer* 3:33:5.
   The *teshuvah* (#16) printed as an addendum to *Minchas Yaakov* (*Toras Chattas*) also rules that <u>hard</u> bones (or shells) are permitted. *Shulchan Aruch* 87:7 says that it is *assur mid'rabannan* to eat the following cooked with milk: עור גידים ועצמות ועיקרי קרנים וטלפים הרכים; *Pri Megadim* SD 87:22 says that the simple reading of this halacha is that the word "הרכים" (*soft*) only qualifies the final item in that list (טלפים), but <u>all</u> עצמות (bones) are forbidden. Accordingly, he is inclined to say that hard bones would be forbidden, and notes that *Minchas Yaakov* would clearly understand that הרכים refers to all the items listed previously. He also references his comments in SD 99:1, where he appears to accept *Minchas Yaakov's* conclusion.
[12] *Mishnah*, *Chullin* 122a, codified in *Rambam*, ibid. 4:21.
[13] *Mishnas Rav Aharon* 1:17.
[14] Rav Yechezkel Abramsky (in the beginning of his *teshuvah* printed as an introduction to Volume 4 of *Tzitz Eliezer*) says that since the process <u>isolates</u> the gelatin found in the bones rather than <u>converting</u> the bones into gelatin, there is no possibility of permitting gelatin based on the lenient opinions regarding *nishtaneh*, since that only applies when *issur* is changed into something different.
[15] *Iggeros Moshe* YD 2:27 (end).

Toras Kohanim), they are forbidden *mid'rabannan*. Therefore, gelatin made from animal bones is also *assur mid'rabannan*.

As noted, nowadays most gelatin is made from pigskins which all agree are *assur mid'oraisah*.

Glucosamine

We have seen that cartilage and soft bones are forbidden, and that is the reason why glucosamine and chondroitin are not considered kosher. These medicinal items, used to treat arthritis, are typically sourced from shark cartilage or the soft shells of crabs, lobsters, or shrimp, which are considered edible parts of non-kosher fish and are therefore forbidden. [The same is true of shellfish broth made from these sources].

Clearly, no reputable *hashgachah* will certify glucosamine made from shark cartilage, etc., but it is possible to purchase kosher glucosamine produced synthetically via fermentation. It also appears that a person can obtain glucosamine at home by creating bone broth – using kosher beef bones – which seems to be a good source of natural glucosamine.

Calcium

We have seen that it is generally accepted that gelatin produced from the bones of animals which did not have *shechitah*, is not considered kosher. This is either because it is currently in an edible form (Rav Aharon Kotler) or is *assur mid'rabannan* even though it comes from an inedible bone (*Iggeros Moshe*). At first glance, we should take the same stance regarding calcium, which is commonly produced from oyster shells. The shell is essentially a hard bone, and the calcium is isolated from it. Seemingly, it should have the same status as gelatin: gelatin made from hard bones is forbidden, so calcium made from hard shells should also be forbidden. But, in fact, it is generally accepted that calcium produced from oyster shells is permitted. What is the difference between gelatin and calcium?[16]

---

[16] One could suggest an alternate answer to what will be noted in the coming text, as follows: *Shulchan Aruch* 87:7 says that if someone cooks one of 6 items (שליא, עור, גידים, עצמות, קרנים, וטלפים) in milk, they are *patur*, and *Shach* 87:22 says that this means it is *patur mid'oraisah* but *assur mid'rabannan*. *Iggeros Moshe* YD 1:37 notes *Shulchan Aruch* is based on *Gemara, Chullin* 114a, which only lists 4 cases (עצמות, גידים, קרנים, טלפים), and says that *Shach's* comments should be understood to refer only to those 4 cases and not the other 2 (שליא, עור). He explains (and cites support to the idea) that the *issur d'rabannan* to cook or eat inedible animal products with milk only applies to those animal products which are referred to as בשר in some context. But since שליא and עור are never considered בשר/meat, *Chazal* would never have given them a status of "meat" as relates to any halachic matter.

Rabbi Eli Gersten suggested that we can find the answer by looking more carefully at *Rambam* cited above. When he records the halacha that it is forbidden to eat the bones, horns, nails (of birds), etc. from a non-kosher animal, he qualifies that it is specific to places where מבצבץ משם הדם כשיחתכו, which means that blood "bubbles out" when the item is cut. This limitation is based on the *Gemara*[17] which explains that the only part of bird nails and animal horns which have a status of "food" (as relates to *tumah*) is the part of the nail which is under the skin, and the part of the horn which bleeds if it is cut. [*Shulchan Aruch*[18] alludes to this when he says that (only) עיקרי קרנים וטלפים (the roots/base of the horns and hooves) are forbidden]. In other words, the prohibition against eating bones etc. is specific to those items which are integrated into the flesh to the point that they bleed when they are cut. Those are (Rabbinically) treated as food items and it is therefore *assur* to eat them. But there are no blood vessels in oyster shells and cracking the shell will not cause any bleeding; therefore, these shells/bones are completely permitted, as is the calcium made from them.

This idea is spelled out by *Aruch HaShulchan*,[19] who quotes *Rambam* and then says:

וקרנים וטלפים וצפרנים בראשם במקום שאין הדם מבצבץ
לא שייך עליהם תורת אוכל כלל וגם איסור אין בזה

This line of reasoning also explains why items isolated from hair and feathers – such as l-cysteine (an amino acid used in dough conditioners) –

---

[17] In this context, *Iggeros Moshe* explains that bones are considered בשר because וגם שהם בתוך הבשר, הם נותנים טעם כבשר ודרכם לבשל כדי ליתן טעם ולכן בכלל בשר הם. Those factors do not appear to be correct for an exoskeleton like an oyster shell, and therefore it might be that gelatin made from hard bones is *assur*, but calcium made from oyster shells is permitted. [Rav Schachter once suggested a possibility along these lines as well]. The issue with this answer is that *Iggeros Moshe* notes that *Pri Megadim* SD 87:22 does not agree with it, and says that even עור is *assur mid'rabbanan*, and although *Iggeros Moshe* believes his personal analysis is correct, he defers to *Pri Megadim* (אבל למעשה יש עכ"צ להחמיר כהפמ"ג). [Furthermore, according to *Iggeros Moshe's* logic, it would be permitted to produce gelatin from beef hides (which did not have *shechitah*), which is not something that is accepted as mainstream].

Nonetheless, one could suggest a variation of *Iggeros Moshe's* principle to differentiate between hides and oyster shells. Perhaps the reason *Chazal* included עור in this *issur*, even though it is generally not בשר, is because *Mishnah*, *Chullin* 122a, lists several types of עור which are בשר. Therefore, it might be appropriate to include all עור in the *issur d'rabbanan* on inedible animal products. But there are no hard exoskeletons which are considered בשר, and therefore they are not *assur mid'rabbanan*. While there is a certain logic to this line of reasoning, it does not have the support of the proofs *Iggeros Moshe* marshalled for his position.

[17] *Gemara, Chullin* 121a.
[18] *Shulchan Aruch* 87:7.
[19] *Aruch HaShulchan* 29:18.

Bone Products 313

is kosher even if the animals or birds did not have *shechitah* or were from non-kosher species.[20] Hair and feathers do not bleed when they are cut, and even the part which is attached to the body is merely in a hair follicle (which has a blood supply) but the hair and feather do not have their own blood supply. Therefore, these are not included in any prohibition associated with meat of non-kosher animals.[21]

The above is a reasonable approach within the position of *Iggeros Moshe* that eating inedible bones is *assur mid'rabannan*. It is not clear if Rav Aharon Kotler – who says that inedible bones which are rendered edible revert to the standard status of "meat" and are *assur mid'oraisah* – would have agreed to permit calcium and l-cysteine. This requires further consideration.

In a mixture

Since it is forbidden to eat hard bones or items made from them, one would logically assume that the *ta'am* coming from a bone is also forbidden. But, in fact, *Shulchan Aruch*[22] says that if bones from a non-kosher animal are cooked with other foods, the status of the other foods is not affected. [This leniency is only true of bones themselves but does not apply to the <u>marrow</u> inside bones].[23] *Pri Megadim*[24] says this is because *Chazal* understood that so little *ta'am* is exuded from the bones that one need not be concerned about its effect on other foods. He compares this to גיד הנשה which may not be eaten but does not compromise other foods it is cooked with, because no (meaningful) *ta'am* comes out of it (אין בגידים בנותן טעם).[25]

---

[20] The use of hair or feathers for this purpose presupposes there are no other issues such as *b'lios* of blood if the feathers are removed from chickens with hot water.
[21] A proof to this point can be seen from the very *Gemara* (*Chullin* 121a) which is the basis for *Rambam's* מבצבץ משם הדם כשיחתכו. The *Gemara* makes its point regarding two cases where *Mishnah, Taharos* 1:2 (חרטום/beak and צפרנים/nails) says that the item is מצטרף/joins with regular food to measure the requisite *kezayis* for טומאת אוכלים. The *Gemara* questioned why those would be מצטרף if they are "just a piece of wood" (i.e., inedible), and to that it answers that the *Mishnah* is referring to the soft part of the beak or nail which bleeds and is edible enough to be מצטרף. Those two items are the second pair of cases in that *Mishnah*. The first pair are כנפים and נוצה, which the *meforshim* explain to be feathers and small hairs, and for those the *Mishnah* says that they are <u>not</u> מצטרף. This means that, in contrast to beaks and nails which have some part which is edible enough to be מצטרף, feathers and hairs have no part which meet that criterion and none of them can be viewed as edible. Accordingly, chemicals etc. derived from them are also permitted.
[22] *Shulchan Aruch* 99:1 (as per *Shach* 99:1).
[23] *Shulchan Aruch* ibid.
[24] *Pri Megadim* MZ 99:1.
[25] *Shulchan Aruch* YD 65:9 and 100:2.

The most direct case where this is relevant is if a piece of meat falls into milk, or if non-kosher meat falls into a pot of kosher food. When calculating whether the meat is *batel b'shishim*, one can "ignore" the volume of the bones and just see if the meat portion is *batel b'shishim*. In this context, it is noteworthy that this only applies if the meat was raw, but if it had been previously cooked, then the bones have already absorbed *ta'am* from the meat and (in most cases) must be *batel* as well.[26]

Below we will see some other situations where this halacha – that one need not be concerned about *ta'am* coming from non-kosher bones – plays some role in a practical issue.

Bone Char

Burned/charred cattle bones are used in the refining process for cane sugar,[27] in that the sugar passes through the "bone char" to whiten the sugar. The bone char does not remain in the sugar.[28] Even if the sugar was hot during this process (which it likely is not), the *kashrus* of the sugar would not be affected because – as we have seen – we do not have to be concerned about *ta'am* coming from a non-kosher bone. An additional factor is that, if the bones are truly burned, they become permitted just as any other non-kosher food which is burned to the point that it is inedible.[29]

The same line of reasoning explains the permissibility of bone china made with bone ash (i.e., ashes of bones). It is forbidden to eat bones, but there is no concern of the bones' *ta'am* transferring into food put onto the china.

---

[26] See *Shulchan Aruch* 99:2-3.

[27] It appears that this process is specific to sugar derived from sugar cane but is not used for beet sugar, coconut sugar, and unrefined sugar, and is also not permitted for sugar which is labeled "organic". Although brown sugar does not have a white color and would seemingly not require bone char, it seems that in some cases bone char is nonetheless used for the sugar before molasses are added (to convert it to "brown" sugar).

[28] See *Tzemach Tzedek* (*Lubavitch*) YD 68-68) who discusses a practice in his time where sugar was whitened with blood (rather than bones), and he considers permitting the sugar based on considerations of נותן טעם לפגם and אין כוונתו לבטל. Those concepts are also relevant to the modern use of bone char.

[29] If it is forbidden to eat bones even though they are inedible, does the prohibition go away if they are burned and rendered even more inedible? See *Imrei Dovid*, *Halachos of Insects*, Chapter 10, and *Animal Products*, Chapter 11.

Bone Products

Other halachos

The following are some other *kashrus*-related halachos relating to bones:

- The status of bee legs (and wings) is similar to that of bones; see *Rema* 103:2 and elsewhere.[30]
- Utensils made of bone do not require *tevillas keilim*; see *Imrei Dovid*, *Tevillas Keilim*, Chapter 1.
- Utensils made of bone can absorb[31] and can be *kashered* with *hag'alah*.[32]
- If there are chicken bones in the *cholent*, it may be forbidden to take the *cholent* off the fire on Friday night and put it back on even if the general conditions of *chazarah* are met. This is because the bones might not be considered fully cooked, and therefore, putting the pot back onto the fire might be a violation of *bishul* for the bones.[33]

---

[30] See *Imrei Dovid*, *Halachos of Insects*, Chapter 43, *Animal Products*, Chapter 24 (beginning), and *Badei HaShulchan* (*Biurim*) 103:2 s.v. *v'chein*.
[31] *Shulchan Aruch* 99:2. This assumption also underlies the point made by *Rema* OC 451:8, noted in the coming text.
[32] *Rema* ibid.
[33] See *Shemiras Shabbos K'hilchaso* 1:20, and the discussion of that ruling in *Iggeros Moshe* OC 4:77-78.

Chapter 28

אין מבטלין איסור לכתחלה

שולחן ערוך סימן צ"ט סעיפים ה-ו

אין מבטלין איסור לכתחלה. ואפילו נפל לתוך היתר שאין בו שיעור לבטלו אין מוסיפין עליו היתר כדי לבטלו. עבר וביטלו או שריבה עליו, אם בשוגג מותר, ואם במזיד אסור למבטל עצמו אם הוא שלו וכן למי שנתבטל בשבילו (ואסורים למכרו גם כן לישראל אחר שלא יהנו ממה שבטלו), ולשאר כל אדם מותר.

הגה: ודוקא שנתערב יבש ביבש, או אפילו לח בלח דאמר שאין אומרים בו חתיכה נעשית נבלה כדלעיל סי' צ"ב, אבל חתיכה שבלעה איסור לא מהני שנתוסף אחר כך היתר דהא אמרינן ביה חתיכה נעשית נבלה. ויש אומרים דאפילו במקום דלא אמרינן חתיכה נעשית נבלה לא מהני ההיתר לבטל אלא אם נתוסף קודם שנודע התערובת אבל אם נודע התערובת קודם לא מהני מה שנתוסף אחר כך. ולפי זה היה צריך החכם המורה לבטל איסור לחקור אם נתוסף ההיתר לאחר שנודע, ולא נהגו כן.

איסור של דבריהם אין מערבין אותו בידים כדי לבטל, ואם עשה כן במזיד אסור, אבל אם נפל מעצמו ואין בהיתר כדי לבטלו מרבה עליו ומבטלו.

הגה: וי"א דאין לבטל איסור דרבנן או להוסיף עליו כמו באיסור דאורייתא, וכן נוהגין ואין לשנות. איסור שנתבטל כגון שהיה ס' כנגדו ונתוסף בו אח"כ מן האיסור הראשון חוזר וניעור ונאסר, לי"ש מין במינו לי"ש בשאינו מינו לא שנא יבש לי"ש לח לא שנא נודע בינתים או לא נודע בינתים.

כזית חלב שנפל למים ונתבטל בס' ואח"כ נפל מן המים לקדירה של בשר מותר, אף על פי שאין ס' בבשר ס' נגד החלב שהרי נתבטל במים, וכל כיוצא בזה.

These halachos[1] are the primary record of the *issur d'rabannan*[2] of אין מבטלין איסור לכתחלה, as well as the related prohibition for a person who violated this to eat the resulting *ta'aruvos*. The following is a brief outline of many relevant details and issues, with sources in the footnotes for where to learn more about each of them.

---

[1] *Shulchan Aruch* 99:5-6.
[2] Although the *Ra'avad* says that the prohibition is *d'oraisah*, most *Poskim* seem to maintain that it is *d'rabannan* (and even *Ra'avad* agrees that the *issur* to eat the mixture is *d'rabannan*); see *Shach* 99:7, *Chochmas Adam* 52:6, and others.

Which foods

1. The prohibition is referred to as אין מבטלין איסור לכתחלה which implies that it might be permitted to be מבטל something which is not yet *issur*, such as milk into water that will later be added to meat, or *chametz* into food before *Pesach*. Some *Poskim* accept that view, but the consensus appears to be that even these actions are forbidden since the result is that the person engineered a way to have a mixture which contains something that it should not (meat with milk in it, or *Pesach* food that contains *chametz*).[3]

   A related question is whether one may dilute fish into a food (e.g., anchovies in Worcestershire sauce, fish oil in orange juice) that will be eaten with meat. That case is somewhat different since eating meat with fish is not a traditional "*issur*" but rather forbidden based on *sakanah*/danger.[4]

   However, many *Acharonim* (including *Mishnah Berurah*)[5] rule that one may add tiny amounts of milk to bread in ways that it is *batel b'shishim*, as long as the person has no specific intention to eat that bread with meat. Although dairy bread is forbidden (even to be eaten without meat), that does not restrict adding dairy in this manner.[6]

2. Is it permitted to add small amounts of rennet from the stomach of a kosher animal (which underwent *shechitah* / קיבת כשירה) to milk, in order to convert that milk into cheese? Is that ביטול איסור לכתחלה since meat is being added to milk? The following is a footnote on that topic from the beginning of Chapter 1 (see there for sources):

   Although the cheese is permitted *b'dieved*, one may not *l'chatchilah* add kosher animal rennet to milk in order to create cheese even if the amount of rennet would be *batel b'shishim*, as doing so would be considered *bitul issur l'chatchilah*. Another halacha is that the dried-out stomach of a cow (which had *shechitah*) is not considered "edible" and therefore if it was used as a source of rennet, the cheese

---

[3] For more on this, see Chapter 12 in the subsection "אין מבטלין איסור לכתחלה", with the footnotes.
[4] Ibid.
[5] *Mishnah Berurah* 447:106 (end).
[6] For more on this, see Chapter 17. Despite the leniency noted in the text, many *hashgachos* will not permit this because the bread would have to be labeled "dairy" (since it contains dairy components, see Point #11 in the coming text) and that would mislead consumers into thinking that dairy bread is permitted (ibid).

is permitted even if the stomach was <u>not</u> *batel b'shishim* in the milk. Here too, one may only rely on this *b'dieved*, but may not add it to milk *l'chatchilah*. However, if one has a combination of these two leniencies – the stomach is dried-out, and it is *batel b'shishim* into the milk – then one may *l'chatchilah* use the kosher stomach to curdle the milk into cheese.

3. Some foods are only restricted because it <u>looks</u> like the person is doing something that they should not be doing (מראית עין). For example, cooking mother's milk with meat (which looks like cooking *basar b'chalav*) and certain bloodspots in eggs.[7] *Aruch HaShulchan*[8] says that since these are not inherently forbidden, there is no prohibition of אין מבטלין איסור לכתחלה, but *Badei HaShulchan*[9] shows that many prominent *Acharonim* disagree with that conclusion.

4. The general rule is that *safek d'rabannan l'kulah*. If so, since אין מבטלין איסור לכתחלה is a *d'rabannan* principle, might it be permitted to purposely add <u>safek</u> issur into food? See *Imrei Dovid*, Alcoholic Beverages, Chapter 22, for different approaches to that question.

> A lenient approach on this issue would justify diluting non-certified liquid medicines in a kosher beverage; it is a *safek* if the medicine is not kosher and therefore אין מבטלין might not be a concern. A second reason to permit this type of dilution is that the *issur d'rabannan* of אין מבטלין might be waived for someone who is (sufficiently) ill. For more on that see *Imrei Dovid* ibid. Chapter 27.

5. *Bitul* is based on the assumption that the additive is insignificant and unimportant. Accordingly, some are of the opinion that any ingredient which is <u>supposed</u> to be in the mixture can never be *batel* even if the situation does not meet the criteria for ביטול איסור לכתחלה. For more on that see *Imrei Dovid, Alcoholic Beverages*, Chapter 15.

---

[7] *Shulchan Aruch* 87:4 (mother's milk) and 66:5 (as per *Shach* 66:11).
[8] *Aruch HaShulchan* 99:39.
[9] *Badei HaShulchan* (Biurim) 99:6 s.v. *v'yesh*, citing *Shach* 66:11, *Rebbi Akiva Eiger* to *Shulchan Aruch* 87:4, and *Yad Yehuda* (Aruch) 66:12 (who reinterprets *Aruch HaShulchan's* proof from *Yerushalmi, Kilayim* 2:1).

Non-food issues

6. A בריה or חתיכה הראויה להתכבד cannot be *batel* (see Chapters 30 and 31) while they are whole, but they can be *batel* if they are chopped or broken. *Shulchan Aruch*[10] says that it is forbidden to break them apart for the specific purposes of making them suitable for *bitul*, as that is a form of ביטול איסור לכתחלה. Nonetheless, it may be permitted to puree broccoli [which is potentially infested with whole/בריה insects] for use in creating a *kugel*, as that might qualify as אין כוונתו לבטל (noted below).[11]

7. In Chapter 13 we saw that *Shulchan Aruch* (95:4) says that if meat and dairy dishes were washed in the same hot water but there was ash/soap in the water, the dishes remain kosher because any *ta'am* passing from one dish to the next will become *pagum* as it passes through the ash. In that context, we noted the following:

   ...*Acharonim* disagree whether it is permitted *l'chatchilah* to setup a situation like the one discussed in *Shulchan Aruch*, where *ta'am* will become *pagum* before it is absorbed into the utensil. *Tzemach Tzedek* assumes that it is forbidden, presumably as a form of *bitul issur l'chatchilah*, while *Chacham Tzvi* understands that it is permitted.

   See the footnotes there for possible explanations for the basis for this *machlokes*.

   See *Imrei Dovid, Halachos of Insects*, Chapter 49, for a related *machlokes* regarding burning an insect to the point that it becomes inedible (at which point the *issur* to eat it will cease). *Minchas Yaakov* says that doing so is a form of ביטול איסור לכתחלה, while *Binas Adam* argues that ביטול איסור only applies if a person finds a "permitted" way to eat the forbidden food. But there is nothing wrong with <u>removing</u> the prohibition from the food altogether, such as by burning it.[12]

8. [The following point assumes that *kitnios shenishtaneh* – *kitnios* dramatically changed into something different – may be eaten on *Pesach*].[13] The prohibition of אין מבטלין איסור לכתחלה applies even

---

[10] *Shulchan Aruch* 101:6.
[11] For more on this, see *Imrei Dovid, Halachos of Insects*, Chapter 45.
[12] See also, *Imrei Dovid, Animal Products*, Chapter 31.
[13] Details of that issue are beyond the scope of this work.

to *issurim d'rabannan*,[14] and even to *kitnios* which is only forbidden based on *minhag*.[15] What about purposely converting *kitnios* into *kitnios shenishtaneh* so that it can be eaten on *Pesach*? [And what about certifying a company doing that?] Is that a violation of אין מבטלין איסור לכתחלה, since the person is taking steps to <u>remove</u> an *issur*? Or is it permitted since the *issur* is "disappearing" rather than becoming *batel*? The answer might depend on the disagreements noted in the previous point.

9. If food was cooked in a non-kosher pot which is *aino ben yomo*, it is permitted *b'dieved*,[16] but it is nonetheless forbidden to use that type of pot without *kashering*.[17] *Pri Megadim*[18] says that if a person knowingly <u>chooses</u> to do that, it would be treated like someone who was מבטל איסור לכתחלה and he would not be allowed to eat the food cooked in that pot (just as one cannot eat a mixture created via ביטול איסור לכתחלה).

Which people

10. If one person chooses to be מבטל איסור for someone else, both cannot eat the mixture.[19] What if a non-Jewish manufacturer is מבטל איסור in something that he produces to sell to the general public? Should we view it as if he is doing that for <u>each</u> of his customers, in which case the Jewish ones would be forbidden to eat the food? It is generally accepted that we view the manufacturer as making his product for the <u>majority</u> of his

---

[14] *Rema* 99:6.
[15] *Pri Megadim* MZ OC 453:1.
[16] *Shulchan Aruch* 103:5 and 122:1.
[17] *Shulchan Aruch* 122:2. If *aino ben yomo* does not give a positive taste into the food, should that not automatically qualify as אין כוונתו לבטל since the person clearly does not <u>want</u> the non-kosher *ta'am* in his kosher food? See below in Point #16 and in the footnotes ad loc.
[18] *Pri Megadim* SD 99:7 (towards the end); see additional support to this position in *Rebbi Akiva Eiger* ad loc., and in *Badei HaShulchan* (*Biurim*) 103:5 s.v. *v'einah*.

Pri Megadim references *Shach* 39:6, who also applies the fine imposed on someone who violates אין מבטלין איסור לכתחלה to cases other than the "traditional" one where *issur* is missed into *heter*. *Shach* is commenting on *Shulchan Aruch* YD 39:6, who rules that if an animal's lungs were accidentally lost before being checked for טריפות, one may eat the meat and assume the animal was not a טריפה. To this *Shach* says that if the person purposely discarded the lungs, the meat is forbidden to him just as our halacha which says this is the penalty for someone who violated ביטול איסור לכתחלה. In that case, no "*issur*" was diluted, yet conceptually it is like ביטול איסור לכתחלה because the person took steps to get around (potentially) forbidden food.

[19] *Shulchan Aruch* 99:5.

customers, and in most cases, this means that the ביטול איסור was not performed for Jewish people, and the food is permitted.[20]

11. Nonetheless, *Iggeros Moshe*[21] said that it is מכוער הדבר (*repulsive*) for a *hashgachah* to allow a non-Jewish company to produce certified kosher items in a way that would be forbidden לכתחלה for a Jew to do. Certifying agencies have accepted this directive and apply it to our halacha as well: a Jew is not allowed to add *issur* to kosher food – since that would be ביטול איסור לכתחלה – and it is therefore inappropriate for the Jew to grant permission to a non-Jew to do the same. [Thus, the leniency noted above, regarding non-Jewish manufacturers, is specific to cases where the *bitul* happens at a company that is not certified kosher.]

> Rav Belsky applied a similar line of reasoning to explain one aspect of why condensate recovered from heating non-kosher materials cannot be used for kosher products; see Chapter 4 footnote 12.

12. If there are two choices – one food has *issur* mixed in at *bitul* proportions (where there was no violation of אין מבטלין איסור לכתחלה) and the other is made with 100% kosher ingredient – it is like ביטול איסור לכתחלה to eat or purchase the one which has *issur* mixed in. This is because the decision to pick that one is similar to "לכתחלה" choosing to have the *issur* mixed in. However, this is limited to cases where both choices are equal. However, if the one that contains *issur* is more available, better quality, less expensive, or otherwise more desirable, there is no need to favor the one which has no *issur* mixed in.[22]

13. Can Person A who is *machmir* on an issue, dilute that "*issur*" for Person B who follows a lenient approach? For example, if Person A only eats *pas Yisroel*, can he use *pas paltar* bread to make kvass (a fermented beverage made with bread) for Person B who eats *pas paltar*?[23] It may depend on whether Person A considers his

---

[20] For more on this, see *Darchei Teshuvah* 108:20.
[21] *Iggeros Moshe* YD 2:41, discussing the use of equipment which is *aino ben yomo* but was not *kashered*.
[22] See *Taz* YD 137:2 (and 138:14) (noted in *Imrei Dovid, Halachos of Insects*, end of Chapter 44), and *Rema* 108:1 (and 122:6). See also below in footnote 29.
[23] In this context it is noteworthy that *pas akum* is *batel b'rov* (and *bitul b'shishim* is not required); see *Shulchan Aruch* 112:14 and *Imrei Dovid, Pas Yisroel and Bishul Yisroel*, Chapter 20.

strict practice to be a *"chumrah"* or required by the letter of the law.[24]

אין כוונתו לבטל

14. The prohibition of אין מבטלין איסור לכתחלה is specific to cases where the person's intention is to dilute the *issur* into the *heter*, but if they have some other intention (אין כוונתו לבטל) there is no concern. Some examples where this might apply are the use of uncertified antifoams,[25] pureeing unchecked produce to create (broccoli) *kugel*, (raspberry) jelly, or (strawberry) smoothies.[26] There are many factors to consider, including: (a) whether אין כוונתו לבטל allows the person to <u>initially</u> add *issur* to *heter* (such as in the case of antifoams) or just lets him add <u>more</u> *heter* (to reach *shishim*), or take some other action (such as pureeing) after the *issur* is already mixed in; (b) does it make a difference if there is a *safek* if the item is even forbidden; (c) must the person take specific steps to show that he does <u>not</u> want the *issur*; and (d) does the presence of alternatives (which have no *issur*) play a role? These issues are discussed in *Imrei Dovid, Halachos of Insects*, Chapters 44-45.

> There was a short time, in approximately the year 1999, when *hashgachos* allowed companies to add non-kosher cooker cream into their milk vats based on a perception that doing so qualified as אין כוונתו לבטל; see the footnote for details on this and why it was eventually rejected.[27]

---

[24] See *Shevet HaLevi* 1:53, *Minchas Shlomo* 1:44, and *Minchas Asher* 1:11.

[25] The antifoam is surely *batel b'shishim* and is just added as a processing aid, rather than because the person <u>wants</u> antifoam in the product.

[26] Pureeing will break apart any בריה and will also make it impossible to "find" the insects, and together this creates a תערובת where *bitul b'shishim* is appropriate. The pureeing is done as a way to prepare the food rather than with <u>intention</u> to break apart the insects.

[27] When cheese is produced as *gevinas akum*, the (leftover) whey generally remains permitted for those who eat *chalav stam*. [For details, see *Imrei Dovid, Animal Products*, Chapters 44 and 46]. But if mozzarella cheese is cooked in water (so that it will be rubbery and stringy), that water absorbs *ta'am* from the cheese and becomes forbidden. Fat which is recovered/separated from the "cookwater" is called "cooker cream", and cheese companies wanted to add this non-kosher cream to the (kosher) milk they used for producing future cheese. As above, the cheese would be non-kosher and the question was whether it would affect the status of the (otherwise) kosher whey.

At first, *hashgachos* allowed this because it is generally assumed that it is undesirable to have fat/cream in the whey since it will make it harder to spray dry the whey and because whey is typically sold as being fat-free. Thus, the cooker cream is being added to the milk so that it will become part of the (non-kosher) <u>cheese</u>, and any small amounts of cooker cream that make their way into the (kosher) whey is unintentional and should qualify as אין כוונתו לבטל. However, with time, the *hashgachos* learned that some cheese companies have specific reasons why they do want fat in their whey (especially if the

15. One application of אין כוונתו לבטל is that equipment used for non-kosher must only be cleaned to the "industrial standard of clean" (כדרך המכבדים) before it is used for kosher, even if that leaves tiny amounts of non-kosher residue in the equipment. For details, including what qualifies as "clean enough", and exceptions where כדרך המכבדים is insufficient, see *Imrei Dovid, Kashering*, Chapter 42.

16. We will see in the upcoming chapter that if so little *issur* was absorbed into a pot that it will always be *batel b'shishim* in any food cooked in that pot (עשוי להשתמש בשפע), there are those who hold that the pot can be used without *kashering*. But if there are times when the *ta'am* will not be *batel b'shishim*, the pot cannot be used without *kashering*, even in situations where the person happens to put in enough food to create *bitul b'shishim*. Presumably, this is because using the pot this way is a form of ביטול איסור לכתחלה. This leads *Pri Megadim*[28] to ask that since no *ta'am* of *issur* will be detectable in the kosher food (since it is *batel b'shishim*), the person clearly has no interest in the *bitul* occurring and this should qualify as אין כוונתו לבטל? See the footnote for some resolutions.[29]

> One situation where one may use non-kosher equipment without *kashering* is that water may be stored in a barrel previously used for non-kosher *stam yayin* even though *ta'am* is absorbed through *kovush*. For more on that, see *Imrei Dovid, Alcoholic Beverages*, Chapter 12.

17. There are situations where tiny amounts of airborne flour from one side of a factory end up in the *Pesach* food being produced on the other side of the factory. There is no question that the *chametz* is

---

whey will be used to produce ricotta cheese). There was no realistic way to know which cheesemakers had this intention and which were אין כוונתו לבטל; therefore, this lenient position was retracted.

[28] *Pri Megadim* MZ 99:7.

[29] *Pri Megadim* appears to answer that the need to *kasher* in such cases is based on *Taz* 137:2 (which is also referenced in *Taz* 99:7 that *Pri Megadim* is commenting on) noted above in Point #12. *Badei HaShulchan* (Biurim) 99:5 s.v. *l'chatchilah* (first one, left column of page 75) suggests an alternate answer based on *Gr"a* 99:18, that *Chazal* specifically forbade use of utensils in this manner out of concern the person would use it with too little kosher food (i.e., without enough for *bitul b'shishim*). This prohibition is like גזירה אינו בן יומו אטו בן יומו rather than based on איסור לכתחלה מבטלין אין. See (a) *Imrei Dovid, Halachos of Insects*, Chapter 44, that this concept appears to be the basis for a disagreement between *Nodah B'yehudah* (YD 1:26 & 2:56-57) and *Nachlas Tzvi* (to *Shulchan Aruch* YD 84:13), and (b) *Imrei Dovid, Kashering*, Chapter 11, where Rav Schachter suggests an idea similar to that of *Badei HaShulchan*.

batel b'shishim[30] and that the situation qualifies as אין כוונתו לבטל. Thus, the food is surely permitted. Rav Schachter said that the food can be used in a certified *Pesach* product, but he said that it is inappropriate to certify the food itself as kosher for *Pesach*. [He ruled similarly when airborne dairy products were going into a pareve food]. Presumably, this is because consumers expect certified products to meet a higher standard than the bare minimum allowed by halacha. It is not clear if *hashgachos* follow this strict latter ruling in practice.

---

[30] *Chametz* is not *batel b'shishim* if it gets mixed in on *Pesach*, but if it happens beforehand, the standard rules of *bitul b'shishim* apply (*Shulchan Aruch* OC 447:1 & 4).

Chapter 29

כלי העשוי להשתמש בשפע

שולחן ערוך סימן צ״ט סעיף ז

אם נבלע איסור מועט לתוך כלי כשר, אם דרכו של אותו כלי להשתמש בו בשפע היתר מותר להשתמש בו לכתחלה כיון שהאיסור מועט וא״א לבא לידי נתינת טעם, ולפיכך איסור משהו שנבלע בקדרה או בתוך קנקנים וכיוצא בהם מותר להשתמש בו לכתחלה ואפילו בן יומו לפי שאי״א לבא לידי נתינת טעם. אבל אם נבלע בכלי שדרכו להשתמש לעתים בדבר מועט בקערה וכיוצא בה אסור להשתמש אפילו בשפע, גזירה שמא ישתמש בה בדבר מועט ויבא לידי נתינת טעם.

Rashba

Our halacha[1] is based on *Rashba*,[2] who introduces the idea that there are some cases where a utensil absorbs non-kosher *ta'am* but nonetheless can be used for kosher food without *kashering*. Specifically, it is a case where so little *issur* was absorbed into a pot or jug, that in all typical ways that the pot is used there will be 60 times as much food as compared to the absorbed *issur*.

> For example, a person has a 4-quart pot that is typically 75% full during cooking, and an ounce of *treif* meat fell onto the inside walls of the pot while it was on the fire. The pot has absorbed an ounce of non-kosher *ta'am*, but since the pot usually has 96 ounces (i.e., 3 quarts, which is 75% of 4-quarts) of food in it, that 1 ounce of *issur* will always be *batel b'shishim* and thus unable to affect the kosher food.

In this type of case, where a relatively small amount of *issur* (איסור מועט) was absorbed into a pot that is usually used with a relatively large amount

---

[1] *Shulchan Aruch* 99:7, and repeated in 122:5.
[2] *Rashba, Toras HaBayis* 4:4 page 36a-b, and *Responsa Rashba* 1:222. He notes that *Ra'avad* ruled similarly, and *Ran* (to *Rif*, *Avodah Zara* 12b) reports that *Rabbeinu Yonah* taught this halacha to *Rashba* in response to a question that *Rashba* asked him. [*Ran* personally disagrees].

of *heter* (דרכו של אותו כלי להשתמש בו בשפע), the pot can be used without *kashering*. This is permitted even *l'chatchilah*, and even if the non-kosher item was absorbed within the past 24 hours. [We will see proofs and explanations for this halacha below].

However, *Rashba* says, if the pot is relatively not so large and there are times when it is used in ways that *bitul b'shishim* is not guaranteed, the pot must be *kashered* even if you choose to use it with enough *heter* to effect the *bitul b'shishim*.[3]

> For example, if the ounce of *issur* was absorbed into a 2-quart pot which is usually used 75% full, the amount of *heter* is then only 48 times as much as the volume of the *issur*. The pot must be *kashered* before kosher use, even if one chooses to fill it completely with 2 quarts of kosher food, which would have 64 times the volume of the *issur* (i.e., enough for *bitul*).

In this context, *Beis Yosef*[4] notes that it is not required that the utensil which is a כלי שעשוי להשתמש בשפע is <u>always</u> used in a way that there will *bitul b'shishim*; it is sufficient if that is the <u>typical</u> way it is used. In fact, we will see below that one of *Rashba's* sources for his halacha is from a *Gemara* which makes exactly this point: in deciding whether the item qualifies as being used בשפע, we ignore the atypical or unusual ways it is used, and only consider the typical usages.[5]

---

[3] If there will be no taste of the forbidden food in the kosher food, the person cooking surely has no intent to dilute this *issur* into the food. If so, why does this not qualify as אין כוונתו לבטל where אין מבטלין does not apply? See Point #16 in the previous chapter.

[4] *Beis Yosef* 122:5, saying דע"כ לא שרי הרשב"א אלא לפי שאינו מצוי להשתמש באותו כלי בדבר מועט וכל דבר שאינו מצוי אין חוששין לו. See also, the next footnote. [It is, however, noteworthy that *Rashba* himself repeatedly uses terms like "אי אפשר לבא לידי נתינת טעם" which imply that it <u>never</u> happens]. See also *Iggeros Moshe* YD 1:60 who suggests that *Tur*, who argues on *Rashba* by saying אף על פי שאין דרך להשתמש בו בהיתר מועט יש לנו לגזור אטו שמא ישתמש בהיתר מועט, would agree that one can be lenient in cases where there will <u>never</u> be a use of the utensil where the *ta'am* is not *batel*. [Other *Poskim* do not note this leniency].

[5] *Gemara, Avodah Zara* 33b, says that one may store water in non-kosher wine barrels – which according to *Rashba* is based on עשוי להשתמש בשפע – but not wine (since *Rashba* is of the opinion that non-kosher wine is אסור במשהו into kosher wine); the *Gemara* then tells that someone mistakenly did put wine in. To that the *Gemara* answers that the original ruling permitting water to be put in still stands, because using the barrels for wine (in which case the *issur* is not *batel*) is אקראי בעלמא הוא (an unusual occurrence). [It is not clear why using a wine barrel to store wine is deemed an unusual occurrence]. Thus, the lenient determination that something qualifies as עשוי להשתמש בשפע is not discredited by the occasional use in ways where *bitul* is not present. See also footnote 7.

The explanation of *Rashba* noted in the text resolves the question noted in *Drishah* 122:2, cited in *Badei HaShulchan* (Biurim) 99:7 s.v. *Im*.

Might להשתמש בשפע, as explained here, justify the use of non-kosher tanker trucks without *kashering*? As noted in *Imrei Dovid, Kashering*, Chapter 35, when the tanker is full, its contents are well more than 60 times the amount of *ta'am* absorbed in the tanker's walls, but sometimes a tanker carries a smaller load which is too small for *bitul*. As noted here in the text, that seemingly qualifies as עשוי

Logic

At first glance, *Rashba's* leniency is hard to understand, and the difficulty with it is evident in *Rashba's* own statement and in the placement of the halacha here in *Shulchan Aruch*. How can someone use a pot without *kashering*? Why does it matter that the non-kosher *ta'am* will be *batel*? Is this not a simple example of אין מבטלין איסור לכתחלה? *Rashba* acknowledges this obvious question, and it also stands out when one sees how this halacha (YD 99:7) is right after the halachos of אין מבטלין (YD 99:5-6). As obvious as the question is, the wording of *Shulchan Aruch* – taken from *Rashba's Toras HaBayis* – does not shed tremendous light on what the answer should be. All it says is that it is permitted because אי אפשר לבא לידי נתינת טעם. How does that explain why this is not ביטול איסור לכתחלה?

We can find explanations for this halacha in two other sources. One is elsewhere in *Rashba*[6] where he says that since it is so rare for there to be a situation where the food will become non-kosher, *Chazal* allowed the person to be מבטל איסור לכתחלה. We can explain that as follows: some understand that the reason the Rabbis forbade ביטול איסור is out of concern that the person might miscalculate; there will be too much *issur* and it will not be *batel b'shishim*. If that is the reason, then in cases where it is almost impossible for the *issur* not to be *batel* (i.e., אי אפשר לבא לידי נתינת טעם), *Chazal* chose to waive this restriction and allowed ביטול איסור לכתחלה.[7]

A similar explanation can be found in *Rivash*.[8] He says that in the second case of *Rashba* – where the *issur* <u>happens</u> to be *batel b'shishim* but the pot does <u>not</u> qualify as עשוי להשתמש בשפע – one could imagine that it would be permitted to use the pot without *kashering*.[9] There the only reason it is forbidden to use the pot is because of a גזרה אטו תבשיל מועט שיהא בו נתינת

להשתמש בשפע. However, in practice, any time the tanker carries a very small load, those products will be forbidden, which means that [even if one accepts *Rashba*, see later in the chapter] in practice this is not something that can be relied upon across the board.

[6] *Responsa Rashba* 1:222 referencing his commentary to *Bava Basra* 87b. The text is based on both of those sources. In the former, he is discussing a case where one is permitted to allow inconsequential residues of *terumah* to become diluted in *chullin* and says, שאין דרכן של בני אדם ללקט וליטפח מבטלין לכתחלה, and in the latter (discussing a case more like ours) he says that אלמא קל הוא שהקלו לבטלו ברוב לפי שלא הטריחו יותר מדאי.

[7] This line of reasoning is very similar to the one *Responsa Rashba* 1:372 uses to explain why one may choose a method of *kashering* based on the primary way a utensil is used (רוב תשמישו) and ignore the occasional use (מיעוט תשמישו) which would require a more robust *kashering*; see *Imrei Dovid, Kashering*, Chapter 20.

[8] *Rivash* 349, referenced in *Beis Yosef* 122:5.

[9] *Rivash* does not clarify exactly why one would think this is permitted, and he may be relying on the logic of אין כוונתו לבטל (see Chapter 28) which is a line of reasoning he considers later in the *teshuvah*.

כלי העשוי להשתמש בשפע   **329**

טעם. In other words, just as *Chazal* forbade the use of an *aino ben yomo* pot [even though food cooked in it will not become non-kosher] because גזירה אינו בן יומו אטו בן יומו,[10] so too, one may not use a pot in a way that the *b'lios* will be *batel* because you might mistakenly use it with a smaller amount of kosher food in which it will not be *batel*. If so, we can understand that in cases where the *issur* will always be *batel* (i.e., עשוי להשתמש בשפע), there is no restriction on using it without *kashering*.

Armed with these explanations, we understand what *Rashba* was referring to when he said the logic is אי אפשר לבא לידי נתינת טעם; there is no concern that someone will miscalculate, so there is no *issur* of using the utensil without *kashering*. We also understand why *Tur*[11] questions this position: he asks that גזירה אינו בן יומו אטו בן יומו is a concern that if you use this *aino ben yomo* pot without *kashering*, you might end up using a <u>different</u> non-kosher pot which was used for non-kosher within 24 hours.[12] If *Chazal* forbade the use of one utensil out of concern you might use a different utensil incorrectly, then surely they would not have allowed the use of a pot where the person could possibly use that same pot in a way that there would be no *bitul*. In other words, *Rashba* (as per either of the explanations given above) is saying that in a case where אי אפשר לבא לידי נתינת טעם, the prohibition of אין מבטלין does not apply, while *Tur* is asking that it is just <u>unlikely</u> for that to happen but not impossible, and therefore it should be forbidden. To that, *Beis Yosef*[13] answers that since it is so unusual for the pot or jug to be used in a way that the *issur* would not be *batel*, there is no need to be concerned for that eventuality.

First Source

The statements above are logical arguments for and against *Rashba's* point, but – as many *Poskim* note – this type of novel suggestion must have

---

[10] See *Gemara, Avodah Zara* 76a (cited in *Shulchan Aruch* 122:2), and below in Chapter 41.
[11] *Tur* 122:5.
[12] In other words, this pot is already *aino ben yomo*, so it is impossible to use it when it is *ben yomo*, so it must be that the concern is that you will use a <u>different</u> pot which <u>is</u> *ben yomo* from non-kosher use. However, see *Bach* ad loc. who questions this assumption and says that maybe the concern is that the person might use the pot thinking it is *aino ben yomo* when in truth it (i.e., that same pot) is *ben yomo*. [*Bach* personally agrees with *Tur's* conclusion to reject *Rashba's* leniency regarding עשוי להשתמש בשפע. He argues that גזרינן היכא דנבלע בו איסור מועט אטו היכא דנבלע בו איסור מרובה].
[13] *Beis Yosef* 122:5. His words are לפי שאינו מצוי להשתמש באותו כלי בדבר מועט וכל דבר שאינו מצוי אין חוששין לו. His reference to this possibility not being "מצוי" is reminiscent of the general standard – relevant to checking vegetables for infestation, animals for טריפות, and other halachos – that one must only concern themselves (and make efforts to discover) possible *issurim* which are מצוי; see more on that topic in *Imrei Dovid, Halachos of Insects*, Chapters 27-30.

a Talmudic source and cannot be proposed based merely on logic. In fact, *Rashba* provides two sources,[14] and we will see that the way others disagree with those sources opens the possibility of all agreeing to be lenient in certain cases.

In *Toras HaBayis*, *Rashba* says that the halacha can be derived from a *Gemara* in *Avodah Zara* (33a-b), which says that one may put water into a barrel in which non-kosher wine had previously been stored. The way *ta'am* transfers when liquids are stored long-term at ambient temperature is via "*kovush*" (see Chapter 48) and *Rashba* understands that this only causes a minimal amount of *ta'am* to be absorbed. That small amount of *ta'am* will surely be *batel* into the (kosher) water put into the barrel, and therefore the reason the barrel can be used without *kashering* is because it is a כלי שעשוי להשתמש בשפע. The *Gemara* never says that this is why it is permitted, but that is how *Rashba* understands it, and it serves as a source for the leniency he expresses.

פגם

Taz, *Ra'ah*[15] and others disagree with this proof because they understand the reason one may put water into the barrel is because there is a negative interaction (פגם) between the water and wine, such that one may use the barrel without *kashering*, if there is <u>also</u> שפע. [See *Imrei Dovid*, *Alcoholic Beverages*, Chapter 12 for more on the disagreement regarding how to understand that *Gemara*]. Below we will see that many of the later *Poskim* are unwilling to rely on *Rashba/Shulchan Aruch*, and to do so they must understand this *Gemara* as per *Taz/Ra'ah*. Accordingly, even they agree that one can be lenient and use the pot, etc., without *kashering* if [a] the taste of the absorbed non-kosher *ta'am* will be לפגם into the kosher food (to accommodate *Taz's* understanding of the *Gemara*), <u>and</u> [b] the pot is used in a way that qualifies as עשוי להשתמש בשפע (as per *Rashba*). If both

---

[14] In fact, *Gr"a* 99:17 suggests that since the first proof is from a *Gemara* that mentions קנקנים and the second is from one that discusses קדירות, that is why *Rashba* and *Shulchan Aruch* cite two different examples of this halacha (איסור משהו שנבלע בקדירה או בתוך קנקנים).

[15] The text is primarily based on *Taz* 99:15, whose reason to disagree with *Rashba* is somewhat different than that of *Ra'ah* (*Bedek HaBayis* 4:4 pages 36a-b). Although both note the point of פגם, for *Taz* it appears to be the main part of his position, while *Ra'ah* just notes it to address one specific point. [Rather, *Ra'ah* focuses on an idea that *kovush* does not cause true absorption but instead just takes in a trace of the item's *ta'am*. Among the things he says is, אלא איסור קנקנים וכלי של יין לא מפני בלע כלל הם נאסרין אלא מפני קליטה שקולטין טעם היין וכשנותנין בהם יין אחר בלא הכשר קולט גם כן מטעם זה ואין בו ממשו של איסור כלל].

conditions are met, then all agree that this is a case where the *Gemara* allows the use of the pot without *kashering*.

One case where we can say with confidence that the absorbed *ta'am* is לפגם into the kosher is the one discussed in the *Gemara*: non-kosher wine (or grape juice) absorbed into a container via *kovush*. For variations of that case, including Scotch in sherry casks, *kovush* of fruit punch which includes grape juice, and whether it applies to hot *b'lios*, see *Imrei Dovid* ibid.

But what about a more typical example of "פגם", which occurs when 24 hours have passed since the pot was used for non-kosher food? After that much time, the *ta'am* is *aino ben yomo* and is נותן טעם לפגם into <u>anything</u> cooked in that pot.[16] If that happens, would *Taz* be lenient? And does that mean that if there is a pot which is עשוי להשתמש בשפע and also *aino ben yomo*, all would agree that it can be used without *kashering*?

Second Source
Seemingly, there is a proof to this question from *Rashba's* second source. This source is not found in *Toras HaBayis* and is not quoted in *Beis Yosef*, but is hinted at in a *teshuvah* from *Rashba* and described in more detail by *Gr"a*.[17] This *Gemara* is in *Pesachim* (30a) and is within the opinion of *Rav*, who holds that (a) pots in which *chametz* was cooked before *Pesach* [and were not *kashered*], must be destroyed on (or before) *Pesach*, and (b) anytime non-kosher is mixed into kosher as מין במינו, it is *assur b'mashehu*. On that the *Gemara* asks, why not let the person keep the *chametz* pot until after *Pesach* and use it to cook foods that are מין בשאינו מינו (where *Rav* agrees that *bitul b'shishim* is effective)? The question presupposes that any *chametz* absorbed into the pot will always be *batel b'shishim*, and *Tosfos*[18] explains that this is because *chametz* is typically just a minor ingredient in this type of pot.

But *Tosfos* is bothered by the *Gemara's* question. Even if the absorbed *chametz* would be *batel b'shishim* into the food, should it not be forbidden to use the pot due to the prohibition of אין מבטלין איסור לכתחלה? That exact question is a proof to *Rashba's* point! The reason the *Gemara* assumes you can use the pot without *kashering* is that no matter what you cook in the pot, the *chametz* will be *batel b'shishim*, and in such cases – i.e., a כלי שעשוי

---

[16] *Shulchan Aruch* 103:5, 122:2, and elsewhere.
[17] *Responsa Rashba* 1:222 and *Gr"a* 99:17.
[18] *Tosfos, Pesachim* 30a ד"ה לשהינהו.

להשתמש בשפע – one may use it without *kashering*. This is *Rashba's* alternate source for his principle.

Seeing how *Tosfos* answers his question will give us an idea of how *Taz* and *Ra'ah* will respond to this proof. *Tosfos* says that in this case, the *ta'am* will surely be *batel b'shishim* and the pot is *aino ben yomo* (since it was not used for *chametz* during the entire *Pesach*), and when both of those conditions coincide, there is no prohibition of אין מבטלין איסור לכתחלה. In other words, while *Tosfos* is not willing to allow every כלי שעשוי להשתמש בשפע to be used without *kashering*, he is lenient when it is also *aino ben yomo*. This is very much like what *Taz* said that when the *ta'am* is [inherently] לפגם one can be lenient, but adds that *aino ben yomo* also qualifies as פגם in this context.

This seems to serve as a resolution to the question posed above: in cases where non-kosher *ta'am* has become *aino ben yomo*, all will agree that a כלי שעשוי להשתמש בשפע can be used without *kashering*. While this appears to be a good proof, *Pri Megadim*,[19] in a very brief comment, says that one can**not** be lenient about this case. He does not give a reason or discuss the apparent proof from *Gemara*, *Pesachim*, but *Yad Yehudah*[20] does. *Yad Yehudah* says that in the *Gemara Pesachim*, the pot was used for *chametz* before *Pesach* when it was still permitted to eat *chametz*. Only in that case is one permitted to be עשוי להשתמש בשפע מבטל איסור לכתחלה if it qualifies as שפע and is *aino ben yomo*. But in a standard case where at the time the non-kosher was absorbed into the pot, it was forbidden to use the pot without *kashering* – since at that point it was just שפע without פגם/*aino ben yomo* – and the fact that 24 hours passed does not suddenly permit one to use the pot without *kashering*.[21]

Yad Yehudah is not the originator of this line of reasoning, and in fact it can be found in *Ra'ah* himself, in the section directly preceding the one

---

[19] *Pri Megadim* SD 99:23.
[20] *Yad Yehuda* 99:28 (Aruch).
[21] Alternatively, perhaps *Ra'ah* would understand the *Gemara Pesachim* as per the second answer in *Tosfos*, ibid. He says that the pot under discussion is made of *cheress* which cannot be *kashered*, and therefore the *Gemara* assumed that since it is already *aino ben yomo* (and שפע?) and there is no way to remove the absorbed *ta'am*, *Chazal* would waive the prohibition of ביטול איסור לכתחלה. That leniency is specific to cases like this, where *kashering* is impossible, but it would not apply for standard pots or utensils.

כלי העשוי להשתמש בשפע

referenced above.²² He says that [although he does not permit עשוי להשתמש בשפע alone] if the *ta'am* would surely be *batel b'shishim* (i.e., שפע), and the *ta'am* was both absorbed and became *aino ben yomo* while it was in a permitted state, one may use it without *kashering*. Furthermore, he says that this is the explanation of the *Gemara Pesachim* that we have been discussing.²³ Thus, *Ra'ah* – a primary source for being *machmir* regarding שפע – says that שפע with "standard" *aino ben yomo* (of a previously forbidden *ta'am*) is not enough to permit the use of the utensil without *kashering*. [We will return to the case of *aino ben yomo* below].

Halacha

As noted, *Shulchan Aruch* accepts *Rashba's* ruling, and it appears that *Rema*²⁴ agrees with this as well. This is also the position of *Pri Chadash* and others.²⁵ However, *Taz*, *Shach*, *Chochmas Adam*, and many others²⁶ say that one should be *machmir* for the strict position and not allow the use of a כלי שעשוי להשתמש בשפע without *kashering*. [They are lenient where it is also פגם, as above].

---

²² Previously, we cited *Ra'ah* in *Bedek HaBayis* 4:4, pages 36a-b, which is on the topic of עשוי להשתמש בשפע, and here in the text we are referring to *Bedek HaBayis* ibid. page 36a which is on a related topic (using an *aino be yomo* meat pot for dairy without *kashering*).

²³ Additionally, *Tosfos* himself offers an alternate explanation for *Gemara Pesachim*, according to which there is no proof regarding *aino ben yomo*.

²⁴ We have seen that *Shulchan Aruch* 99:7 and 122:5 cites *Rashba's* ruling, and in both locations, *Rema* does not comment or disagree, which indicates that he agrees with it; see *Iggeros Moshe* YD 1:60 (and *Toras Ha'asham* to *Toras Chattas* cited below). There are two other indications to this position. Firstly, in *Toras Chattas* 85:12, *Rema* cites *Tur* (who cites *Rashba* and disagrees with him), *Beis Yosef* (who defends *Rashba*), and *Shulchan Aruch* (who accepts *Rashba*), which implies that he (*Rema*) agrees with this conclusion. However, in the related "*Simanim*" of *Toras Chattas*, he first says that one should be *machmir* and then notes that some are lenient, which gives the impression that he favors the strict position.

Secondly, *Tur* discusses *Rashba* in YD 122, and *Beis Yosef* on this is in YD 99 and 122. *Darchei Moshe* 99:5 (end) directs the reader to "YD 122" to see when one may cook in a pot that has *b'lios* of *issur*. This line appears to be a direct response to *Beis Yosef's* discussion of *Rashba*. When we turn to YD 122, we find (a) the only case noted where one can use a non-kosher pot (without *kashering*) is the case of שפע, and (b) *Darchei Moshe Ha'aruch* 122:5 cites *Beis Yosef's* defense of *Rashba* without adding any of his own comments. [*Darchei Moshe Ha'aruch* is what *Rema* wrote, and it was printers who chose to print only certain parts of that commentary in the volumes of *Tur*. They saw nothing added in this *Darchei Moshe Ha'aruch* so they did not include it, but *Darchei Moshe* 99:5 was seemingly referring to this]. Once again, this implies that *Rema* agrees with *Shulchan Aruch*/*Rema* on this point.

²⁵ *Pri Chadash* 122:3, *Levush* 99:7 (see also 122:4-5, and *Pri Megadim* MZ 99:15, who questions why *Taz* says *Levush* is *machmir*), and Gr"a 99:17. Additionally, we have seen previously that *Rivash* agrees with *Rashba*, and that they (and *Ran*, who personally disagrees) cite this ruling from *Ra'avad* and *Rabbeinu Yonah*.

²⁶ *Taz* 99:15, *Shach* 99:23 and 122:3, *Chochmas Adam* 52:10 (who says "all the *Acharonim*" disagree with *Rashba/Shulchan Aruch*), *Bach* 122, *Pri Megadim* MZ 99:15 & SC 99:23, and *Minchas Yaakov* 85:43. Additionally, we have previously seen that *Ra'ah*, *Ran*, and *Tur* are *machmir*. [*Aruch HaShulchan's* position will be noted below].

Nonetheless, *Chochmas Adam*[27] and others consider *Rashba* as a factor/צירוף when there are other reasons to be lenient and/or when *kashering* is somehow impossible to accomplish. Furthermore, *Aruch HaShulchan*[28] says that one can always be lenient if the item in question is *aino ben yomo* and says that this is partially based on the fact that – as we saw above – all agree that if the *ta'am* is *pagum*, one can be lenient. In other words, all are lenient if the *ta'am* is inherently לפגם and there is a question whether the same applies when it is "just" *aino ben yomo* (which is לפגם but not inherently לפגם), and he is ruling that at least in that case one can be lenient.[29] *Iggeros Moshe*[30] echoes this ruling, saying that מנהג מורי הוראה להתיר בשפע היתר דוקא לאחר מעת לעת.

As relates to certified facilities, Rav Belsky said that although halachically one could be lenient and not *kasher* a כלי שעשוי להשתמש בשפע, especially if it was *aino ben yomo*, as a matter of policy we should not rely on that except in cases where there was an added צירוף or where *kashering* was impossible. For example, some stainless-steel tanks (or pipes) have a "sight glass" which is basically a small glass window through which the operator can see into the tank. *Ashkenazim* generally do not *kasher* glass,[31] but since that position is a *chumrah*[32] and the sight glass qualifies as a עשוי להשתמש בשפע (since it is such a small part of the tank), one can be lenient and *kasher* the tank despite the glass present. Similarly, if *Mashgichim* with experience in these matters determine that there are technical reasons

---

[27] *Binas Adam*, *Sha'ar Issur V'heter* 41 (58). In that case, the צירופים were עשוי להשתמש בשפע, *aino ben yomo*, and נ"ט בר נ"ט על ידי בישול לכתחלה.
[28] *Aruch HaShulchan* 99:49. See also *Gilyon Maharsha* 99:18.
[29] It is worth bearing in mind that the two potential *issurim* to use the utensil without *kashering* – אין לכתחלה מבטלין and גזירה אינו בן יומו אטו בן יומו – are both *issurim d'rabannan*. Thus, there is reason to say that the *Acharonim* are only *machmir* regarding כלי שעשוי להשתמש בפשע within 24 hours of non-kosher use when there is some element of *issur d'oraisah* present. But they might be willing to accept *Rashba* when the utensil is *aino ben yomo* and surely not more than an *issur d'rabannan*.
In this context it is noteworthy that (a) *Pri Megadim* MZ 99:15 at first considers whether *Taz* would be lenient for שפע if the non-kosher *ta'am* was only *assur mid'rabannan* (e.g., *stam yayin*), saying משמע ולדינא צ"ע באיסור דרבנן בכלי גדול, but then seems not as sure, saying באיסור מועט דרבנן שומעין להרשב"א להקל עכ"פ שדרכו להשתמש בשפע אולי יש לצדד, and (b) we saw earlier that *Pri Megadim* SD 99:23 says that one should not be lenient on עשוי להשתמש בשפע even if the item is *aino ben yomo*.
[30] *Iggeros Moshe* YD 3:28. See also the leniency suggested by *Iggeros Moshe* YD 1:60, noted above in footnote 4.
[31] See *Rema* OC 451:26 and *Imrei Dovid*, *Kashering*, Chapter 56.
[32] Ibid.

why it is impossible to *kasher* a specific very large storage tank, one could rely on עשוי להשתמש בשפע if the tank is *aino ben yomo*.[33]

Questions

We have seen that *Shulchan Aruch* accepts the leniency of *Rashba* that a כלי שעשוי להשתמש בשפע can be used without *kashering*. However, there are at least two halachos which seem to suggest that *kashering* is required even though there is just a tiny *b'liah* which will surely be *batel* each time the utensil is used.

The first of those is that *Shulchan Aruch*[34] cites two opinions whether a utensil used for *bishul akum* must be *kashered* before it is used for kosher food. [In fact, the source of the strict opinion there is *Rashba*].[35] *Bishul akum* is *batel b'rov* and any *ta'am* absorbed into the utensil will surely be *batel b'rov* into food subsequently used in that utensil. If so, it should automatically qualify as עשוי להשתמש בשפע and *kashering* should not be required?

The second is that *Shulchan Aruch*[36] rules that one cannot *kasher* a utensil without first removing the rust that is on it, and two reasons are given for that requirement. Some understand that it is because the rust blocks the *hag'alah* water from contact with the utensil, while others say that the issue is that there might be food stuck underneath the rust (and *hag'alah* is not effective on tangible residue). If there is rust on just a small part of the utensil (as one might expect), then *hag'alah* will be perfectly effective on the non-rusted part, meaning that the part which was not *kashered* properly (i.e., where the rust is) should qualify as עשוי להשתמש בשפע. So, why can you not use the utensil even though there is some rust, and that part was not *kashered*? Is *Shulchan Aruch's* ruling regarding rust only applicable in the unusual cases where a very large part of the utensil is covered with rust?

---

[33] See also *Imrei Dovid, Kashering*, Chapter 49, where עשוי להשתמש בשפע is one factor used in determining the proper way to *kasher* storage tanks in which non-kosher was *kovush* (at ambient temperatures). See other examples there in Chapters 2 and 11 (end).
[34] *Shulchan Aruch* YD 113:16.
[35] *Rashba, Toras HaBayis* 3:7, page 95b (end).
[36] *Shulchan Aruch* OC 451:3.

Both these halachos appear to say that *kashering* is required even though the *b'liah* seemingly qualifies for *Rashba's* leniency of שפע. Elsewhere,[37] we have discussed these questions and noted Rav Schachter's suggestion that there is a supra-halachic requirement to *kasher* utensils even when עשוי להשתמש בשפע says that it is not necessary. Clearly, sources are required to support this assertion, and the fact that none of the *Poskim* mention this in connection with our halacha (עשוי להשתמש בשפע) appears to be an implicit rejection of that notion.

These questions require further consideration.

---

[37] See *Imrei Dovid, Pas Yisroel and Bishul Yisroel*, Chapter 48 (for the question about *bishul akum*) and *Imrei Dovid, Kashering*, Chapter 11 (for the question about rust). In the latter source, we noted the following (the second of which only addresses the issue of rust):

[Footnote 17] Rav Belsky suggested that *Rashba* is only lenient in cases where the non-kosher was absorbed into a small portion of the pot (for example) such that if the pot was filled that high with food there would be enough food to be *mevatel* the non-kosher *ta'am*. But if *ta'am* was absorbed into all parts of the pot but it happens to be that the *ta'am* will always be *batel* (due to the size of the pot or the percentage of non-kosher in the original food), then *Rashba* would not be lenient. Not only is there no indication in *Rashba* (or others) to support this, but Rav Schachter pointed out that *Rashba's* two proofs (*Gemara, Pesachim* 30a and *Avodah Zara* 33b) are from exactly those types of cases where *ta'am* was absorbed into all parts of the utensil.

[Footnote 25] A possible answer might be that when just a small amount of *ta'am* is absorbed into a utensil, there is no requirement to *kasher* it (assuming it qualifies as a עשוי להשתמש בשפע). But if enough *ta'am* is absorbed to require *kashering*, then a full *kashering* must be done and it is not sufficient to just remove "enough" to get it below the threshold of being *nosein ta'am*. For this reason, once a utensil is non-kosher, the rust must be removed even though the amount of *ta'am* left underneath the rust is not enough to affect food cooked in the utensil afterwards. Such a concept is cited by *Shevet HaLevi* 2:33d from *Ritva* (*Avodah Zara* 76a). *Shevet HaLevi* shows that other *Rishonim* disagree with the premise which underlies *Ritva's* opinion, and that *Pri Megadim* (MZ 451:16) proves that *Shulchan Aruch* YD 121:5 follows that approach. That said, they may still agree with the final concept that once *kashering* is required, one cannot be satisfied with a partial removal of *ta'am*, and every last bit must be taken out.

See also *Imrei Dovid, Animal Products*, Chapter 48, footnote 6.

Chapter 30

בריה

שולחן ערוך סימן ק' סעיף א
בריה, דהיינו כגון נמלה או עוף טמא וגיד הנשה ואבר מן החי וביצה שיש בה אפרוח וכיוצא בהם, אפילו באלף לא בטל. ואין לו דין בריה אלא אם כן הוא דבר שהיה בו חיות, לאפוקי חטה אחת של איסור. וכן צריך שיהא דבר שאסור מתחלת ברייתו, לאפוקי עוף טהור שנתנבל ושור הנסקל, וכן צריך שיהיה דבר שלם שאם יחלק אין שמו עליו, לאפוקי חלב, וכן צריך שיהיה שלם.

הגה: ועיקר גיד הנשה אינו אלא על הכף בלבד, והוא כרותב ד' אצבעות, ואם הוא שלם מקרי בריה.

Bitul is a process of nullification, which is to say that the forbidden item is so insignificant that it does not affect the other parts of the mixture. Therefore, there are certain times when the issur is either inherently important or plays a noteworthy role in the mixture, and therefore is not suited for bitul. This chapter discusses one such example (בריה), and others are discussed in Chapters 1 (דבר דבר), 31 (המעמיד), 33 (חתיכה הראויה להתכבד), 35 (דבר שיש לו מתירין), (חזותא), and 62 (חשוב, דבר שבמנין).

מלקות

The current halacha[1] says that a non-kosher *beryah* which is mixed into other foods cannot become *batel* regardless of how diluted the *beryah* is. [*Beryah* is roughly translated as an "entire item"; more details below]. The *Gemara*[2] records this halacha for a very specific case – גיד הנשה – without much detail. However, the status of *beryah* is also relevant for the halacha that someone who eats a *beryah* of forbidden food receives the punishment of מלקות even if the *beryah* is not a *kezayis* in size (which is the

---

[1] *Shulchan Aruch* 100:1.
[2] *Gemara, Chullin* 99b-100a, explaining *Mishnah, Chullin* 96b.

typical amount one must eat to receive מלקות).³ *Rishonim* understood that the criteria for both of these halachos are identical. In fact, it is suggested that the reason *Chazal*⁴ created the restriction that a *beryah* cannot be *batel* is <u>because</u> one receives מלקות for eating a *beryah*; the מלקות indicates that there is something special about the *beryah* even in small amounts, and it is due to that distinctiveness that it cannot be *batel*.⁵ Based on several sources regarding *beryah* and מלקות, and known cases where forbidden items <u>can</u> be *batel b'shishim*,⁶ the *Rishonim* clarify that there are four criteria to define a *beryah*, and those are recorded in our halacha.⁷

Four Criteria

~ **Living**

The גיד הנשה is part of a living animal and is considered a *beryah*, but a kernel of wheat⁸ is not and therefore it can be *batel*. An example of a forbidden kernel of wheat is one which is *chodosh*, but we will see in Chapter 33 that there is a separate reason why it cannot be *batel*.⁹ Therefore, a better example is that eggs laid by an insect are not considered *beryos* and can be *batel* since there is no living being inside them.¹⁰

---

[3] For another case where a forbidden item's special status for מלקות potentially translates into a stricter status regarding *bitul* (somewhat similar to *beryah*), see *Rema* 104:1 as per *Badei HaShulchan* 104:12.
[4] Most assume that this principle, that *beryah* is not *batel*, is Rabbinic in nature; see for example, *Taz* 100:1 and *Pri Megadim* ad loc. If so, does it maybe not apply to foods which themselves are only *assur mid'rabbanan*? See *Badei HaShulchan* (Biurim) 100:1 s.v. *beryah* who discusses this issue. However, the question is primarily academic, as there are few practical cases of *issurim d'rabbanan* which meet the criteria for *beryah* (discussed further in this chapter).
[5] *Taz* 100:1. In other words, *bitul* is an assumption that the minor ingredient is unimportant and nullified, but if there is something unusual about this ingredient, that prevents us from viewing it as unimportant and suited for *bitul*.
[6] Among the sources are: [1] גיד הנשה is the one case where the *Gemara* (*Chullin* 99b-100a) says that it cannot be *batel* since it is a *beryah*; [2] a person receives מלקות for eating a whole living kosher bird even if it is not a *kezayis* in size (*Gemara*, *Chullin* 102b); [3] if the kosher bird is dead, or they eat a whole non-kosher bird (alive or dead), they only receive מלקות if they eat a *kezayis* (ibid.); [4] the forbidden fats of an animal (חלב), *arlah*, and כלאי הכרם can be *batel b'shishim*; [5] a שור הנסקל can be *batel* into non-*kodashim* (*Gemara*, *Zevachim* 70b-72a); and [6] a kernel of wheat is not considered a *beryah* (regarding מלקות) since it is not a living being (*Gemara*, *Makkos* 17a).
[7] See *Pri Megadim* SD 100:3 (and *Rebbi Akiva Eiger* ad loc., as printed in the *Machon Yerushalayim* edition of *Shulchan Aruch*) regarding the source and necessity for all four criteria.
[8] See Source #6 in footnote 6.
[9] However, we will see there that a דבר שיש לו מתירין <u>can</u> be *batel* if it is mixed מין בשאינו מינו (but *beryah* cannot, see below). Thus, if a *chodosh* grain was mixed into other items מין בשאינו מינו, it would be relevant to know that it is not considered a *beryah*.
[10] *Machzeh Eliyahu* 1:95; see more on this in *Imrei Dovid, Halachos of Insects*, Chapter 10.

~ אסור מתחלת ברייתו

Only items which are inherently forbidden from the time they are created are deemed *beryos*, but those which were born "kosher" and only became *assur* at some later point, can be *batel*. This is one reason why a piece of נבילה (meat that did not have *shechitah*) can be *batel*; the status of נבילה began when the animal died, so it is not אסור מתחלת ברייתו.[11] A common example of a food that appears to be אסור מתחלת ברייתו is an insect, and for that reason it is commonly assumed that whole insects cannot be *batel* when they get mixed into a food. But Rav Shlomo Kluger[12] asks that most insects are permitted until they walk on the ground, which means that for the first second they were born they were not *assur*; if so, they are not אסור מתחלת ברייתו?

We discussed this question in *Imrei Dovid, Halachos of Insects*, Chapter 3, where [among other things] we quoted *Chavos Da'as* and *Pri Megadim*,[13] who responded that:

> ...the real criterion is that the *beryah* must be <u>inherently</u> forbidden, and אסור מתחלת ברייתו is merely a common way of measuring if the item meets that requirement. Accordingly, *Chavos Da'as* argues that an insect is considered "inherently forbidden" even before it fulfills the technical requirement of walking on the ground, and, therefore, it is a *beryah* which cannot be *batel*.

> ...before a land-based insect leaves its birthplace it is considered a part of the vegetable, and therefore as a "vegetable" it is permitted.[14] Only when the insect leaves the vegetable is it viewed as a separate entity, which is then forbidden as an "insect". Accordingly, as soon as the creature becomes an "insect" it is forbidden and qualifies as אסור מתחלת ברייתו.

~ אם יחלק אין שמו עליו

One of the cases which seems to meet both preceding criteria is חלב (the forbidden fats of an animal); it is part of a living animal and is inherently non-kosher from the moment the animal is born. Why then is it that חלב can be *batel b'shishim*?[15] The answer to this question goes to the heart of why a person typically receives מלקות for eating a *beryah*, but otherwise must eat a *kezayis* to deserve that punishment. The general rule is that a person is not considered to have truly "eaten" something – whether that

---

[11] See Sources #3 and #5 in footnote 6.
[12] *Tuv Ta'am Vada'as* 1:160.
[13] *Chavos Da'as* 100:5 and *Pri Megadim* SD 100:31.
[14] Accordingly, there is no *timtum halev* from eating the insect before it walks (Rav Gissinger, cited in *Imrei Dovid, Animal Products*, Chapter 22).
[15] See Source #4 in footnote 6.

is for a *mitzvah* (e.g., *matzah* on *Pesach*) or an *aveirah* (e.g., non-kosher food) – unless they eat a *kezayis*. But when the *Torah* says, "do not eat X", that is understood to mean that if someone eats an <u>entire</u> "X" they have surely violated the *Torah's* precept. For this reason, if a person eats an entire insect, for example, they receive מלקות even if the insect is not as large as a *kezayis*.

The above is true only if the forbidden item comprises a unit that the *Torah* forbade. In that case, the prohibition applies to the unit even if it is not a *kezayis* in size. A way of determining if something is actually a "unit" is by seeing how you refer to a <u>part</u> of that item. In the case of an insect, you would say that this is part of a forbidden insect, and the fact that when the insect is divided you describe it differently – אם יחלק אין שמו עליו / *if it is divided, it does not retain its appellation* – that indicates that the undivided insect is the unit that the *Torah* forbade, and it is considered a *beryah*.

But in the case of חלב, each small piece of the fat is referred to as חלב just like the larger, complete piece of חלב. This means that any piece of חלב – even if it is a "complete" piece of חלב delineated in the *Torah* (e.g., חלב המכסה את הקרב) – is not a *beryah*.

Rav Schachter said that this is another reason why insect eggs are not *beryos* and therefore can be *batel*. While it true that half an egg is not called an "egg", the *Torah* does not say "do not eat insect eggs". Rather, the prohibition is "do not eat excretions/*yotzeh* from a non-kosher animal or insect". In that context, half an insect egg or a whole insect egg are both referred to as a *yotzeh*, and no one would say that the half egg is a "partial *yotzeh*". Therefore, he said that insect eggs are not *beryos*.[16]

~ **Complete**
The most obvious requirement for a *beryah* is that it be complete, and the following is a quote from *Imrei Dovid, Halachos of Insects*, Chapter 8, regarding that issue: [See there for sources].

> The previous chapter mentioned the concept of "*beryah*", which literally means a "creation" but is used to refer to a complete insect, and that status

---

[16] See *Imrei Dovid, Halachos of Insects*, Chapter 10, cited above. See also *Pri Megadim* and *Rebbi Akiva Eiger* to *Shach* 86:10 (discussed in *Imrei Dovid, Animal Products*, Chapter 28, footnote 20) who essentially raise the same question on the possibility that ova (partially formed eggs taken from inside a chicken after it is slaughtered) are *beryos*. [In turn, they are questioning *Shulchan Aruch* 86:3 who rules that ova cannot be *batel*].

relates to two halachos: Firstly, there is a special *issur* to eat a complete insect even if it is not a *kezayis* in size. Secondly, a complete insect cannot become *batel*.

As relates to the former, the *Gemara*[17] questions how much of an insect must be missing before it is no longer considered "complete". Does the term "*beryah*" refer to an insect which is 100% complete or one which is complete-enough to be viable? If it means "complete" then even if the insect is missing a leg or some other non-critical body part (אבר שאין הנשמה תלויה בו) it is no longer a *beryah*, but if the term "complete" refers to a viable being, then it only loses that status if it is missing a part of the body that it cannot live without. The *Gemara* does not resolve this question.

The *Gemara* is discussing the first issue (eating a whole insect), and the *Rishonim* understand that this same issue also relates to the second issue (*bitul*). Accordingly, *Shach*[18] rules that since this question is unresolved and since it is a mere Rabbinic principle that a *beryah* cannot be *batel*, one may be lenient and assume that as soon as an insect is missing any part of its body – even a non-critical part – it is no longer a *beryah* and can be *batel b'shishim*.

Beis Yosef also cites *Haga'os Sha'arei Durah* as saying that if part of a whole non-kosher fish dissolved during cooking, it is still considered a *beryah* because that shrinkage is common and typical. If we were to accept this opinion it would mean that an insect whose leg was cut off as part of the cooking process might still be considered a *beryah* and not be *batel*.

Although *Beis Yosef* does not cite anyone who disagrees with this position, *Magen Avraham* says that it is actually dependent on a *machlokes Rishonim*. Accordingly, *Mishnah Berurah*[19] rules that since *Rema* appears to follow the *Rishonim* who "argue" on *Haga'os Sha'arei Durah*, one may be lenient as it relates to the *Hilchos Berachos* aspect of *beryah*, and assume that something is not a *beryah* even if it is only incomplete due to cooking. Similarly, *Binas Adam*[20] rules that one may be lenient as relates to the *bitul* of a *beryah* which has lost a leg or other body part during cooking.

This is why there are certain leniencies when infested produce is cooked or pureed; the possibility that the insects were broken apart and are no longer *beryos* means that they are now potentially suitable for *bitul*.[21]

---

[17] *Gemara, Nazir* 51b-52a.
[18] *Shach* 100:6.
[19] *Mishnah Berurah* 210:8 as per *Sha'ar HaTziun* 210:23.
[20] *Binas Adam* 53 (72).
[21] See *Shach* 84:29 cited in *Imrei Dovid, Halachos of Insects*, Chapter 31. See also ad loc. Chapter 16 footnote 10.

Other details

Although the principle that a *beryah* cannot be *batel* is Rabbinic in nature, many suggest that it also applies to foods that themselves are only *assur mid'rabannan*.[22] However, since it is a *d'rabannan* if one is unsure if there is a *beryah* present, they may apply the rule that *safek d'rabannan l'kulah* and permit the mixture.[23] [We discussed a possible practical application of this *Imrei Dovid, Halachos of Insects*, Chapter 32].

Some *Rishonim* say that a *beryah* can be *batel* if it is diluted in 960 times its volume,[24] but *Shulchan Aruch* rules that it can never be *batel*, and for that reason he says that "it is not *batel* even in 1,000".[25]

Beryah is not *batel* regardless of whether it is mixed as מין במינו or מין בשאינו מינו.[26] However, it is only the *beryah* itself which is not *batel*. If a person is able to remove the non-kosher *beryah* from the mixture, the *ta'am* that *beryah* exuded is *batel b'shishim* just like *ta'am* coming from any other food.[27] It therefore follows that even if the *beryah* was not removed, but is small enough that it would be *batel b'shishim*, there is no need to *kasher* the utensil that the mixture was in. The mixture itself is forbidden since it has a *beryah* mixed into it, but the utensil has no *ta'am* of *issur* and therefore can be used without *kashering*.[28]

See in Chapter 46 where we consider whether the insect's negative taste (נותן טעם לפגם) should mean that it can be *batel* despite its being a *beryah*.

Berachos

The concept of *beryah* also has relevance to *hilchos berachos*. The general rule is that one does not recite a *bracha* after eating food unless they ate a

---

[22] See above in footnote 4.
[23] *Taz* 100:1. One may only be lenient if there is a *safek* whether the forbidden item is a *beryah* or not (e.g., one is unsure if it is complete), but if it is a *beryah* and the *safek* is if it is a forbidden item at all (e.g., it is a full גיד but one is unsure if it is a גיד הנשה), then one must be *machmir* since the "*safek*" relates to a question of a *d'oraisah* (i.e., is this item forbidden) (ibid., and see also *Shach* 101:2).
[24] *Rashba, Toras HaBayis* 4:1 page 14b, cited in *Beis Yosef* to 100:4.
[25] See *Imrei Dovid, Halachos of Insects*, Chapter 33, that some considered the opinion (that *beryah* is *batel* in 960) as a partial justification for certain leniencies. There it also discusses the possibility that the principle that a *beryah* cannot be *batel* might not apply to the tiny and unappetizing insects found in vegetables.
[26] *Rema* 101:6.
[27] *Shulchan Aruch* 100:2. What if something separates from the mixture and we are not sure if it is the *beryah* or not? See *Shulchan Aruch* 110:6-8 and Chapter 63.
[28] See above in Chapter 1, Part 2.

kezayis, and *Shulchan Aruch*[29] records that some say that if a person eats a *beryah* they should recite a *bracha* even if it is not a *kezayis* in size. However, he notes that since not all *Poskim* agree with this position, one should avoid the issue by never eating a *beryah* (unless they eat a *kezayis* of the food).

In this context, *Shulchan Aruch*, *Rema*, and *Mishnah Berurah*, say that the definition of *beryah* is different for *berachos* than for (מלקות or) *bitul*. The first three criteria – from a living being, אסור מתחלת ברייתו, and אם יחלק אין שמו עליו – do not apply, and a whole grape, cherry, bean, or small fish,[30] are also considered a *beryah*. The one requirement that there is, is that the item must be complete (like for *bitul*). From that perspective, if part of the fruit or vegetables is missing, it is not a *beryah*, and this means that even if an inedible pit was not eaten with the food, the person has not eaten the complete *beryah*.[31]

---

[29] *Shulchan Aruch* OC 210:1.
[30] *Shulchan Aruch* (grape), *Mishnah Berurah* 210:5 (cherry, bean), and *Sha'ar HaTziun* 210:20 (fish).
[31] *Rema* 210:1 as per *Mishnah Berurah* 210:9.

Chapter 31

חתיכה הראויה להתכבד

שולחן ערוך סימן ק"א סעיף א
חתיכה הראויה להתכבד דינה כבריה דאפילו באלף לא בטלה. ואפילו אם היא אסורה בהנאה כיון שאם תתבטל היתה מותרת וראויה להתכבד.

הגה: ואפילו אינה אסורה רק מדרבנן אינה בטילה. ואם הוא ספק אם ראויה להתכבד או לא אזלינן לקולא אפילו היא אסורה מדאורייתא.

Basic halachos

A food which is so respectable that it would be served to honored guests (חתיכה הראויה להתכבד, defined below) is too significant to become *batel*, even if it is just 1/1000th of a mixture.[1] This strictness applies whether the forbidden item is מין במינו or מין בשאינו מינו with the rest of the items,[2] and even if the item itself is only *assur mid'rabannan*.[3] [An exception is that *pas akum* and *bishul akum* can be *batel b'rov* even if they are a חתיכה הראויה להתכבד.][4]

Since the concept of חתיכה הראויה להתכבד is Rabbinic in nature, if one is unsure whether a given food qualifies, they can be lenient and assume it does not.[5] However, if the food is surely ראויה להתכבד but we are unsure

---

[1] *Shulchan Aruch* 101:1.
[2] *Rema* 101:6.
[3] *Rema* 101:1.
[4] *Shach* YD 112:23.
[5] *Rema* 101:1.
  However, the general leniency of תולין בדרבנן (see *Imrei Dovid, Alcoholic Beverages*, Chapter 20) does not allow us to assume that if some of the pieces became broken (i.e., no longer ראויה להתכבד) that it was the forbidden one which was broken (*Shulchan Aruch* 101:7); rather, כל דפריש (see Chapter 63) dictates that it was one of the permitted ones that broke (*Taz* 101:14).

whether it is forbidden at all, then we must be *machmir*.⁶ For example, if a *pegimah* is discovered in the knife used for *shechitah*, the animal is forbidden based on a safek that the *pegimah* might have rendered it a נבילה,⁷ and if part of that animal which is ראויה להתכבד is mixed into other meat, it cannot be *batel*. The meat is surely ראויה להתכבד and the *safek* is whether it is forbidden; in that case, the meat cannot be *batel*.

The חתיכה הראויה להתכבד must be inherently forbidden, such as a piece of meat which is a נבילה or בשר בחלב.⁸ But if there is a food which is inherently permitted but cannot be eaten due to some external factor, it can be *batel*. Some examples of this are kosher meat which absorbed non-kosher *ta'am*,⁹ meat which was never salted and is therefore saturated with (non-kosher) blood,¹⁰ or a vegetable which is infested with insects. In each of these cases, the food which is ראויה להתכבד (i.e., the meat or vegetable) is actually permitted, but there it is something else (i.e., the *b'liah*, blood, or insect) that prevents people from eating it; therefore, it can be *batel* into other foods as per the standard rules of *bitul*.

Lastly, if a food is only ראויה להתכבד when it is whole or in a large piece, then that food can be *batel* if it has already been cut into smaller pieces.¹¹ For example, if salmon steaks are ראויים להתכבד, then they cannot be *batel* when they are in that form, but if the fish is cut into small pieces or ground up to the point that it is no longer ראויה להתכבד, then it can be *batel*. Furthermore, *Chochmas Adam*¹² says that if individual small pieces of meat are not ראויים להתכבד but multiple small pieces served together are, the small pieces can be *batel* since that form of meat is not ראויה להתכבד as is.

An example where this last point is relevant is for Chinese-style restaurants. They commonly cut up all meat and chicken into small pieces before they cook and prepare them for serving. No one would serve one small piece of meat to an honored guest, so if the store mistakenly had non-kosher meat which was cut up in this manner, it could be *batel* into

---

⁶ *Shach* 101:2. Since the halacha is that one must be *machmir* on the *safek issur* (before it was mixed into the other items), that is considered a "decided" fact; therefore, when it becomes mixed into other foods the principle of חתיכה הראויה להתכבד comes into effect.
⁷ See *Shulchan Aruch* YD 18:11 and *Shach* 18:1.
⁸ *Shulchan Aruch* 101:2. Although the meat and milk are not individually *assur*, the mixture is considered inherently forbidden and therefore can qualify as a חתיכה הראויה להתכבד.
⁹ *Shulchan Aruch* ibid.
¹⁰ *Rema* 101:2.
¹¹ *Shulchan Aruch* 101:6 as per *Shach* 101:15.
¹² *Chochmas Adam* 53:11. See also *Nekudos HaKesef* to *Taz* 101:10 and *Pri Megadim* MZ 101:10.

the kosher meat that they have. This is true even if the finished dish prepared by the restaurant is ראויה להתכבד, since the small pieces are not.

Defining ראויה להתכבד

The *Poskim*[13] provide many examples of foods that are or are not considered ראויה להתכבד, and they also tell us that the criterion for which foods qualify is not the same in all times and places.[14] While those discussions are helpful in intuiting which foods are ראויה להתכבד, we may be able to get a more specific definition by considering a statement of *Darchei Moshe*[15] which, at first glance, seems hard to understand.

There are two halachos which have similar standards. The first is that food which is [not edible raw and is] fit for a royal table (*oleh al shulchan melachim*) is only kosher if a Jew participates in the cooking (*bishul Yisroel*). Second is our halacha that a food that is so special that it would be served to honored guests cannot be *batel* if it gets mixed into other foods. Seemingly, any food that qualifies for the first halacha, should also qualify for the second one; if you would serve it to a king then it would obviously be appropriate for any guest. Why then does *Darchei Moshe* say that a *kurkuvan* (gizzard) is *oleh al shulchan melachim* even though it is not a חתיכה הראויה להתכבד? How can a food be suitable for a king's feast but not be appropriate to serve to honored guests?

We need two pieces of information to answer this question. One is from the source[16] for the statement that a *kurkuvan* is not a חתיכה הראויה להתכבד. The *Gemara*[17] says that אוכליהן לאו בר אינש which literally means that people who eat *kurkuvans* are subhuman. But the *Gemara* then explains that אוכליהן כבשר לענין זביני לאו בר אינש which means that no one (literally, no

---

[13] See *Shulchan Aruch* 101:3-5 and the *Poskim* ad loc.

[14] *Taz* 101:9 (based loosely on *Shulchan Aruch* 110:1), *Shach* 101:12, and others.
   If חתיכה הראויה להתכבד changes from place to place and from time to time, why do the *Poskim* list specific foods that do or do not qualify? Why would that information be relevant to future generations? *Minchas Yaakov* 40:8 suggests two answers which both say that there is a special strictness to any food which *Poskim* recorded as being חתיכה הראויה להתכבד. Either one must always be *machmir* about those foods (even if they are not ראויה להתכבד in a given location), or that if one is unsure, they should be *machmir*. [It is not clear what the basis for this strictness would be, but see *Shulchan Aruch* 110:1 who says something similar in a somewhat different context]. *Pri Megadim* MZ 101:9 says that one should (at least) follow the latter approach. Neither *Minchas Yaakov* nor *Pri Megadim* clarify if this applies only to statements of the earliest *Poskim*, or to any written record of a *Posek* who considered a specific food חתיכה הראויה להתכבד in his time and place.

[15] *Darchei Moshe* 113:3, cited by *Shach* 113:2.

[16] See *Beis Yosef* to *Shulchan Aruch* 101:5 and *Gr"a* 101:15.

[17] *Gemara*, *Nedarim* 54b.

"human") would choose to buy *kurkuvan* if they could just as easily buy a standard piece of meat. In other words, it is not that people do not eat *kurkuvan*,[18] but rather that it is always a second choice to a "regular" piece of meat.

The other piece of information we need is a more accurate definition of the term חתיכה הראויה להתכבד. While it is true that it means "a food that would be served to honored guests",[19] the implication of that simple translation would be that the word "להתכבד" means "honored". In fact, the complete term in the *Gemara*[20] is חתיכה ה...ראויה להתכבד בה לפני האורחים and להתכבד is a reflexive verb (לשון התפעל) which means it reflects back on the subject of the sentence. It is not clear if the subject of the sentence is the food (חתיכה) or the unspoken person serving the food, but it is surely not the guest. In other words, the phrase means, the food is of a nature that when you serve it to guest it brings respect to the person serving it (or that it is a "respectable" food).

Based on the *Gemara* of אוכליהן לאו בר אינש this means as follows. *Kurkuvan* is a "second choice" food (אוכליהן כבשר לעניני זביני לאו בר אינש); it is therefore axiomatic that when it is served to guests it will not engender admiration for the host. That does not mean that it would not be served to them, just that it is not the part of the meal that causes them to applaud the person who gave it to them. For example, one might serve their honored guest a steak together with rice and salad. All three are appropriate and all three are therefore considered *oleh al shulchan melachim*, but the steak is the only one which is ראויה להתכבד. Just as the side dishes in this example are *oleh al shulchan melachim* but are not ראויה להתכבד, so too any food, like *kurkuvan*, which is a second-choice food, is not ראויה להתכבד.

In summary: if the focus of ראויה להתכבד was on the person <u>receiving</u> the food (the honored guest), then we would have a hard time understanding

---

[18] In fact, *Gemara*, *Beitzah* 7a, says that some people eat קורקבן and others do not.
   When *Gr"a* ibid. cites the basis for the halacha that קורקבן is not a חתיכה הראויה להתכבד he cites three sources: 1 – this *Gemara*, *Beitzah*, 2 – *Gemara*, *Nedarim* ibid., and 3 – *Gemara*, *Me'ilah* 20b. Of these, #1 does not say אוכליהן לאו בר אינש or anything else "negative" about eating them, and #3 says that line but does not explain it (and only #2 does). Possibly, as per the text here, *Gr"a* is citing #1 as the "introduction" to the actual sources which is #2, and then adds in #3 because there *Rashi* explains what אוכליהן כבשר לעניני זביני לאו בר אינש means (and there is no *Rashi* in *Nedarim* to explain it).
[19] See *Pri Megadim* MZ 101:1 who says it refers to אורחים יקרים וחשובים. See also *Issur V'heter* 43:2 (which is a partial source for *Darchei Moshe* ibid.) who uses the term אורחים נכבדים.
[20] *Gemara*, *Chullin* 100a.

how a food which is not ראויה להתכבד can possibly be *oleh al shulchan melachim*. But we have now seen that ראויה להתכבד refers to a food that reflects honor on the person serving it, and that is limited to the finest foods. This is a much higher standard than what qualifies as *oleh al shulchan melachim*. Accordingly, the ruling of *Darchei Moshe* is understandable.[21]

This understanding provides us with a more accurate definition of חתיכה הראויה להתכבד. It is not any food that one would serve to honored guests, but rather certain special foods that are (typically) the finest main dishes which reflect honor on the person serving them.[22] It also helps us understand that – at least in the modern era – the primary foods which qualify as חתיכה הראויה להתכבד are pieces of meat, poultry, and fish.

Raw Meat

Does the piece of meat (or other food) have to be fit for honored guests as-is, or does it even include pieces that will only be ראויה להתכבד when they are cooked or otherwise prepared? *Shulchan Aruch*[23] rules in accordance with the former position, and therefore meat which is raw or too large to serve respectably, is not considered ראויה להתכבד and can be *batel*. But *Rema* argues that if all that is required is some small amount of preparation, the meat is considered ראויה להתכבד. This includes meat which requires *melichah*, or dividing into serving-sized pieces, or cooking. For example, a forequarter of beef is a חתיכה הראויה להתכבד which cannot

---

[21] It may be that the explanation given in the text is included in how *Avnei Nezer* YD 96:2 explains *Darchei Moshe/Shach*, as follows:

ונראה דטעם דברים חשובים שאין בטלים משום שמחמת חשיבותם עומדים בפני עצמם ואינם מתבטלים לאחרים, אבל אלו שחשיבותם רק לפרפרת הפת לא לעצמם שפיר בטלים.

[22] An alternative answer to the questions posed in the text can be suggested based on the words of *Issur V'Heter* ibid. who leads up to the discussion of *kurkuvan* by saying, ...ודרך אדם להזמין חבירו עליו וה"ה בני מעיים של בהמה וכה"ג אף על פי שאין הדבר ראוי ליתן לפני אורחים נכבדים One could understand that he means to differentiate between the prohibition of *bishul akum* and the inability for חתיכה הראויה להתכבד to be *batel*. *Bishul akum* is forbidden because it encourages friendship which might lead to intermarriage (see *Imrei Dovid, Pas Yisroel and Bishul Yisroel*, Chapter 1), so it includes any food which might be served in a social setting (ודרך אדם להזמין חבירו עליו). In contrast, חתיכה הראויה להתכבד is a food that is so significant that it cannot be *batel*. Those are not the foods one would serve to their "friends", but rather what they would present to distinguished guests (הדבר ראוי ליתן לפני אורחים נכבדים). For example, the foods someone serves at a neighborhood barbecue are very different from what they would have when a dignitary was eating at their home. The former meets the criterion for *bishul akum* but are not חתיכה הראויה להתכבד, while the latter are חתיכה הראויה להתכבד (and might be "too fancy" for *bishul akum*?). Thus, the standards for these two halachos might seem similar but once we probe the reasons for these Rabbinic enactments, we realize that they are not identical. The weakness of this answer is that it seems to be inconsistent with the way all the *Poskim* describe the criterion for *bishul akum* as "עולה על שולחן מלכים"; see also *Imrei Dovid* ibid., Chapter 27.

[23] *Shulchan Aruch* 101:3, citing the strict opinion only as a "ויש חולקים בכל זה".

be *batel* even though it cannot be served to guests without being salted, cut up, and cooked. However, if significant effort is needed to prepare the meat – such as removing the hide from an animal[24] or removing the feathers from a chicken[25] – then it is not ראויה להתכבד.[26]

This *machlokes* is relevant to many situations where the question of חתיכה הראויה להתכבד arises. Here are some examples of this which we will see in future chapters:

- After many animals' lungs were checked and the kosher carcasses were segregated, someone noticed that there was a worm inside one of the skulls, which means that one of the "kosher" carcasses is actually a *teraifah* (Chapter 62).

- A proprietor is caught sneaking non-kosher meat into his store, and at this point no one can tell which meat is kosher and which is not (Chapter 64).

- 200 animals had *melichah* and it was determined that, for a handful of them, more than 72 hours passed between the time of *shechitah* and *melichah*, but at this point no one can identify the meat which was salted too late (Chapter 33).

In these cases, the mixture of kosher and non-kosher meat occurred when the meat was raw. *Shulchan Aruch* would not consider this an example of חתיכה הראויה להתכבד, while *Rema* would say that it potentially is and therefore *bitul* is not possible.

The case where [even] *Rema* is lenient can also be relevant in a slaughterhouse. For example, if *shechitah* was not performed properly, but the animal was mistakenly not marked as being a נבילה, and now we do not know which of the carcasses is the forbidden one. Similarly, it is common that at a commercial chicken *shechitah*, the *shochet* will not check his knife after each bird, but instead might only check it after every 50.[27] If

---

[24] *Rema* ad loc., as per *Taz* 101:6 and *Shach* 101:10.
[25] *Rema* ibid.
[26] *Shach* 101:7 says that the need for much effort to prepare the meat for eating is also a reason it does not qualify as a דבר שבמנין (see Chapter 62).
 What if the hide was removed but the animal still requires *nikkur*? See below in footnote 35.
[27] This is because it is rare to find a *pegimah* in the knife after *shechitah* of birds, so it is financially worthwhile to check less often and be willing to occasionally throw out many birds (i.e., all those *shechted* since the previous time the knife was checked), rather than spend a few seconds after each *shechitah* to check the knife.

he finds a significant *pegimah*, all birds *shechted* since the last time he checked the knife are all considered non-kosher. But what if there are several *shochetim* present and all their chickens end up on the same processing line? That line now has 50 chickens from this *shochet* which are not kosher and might have 250 chickens from other *shochetim* which are kosher (since their knives did not have *pegimos*). In both of these cases, it is likely that as a matter of policy, the *hashgachah* will not allow any of the questionable meat or chicken to be sold as kosher, but what is the baseline halacha?

We have seen that *Rema* is lenient not to consider a whole animal or bird to be a חתיכה הראויה להתכבד if the hide (for an animal) or feathers (for a bird) have not been removed. What about in the examples we gave? Any carcasses which still have their hide or feathers on are surely *batel*, since even *Rema* agrees that they are not a חתיכה הראויה להתכבד. However, those carcasses which are further along in their processing and already had their hide or feathers removed, are considered a חתיכה הראויה להתכבד and are not *batel*. Although the תערובות of carcasses began <u>before</u> the hide or feathers were removed [at which time the forbidden ones could be *batel*], the decision whether *bitul* occurs is made at the time that people became aware of the issue (ידיעת התערובות). Any animals or birds which are חתיכה הראויה להתכבד at that time are not *batel*, even though they were not חתיכה הראויה להתכבד (since they still had a hide or feathers) when the תערובות was first created.[28]

൙ ൞

This ruling of *Rema* is the starting point for many *chumros* when there is a תערובות of non-kosher and kosher meat or poultry, such as in the cases noted earlier. Sometimes, being *machmir* on this issue will lead to a significant financial loss for the people involved, and at times there may be other mitigating factors to consider being lenient. In that context, it is worth noting *Pri Megadim's*[29] interpretation of the subtle differences between how *Rema* chooses to argue with *Shulchan Aruch* in different locations. If he cites an opinion and says "וכן עיקר", that means he is firmly accepting that position, and we – Ashkenazim – follow that as well. But

---

[28] *Teshuvos Radvaz* 1:267 (cited in *Pischei Teshuvah* 101:5), and *Pri Megadim* SD 101:8 (and 110:13). However, meat which was *batel* at the time of ידיעת התערובות remains permitted even if the hide or feathers are later removed (*Shulchan Aruch* 101:3).

[29] *Pri Megadim*, סדר והנהגת השואל עם הנשאל באיסור והיתר 3:6 and elsewhere, including SD 101:8 where he is commenting on *Rema* 101:3.

when he just says וכן נוהגין, or והכי נוהגין, or וכן המנהג, or [as he says in our case] וכן נוהגין, that means that it is merely a custom to be *machmir*, but it is not a decisive ruling.³⁰ Accordingly, if there is some other *safek* or reason to be lenient, it is possible to follow the more lenient approach.

Our halacha – where *Rema* says that raw meat, etc., is considered a חתיכה הראויה להתכבד – is one of the instances where *Pri Megadim* notes this idea, suggesting that under the right circumstances it might be appropriate to follow the ruling of *Shulchan Aruch* that only meat which is fully cooked and ready to eat can possibly qualify as חתיכה הראויה להתכבד.³¹

Blends

Thus far, we have considered which foods qualify as חתיכה הראויה להתכבד, and we now turn to two types of cases where that determination is potentially affected by the blending of two items.

~ Part is and part is not

We have seen that an animal carcass in the slaughterhouse might or might not be a חתיכה הראויה להתכבד depending on whether or not the hide has been removed. But what about the fact that even if the hide was removed (and the meat was fully cooked), certain parts of the animal will never be ראויה להתכבד? *Pri Megadim* addresses this issue and divides it into three different cases, as follows.

1. The animals' hides were removed, and the carcasses were butchered into separate pieces, some of which are ראויה להתכבד and others are not. For example, we might say that the rib eye is ראויה להתכבד, but the hooves are not. The rib eyes in the mixture are surely forbidden since the one non-kosher rib eye that is there cannot be *batel*. As far as the hooves, *Shach* says that they are permitted, since the forbidden hoof is not a חתיכה הראויה להתכבד, and so it is *batel* in the other hooves. But *Taz* argues that if part of animal is non-kosher, then the entire animal must be non-kosher. Therefore, if every rib eye is "not kosher" (since the one truly non-

---

³⁰ *Pri Megadim* also says that he is unsure how to categorize those situations when *Rema* says " והכי נהוג".

³¹ For example, see *Chasam Sofer* YD 91, cited in *Pischei Teshuvah* 101:4, who leniently follows *Shulchan Aruch's* ruling that a large piece of raw meat is not considered תתיכה הראויה להתכבד, in conjunction with (a) a *safek* if the animal was even a *teraifah* altogether, and (b) a situation where being *machmir* would lead to a הפסד מרובה מאוד.

kosher rib eye cannot be *batel*), then the hooves from those same animals must also be non-kosher.³²

2. The hide was not yet removed, and the overall carcass is therefore not a חתיכה הראויה להתכבד, but it is possible to cut out one of the internal organs (e.g., the liver) which would be ראויה להתכבד. *Pri Megadim*³³ is unsure whether *Taz* might agree in this case, since the liver is just a minor part of the overall animal and, therefore, should potentially be judged as being part of the "whole" which is not ראויה להתכבד (due to the hide).

3. The last case is where one piece of meat contains two parts, one of which is ראויה להתכבד and the other is not. His example is an animal's head which still has the tongue attached to it; tongue is a חתיכה הראויה להתכבד, but the rest of the head (e.g., the cheek meat) is not. *Pri Megadim*³⁴ says that in this case, where the pieces are <u>attached</u>, even *Shach* would agree that the entire head is forbidden. He opines that it would be preposterous (דזה הוה כחוכא) to say that two halves of the exact same piece of meat have different statuses — one kosher (the cheek) and the other non-kosher (the tongue).³⁵

~ **Only together**

Another questionable case is where the components of a food are individually not ראויה להתכבד, but the food as a whole is. The example given by the *Poskim* is of cheese-filled *kreplach* (dumplings), where neither the dough wrapping nor the cheese filling are ראויה להתכבד, but the overall *kreplach* are. As noted at the beginning of the chapter, the only foods which can be considered חתיכה הראויה להתכבד are those which are <u>inherently</u> forbidden (אסור מחמת עצמו), and in this case that only applies to

---

³² *Pri Megadim* MZ 101:8 based on *Taz* 110:5 and *Shach* 110:31.
³³ *Pri Megadim* SD 110:13.
³⁴ *Pri Megadim* MZ 101:8.
³⁵ *Nodah B'yehudah* YD 16 says that if the hindquarter of an animal did not yet have *nikkur*, even *Rema* would agree that it is not a חתיכה הראויה להתכבד since it takes tremendous effort to remove the *gid hanasheh* and *chailev* from it. [See also *Yad Yehudah* 101:10 (*Aruch*)]. Nonetheless, he explains, *Rema* says a <u>whole</u> animal which merely had its hide removed (i.e., it did not yet have any *nikkur*) is considered a חתיכה הראויה להתכבד, since the forequarter (which needs much less *nikkur* than the hindquarters) just needs a relatively small amount of effort to make it ראויה להתכבד. *Nodah B'yehudah* does not explain if the reason the hindquarter cannot be *batel* in this case is because it still attached to the forequarter (as in case #3 in the text) or if he would take that position even if they had already been separated (as per *Taz* in case #1).

the cheese portion of the *kreplach* which became forbidden when they absorbed *ta'am* of meat (and became *basar b'chalav*).

Chavos Da'as[36] says that since only the cheese is אסור מחמת עצמו but the dough is not, it is only the cheese which can be considered in the calculation for being חתיכה הראויה להתכבד, and since the cheese alone is not ראויה להתכבד, the *kreplach* can be *batel*. But *Imrei Boruch*[37] argues that since the cheese is part of an overall food which is suitable for honored guests, and the cheese is אסור מחמת עצמו, the *kreplach* cannot be *batel*. *Badei HaShulchan*[38] shows that *Pri Megadim* agrees with the lenient approach of *Chavos Da'as*, and therefore rules in accordance with that opinion.

---

[36] *Chavos Da'as* 101:7 (*Biurim*). *Chavos Da'as* is commenting on the ruling of *Nodah B'yehudah* YD 1:30, but there are significant differences between what that *teshuvah* says and how it is quoted in *Chavos Da'as*; it is not clear what *Nodah B'yehudah's* position is on the issue discussed here in the text.
[37] *Imrei Boruch* to *Chavos Da'as* ibid.
[38] *Badei HaShulchan* (*Biurim*) 101:2 ד"ה נאסרה, based on *Pri Megadim* MZ 101:4; see also *Badei HaShulchan* 101:48 (with *Biurim* ad loc.) with *Pri Megadim* MZ 110:1

Chapter 32

Comparing Fish Fillets

שולחן ערוך סימן ק"א סעיפים ח-ט

קורקבן שנמצא נקוב ונתערבה אותה תרנגולת עם אחרות, מדמין שומן שבקורקבן לשומן התרנגולת של מקום חיבור הקורקבן, ואם דומים לגמרי מכשירים האחרות. (וכן כל כיוצא בזה).

ראש כבש שנמצא טריפה ולא נודע מאיזה כבש הוא והקיפו הראש לצוארו של אחד מהכבשים ונמצאו החתיכות דומות ומכוונות יפה, יש לסמוך על זה להתיר האחרות.

Background

The entire *Yoreh Deah* 101 is about חתיכה הראויה להתכבד, and the final two halachos[1] speak about a case where a forbidden חתיכה הראויה להתכבד (a bird or sheep) was mixed with other animals, but someone thinks they can detect which is the forbidden one. Specifically, a סימן טריפה was found in the bird's *kurkuvan* or the sheep's head after they were separated from the rest of the carcass, and the plan is to compare the forbidden *kurkuvan* or head to the carcasses to figure out which one the *kurkuvan* or head came from. The source of this halacha is a *Gemara* cited earlier in *Yoreh Deah*,[2] that if a person receives several pieces of fish and there are scales on only some of them, they can eat all the pieces if they can determine that they are all from the same (kosher) fish.

How are these comparisons made? How does one determine which carcass the *kurkuvan* or head is from, or whether the pieces are all from the same fish? Generally, one can be lenient only if they can align the pieces together like a jigsaw puzzle to prove which pieces originally

---

[1] *Shulchan Aruch* 101:8-9.
[2] *Gemara, Avodah Zara* 40a, codified in *Shulchan Aruch* YD 83:4.

belonged together,[3] but *Taz*[4] says that there are some situations when it is sufficient to have just a visual comparison (e.g., that the fat of the forbidden *kurkuvan* looks like the fat on a given carcass). However, *Taz*[5] adds that nowadays we never consider ourselves skilled enough to rely on a visual comparison, and the only possibility of being lenient is when the pieces can be aligned together into a whole.

Furthermore, the cases of a *kurkuvan* or sheep's head are ones where *mid'oraisah* the meat is all permitted, since the forbidden carcass is *batel b'rov* in the other ones. The entire issue is that the forbidden animal is a חתיכה הראויה להתכבד, which *mid'rabbanan* cannot be *batel*. *Chasam Sofer*[6] says that only in this case can one possibly rely on a "comparison" to identify the forbidden animal, thereby permitting the other ones. But if *mid'oraisah* the forbidden animal was not *batel* – such as if there were only two animals, one kosher and one non-kosher – then one can never rely on "comparing" to determine which is the permitted carcass. *Rebbi Akiva Eiger*[7] appears to disagree, citing the aforementioned *Gemara* regarding fish, as a proof that aligning pieces with one another is a solid proof even when one is considering a possible *issur d'oraisah*.[8]

Fish Fillets

All this was relevant when the following *shailah* arose:

> A caterer ordered hundreds of fillets[9] of sea bass and requested that the company leave a "skin tag" on them so he could see the scales and determine that the fillets are from a kosher fish. There was a miscommunication and the company only left skin tags on some of the fillets and not on the rest. The *Mashgiach* compared the fillets with and without the skin tags, and they seemed to have identical features

---

[3] *Shulchan Aruch* 83:4 and 101:9, as per *Taz* 83:4, 101:15, and *Shach* 83:4.
[4] *Taz* 101:15, reconciling *Shulchan Aruch* 101:8 and 101:9.
[5] *Taz* 101:15.
[6] *Chasam Sofer* to *Shulchan Aruch* 101:8.
[7] *Rebbi Akiva Eiger* to *Shulchan Aruch* 101:8. See other *Poskim* cited in *Darchei Teshuvah* 101:106.
[8] How would *Chasam Sofer* respond to this proof? See *Badei HaShulchan* (*Biurim*) 101:8 s.v. *shuman*.
[9] Fish can be prepared for eating in two basic ways: steaks and fillets. In both cases, the fish is scaled, and the intestines are removed beforehand. Steaks are cut from fish with thick flesh (e.g., salmon, shark), and the fish is cut perpendicular to the spine into several pieces/steaks. Fish that have thinner flesh (e.g., flounder) are cut parallel to the spine so that all the flesh on one side (or both sides together) of the fish can be cooked as one fillet. [Other sea creatures, such as crabs, shrimp, and oyster, are processed differently]. Many types of fish steaks are from non-kosher fish. However, the vast majority of fillets sold commercially are from kosher fish, and one notable exception is the different varieties of catfish.

(fat lines, size, shape, etc.). Is that enough proof to say that all the fillets are kosher?

In this case, there was no possibility of aligning the fillets like a jigsaw puzzle, since that is only effective when the possibility is that the various pieces might be from the same fish. However, these hundreds of fillets were obviously from many different fish and not part of the ones which had the skin tags. The only way to identify them as kosher fish was through a visual comparison (fat lines, size, shape, etc.) and, as we saw above from *Taz*, that is not relied upon nowadays. Additionally, this was not a case of חתיכה הראויה להתכבד, where *mid'oraisah* the non-kosher fish were *batel*. Rather, the "comparison" would have to permit hundreds of fillets which might be *assur mid'oraisah*, and we saw above that some *Acharonim* say that this cannot be relied upon in those cases.

Thus, there was no way to permit the fillets, and they had to be sold to be used at a non-kosher event.[10]

Skin Tags

The original plan was to permit the fillets based on the skin tags which the processor would leave on them. It seems that a skin tag is effective only if it has scales on it that the *Mashgiach* can pull off to see that they come off without ripping skin. But if the tag has no scales on it, then at first glance it would appear to be worthless. In fact, in most cases there are no scales on the skin tag.

Nevertheless, it has been suggested that even without scales, it is possible to identify the fish by merely looking at the skin to identify the breed. This type of identification would require the *Mashgiach* to have considerable expertise, where he would be able to look at a small patch of skin – typically an inch by an inch at most – and know which fish it comes from. Additionally, we have seen that *Taz* says that visual comparisons are not something which one should rely on nowadays. Thus, this idea, that one can identify fish by looking at the skin tag even if there are no scales, is something which seems quite questionable.

In this context, it is worth noting that some unscrupulous processors have been caught gluing skin tags taken from kosher fish onto non-kosher fish,

---

[10] Without knowing more about the business practices of the processor, there was no way to rely on אומן לא מרע נפשיה to permit the fish (see *Imrei Dovid, Alcoholic Beverages*, Chapter 19) (Rav Schachter).

to make them appear kosher! *Mashgichim* caught these when they saw that the tags were on "backwards" or on the wrong side of the fillet (see the footnote),[11] and it is worthwhile to be alert for this.

---

[11] A fish's scales are attached on just one side of the scale, and that side is always the one that faces the fish's head. [This way, when the fish swims, the water presses the scale down on the flesh. If the scale was attached on the side facing the tail, the water would lift the scale up and rip it out of the skin]. Thus, if the attached side of the scale is facing the tail, it is on "backwards". How do you know which side of the fillet is the head? Generally, fish are wider at the head than at the tail, and therefore by looking at the fillet you can tell which side was the fish's head. [Also, processors tend to leave the skin tag on the tail area].

A fillet is a long flat piece of flesh, but the top and bottom are not identical. The bottom – which faced the inside of the fish – is flat, while the top – which faced the outside of the fish – is rounded. Scales are only found on the outside of the fish, and therefore should only be on the top of the fillet rather than on the bottom.

Chapter 33

דבר שיש לו מתירין

שולחן ערוך סימן ק"ב סעיף א'
כל דבר שיש לו מתירין כגון ביצה שנולדה ביום טוב שראויה למחר, אם נתערבה באחרות בין שלימה בין טרופה אינה בטלה אפילו באלף. ואפילו ספק נולדה ביום טוב ונתערבה באחרות אסורות. ואם נתערבה בשאינה מינה בטלה בס'

הגה: מיהו אם לבנו בה מאכל או נתנו בקדירה לתקן הקדירה כגון שמלאוה בתרנגולת אינה בטלה, ועיין בא"ח סימן תקי"ג.

We will begin with some of the basic halachos and examples, and then follow with others which are more practical and/or contentious

Basics

In earlier chapters we saw examples of foods which cannot be *batel* due to their prominence or the significance of their role in the mixture. This included חתיכה הראויה להתכבד (Chapter 30), בריה (Chapter 1), דבר המעמיד (Chapter 31), and others. This chapter is about something which cannot be *batel* for a very different reason: it is a food that is currently forbidden but will become permitted in the future[1] (דבר שיש לו מתירין). Due to this unusual status, *Chazal* legislated that instead of the person consuming the food as part of the *ta'aruvos*, they should wait for it to become permitted and then eat it (עד שתאכלנו באיסור תאכלנו בהיתר).[2]

---

[1] *Shulchan Aruch* 102:1 discusses an egg which is forbidden one day and will become permitted the next day. However, the same is true if the food will become permitted after an extended amount of time. This point can be seen in (a) *Shulchan Aruch* 102:2 (as per *Tur* end of 102) who considers whether a ביצת ספק טריפה is a יש לו מתירין even though it will take 12 months for it to [possibly] become permitted, and (b) *Magen Avraham* 677:12 says that unused *Chanukah* candles are considered יש לו מתירין since they have a permitted use during the next *Chanukah*.

[2] *Shulchan Aruch* 102:1 as per *Rashi*, *Beitzah* 3b, s.v. *afilu*, cited by *Taz* 102:1 and many others.

This principle is Rabbinic in nature,[3] and one might think that we would apply the principle of *safek d'rabbanan l'kulah* to permit all cases where there is some doubt whether the mixture contains a דבר שיש לו מתירין. However, the rationale of the halacha – עד שתאכלנו באיסור תאכלנו בהיתר – dictates that one must be *machmir* if there is even a *safek* whether the item is forbidden.[4] It is logical that a person should avoid *safek issur* if there is an easy option to do so; therefore, a *safek* דבר שיש לי מתירין is also not *batel*, and one is required to wait until the (possible) *issur* disappears before eating the mixture. [Similarly, a דבר שיש לו מתירין is not *batel* even if the forbidden item is only *assur mid'rabbanan*].[5] We will consider practical applications of this when we discuss *chodosh*, below.

מין במינו

We have seen the rationale for <u>why</u> *Chazal* dictated that a דבר שיש לו מתירין is not *batel*, and *Ran*[6] adds an extra understanding of <u>how</u> *Chazal* structured that halacha, as follows: The opinion of *Rebbi Yehuda* is that *min b'mino* is never *batel*; *Ran* suggests that theoretically all would agree to that, and the only reason we reject it is because any time *issur* is mixed into *heter*, the very fact that the item is "*issur*", is itself a reason why it is not *min b'mino* with the *heter*. The two items might be physically identical, such as meat in meat, but the fact that one piece is not kosher and the others are kosher, means they are different enough from one another to not qualify as a pure *min b'mino*. But in cases where the *issur* itself will one day become permitted, *Chazal* told us to view that as a "better" *min b'mino* and in that case we agree with *Rebbi Yehuda* that it cannot be *batel*.

Ran's explanation leads to a significant detail within this halacha, which is that the only time דבר שיש לו מתירין is not *batel* is if the *issur* and *heter* are *min b'mino*, since only then does the above logic apply.[7] For example, if *shemittah* apples were cooked with non-*shemittah* apples, the *shemittah*

---

[3] See, for example, *Rashi* and *Taz* ibid.
[4] *Shulchan Aruch* ibid., based on *Gemara*, *Beitzah* 3b-4a. Towards the end of the chapter, we will see an exception where דבר שיש לו מתירין is *batel* when there is a specific type of *safek*.
[5] *Shulchan Aruch* ibid., as explained by *Taz* 102:3. The דבר שיש לו מתירין is also not *batel* even if it is both a *safek* <u>and</u> not more than an *issur d'rabbanan* (*Shach* 110:59, based on *Gemara*, *Beitzah* ibid).
    Related to this are the positions of (a) *Shach* 69:56 and 102:11 that דבר שיש לו מתירין is forbidden even if it is not עצמו מחמת אסור, discussed towards the end of this chapter regarding Meat Without *Melichah*, and (b) *Shach* 102:9 that even the absorbed *ta'am* of a דבר שיש לו מתירין is forbidden, discussed in *Imrei Dovid*, Animal Products, Chapter 30. [As noted in each of those citations, *Rema* disagrees with *Shach* on both points].
[6] *Ran*, *Nedarim* 52a ד"ה וקשיא, cited in *Taz* 102:5.
[7] *Shulchan Aruch* 102:1.

apples are not *batel* regardless of how few there are of them. *Shemittah* fruit is a דבר שיש לו מתירין, since they can be eaten if one follows the rules of *kedushas shevi'is*, and a mixture of apples in apples is *min b'mino*.[8] Therefore, all the apples in the mixture must follow the rules of *kedushas shevi'is*. But if the *shemittah* apples were cooked with non-*shemittah* pears, that is a mixture of מין בשאינו מינו, which is not treated as a דבר שיש לו מתירין, and the standard rules of *bitul b'shishim* apply.[9]

We saw in Chapter 21 that as relates to most *halachos*, the criterion for whether foods qualify as *min b'mino* is whether they have a similar taste, but as relates to דבר שיש לו מתירין (and certain other cases) the criterion is whether the foods are referred to by the same name.[10] [Below, in the discussion of *chodosh* malt, we will see more details about this criterion].

Within the requirement that a דבר שיש לו מתירין be *min b'mino*, there is a *machlokes* how to treat *chametz* on *Erev Pesach*. There is a special halacha that *chametz* which gets mixed into other foods <u>on</u> *Pesach* is not *batel* regardless of whether it is *min b'mino* or *min b'sheaino mino*.[11] However, that halacha does not apply <u>before</u> *Pesach* even at the times on *Erev Pesach* when *chametz* is already forbidden.[12] But what about it qualifying as a דבר שיש לו מתירין when it is *assur* (on *Erev Pesach*) due to the fact that it will become permitted as soon as *Pesach* ends?[13] Some *Rishonim* agree with this proposal, and therefore rule that *chametz* mixed into other foods (*min b'mino*) on *Erev Pesach* cannot be *batel*.[14] But *Rema*[15] accepts the ruling that it is not a דבר שיש לו מתירין, since the *heter* to eat the *chametz* after *Pesach* is not a permanent one, as the *issur* will return a year later when *Pesach* returns. Within the context of *Ran's* explanation this is understood to mean that since the *chametz* will always retain some

---

[8] *Derech Emunah* 7:144. For more details, see *Imrei Dovid*, *Shemittah*, Chapter 21.
[9] Ibid.
[10] Aside from the sources noted above in Chapter 21, *Shach* 102:3 specifically makes the point as relates to דבר שיש לו מתירין.
[11] *Shulchan Aruch* OC 447:1.
[12] *Shulchan Aruch* OC 447:2.
[13] After *Pesach*, *chametz* owned by a Jew will also be forbidden as *chametz she'avar alav haPesach*. However, that prohibition is Rabbinic in nature, while from the *d'oraisah* perspective, the *chametz* is forbidden on *Erev Pesach* (and on *Pesach*) but will be permitted after *Pesach* (*Pri Megadim* SD 102:8, towards the end).
[14] See *Rambam*, *Hil. Ma'acholos Assur* 15:9, cited in *Taz* 102:13.
[15] *Rema* 102:4, as per *Taz* 102:13 and *Shach* 102:14. See also *Shulchan Aruch* OC 447:2 as per *Biur Halacha* ad loc.

element of *issur* (i.e., that it cannot be eaten next *Pesach*), it is lacking in the *min b'mino* aspect of being identical to the *heter* into which it is mixed.

₪ ₪

There are several other important details as to when דבר שיש לו מתירין does and does not apply, and we will discuss most of them in the context of contemporary applications regarding *chodosh/yoshon*. Briefly, the *Torah* says that any of the five primary grains – wheat, rye, spelt, oats, barley – which took root after the first day of *Chol HaMoed Pesach*, cannot be eaten until the next *Korban HaOmer* is brought (on the first day of *Chol HaMoed Pesach*). Grains which took root after the cutoff date are referred to as "*chodosh*" (new) until the next *Chol HaMoed Pesach* comes, at which point they become "*yoshon*" (old) and are permitted.

> The question of whether one is required to eat only *yoshon* nowadays is beyond the scope of this chapter,[16] and our discussion assumes that it is obligatory.

The *Gemara*[17] says that *chodosh* is a דבר שיש לו מתירין, since the prohibition against eating it will lift automatically on *Chol HaMoed Pesach*.[18] We will focus on several outgrowths of that status.

Chodosh Malt

Barley is one of the grains which must be *yoshon*, and when barley is steeped in warm water, an enzyme is released which converts the barley's starch into a sweet liquid known as malted barley, or just "malt". Very small amounts of malt are sometimes added to flour as an "enrichment", and somewhat larger amounts might be added to breakfast cereals (e.g., Corn Flakes, Rice Krispies), pretzels, and other foods to contribute sweetness and flavor. Malt made from barley that was planted after *Pesach* does not come to the retail market until some time in the winter,

---

[16] Some of those who discuss this are *Responsa Maharam Rutenberg* (Lvov edition) 199, *Responsa Rosh* 2:1, *Shulchan Aruch* OC 489:10 & YD 293:1-3 and the *Poskim* ad loc., *Bach* YD 293, *Magen Avraham* 489:17, and *Mishnah Berurah* 489:45.

[17] *Gemara*, *Nedarim* 58a.

Previously we noted that some maintain that *chametz* before *Pesach* is not a דבר שיש לו מתירין because it will become forbidden again next *Pesach*. Those *Poskim* agree that *chodosh* is a דבר שיש לו מתירין because although the overall the prohibition of *chodosh* will return next year (for grain that is planted then), the current *chodosh* grain will become permanently permitted once *Chol HaMoed Pesach* arrives (*Pri Megadim* MZ 102:13).

[18] *Ran*, *Nedarim*, ad loc., says that it is יש לו מתירין since the *korban omer* will render it *yoshon*. The text here gives an alternate reason which applies nowadays when there is no *korban omer*.

which is relatively late in the "*chodosh*" season". If it is present in flour or cereal, can it be *batel* or is that food automatically forbidden?

~ Chametz

One reason not to consider malt as a דבר שיש לו מתירין is because malt is *chametz* due to its being produced by soaking barley in water for an extended period of time. This means that the *chodosh* malt will <u>never</u> become permitted (i.e., it is not יש לו מתירין) since the time it becomes permitted is on *Chol HaMoed Pesach*, and a few days before that time (i.e., on *Erev Pesach*) the Jew will have to dispose of the malt as *chametz*. Thus, it is not יש לו מתירין since there will <u>never</u> be a time when the owner can eat it.[19]

This is comparable to the case discussed in *Shulchan Aruch*[20] of a food which will spoil before it becomes permitted. That food is not a דבר שיש לו מתירין since, in practice, it will not be edible when the prohibition against eating it finally lifts. So too, with *chametz* such as *chodosh* malt. By the time the *issur* of *chodosh* is removed, the person will have had to destroy it since it is *chametz*; such foods are not considered a דבר שיש לו מתירין and, therefore, can be *batel*.

While this point is theoretically accurate, it seems to be no longer true in practice. That is because *Shulchan Aruch*[21] says that דבר שיש לו מתירין applies not only in cases where the *heter* comes automatically with time, but even in cases where the person can easily "create" a *heter* for the food.[22] [We will consider examples of that in Chapter 36]. If so, maybe the malt should be considered a יש לו מתירין since the owner can sell it to a non-Jew before *Pesach* and then buy it back after *Pesach*? This idea is discussed in the *Poskim*,[23] and they give two primary reasons to reject it. Firstly, selling food to a non-Jew is not simple enough to qualify as an "easy" way to create a *heter*. Secondly, דבר שיש לו מתירין implies you will be able to

---

[19] See, for example, *Chochmas Adam* 53:28, and *Aruch HaShulchan* 102:27.
   Accordingly, the *Gemara's* statement that *chodosh* is a יש לו מתירין is understood only to apply to wheat, barley, etc., which have not yet come into contact with water and are not *chametz*.
[20] *Shulchan Aruch* 102:4.
[21] *Shulchan Aruch* 102:2.
[22] The source for this is *Gemara, Nedarim*, 58a, which says that *tevel* is a דבר שיש לו מתירין because (as *Ran* ad loc. explains) the person can separate *terumah* and *ma'aser* from the *tevel* (rendering it *chullin*) using other produce. This shows that although the *tevel* requires intervention to become permitted, it is nonetheless considered יש לו מתירין if that change can happen without much effort or loss.
[23] See the coming footnote.

enjoy this item at some point in the future, and if you sell it then you clearly will never have the item.[24]

Both of those reasons do not seem to apply nowadays to the standard way people sell their *chametz*, using their local Rabbi as their agent (colloquially known as *mechiras chametz*). The process is very easy (and, in fact, most people are doing it anyhow, so that adding one more food to the sale is effortless), and it is essentially guaranteed that the Jew will get his *chametz* back after *Pesach*. Thus, both objections raised against this idea do not appear to apply in the modern era. If so, the *chodosh* malt should be viewed as a דבר שיש לו מתירין even though it is *chametz*.

From a different angle, Rav Schachter pointed out that the idea that the malt is *chametz* is only relevant to cases where a Jewish person has the food which has malt mixed into it. He does not have to treat it as a דבר שיש לו מתירין since it will never become permitted for him to eat it. But in most cases this issue is raised for a very different scenario, where a manufacturer wants a product certified as suitable for people who avoid *chodosh*, even though it contains a small amount of malt. In the typical case where that manufacturer is owned by someone non-Jewish, the malt surely is a דבר שיש לו מתירין, since it will become permitted (as *yoshon*) on *Chol HaMoed Pesach*. The non-Jew will not be required to dispose of the malt before *Pesach* since he is not obligated in the *mitzvah* to destroy all of his *chametz*. In such cases, it remains a דבר שיש לו מתירין, and the fact that the malt is *chametz* does not affect that status.

~ **Bitul**

Having established that if a non-Jew owns the food that contains *chodosh* malt it is a דבר שיש לו מתירין, we have also shown that the same seems to be true even if a Jew owns it. Let us now consider how that applies to breakfast cereal and flour which contains *chodosh* malt.

For malt in breakfast cereal, the decision appears to be straightforward, because even if it were not a דבר שיש לו מתירין, it would not be *batel* because the malt is typically 2-3% of the cereal, which is to say that it is not *batel*

---

[24] *Darchei Teshuvah* 102:1 cites several *Poskim* who discuss this issue. The one who gives the clearest explanation why the option of selling the *chametz* is not a reason to qualify as דבר שיש לו מתירין is *Binas Adam* (*Sha'ar Issur V'heter* 54/73), who gives the two reasons noted here in the text. [See also *Pri Toar* 102:1 (end), who suggests a third reason (which would apply nowadays) without coming to a conclusion]. Other prominent *Poskim* who follow that position, but do not explain what it is based on, include *Pri Megadim* (*Sha'ar HaTa'aruvos* 3:2) and *Aruch HaShulchan* 102:16.

b'shishim. That means that, regardless of whether it is a דבר שיש לו מתירין, it does not meet the standard requirements of bitul b'shishim required of every forbidden food.

But this is not true regarding malt in flour, because it is added in such small amounts (e.g., 2/10th of 1%)[25] that it is surely batel b'shishim. What about the fact that in just about every case the malt is a דבר שיש לו מתירין which cannot be batel even at 1 in 1,000? The apparent answer is that we have seen that דבר שיש לו מתירין is only not batel when it is in a mixture which is מין במינו, and that for these purposes the criterion for מין במינו is whether the foods have a similar name. Barley malt and wheat flour do not satisfy this criterion as they are very different names, and therefore even though the malt is a דבר שיש לו מתירין, it should seemingly qualify for bitul.

However, there is yet another wrinkle to this discussion. This is because as relates to the halachos of techum, the Gemara[26] says that water, salt, and spices are not batel in a dough since they are דבר שיש לו מתירין. Tosfos[27] questions this, since דבר שיש לו מתירין only applies in cases of min b'mino, which these items are not, and he suggests two answers: either it is a special chumrah for hilchos techum to consider this min b'mino, or whenever ingredients are part of a food's recipe, they are automatically considered to be min b'mino with one another (since they join together to form one unified item). Taz and Shach[28] accept Tosfos' second answer, in which case the chodosh malt is not batel since it is a functional part of the flour which automatically qualifies it as min b'mino. But Magen Avraham[29] favors the first answer of Tosfos. According to Magen Avraham, chodosh malt is not min b'mino with flour and can be batel even though it is a דבר שיש לו מתירין.

> In general, hashgachos will not certify an item as kosher if that status depends on bitul. Many hashgachos follow that same policy for flour certified as yoshon and will only provide certification if the malt is also yoshon. Others will certify that the flour is yoshon but inform clients (and other hashgachos) that their oversight is limited to the status of the flour, but they take no responsibility for the malt.

---

[25] 2/10th of 1% is equivalent to 500 parts flour/heter for every 1-part malt/chodosh.
[26] Gemara, Beitzah 39a, explaining Mishnah, Beitzah 37a.
[27] Tosfos, Beitzah 39a, s.v. mishum.
[28] Taz 102:6 and Shach 102:6.
[29] Magen Avraham 513:7, explaining (as per Machatzis HaShekel) that this is the opinion of Shulchan Aruch 513:3, Rema (Toras Chattas 74:2), and others.

~ ספק ספיקא

There is one last thing to consider. *Rema*[30] says that a justification for permitting all foods of unknown *yoshon* status is that there is always a *sfek sfekah*: maybe the grain was from a previous year (and is therefore *yoshon*), and maybe it grew this year but was planted before *Pesach* (which would also render it *yoshon*). If that is correct, then we can permit the foods that have malt in them, since *sfek sfekah* would allow us to ignore the possibility that the barley is *chodosh*.

Nowadays in the United States, it is generally highly questionable if one can rely on that *sfek sfekah* as relates to wheat, for the simple reason that there is little spring wheat and durum wheat left from one year to the next, and by late fall it is reasonably clear that all producers of bread, pasta, and certain other foods are using spring wheat from the current year's crop. Additionally, most manufacturers are very sensitive to know when they start receiving grain from the "new" crop, and consumers can potentially access that information by contacting the company. Thus, the first *safek* does not apply, and we are left with just one *safek* – whether the wheat used in this product was planted before *Pesach*.

All this applies to wheat and flour, but the same is not true for malt, for several reasons: Each year's barley crop lasts well into the next year, there is no significant quality variance between malts from different years, and it takes considerable time for each year's barley to be converted into malt, shipped to manufacturers, and finally arrive on store shelves. This means that even when it is close to *Pesach* (i.e., the end of the "*chodosh* season") there is a legitimate *safek* that the malt in a given box of cereal or bag of flour might be from the previous year's crop. This combines with the *safek* that even if the barley is from this year, it might have been planted before *Pesach*, and there is a *sfek sfekah*. If so, once again, we have a basis for permitting the cereal, since *sfek sfekah* allows us not to worry that the barley was *chodosh*.

---

[30] *Rema* YD 293:3.

Shach (*Klalei Sfek Sfekah* #11) says that if the two *sfekos* permit the item for the exact same reason (משם אחד) that does not qualify as a *sfek sfekah*. This leads several *Acharonim* to question *Rema's* reliance on *sfek sfekah* for grain of unknown *yoshon* status, since both *sfekos* (previous year, planted before *Pesach*) permit the grain for the same reason, that it was not planted after this *Pesach* (see, for example, *Rebbi Akiva Eiger* to *Rema* ibid). *Chavos Da'as* (to *Shach* ibid.) answers that the requirement of משם אחד does not apply to situations, such as ours, where the two possible *sfekos* are naturally occurring happenstances (דבר ההווה ורגיל כך ואינו במקרה ומזדמן).

But *Shach*[31] questions this ruling of *Rema*. How can *Rema* say that food of unknown *chodosh* status is permitted based on *sfek sfekah*, when *Rema*[32] himself says that one should preferably not rely on *sfek sfekah* to permit a דבר שיש לו מתירין? As we have seen, *chodosh* is a דבר שיש לו מתירין, so a *sfek sfekah* should not be effective? *Shach* suggests several answers. One is that *Rema*[33] says that if there is a "need" (צורך), one may follow the *Poskim* who leniently rule that *sfek sfekah* can be relied upon even for a דבר שיש לו מתירין. *Shach* says that the ability to eat food during many months of the year often qualifies as a meaningful "need", and therefore *sfek sfekah* can justify being lenient.

Shach says that an even better answer is based on *Rosh*,[34] who says that there are different types of *sfek sfekah*. A *sfek sfekah* which suggests that there may never have been *issur* present, can be relied upon even when the potential *issur* is a דבר שיש לו מתירין. The *sfek sfekah* regarding *chodosh* is an example of this, since it indicates that this grain is actually *yoshon* (since it is from a previous year or from a crop planted before *Pesach*). The other type of *sfek sfekah* is where we know there was *issur*, but due to the way it was mixed into other foods, we have reason to believe it is no longer present in the sample presently in front of you. That is the case where *Rema* says that one should avoid relying on *sfek sfekah*, since *Chazal* specifically said that a דבר שיש לו מתירין remains forbidden even if it was diluted in ways that would permit standard forbidden items.

ଓଃ ଃଠ

In summary, we have considered whether *chodosh's* status as a דבר שיש לו מתירין should preclude malt from becoming *batel* in flour. [It is not minute enough to be *batel b'shishim* in cereal]. Some reasons to think it might indeed be *batel* are that (a) it is *chametz*, which means that the Jewish owner must dispose of it before *Chol HaMoed Pesach* when it will become *yoshon*, (b) malt is מין בשאינו מינו in flour, and (c) *Rema's* general *sfek sfekah* to permit all possible *chodosh* might apply to malt. We have delineated challenges to each of these lines of reasoning.

---

[31] *Shach* 110:56, who begins by asking from the way *Rema* accepts the ruling of *Shulchan Aruch* OC 497:4 that *sfek sfekah* can permit a דבר שיש לו מתירין, and later notes the question from *Rema's* ruling regarding *chodosh*.
[32] *Rema* 110:8.
[33] *Rema* 110:8.
[34] *Responsa Rosh* 2:1.

Yoshon Flour Milling & Barley Pearling

~ **The concern**

One way to obtain *yoshon* flour and barley is to identify product which was processed and bagged before any

Winter Wheat
Winter wheat[35] is always *yoshon* since it is planted in the fall and harvested after *Pesach*, and it is commonly sold as "cake flour".[36] However, one must still consider the typical scenario that the mills which process winter wheat are doing the same for spring wheat, which would raise the same concerns noted in the text.

chodosh grain came to market. While this is surely the safest way to avoid *chodosh*, it raises quality and halachic issues because these items can become infested with insects if they are stored for too long. [One way to avoid this issue is to place the items in refrigerated storage, but that is not realistic for most consumers or bakeries]. Accordingly, most *yoshon* flour and barley is stored as grain, and not processed for further use until close to the time when it will be used. By that point, the factories are already working with *chodosh* grains as well, and that leads to potential contamination of the *yoshon*, as follows.

Converting wheat into flour involves not only grinding the kernels, but also repeatedly passing them through filters/sieves, and moving the wheat and flour from place-to-place multiple times.[37] None of this equipment is ever cleaned with water, and the minimal amount of cleaning done will invariably leave behind some kernels and a dusting of flour in many places. These tiny amounts of *chodosh* residue would theoretically be *batel b'shishim*, except that we must consider whether they should not be *batel* due to their being a דבר שיש לו מתירין.[38] Similarly, the pearling of barley (scraping off an outer layer to prepare it for human consumption) is done

---

[35] A small percent of barley is planted in the fall, but the overwhelming majority of barley is a spring crop planted around *Pesach*-time.
[36] Much of "all purpose" flour is made from winter wheat, but this is not necessarily always true.
[37] Some of the common steps are railcar to grain pit to elevator to silo to steel bin to separator to tempering bin to mill to shaking sifters [milling and sifting are often repeated several times] to storage bin to bag filler or tanker. The first and last of these (railcar and tanker) can/are cleaned with water, but all the rest are not.
[38] As relates to standard *issurim*, it is sufficient to clean equipment to the industry standard of cleanliness (כדרך המכבדים), even if some residue remains, but that is based to a great extent on *bitul* which is ineffective for a דבר שיש לו מתירין like *chodosh*. For more on that, see *Imrei Dovid, Kashering*, Chapter 42.

on equipment that is never perfectly clean, leaving behind bits of *chodosh* barley that seemingly are not *batel*, since they are a דבר שיש לו מתירין.

The first angle noted above – that malt is *chametz* – does not apply to pearled barley, since the pearling process does not involve water and the barley per se is not *chametz*. On the other hand, flour goes through a process known as tempering, which is very similar to what *Chazal* refer to as לתיתה, and it is therefore treated as *safek chametz*.[39] Therefore, any points noted above regarding malt's *chametz* status, and whether that might render the יש לו מתירין consideration moot, also apply to flour.

Let us now consider the other two angles noted above (*bitul* and *sfek sfekah*) as well as other possible reasons to be lenient.

~ סלק את מינו

Earlier we considered that *chodosh* malt might be suitable for *bitul* in flour [even though malt is a דבר שיש לו מתירין] because malt is not *min b'mino* with flour. At first glance, that line of reasoning does not seem applicable to the *bitul* of *chodosh* flour residue in *yoshon* flour or the *bitul* of *chodosh* barley residue in the *yoshon* barley, because those cases seem like classic examples of *min b'mino*. What could be more *min b'mino* than flour in flour or barley in barley?

However, Rabbi Eli Gersten suggested a reason why this might be viewed as not being *min b'mino*. When farmers harvest their fields, there is a certain amount of dirt and other foreign material which gets swept up together with the grain. Processors put in considerable effort to remove as much of this unwanted debris as possible, but they are never 100% successful. This means that the *yoshon* flour and barley have (a) a tiny amount of non-grain mixed in, and (b) a tiny amount of *chodosh* residue mixed in. The *chodosh* residue ("b") is not *min b'mino* with the non-grain ("a"), and therefore if there is 60 times as much non-grain as there is *chodosh* residue, the *chodosh* will be *batel*. Although the *chodosh* is *min b'mino* with the *yoshon* flour, it is not *min b'mino* with the non-grain residue, and the principle of סלק את מינו כמי שאינו ושאין מינו רבה עליו ומבטלו (see Chapter 22) allows it to be *batel* in the non-*mino*.

---

[39] See *Shulchan Aruch* OC 453:5 with *Mishnah Berurah* 453:26-27. In more recent years, R' Yosef Herman took a sample of wheat which had been tempered in a modern factory and showed it to Rav Neuschloss of New Square. He determined that a small minority of kernels had signs of *chimutz*, and based on that Rav Moshe Feinstein said that flour should be treated as no worse than *safek chametz*.

One challenge to this creative suggestion is that it assumes there is some way to calculate the ratio of non-grain residue to *chodosh* residue, to determine that it is at least 60:1. It is not at all clear how that would be established, especially since factories make considerable efforts to remove as much non-grain as possible (thus there is likely very little of it left), and the flour and barley go through multiple tanks, pipes, etc., which are each places where more *chodosh* residue might get mixed in.

But one can also question this idea's halachic assumption that the non-grain residue is distinct from the flour. One could argue that after all the efforts made to clean the grain, anything that is left is just treated as "grain" rather than as something else.[40] This idea requires further consideration.

Another possible reason to be lenient also relates to the concept of סלק את מינו, not on the factory level but rather for the consumers. Namely, the baker or cook who will use the flour or barley will not use it alone but will mix it with other ingredients. For example, flour will be mixed with water, sugar, eggs, and chocolate to produce a cake, or barley will be added to meat, potatoes, beans, water, and spices to create a *cholent*. The decision if those qualify as מין בשאינו מינו with the *chodosh* residue depends on the disagreement cited earlier, whether items added together to create a recipe are automatically considered *min b'mino* (Taz, Shach) or not (Magen Avraham). According to *Magen Avraham*, the אינו מינו water, sugar, etc., will be able to create *bitul* for any tiny bits of *chodosh* residue in the *yoshon* flour or barley, based on the principle of סלק את מינו. [This would permit the food but would seemingly not justify the certification of the flour or barley as *yoshon*].

---

[40] This idea would be similar to the statement of *Pri Megadim* SD 100:31 (noted briefly in Chapter 30) who says that until an insect crawls it is considered "vegetable" (which is why it is permitted), and it is only considered an "insect" (and forbidden) when it starts walking. Here too, the tiny bits of non-grain which cannot be removed no longer have their own identity and are just considered "grain".

When this point was brought to Rabbi Gersten's attention he marshalled two sets of proofs that undesirable additives retain their אינו מינו status. One was from *Shulchan Aruch* YD 126:7 and 123:20 where it states that although [*Shulchan Aruch* is of the opinion that] non-kosher wine cannot be *batel* when mixed into other wine (i.e., מינו במינו), if the wine still has some grape peels and pits in it, these are considered אינו מינו and סלק את מינו applies to permit *bitul*. The other was from several sources (*Gemara*, *Avodah Zara* 73a; *Haga'os Ashri*, *Avodah Zara* 5:28; and *Tur* YD 126 (end)) that if there is water in the wine, then non-kosher wine can be *batel* into that water, based again on סלק את מינו. In both these cases, the אינו מינו (i.e., peels, pits, and water) are undesirable additives and retain their own identity as relates to סלק את מינו and are not "reclassified" as being wine. The argument against this is that in all these cases, the additive is separate from the wine – in the first case because it will still be removed, and in the second case because it was added to the wine (purposely or accidentally) – which is quite different from our case where the dirt, etc., is basically a natural part of the grain which cannot and will not ever be removed. Seemingly, that should mean that we view the non-grain as "grain" and not think of it as a separate item that qualifies for סלק את מינו.

~ תרי משהו ~

The previous section considered treating the mixture of *chodosh* and *yoshon* flour or barley as אינו מינו based on the principle of סלק את מינו, and Rav Belsky suggested an alternate way to view them as אינו מינו as per the way *Shach*[41] explains a concept called תרי משהו לא אמרינן. As we have seen, a דבר שיש לו מתירין is *assur b'mashehu* (i.e., never *batel*) if it is in a mixture which is *min b'mino*. *Shach* says that this is true the first time some *issur* is mixed into *heter*, but not when some of that mixture falls into another batch of *heter* (where, again, it is *batel b'shishim*). In other words, certain foods are *assur b'mashehu* but only once; we do not employ the *issur mashehu* twice.

Shach explains that when (for example) *chodosh* grain is mixed into *yoshon* grain, that is *min b'mino*, since grain and grain have the same "name". But since that mixture contains both *chodosh* and *yoshon*, it is deemed "*aino mino*" with other batches of grain, since it is somewhat different from them! If so, the *issur mashehu* does not apply in the second mixture since at that point it is not *min b'mino*.[42]

Rav Belsky said that the concept of תרי משהו can apply in a flour mill or barley pearling facility if the equipment is first flushed with significant amounts of *yoshon* grain (which is not sold as *yoshon*). He reasoned that during the flush, the *chodosh* residue on the equipment becomes diluted in the grain passing through, and if/when some residue of the flush gets mixed into the *yoshon* flour or barley (i.e., the produce after the flush, which will be sold as *yoshon*), that is a second *mashehu* which *Shach* has indicated is permitted.

One question on this line of reasoning is that it seems appropriate for the milling or pearling equipment, and for certain pipes where the "flush" seems likely to reach all parts of the equipment and we can be confident that any *chodosh* is diluted in the flush's grain. But the same is not true of the bins and (many of) the conveyors which are only partially filled during the flush, likely leaving many parts of the equipment with no contact with the flush's grain. Some of the *chodosh* residue might get carried away with the flush, but there is also likely much *chodosh* residue left behind. That residue does not qualify as תרי משהו and would not be *batel*.

---

[41] *Shach, Nekudos HaKesef*, to *Taz* 92:16.
[42] Therefore, if the item which is *assur b'mashehu* is forbidden even for *aino mino* (e.g., *chametz* on *Pesach*), then תרי משהו would be forbidden (*Shach*).

דבר שיש לו מתירין   373

One can also question Rav Belsky's proposal on halachic grounds: *Shach* himself says that the leniency of תרי משהו does not apply to mixtures which are לח בלח. Most (including *Shach*) assume that mixtures of flour with other flour is considered לח בלח since the individual pieces of flour are not distinguishable from one another.[43] If so, we might be able to apply the leniency of תרי משהו to the case of barley pearling, but how can it be suitable for a flour mill? This requires further consideration.[44]

~ ספק איסור משהו

Rav Elyashiv is reported to have proposed a different reason why the produce is permitted after a flush. His reason was that at that point it is not even clear that there is any *chodosh* residue left, since it might all have been removed; therefore, one can be lenient about the Rabbinic principle of דבר שיש לו מתירין. The obvious question on this is that we have seen that even <u>safek</u> of דבר שיש לו מתירין cannot be *batel*. It has been suggested that maybe the *chumrah* is limited to cases where we know the possible *issur* was mixed into the other food, and we are just unsure if the item was forbidden. But our case is different, since we do not know if there is any *chodosh* here at all.[45] We saw earlier that *Shach* cites *Rosh* who suggests a very similar difference between different types of *sfekos*,[46] and this may be a source for Rav Elyashiv's position.[47]

> *This idea touches on a topic known as* ספק איסור משהו,
> *which is the subject of the coming chapter.*

---

[43] See below in Chapter 61.

[44] Some have suggested that since the entire lack of *bitul* is based on a *d'rabannan* principle (i.e., דבר שיש לו מתירין), we can rely on the opinion in the *Poskim* that even flour is יבש ביבש. Others report that Rav Belsky said that flour mixed into flour is only לח בלח when the flours are blended together, but when permitted flour <u>pushes</u> forbidden flour out of a pipe, the flours do not mix together, and it is not treated as לח בלח. Even if one were to accept this novel line of reasoning, it would seemingly only apply to very specific pipes, but not to the bins and conveyors where much of the *chodosh* residue remains.

[45] See *Imrei Dovid*, *Shemittah*, Chapter 19, footnote 8, where we cite *Minchas Yitzchak* 6:129 regarding the *bitul* of coins that have *kedushas shevi'is*, who also says that דבר שיש לו מתירין does not apply when we have no firm reason to believe there is any *issur* present. However, that case is quite different from ours in that it is a mere suspicion that the storekeeper had money with *kedushas shevi'is*, as opposed to our case where we <u>know</u> that there was *chodosh* flour or barley processed in the factory.

[46] In *Shach's* case, there was no "*mashehu*", and therefore the case where he says one can be lenient requires relying on *sfek sfekah*. In our case, there is not more than the tiniest amount of *chodosh*, so the most significant potential concern is that it is *assur b'mashehu*; hence, one *safek* is potentially enough to permit the flour.

[47] See *Shulchan Aruch* 102:2, that if one is unsure whether the food will eventually become permitted, that food does not have the status of a דבר שיש לו מתירין. Thus, there is clearly precedent that sometimes a "*safek*" דבר שיש לו מתירין can be *batel*, and the text is explaining a source that there may be other cases as well.

~ **Limits to Mashehu**

Rav Schachter suggested a different type of possibility which seems to obviate this entire concern. The halacha is clear that דבר שיש לו מתירין cannot be *batel b'shishim* and cannot even be *batel* when diluted in 1,000 times its volume of *heter* (e.g., *chodosh* malt at 2/10th of 1% of flour). We refer to this by saying that a דבר שיש לו מתירין is *"assur b'mashehu"*, which literally means that even the tiniest amount of it causes a mixture to become forbidden. But, Rav Schachter argued, the term *"mashehu"* should not be taken literally, and even a *mashehu* has limitations. *Chazal* forbade these mixtures when the *issur* is diluted in thousands of times its volume, but when it comes to the point that there are millions of times as much *heter* as *issur*, then even a דבר שיש לו מתירין can be *batel*. After the factory personnel clean their equipment as well as they can – by blowing air, brushing, and flushing the equipment with *yoshon* product to be sold as non-*yoshon* – the amount of residue will be so minute that it will be *batel* in millions of times its volume of *yoshon*. Therefore, according to this line of reasoning, it can be *batel* even though it is a דבר שיש לו מתירין.[48]

ଓଃ ଃଠ

In summary, the issue being considered was whether *yoshon* flour or barley can be milled or pearled on equipment previously used for *chodosh* and still maintain its *yoshon* status, or should we be concerned that the bits of *chodosh* residue cannot be *batel* since it is a דבר שיש לו מתירין. We considered four possible reasons to be lenient: (a) the bits of dirt mixed into the flour is מין בשאינו מינו with the *chodosh*, and can effect *bitul* based on the principle of סלק את מינו, (b) if we flush the system with *yoshon* grain that is not sold as *yoshon*, it might be permitted based on the concept of תרי משהו לא אמרינן, or (c) because it is possible that there is not even any *chodosh* left after the flush, and (d) it may be that the amount of residue is so small that it is too little to even be considered a *mashehu*. Once again, each of these lines of reasoning have reasons why one might disagree and/or are novel interpretations that others might not agree with.

---

[48] See a similar idea in *Halichos Shlomo, Pesach* 4:5 (discussing the *issur mashehu* for *chametz* on *Pesach*), and there in footnote 20, citing several sources. In contrast, see *Gra"z* OC 447:16, who says that a *mashehu* is forbidden even if it is diluted in millions of times its volume of *heter* (שמשהו אין לו שיעור ויכול הוא להתפשט ולהתחלק לאלפי אלפים משהויין).

Meat Without Melichah

The following is summarized from Imrei Dovid, Meat and Poultry, Chapter 35, and particularly there in footnote 25

Shulchan Aruch and *Rema*[49] say that meat which did not have מליחה and is therefore not kosher due to the blood absorbed in it, is not a חתיכה הראויה להתכבד or a דבר שבמנין, since the meat per se is kosher and it is only the blood inside it which is not permitted (אינו נאסר מחמת עצמו). [For more on those points, see Chapters 31 and 62]. Why is the meat not a דבר שיש לו מתירין since – even if 72 hours have passed since *shechitah* and מליחה is no longer an option – you can still eat the meat via roasting (which can remove blood even after 72 hours)?

Rema[50] answers that the exception of אינו נאסר מחמת עצמו applies to דבר שיש לו מתירין as well, and that is why the meat can be *batel*. *Shach*[51] agrees with the halachic conclusion, but says it is based on a different reason. He argues that דבר שיש לו מתירין is not *batel* because of the concept that עד שתאכלנו באיסור אכלו בהיתר, and that applies even if the food is not inherently forbidden. Rather, he says, the reason it is not a דבר שיש לו מתירין is because the ability to eat the meat roasted existed all along, so that there is no way to avoid the *issur* in the desired manner (via cooking) without relying on *bitul*. Accordingly, עד שתאכלנו באיסור אכלו בהיתר does not apply, and it can be *batel*.[52]

This leniency, that meat without מליחה is not considered a דבר שיש לו מתירין, was relevant in a situation where many lambs had מליחה, but it was later determined that for several of the carcasses the מליחה started more than 72 hours after *shechitah*. Thus, of the dozens of lambs which had מליחה, a few were not considered kosher due to blood which the מליחה could not remove, and there was no way to identify those problematic carcasses. This is exactly the case discussed above: all the lambs are inherently kosher, but some have non-kosher blood absorbed in them. As we have seen, the non-kosher lamb can be *batel* into the kosher ones and they are not a דבר שיש לו מתירין. [Other factors that were relevant in that situation are beyond the scope of this work].

୧୦ ଓଃ

Two other potential examples of דבר שיש לו מתירין are when utensils which require *tevillah* or *hag'alah* become mixed with other utensils. Those issues will be discussed in Chapter 36.

---

[49] *Shulchan Aruch* 69:14 and *Rema* 101:2.
[50] *Rema* 102:4.
[51] *Shach* 69:56 and 102:11.
[52] See Gr"a 102:15 that this idea – that even without *bitul* the meat is permitted to be roasted, and therefore it is not a יש לו מתירין – is a *machlokes Rishonim*, and *Rema* 108:1 rules that it is not considered יש לו מתירין (as *Shach* says here). [Thus, *Rema* 102:4 is merely providing a second reason why the meat can be *batel*]. Another application of this leniency would be if a dairy food was mixed into pareve ones; the ability to eat all the foods with milk or parve, is not enough to qualify the dairy item as יש לו מתירין, since that use was permitted even without *bitul*, and the discussion about *bitul* revolves around the option to eat it with meat.

Chapter 34

ספק איסור משהו

שולחן ערוך סימן ק"ב סעיף א'
כל דבר שיש לו מתירין כגון ביצה שנולדה ביום טוב שראויה למחר, אם נתערבה באחרות בין שלימה בין טרופה אינה בטלה אפילו באלף. ואפילו ספק נולדה ביום טוב ונתערבה באחרות אסורות. ואם נתערבה בשאינה מינה בטלה בס'

הגה: מיהו אם לבנו בה מאכל או נתנו בקדירה לתקן הקדירה כגון שמלאוה בתרנגולת אינה בטלה, ועיין בא"ח סימן תקי"ג.

The previous chapter cited Rav Elyashiv's position that *yoshon* flour milled on equipment which had previously been used for *chodosh* is permitted after a flush of *yoshon* flour (which will not be sold as *yoshon*). The logic presented there is related to the issue of whether *safek issur mashehu* is permitted. This chapter explores that issue, which is most relevant on *Pesach*.

Introduction

Mid'oraisah, *chametz* is *batel b'shishim* just like any other forbidden item.[1] However, *mid'rabbanan*, any *chametz* which is mixed into food <u>on</u> *Pesach* is not *batel* regardless of how little *chametz* is in the mixture.[2] This is known as *"issur mashehu"* and applies whether the mixture is לח בלח or יבש ביבש. This *chumrah* is limited to cases where the *chametz* was mixed in on *Pesach*, but if the *ta'aruvos* was created <u>before</u> *Pesach* – and even if it occurred on *Erev Pesach* after midday[3] – the standard rules of *bitul* apply. Therefore, assuming the *chametz* was *batel* before *Pesach*, it remains permitted to eat that food on *Pesach*.[4] The exception to this leniency is if the *ta'aruvos* is *yavesh b'yavesh*; in that case, even if the *chametz* was *batel*

---

[1] See *Mishnah Berurah* 447:1.
[2] *Shulchan Aruch* OC 447:1.
[3] *Shulchan Aruch* OC 447:2.
[4] *Shulchan Aruch* OC 447:4.

before *Pesach* (and may be eaten on *Erev Pesach*),[5] once *Pesach* begins the *chametz* is חוזר וניעור, and the mixture is forbidden.[6]

The *Poskim* discuss several variations of a similar issue: someone discovered a kernel of wheat or barley mixed into their food on *Pesach* but is uncertain whether the kernel is *chametz* or whether it was *nosein ta'am* in the food. The kernel will obviously be discarded and not eaten, and the issue is whether the rest of the food is forbidden. There is no question that any *ta'am* extracted from the grain will be *batel b'shishim* in the food, such that the *issur mashehu* is the only possible reason the food might be forbidden. May one eat that food on *Pesach*? In other words, what is the status of a food where there is a *safek* which – at worst – will only be forbidden based on the *issur mashehu*?

> Although the cases discussed by the Poskim are not so relevant nowadays, the principles regarding safek issur mashehu drawn from their rulings will nonetheless help resolve a common contemporary issue, noted at the end of the chapter.[7]

נתבקעו

The discussion begins with a *Gemara*[8] which has a *machlokes* regarding grains of barley which had some contact with water and were possibly "נתבקעו" (*cracked*, a sign that they became *chametz*). *Rif*[9] rules that since the *machlokes* is unresolved, the principle of *safek d'oraisah l'chumrah* dictates that one should refrain from eating the barley. However, if a few pieces of this barley were mixed into a food on *Pesach*, one may eat the food (after discarding the barley) since the *issur mashehu* is only a *d'rabannan*.[10]

Rif is essentially ruling that one can be lenient when there is a *safek* about an *issur mashehu*, and *Shulchan Aruch*[11] accepts this lenient ruling. However, *Rema* says that *Ashkenazim* are strict on this matter, and the

---

[5] See *Shulchan Aruch* OC 447:2.
[6] *Rema* OC 447:4. Additional details on some of the points noted in this paragraph can be found in Chapter 61.
[7] See another example in *Imrei Dovid, Meat and Poultry*, Chapter 47.
[8] *Gemara, Pesachim* 40a.
[9] *Rif, Pesachim* 12a.
[10] The text explains *Rif* as per the simple reading of his words, and as explained by *Ran* ad loc. This is also the explanation recorded in *Magen Avraham* 467:12, cited in *Mishnah Berurah* 467:36. However, *Rambam* (*Hil. Chametz U'matzah* 5:8) understands that the "*d'rabannan*" relates to the status of grains which were נתבקעו.
[11] *Shulchan Aruch* OC 467:9.

Acharonim offer three explanations for that position. The first is from *Avnei Nezer*[12] who says that *Rema* is of the opinion that the reason *Chazal* created an *issur mashehu* is because people are used to eating *chametz* all year round (לא בדילי מיניה) and therefore need special restrictions to help keep them from accidentally eating it on *Pesach*. As such, the *issur mashehu* is particularly strict, and the principle of *safek d'rabannan l'kulah* does not apply. Therefore, even if there is a *safek* that food might be forbidden based on the *issur mashehu*, one may not eat it.

A second explanation is offered by *Rebbi Akiva Eiger*,[13] who also says that *Rema* is *machmir* about *safek issur mashehu* in this case based on the position of *Tosfos*,[14] which the later *Acharonim*[15] explain as follows: In theory, *safek issur mashehu* is permitted just like any other *safek d'rabannan*, but in this case the sole *safek* is on the status of the kernel of barley. If the barley is *chametz*, then the food is forbidden and there is no other *safek*. That *safek* is a *safek d'oraisah* and we must be *machmir* and assume that the kernel is forbidden. If so, once the *safek* has been "resolved" from that perspective, the status of the *d'rabannan* issue that follows (i.e., the *issur mashehu*) must go along with that decision.[16] Thus, in many cases, *safek issur mashehu* is forbidden, but in situations where the true *safek* is a *d'rabannan*, one can be lenient.

However, most *Poskim* understand that *Rema* agrees with the conclusion of *Rif* that *safek issur mashehu* is permitted in [basically] all cases.[17] The reason he is *machmir* in this specific case is because he understands that the halacha follows the strict opinion in the *Gemara*, so that this barley kernel is treated as <u>surely</u> being *chametz*. But in any case where there truly is a *safek*, the food is permitted.

---

[12] *Avnei Nezer* OC 361:3-4. *Avnei Nezer* suggests an overall approach to the disagreement between *Shulchan Aruch* and *Rema*, which sees them as having a fundamental disagreement about the basis for the *issur mashehu*. *Avnei Nezer* notes that this understanding of *Shulchan Aruch* appears to be contradicted by *Shulchan Aruch* YD 102:4 (and see more on this in a footnote to *Yabeah Omer* OC 9:39). That question does not affect his explanation of *Rema* noted in the text.

[13] *Rebbi Akiva Eiger* to *Magen Avraham* 467:12, and see also *Responsa* 1:26.

[14] *Tosfos, Chullin* 97a s.v. *Amar Rava*.

[15] *Toras Chesed* OC 20:9 and *Achiezer* 2:15:7.

[16] This is known as נתגלגל (*the status decided on the d'oraisah level* <u>rolls over</u> *to the d'rabannan issue*); for more on that see *Imrei Dovid, Alcoholic Beverages*, Chapter 22 Part 2, and below in Chapter 65.

[17] See *Pri Megadim* AA 467:13 citing *Bach* and *Pri Chadash* OC 467:9. See also *Gr"a* 467:9 s.v. *v'ein, Chazon Ish* (OC 117:4 s.v. *vegam*, OC 119:10 s.v. *v'haRema*, and OC 119:12 s.v. 447:4), and *Chok Yaakov* 467:26 cited in *Mishnah Berurah* 467:38 and in *Biur Halacha* s.v. *afilu*.

ספק איסור משהו

Questions

According to this understanding, *Rema* essentially agrees with *Shulchan Aruch* that *safek issur mashehu* is permitted (and is only strict in the specific case of נתבקעו). The *Acharonim* note several apparent contradictions to this lenient ruling of *Rema*, and their solutions help us get a more nuanced understanding of exactly when *Rema* is lenient.

~ יבש ביבש

One question is from the halacha, noted above, that חוזר וניעור applies to mixtures of יבש ביבש. The case *Rema*[18] gives for that halacha is that bread fell into a container of wine and was removed from the wine before *Pesach*. It is possible that some breadcrumbs remain in the wine, and therefore one may not drink the wine on *Pesach* since the mixture of crumbs in wine is considered יבש ביבש. Any crumbs in the wine are *batel b'shishim*, so the only reason to forbid the wine is because of the *issur mashehu*; if so, since we do not <u>know</u> that there are crumbs, should this be a case of *safek issur mashehu* and be permitted? In other words, חוזר וניעור might apply to a case of יבש ביבש, but this case is permitted for a different reason (*safek issur mashehu*).[19]

Olas Shabbos[20] answers that if bread falls into wine, it is so likely that crumbs will flake off into the wine that there is not much of a *safek* that they are present. Thus, whereas *safek issur mashehu* is permitted in cases where there is only a small chance that the *mashehu* is present (or forbidden), if there is good reason to believe that there is a *mashehu* of *chametz*, then *Rema* will not be lenient. *Mishnah Berurah*[21] and others cite this ruling of *Olas Shabbos*.

~ סכין

A second question on *Rema* comes from his ruling[22] regarding food cut with a dirty knife which had previously been used for *chametz*. *Rema* says that one may not eat the food since some *chametz* may have transferred from the knife to the food, but if the food gets mixed into other food, one may

---

[18] *Rema* OC 447:4.
[19] Previously, we noted three ways to explain why *Rema* is *machmir* in the case of נתבקעו. The second and third explanations must deal with the question noted here in the text, but not the first one (*Avnei Nezer*, that *Rema* is *machmir* about *safek issur mashehu*).
[20] *Olas Shabbos* OC 447:4 (end), cited in *Pri Megadim* AA 447:12. The relevant words are:
ומה שכתב דחיישינן שמא נשארו פרורין וכו'. אף על גב דספק משהו הוא מכל מקום החמירו בו, משום דהאי ספיקא קרוב לודאי הוא דמסתמא נשתייר בו פרורין
[21] *Biur Halacha* 447:4 s.v. *shemah*.
[22] *Rema* OC 447:7.

eat the combined foods. This is because there cannot be very much *chametz* left on the blade of a dirty knife, and presumably whatever is there will be *batel b'shishim* into the food cut with that knife. This means that the only possible reason to forbid the food cut with the knife is the *issur mashehu*. We do not <u>know</u> that there is *chametz* residue on the knife. If so, *Chazon Ish*[23] asks, this should be another example of *safek issur mashehu*, and *Rema* should permit even the food cut with the knife (and not just the food into which that original food was mixed in)?

He answers that *safek issur mashehu* is only permitted when the "*mashehu*" is thoroughly mixed into a food and there is no chance a person will eat the *chametz* itself. But in this case, any residue that transfers from the knife will rest on the surface of the food, and the person eating it will unwittingly consume the *chametz* "by itself" (while it is perched on top of the food). Only when the food that was cut with the *chametz* knife is mixed into other foods[24] does *safek issur mashehu* come into play and permit the food. Thus, from this halacha we learn that *issur mashehu* is only permitted when there is a *ta'aruvos*, but if there is a chance that the person will eat even a bit of *chametz* as is, then the food is forbidden.

~ **ירדו גשמים**

Chazon Ish[25] asks another question on *Rema* based on a ruling he gives[26] in a case where water dripped onto a pile of wheat. Some of the kernels were obviously affected by the water and cannot be used on *Pesach*. As far as the remaining kernels are concerned, *Rema* describes a case where there is a *sfek sfekah* that indicates that they are permitted, and rules that one may retain ownership of them for *Pesach* but should not eat them. Why should we be stricter about <u>eating</u> the kernels than <u>owning</u> them? *Beis Yosef* explains that:

דאף על גב דלענין בל יראה יתבטלו הספיקות ברובן
לגבי אכילה דהוי במשהו לא מקילין

Chazon Ish takes this literally and says that the reason not to eat these kernels is an extension of the *issur mashehu*. But even if it is treated as *mashehu*, have we not seen that *safek issur mashehu* is permitted? So, in this case, where there is just a *safek* if these kernels became wet (and

---

[23] *Chazon Ish* OC 119:16 ד"ה ס"ז בהגה'.
[24] For that matter, if the food cut with the *chametz* knife had itself been blended to the point that any residue would be mixed in, the food is also permitted (*Chazon Ish*).
[25] *Chazon Ish* OC 121:25 ד"ה תס"ו ב.
[26] *Rema* OC 467:2.

chametz), they should be permitted? *Chazon Ish* says that this indicates that *safek issur mashehu* is only permitted in cases of לח בלח, but not in cases of יבש ביבש. That is to say that the wheat kernels are distinguishable one from another, and the reason they are a "*ta'aruvos*" is because no one can tell which kernel is *chametz* and which is not. For that type of *ta'aruvos* (יבש ביבש), the leniency of *safek issur mashehu* does not apply.

Chazon Ish does not explain [or provide a source] why יבש ביבש should be treated stricter than לח בלח. At first glance, one might think that it is based on the previously mentioned point of *Chazon Ish*, that *safek issur mashehu* is not permitted when there is a chance the person might eat *chametz* as is (not in a *ta'aruvos*). That is definitely true in many cases of יבש ביבש, but surely does not explain this broad ruling of *Chazon Ish* because this is a case of wheat <u>kernels</u> which possibly became wet. No one will eat the grains in their current form, and they will obviously be milled into flour and baked into *matzah* or something similar. If so, we can be confident that no one will ever eat a bit of *chametz* that is not mixed with other foods. Thus, we are left unsure why *Chazon Ish* maintains that יבש ביבש should be treated more strictly than other cases of *safek issur mashehu*.[27]

But a more significant point is that the other *Poskim* implicitly reject *Chazon Ish's* approach. Many[28] pose the same question as *Chazon Ish* – why is eating those kernels stricter than retaining ownership – and they find this question so compelling that they essentially say one should ignore this ruling of *Rema*![29] At most, they see *Rema* as saying that if there is no bother to save these grains until after *Pesach*, then it is commendable to

---

[27] One could potentially suggest that *Chazon Ish* is based on a combination of (a) the concern that the person will eat *chametz* as is (as per *Chazon Ish* noted above), which becomes (b) a pseudo-נתגלגל (as per *Rebbi Akiva Eiger* noted above), as follows. When the mixture is in a יבש ביבש form – before the grains are milled into flour – we cannot be lenient based on *safek issur mashehu* since a person eating the kernels might eat the *chametz* kernel as-is. Once that determination is made, it remains in force (as a pseudo-נתגלגל) even when the grains are milled into flour. The obvious issue with this explanation is that we previously cited *Rema* who says that even though it is forbidden to eat the food cut with the *chametz* knife, once that food is mixed into other food (or even blended by itself) it becomes permitted. Thus, it is clear that this pseudo-נתגלגל is not a meaningful concern.

[28] See, for example, *Taz* OC 467:4, *Chok Yaakov* 467:10, and *Mishnah Berurah* 467:11 (with *Sha'ar HaTziun* 467:19).

[29] Although *Beis Yosef* notes a reason to be stricter about eating, these *Poskim* assume that it is based on a general position that *sfek sfekah* cannot be relied upon as relates to <u>eating</u> *chametz*. [And this is what *Beis Yosef* refers to when he says that "eating is subject to the *issur mashehu*"; eating *chametz* is stricter and cannot rely on *sfek sfekah*, just as *issur mashehu* applies to eating and not to בל יראה]. But they note that in several places *Rema* rules that one <u>may</u> rely on *sfek sfekah* even to permit eating a food that might be *chametz*, and therefore *Rema's* ruling in this case cannot be taken "literally".

do so and avoid even the smallest question of partaking from forbidden *chametz*, but really the halacha is that one may even eat them on *Pesach*. *Mishnah Berurah's*[30] acceptance of this position is an implicit rejection of *Chazon Ish's* strict stand regarding *safek issur mashehu* for cases of יבש ביבש.

Infant rice cereal

In Imrei Dovid, Kashering, Chapter 57 we discussed the use of infant rice cereal on Pesach and came to a strict conclusion. In the upcoming paragraphs we reexamine the issue based on the sources noted in this chapter.

We have seen that [other than *Avnei Nezer*] it is assumed that *Rema* agrees that *safek issur mashehu* is permitted. Some of the later *Poskim* say that this does not apply if [1] the primary *safek* is a *d'oraisah* (*Rebbi Akiva Eiger*), [2] there is a strong chance that the item is truly forbidden (*Olas Shabbos*), or that [3] the person might eat the *chametz* as is (not mixed into other foods) (*Chazon Ish*). However, most reject the other position of *Chazon Ish*, that *safek issur mashehu* does not apply in cases of יבש ביבש. Let us now see how this applies to the case of infant rice cereal.

Infant rice cereal is made by cooking rice until it develops a porridge-like consistency, and then the watery mixture is poured onto a hot drum dryer so that all the water boils out. The result is flakes of cooked rice, which can easily be converted back into porridge by simply adding water. Assuming the rice does not contain any *chametz* ingredients, it would appear to be suitable for infants on *Pesach*. Although rice is *kitnios*, infants are permitted to eat *kitnios*,[31] and thus it should not pose a problem.

However, some of the same companies that package rice cereal also produce a similar product made of oats, which are *chametz*. If even one flake of oat cereal was to be mixed into the rice cereal, it would not be permitted to eat the rice cereal on *Pesach*. Although the oat flakes were mixed in before *Pesach* and are surely *batel b'shishim*, each flake is free-standing and distinguishable from the next. The mixture of one oat flake in thousands of rice flakes is יבש ביבש and – as we saw – that is the case where *Rema* says that even if the *chametz* was mixed in before *Pesach*, it is חוזר וניעור, and the food may not be eaten on *Pesach*.

---

[30] *Mishnah Berurah* 467:11.
[31] See *Mishnah Berurah* 453:7.

It is reasonable to assume that – despite the manufacturer's vigilance to avoid allergens and contamination – there is one flake of oat cereal in one of the boxes of rice cereal, but it is obviously not at all clear that there are any oat flakes in any individual box of rice cereal.[32] That is a simple case of *safek issur mashehu*, because we do not know if there is an oat flake in the box (*safek*) and, if it is there, it is only forbidden based on the *issur mashehu*. The three exceptions when *safek issur mashehu* is forbidden also do not apply in this case: [1] there is no question about the status of the oat flake, and the *safek* is rather whether it is present; [2] there is a very small chance that an oat flake is mixed into any given box of rice cereal; and [3] rice cereal is eaten after being reconstituted into porridge, so there is no chance someone will eat the oat flake as is. The only potential reason to be *machmir* is based on the latter ruling of *Chazon Ish*, that *safek issur mashehu* does not apply in cases of יבש ביבש, but it appears that the other *Poskim* do not accept that position.

Consequently, it seems that if one can determine that the infant rice cereal is free of *chametz* ingredients,[33] one may retain ownership of it on *Pesach* and feed it to a child.

---

[32] The text explains a basis for being lenient based on *safek issur mashehu*. Another reason to permit it is based on *Chayei Adam* 121:20 (citing *Magen Avraham* 467:4, which in turn, is based on *Shulchan Aruch* YD 110:7) that since *issur mashehu* is only *assur mid'rabannan* one is entitled to "assume" (תולין בדרבנן) that the forbidden oat flake is in a different box of cereal. For more on the principle of תולין בדרבנן, see *Imrei Dovid, Alcoholic Beverages*, Chapter 20.

[33] The text discusses the concern that an oat flake might be mixed into the rice. What about the possibility that the vitamins added to it are *chametz*? The vast majority of them are not *chametz*, and presumably one may rely on כל דפריש מרובא פריש to assume the vitamins in any given container are not *chametz*-based; see the end of Chapter 63.

Chapter 35

חזותא

שולחן ערוך סימן ק"ב סעיף א'
כל דבר שיש לו מתירין כגון ביצה שנולדה ביום טוב שראויה למחר, אם נתערבה באחרות בין שלימה בין טרופה אינה בטלה אפילו באלף. ואפילו ספק נולדה ביום טוב ונתערבה באחרות אסורות. ואם נתערבה בשאינה מינה בטלה בס'

הגה: מיהו אם לבנו בה מאכל או נתנו בקדירה לתקן הקדירה כגון שמלאוה בתרנגולת אינה בטלה, ועיין בא"ח סימן תקי"ג.

Sources and Opinions

In previous chapters, we saw several examples of *issur* which cannot be *batel* because it is too prominent (להתכבד הראויה חתיכה, בריה), has a significant role in the food (דבר המעמיד), or due to another reason (דבר שיש לו מתירין). In each of those cases, the halacha is based on a *Gemara* which unambiguously makes the point that *bitul* is inappropriate for that case. In contrast, this chapter will be about a similar concept – that *issur* which changes the color or appearance (חזותא) of the food cannot be *batel* – but this one has no clear *Gemara* source, and some question if the halacha is true at all.

The *Gemara* (*Bava Kama*)[1] which seems to be most relevant discusses a thief who stole cloth and dye, applied the dye to the cloth, and then returned the dyed cloth to the original owner. Should we say that since חזותא מילתא (*when something affects the color of an item, it is as if the color is still present*), the thief has returned both the cloth and dye? Or should we say that חזותא לאו מילתא, and all that has been returned is the cloth, which means that the thief must still repay the stolen dye? The *Gemara* attempts to prove that חזותא מילתא from sources that clothing dyed with *arlah* or *shevi'is* items are forbidden and rejects these since the *pesukim*

---

[1] *Gemara, Bava Kama* 101a.

upon which those halachos are based, might be specific to *arlah* and *shevi'is* and not be relevant to other halachos. The *Gemara* leaves the question unresolved. [The continuation of the *Gemara* will be discussed below].

Pri Chadash[2] says that since the *Gemara* does not resolve the question of whether חזותא מילתא, we should apply the general rule for unsettled halachic issues: we are *machmir* when that relates to a *d'oraisah* issue and are lenient when there is not more than an *issur d'rabannan*.[3] For example, if a tiny bit of carmine was used to color a candy red, orange, or purple, the candy would be forbidden since carmine — which is made of crushed cochineal insects — is *assur mid'oraisah*.[4] But if the purple coloring was created using non-kosher enocianina, the candy would *b'dieved* be permitted (assuming the enocianina was *batel b'shishim*) since enocianina — made from the residue of grape juice production — is (only) *assur mid'rabannan* as *stam yayin*[5] and can therefore be *batel b'shishim* even if it provides color.

But *Minchas Yaakov*[6] argues that this *Gemara* is not at all relevant to forbidden foods. He notes that the *Gemara's* cases of a thief, *arlah*, and *shevi'is* were all about cloths and clothing, where it is typical that they are dyed, and where taste is obviously meaningless. In those cases, it is possible that חזותא might be significant enough to prevent *bitul*. In contrast, taste is the primary feature of a food, and color is relatively

---

[2] *Pri Chadash* 102:5.
[3] It is generally assumed that *mid'oraisah* every *issur* can be *batel b'shishim*, and it is always a Rabbinic restriction which says *bitul* is not possible (or that *shishim* is not enough for *bitul*). If so, every case of חזותא is one where *mid'oraisah* the *issur* is *batel*, and according to Pri Chadash's logic we should never be *machmir*? See *Pri Megadim* MZ 100:1, who shows that while many agree that חזותא is a Rabbinic principle (and might therefore be lenient), *Pri Chadash* is of the opinion that items which provide color are *mid'oraisah* not *batel* (because it is as if the *issur* is detectable and not considered as a *ta'aruvos*). Therefore, where the forbidden food was inherently *assur mid'oraisah*, Pri Chadash says one should be *machmir* regarding חזותא.
[4] For more on carmine and its kosher status, see *Imrei Dovid, Halachos of Insects*, Chapter 49.

Pasta colored with black squid ink is not a good example of חזותא of an *issur d'oraisah* because the squid ink also provides flavoring to the pasta. Thus, even if חזותא does not prevent *bitul*, the ink is not *batel* because it is a מילתא דעבידא לטעמא. [Even those who say that the prohibition against eating a *yotzeh* (byproduct) of a forbidden item is less severe than eating the *issur* itself (see *Imrei Dovid, Animal Products*, Chapters 2 and 36) agree that it is nonetheless an *issur d'oraisah* to do so].
[5] For more on enocianina (a.k.a., eno) and its kosher status, see *Imrei Dovid, Alcoholic Beverages*, Chapter 37.
[6] *Minchas Yaakov* 74:5. He also supports his position from the fact that none of the early codifiers mention that something which provides color cannot be *batel* (והרמב"ם הרי"ף הראשונים הפוסקים כל וגם עביד שלא כל דבטל משוע דין זה כלל כתבו לא בטילים שאינם דברים שכתבו פוסקים גדולי ושאר והרש"ב"א והטור והרא"ש חזותא דאיכא אף לטעמא).

unimportant. Therefore, the *Gemara* never even considered that חזותא should prevent *bitul* when *issur* is mixed into food, and one can completely ignore חזותא in those contexts. According to *Minchas Yaakov*, the candy colored with carmine (note above) would be permitted *b'dieved*; although carmine is *assur mid'oraisah*, it can be *batel b'shishim* like any other *issur*, irrespective of the fact that it provides coloring/חזותא to the candy.

There is another *Gemara* (*Zevachim*)[7] that mentions the term חזותא, and *Minchas Yaakov* says that *Rashi's* interpretation of that *Gemara* supports his position. The *Gemara* says that there are times when *bitul* depends on taste, other times it is based on *rov*, and there are cases where it depends on חזותא (אמור רבנן בטעמא ואמור רבנן ברובא ואמר רבנן בחזותא). The *Gemara* says that the first two (taste, *rov*) relate to the *bitul* of different examples of forbidden foods, and *Rashi*[8] explains that the third one (חזותא) is relevant to a halacha specific to *mikvah*. Why would *Rashi* say that this third halacha is different than the other two? Why not say that חזותא is also relevant for *bitul* of *issur* which provides color? This implies that חזותא has no possible relevance to *bitul* of forbidden foods, leaving *Rashi* no choice but to say that it relates to *mikvah*. [*Pri Chadash* responds to this proof by saying that since the other *Gemara* (*Bava Kama*) leaves the question of חזותא מילתא unresolved, *Rashi* chose a "safe" case where חזותא is the criterion for *bitul*].

Previously we noted that the *Gemara*, *Bava Kama*, does not resolve the question of חזותא מילתא for a thief. However, the very next text in the *Gemara*[9] cites *Rava* who raises a question from the previously noted case of clothing dyed with *arlah* (which implies that חזותא מילתא) to a source regarding clothing which absorbed *tamei* blood (which indicates that חזותא לאו מילתא). To this question, the *Gemara* responds that the source regarding *tumah* is discussing blood which is only *tamei mid'rabannan*, and for that reason it is lenient regarding חזותא.[10] *Rava's* question is very unexpected, because it is based on the strict halacha regarding *arlah* and the *Gemara* had just suggested that this might be a halacha that is unique to *arlah* (and *shevi'is*). So why is *Rava* asking from a stance regarding *arlah* which might not apply to other halachos?

---

[7] *Gemara, Zevachim* 79a.
[8] *Rashi, Zevachim* ibid. ד"ה והיכא.
[9] *Gemara, Bava Kama* 101b.
[10] Those who say that חזותא is not *batel* even for *issurim d'rabannan* (see the upcoming text), will presumably understand that this *Gemara* is limited to this specific *issur d'rabannan*, and is not saying that חזותא is *batel* for any *issur d'rabannan*.

This question of *Rava* supports *Shach* and others,[11] who say that חזותא is never *batel*. In other words, the beginning of the *Gemara* suggests that *arlah* is different from other *issurim*, but *Rava* rejects that possibility and therefore questions it based on a source regarding *tumah*.[12] [*Pri Chadash* responds to this proof that *Rava* is suggesting that maybe the halacha of *tumah* is a proof that *arlah* is unique because if not, there is a contradiction between those halachos]. According to *Shach*, the candy will be forbidden *b'dieved* even if it was colored by enocianina; although enocianina is only *assur mid'rabannan*, it cannot be *batel* since it changes the color of the food.

In addition to the opinions we have cited – חזותא is never *batel* (*Shach*), חזותא does not prevent *bitul* (*Minchas Yaakov*), and *issur d'oraisah* which affects חזותא cannot be *batel* (*Pri Chadash*) – others suggest that חזותא is only significant when discussing food which is *assur b'hana'ah*[13] or only when it is a דבר שיש לו מתירין.[14] There are very few cases where a forbidden

---

[11] *Toras Chattas* (*Rema*) 74:2 (as understood by *Minchas Yaakov* ibid.), *Minchas Kohen* (*Sha'ar HaTa'aruvos* 3:3), and *Shach* 102:5 (as understood by *Pri Megadim* ad loc. and *Minchas Yaakov*). However, see footnote 14 for *Chasam Sofer's* alternate understanding of *Shach*.

[12] This proof can be found in *Responsa Ran* 70, parts of which are cited in *Pri Chadash* ibid.

It is noteworthy that *Rava* is also the person who makes the statement noted in the previous text (in *Zevachim*) that אמור רבנן בטעמא...ואמור רבנן בחזותא. If *Rava* in *Bava Kama* takes the position that חזותא is never *batel*, that strengthens the question noted above, of why *Rashi* chooses a case of *mikvah* to explain *Rava's* statement in *Zevachim*.

[13] *Gr"a* 102:6. [See the coming footnote that *Gr"a* also agrees that חזותא מילתא when the forbidden item is a דבר שיש לו מתירין]. *Chochmas Adam* 53:41 combines *Gr"a* and *Pri Chadash*, saying that one can be lenient anytime an *issur d'rabannan* creates חזותא (as per *Pri Chadash*), and that for *issurim d'oraisah* one need only be *machmir* if the item is also *assur b'hana'ah* (as per *Gr"a*).

Gr"a says that when the *Gemara*, *Bava Kama* says that we only say חזותא מילתא for *arlah*, it means to say that חזותא מילתא is for cases like *arlah* which are *assur b'hana'ah*. [The logic would be that one derives benefit from the color and that is why it is a violation of the *issur hana'ah*]. However, see *Responsa Ran* 70, who says that if that were true, the *Gemara* would not have asked a second question from *shevi'is*.

[14] An egg laid on *Yom Tov* is forbidden until after *Yom Tov* and is also a דבר שיש לו מתירין (since it will become permitted on the next day). *Shulchan Aruch* OC 613:3 says that if the egg is used to whiten a food, it cannot be *batel*, since something that provides color and taste cannot be *batel* (מידי דלחזותא וטעמא עביד לא בטיל). [*Rema* YD 102:1 makes a similar point]. The *Poskim* take different approaches as to what this is referring to [and those opinions are reflected in the opinions noted in this chapter]; one of them is that חזותא מילתא is only for cases of דבר שיש לו מתירין. In other words, the basic halacha is that חזותא לאו מילתא (as per *Minchas Yaakov*), but for a דבר שיש לו מתירין, the fact that it provides color automatically qualifies it as *min b'mino* (even if it is not physically *min b'mino*). This is consistent with the second answer in *Tosfos, Beitzah* 39a, s.v. *mishum* (discussed in Chapter 33), that anything used to create a food is ipso facto *min b'mino*.

Some of those who follow this approach are *Gr"a* 102:6 (who also says חזותא מילתא for *issurei hana'ah*, see the previous footnote), *Chavos Da'as* 102:1 (*Biurim*), and *Aruch HaShulchan* 102:8. *Chasam Sofer* (in his glosses to *Shach* 102:5) says that this is also the position of *Shach*, but see above in footnote 11.

item that provides color is also *assur b'hana'ah* (see an example in the footnote)[15] or a דבר שיש לו מתירין, and, therefore, those who restrict חזותא to one of those situations are basically saying that, in practice, חזותא is rarely a factor to prevent *bitul*.

Rav Schachter said that it is appropriate to follow the ruling of *Pri Chadash*, that when dealing with an *issur d'oraisah*, if something provides color, it cannot become *batel*.[16]

Other details

Several *Poskim* note that the entire previous discussion is limited to cases where the person intentionally used the (forbidden) item to color his food. But if that outcome was unplanned (or, presumably also, if the non-kosher ingredient fell into the food by mistake), then the fact that it changes the color of the food is not relevant and it can be *batel*.[17]

We have seen that – per *Pri Chadash* – a food colored with carmine is forbidden even if there is very little carmine in the recipe. Carmine is *issur d'oraisah* and when it is present it provides חזותא and cannot be *batel*. That is true for the food itself, but the carmine's presence does not mean that the equipment must be *kashered*. *Kashering* is performed to remove non-kosher taste, and since there is less than 1/60th carmine in the recipe, there is no *ta'am* of carmine absorbed into the equipment, so no *kashering* is required.[18]

---

[15] We saw in Chapter 33 that *chametz* is not a דבר שיש לו מתירין, and before *Pesach* it is also not *assur b'mashehu*. However, even before *Pesach* it still qualifies as something which is *assur b'hana'ah*. This leads to the following potential case of a food that is *assur b'hana'ah* which provides color: Olives which stay on the tree for an extended time will be black, but these olives are not sold to consumers for eating (but are rather used to produce olive oil). The natural color of the black (oxidized) olives which are available for sale, is green, and processing of the olives (with lye) changes their color to a shade of brown. At the end of the processing, they are exposed to a tiny amount of ferrous gluconate which changes their color to the uniform black color which consumers expect. Certain European manufacturers of ferrous gluconate use wheat-based glucose to create the gluconic acid which is later reacted with iron to create ferrous gluconate. Thus, these olives are an apparent example of a food whose color was changed by something which is *assur b'hana'ah* (*chametz*).

While this is factually correct, we saw in Chapter 2 that it seems this is an example of זה וזה גורם, since the gluconic acid (i.e., the *chametz*) itself would not affect the color of the olives, and it is only the combination of gluconic acid with iron (i.e., *chametz* with non-*chametz*) which has that effect. This means that the *b'dieved* status of the olives depends on the *machlokes* whether the leniency of זה וזה גורם applies to חזותא; for more on that see *Pri Chadash* 102:1 and *Pri Megadim* MZ 100:1.

[16] As *Chasam Sofer* ibid. says, אין לזוז מפסק הפרי חדש. See also *Shevet HaLevi* 8:184.

[17] *Pri Chadash* 102:5, cited in *Pri Megadim* MZ 100:1.

[18] This point was also noted in Chapter 1, regarding a דבר המעמיד which is in tiny proportions but cannot be *batel*.

How does this apply to a company that produces colors, including some made with carmine? That factory's formulations are likely to contain very high percentages of carmine, where the carmine is not *batel b'shishim*. At first glance, one would assume that since the equipment absorbs a *ta'am* of carmine, it must be *kashered* before kosher colors are produced. We will consider the different aspects of that question in Chapter 38.

Chapter 36

Bitul of Keilim

שולחן ערוך סימן קי"ב סעיפים ב'-ג'

יש מי שאומר שלא אמרו דבר שיש לו מתירין אלא
כשהמתיר עתיד לבא על כל פנים או אם המתיר בידו
לעשותו בלא הפסד, אבל דבר שאינו בידו ואינו ודאי
שיבא המתיר אינו בדין דבר שיש לו מתירין. לפיכך
ביצה של ספק טריפה שנתערבה באחרות אינו בדין
דבר שיש לו מתירין לפי שאין המתיר בודאי ואינו
בידו.

כלי שנאסר בבליעת איסור שנתערב באחרים ואינו
ניכר, בטל ברוב ואין דנין אותו כדבר שיש לו מתירין
(לפי שצריך להוציא עליו הוצאות להגעילו, וכל כיוצא בזה).

Non-Automatic Heter

In Chapter 33 we discussed the typical cases of דבר שיש לו מתירין and considered whether *chodosh* and *chametz* qualify. Those cases share a common feature with the classic case of דבר שיש לו מתירין – an egg laid on *Yom Tov* which is forbidden on *Yom Tov* but permitted right after[1] – in that for each of them, the forbidden item automatically becomes permitted with the passage of time. *Chodosh* becomes *yoshon* on the first day of *Chol HaMoed Pesach*, *chametz* may be eaten when *Pesach* ends, and the egg is permitted after *Yom Tov*. In this chapter, we branch into a different type of דבר שיש לו מתירין where the item can become permitted, but to reach that new state, some action must be taken. Does עד שתאכלנו באיסור אכלו בהיתר apply in those cases as well?

The discussion begins with cases which are not so practical for us, but which teach principles for dealing with two situations which are very relevant. The *Gemara* (*Nedarim*)[2] says that the following five items are considered a דבר שיש לי מתירין – *tevel*, an item forbidden based on a

---

[1] See *Shulchan Aruch* OC 513 and YD 102:1.
[2] *Gemara*, *Nedarim* 58a and 59a.

Bitul of Keilim 391

neder/vow, *ma'aser sheini, hekdesh*, and *chodosh*[3] — but the following five are not – *terumah, terumas ma'aser, challah, arlah*, and *klai hakerem*.[4] All these cases (other than *chodosh*) are items which are permanently forbidden, so how can they possibly be a יש לו מתירין? The subsequent *Gemara*[5] explains that since a *neder* can be undone through the process of *hataras nedarim*, that is enough to qualify it as a יש לו מתירין. That raises an obvious question: *terumah* (and *terumas ma'aser* and *challah*) should also qualify as יש לו מתירין since *hataras nedarim* can also be used to undo the designation of this item as *terumah*? To that the *Gemara* answers that there is a *mitzvah* to undo standard *nedarim*; therefore, it is taken as a virtual "given" that the person will eventually do so, and that is why a *neder* is יש לו מתירין. No such *mitzvah* applies to *terumah*;[6] therefore, it will likely remain *terumah* forever and is not a יש לו מתירין.[7]

This *Gemara* indicates that there are situations which qualify as דבר שיש לו מתירין even though the *issur* does not expire automatically (as it does with *chodosh, chametz*, and the egg) but rather requires some action to make that happen. However, the mere possibility that the *issur* <u>can</u> be undone is not sufficient, and only certain possible actions (e.g., ones that are a *mitzvah*) qualify.

If the criterion is that it must be <u>assumed</u> that the *issur* will be undone, we can easily understand why *tevel* is יש לו מתירין, since it is typical that

---

[3] [Four of these are listed on 58a, and *neder* is on 59a]. *Tevel* is an item from which *terumah* and *ma'aser* were not yet separated and may not be eaten until that separation occurs. Produce designated as *ma'aser sheini* must be eaten in *Yerushalayim* unless the person transfers (*podeh*) the *kedushah* onto money (which he uses to buy foods that he will eat in *Yerushalayim*). One may not use an item forbidden via a *neder* or donated to the *Beis HaMikdash* (*hekdesh*). *Chodosh* was defined in Chapter 33.

[4] *Terumah* and *terumas ma'aser* are portions of produce designated for *Kohanim*, and *challah* is similar to them but it is separated from dough rather than produce. *Arlah* is fruit that grew during the first three years after a tree was planted, and *klai hakerem* is produce that grows in close proximity to grapes; both of these items are forbidden.

[5] *Gemara, Nedarim* 59a.

[6] *Gilyon Maharsha* (to *Taz* YD 323:2) goes one step further and says that if the person is *matir neder* for *terumah*, he loses the *mitzvah* he previously earned for separating the *terumah*, plus the *bracha* that he recited on that *hafrashah* is now retroactively considered a *bracha levatalah*. [However, see *Responsa Chasam Sofer* YD 320 who rules that it would not be a *bracha levatalah*].

[7] If the *Gemara* had not listed *terumah, terumas ma'aser*, and *challah* as not being יש להם מתירין, we might never have known the concept that although *hataras nedarim* is possible, they are not יש להם מתירין since there is no *mitzvah* to do this *hataras nedarim*. That could explain why these three cases are listed, but not (a) why we need all three, or (b) why *arlah* and *klai hakerem* are listed. Thus, it may be that the main reason to list all these cases is for another element of the *Gemara's* statement: that although they can be *batel* (and are not *assur b'mashehu* like a יש לו מתירין), they are not *batel b'rov* or *batel b'shishim* like most other forbidden foods, but instead require 100 or 200 times their volume for *bitul* (100 for *terumah, terumas ma'aser*, and *challah*, and 200 for *arlah* and *klai hakerem*).

people will separate *terumah* and *ma'aser* to remove the *tevel* status. What about *hekdesh* and *ma'aser sheini*? *Ran*[8] says that the case of *hekdesh* is one where an object was donated to the *Beis HaMikdash's* general fund (קדשי בדק הבית); since the *Beis HaMikdash* has no particular use for the item itself, they will be *podeh*/transfer its *kedushah* onto money (which will be used for upkeep); thus, the object will eventually lose its *kedushah*. See the footnote regarding *ma'aser sheini*.[9]

Rashba[10] asks that this *Gemara* that considers *tevel* a יש לו מתירין, seems to be contradicted by another *Gemara* (*Avodah Zara*)[11] which wonders why *tevel* is *assur b'mashehu* if it is mixed into standard food as *min b'mino*. What is the question? That status is exactly the one given to every דבר שיש לו מתירין – it is not *batel* when *min b'mino* – so it should be obvious that *tevel* also has that halacha? *Rashba* answers based on a third *Gemara* (*Bava Metziah*)[12] which says that the reason *ma'aser sheini* is a דבר שיש לו מתירין is because the person can remove its *kedushah* by being *podeh* it, but if the person does not have the right type of coin available then it is not a יש לו מתירין and can be *batel*.

Rashba explains that just like the lack of access to a coin is enough to negate *ma'aser sheini's* status as a יש לו מתירין, so too, if *tevel* was mixed into other food and the person has no other *tevel* to use for the separation,[13] the *tevel* in the mixture is not considered a יש לו מתירין. The

---

[8] *Ran Nedarim* 59a, s.v. *terumah*.
[9] *Rambam* (*Hil. Ma'aser Sheini* 6:14) (as per *Pri Chadash* 102:8) understands that the case of *ma'aser sheini* is where the mixture is in *Yerushalayim*, so it is יש לו מתירין because you can eat all of it right there as if it was all *ma'aser sheini*. However, *Ran* (*Nedarim* 58a s.v. *kol*) says that *ma'aser sheini* is יש לו מתירין because you can be *podeh* it (which clearly means that it is not yet in *Yerushalayim*). How is that different from *terumah* which – as noted in the text – is not יש לו מתירין since there is no expectation its *kedushah* will be removed (via *hataras nedarim*)? *Sha'ar HaMelech* (*Hil. Ma'acholos Assuros* 15:10) gives two answers. The first is that it is common to be *podeh* one's *ma'aser sheini* since it is difficult to carry it all to *Yerushalayim* to eat there. The second is that anytime the person can easily remove the *issur* by himself (such as when one is *podeh ma'aser sheini*) it is יש לו מתירין, even if there is no *mitzvah* to do so, and the *Gemara* only required "*mitzvah*" for situations where removing the *issur* requires other people, such as for *hataras nedarim* (for *neder*, *terumah*, *terumas ma'aser*, and *challah*) which is accomplished with 3 outsiders.
  Nowadays, since we no longer can eat *ma'aser sheini* in *Yerushalayim*, everyone is *podeh* their *ma'aser sheini*, and therefore it is obvious why it is a דבר שיש לו מתירין (*Sha'ar HaMelech*).
[10] *Toras HaBayis* 4:4 pages 38a-b.
[11] *Gemara, Avodah Zara* 73b.
[12] *Gemara, Bava Metziah* 53a.
[13] *Mid'oraisah*, the *tevel* is *batel* in this mixture and no longer requires *hafrashah* to remove the *tevel* status. [In fact, it would be forbidden to be *mafrish* for that *tevel* from another standard piece of *tevel* since – from a *d'oraisah* perspective – that would be מן החיוב על הפטור]. It is only a Rabbinic principle (דבר שיש לו מתירין) which prevents *bitul* and forces the *tevel* to retain its status. Therefore, the "other *tevel*" which the person must have, is a very specific type of produce which itself is only *tevel*

Bitul of Keilim 393

option to remove the *issur* is not readily available, and therefore it is not a דבר שיש לו מתירין. It is for those cases that the *Gemara* in *Avodah Zara* wonders why *tevel* should be *assur b'mashehu*.

We will return to *Rashba's* understanding of the case of *tevel* below, but for now we will consider the practical cases which *Rashba* and others discuss.

Kashering

~ Expense

Thus far, we have seen *Rashba's* clarification of when something is considered יש לו מתירין (because a person can do something to convert it to *heter*), and when it is not. He then applies these principles to the case where a non-kosher dish was mixed into kosher ones, and no one can tell which is which. It is possible to *kasher* all the dishes, which will surely remove the non-kosher *ta'am* and render them all suitable for use. But *kashering* requires fire – either for *libun* or to heat the *hag'alah* water – and the fuel to create that fire costs money; therefore, *Rashba* rules that the possibility for the person to *kasher* the dishes is not enough to qualify the non-kosher one as a דבר שיש לו מתירין. Accordingly, we apply the standard rules of *bitul*, which state that a non-kosher dish is *batel b'rov* in the kosher ones, and all of them can be used without *kashering*.

Several objections are raised to *Rashba's* application of his principles to this case,[14] and we will focus on the one noted in *Maharil* (cited in *Shach*):[15] If a person has *ma'aser sheini* that is far away from *Yerushalayim*, the fact that he could bring it to *Yerushalayim* is not enough to qualify it as a דבר שיש לו מתירין, since it takes considerable effort to bring the produce there.

---

mid'rabannan, such as דמאי or something that grew in an עציץ שאינו מנקוב; see *Tosfos* and *Rosh* to *Gemara*, *Nedarim* 58a.

[14] One reason given to be stricter than *Rashba*, and require *kashering* in all cases, is from *Ra'ah* (*Bedek HaBayis* 4:4 page 38a), cited in *Shach* 102:8, who says that since the non-kosher *ta'am* can be removed with *hag'alah*, it is an example of אפשר להסירו and does not qualify as a *ta'aruvos* at all; for more on this see Chapter 24, and there in footnote 5. See also (a) *Taz* 102:8 that even when *Rashba's* principle applies, the dishes must eventually be *kashered* to avoid cooking one food in all the dishes, where it will be certain that non-kosher *ta'am* was absorbed into this food, and (b) *Bach*, cited in *Shach*, that even when *Rashba's* principle applies, the person should discard one of the dishes.

In contrast, *Yad Shel Shlomo* (*Chullin* 8:86, end), cited in *Taz* and *Shach* ibid., disagrees with *Rashba's* entire premise that something which requires "action" (e.g., *kashering*) can qualify as יש לו מתירין (except in cases where that action is a *mitzvah*, such as being *matir neder* – see *Pri Megadim* to *Shach*).

[15] *Responsa Maharil* 164, cited in *Shach* 102:8.

Nonetheless, *Tosfos*[16] says that if the *ma'aser sheini* is just outside the *Yerushalayim* city limits, it is so easy to bring it into the city that that itself qualifies it as a יש לו מתירין. This shows that if it takes minimal effort or expense to convert or use the forbidden item as *heter*, that possibility is enough to render it a דבר שיש לו מתירין. *Maharil* argues that in most cases the cost to *kasher* a utensil is a perfect example of this concept. For most people, that tiny expense is not a meaningful factor, and therefore the non-kosher dish cannot be *batel* since there is a way to make it kosher (i.e., יש לו מתירין) via *kashering*. [*Chochmas Adam*[17] accepts this ruling].

There is reason to believe that *Rema* agrees with this point, because after *Shulchan Aruch*[18] cites *Rashba's* halacha – that a non-kosher dish mixed into kosher ones is *batel b'rov* and can be used without *kashering* – *Rema* adds an explanation that this is because it costs money to *kasher*. Adding an explanation for the halacha seems superfluous, unless he means to indicate that the leniency only applies when there is an expense to *kasher*. But in cases where there is no significant cost to *kasher*, the non-kosher dish should be treated as a דבר שיש לו מתירין which is not *batel*.[19]

This point seems quite logical, and to understand why *Rashba* [and *Shulchan Aruch*] appear to disagree we will have to look more carefully at how *Rashba* describes the case when *tevel* is not considered a יש לו מתירין. He says:

ותירץ רבנו תם ז"ל דההיא דר' יוחנן בשאין לו טבל אחר להתירו...
שאילו אתה מזקיקו לקנות ממקום אחר **פעמים אין לו** והרי הוא נפסד כדי להתירו

He does not say that it is יש לו מתירין when it is difficult to obtain the "other" *tevel* for *hafrashah*, but rather that it is always יש לו מתירין since in some cases that will be true. In other words, since there will be times when it would be difficult for the person to obtain other *tevel* for the *hafrashah*,[20]

---

[16] *Tosfos, Bava Metziah* 53a ד"ה וליהדר.
[17] *Chochmas Adam* 53:23.
[18] *Shulchan Aruch* 102:3.
[19] See also *Toras Chattas* (*Rema*) 74:5 who uses the term לפזר מעותיו ולהגעילו (*to discard/waste his money to kasher*) which has an even stronger implication that the leniency is limited to cases where there is significant cost to *kasher*. [The term לפזר מעותיו is taken from *Toras HaBayis HaKatzar* 4:4 page 38a, cited in *Tur* YD 122 and *Beis Yosef* to 102:3. It is not found in *Toras HaBayis HaAruch* cited in *Beis Yosef* 122]. Why does *Rema* need the reason of *Rashba* when he rules (*Rema* 102:4) that *b'lios* are never a דבר שיש לו מתירין? See *Badei HaShulchan* (*Biurim*) 102:3 ד"ה ואין דנין.
[20] This is especially true as per the requirements needed for this "other" *tevel*, as noted in footnote 13.

we do not differentiate between those cases where it is difficult and others where it is easy; rather, <u>all</u> are not a דבר שיש לו מתירין.[21]

This indicates that even though it is most common for the cost of *kashering* to be negligible (as *Maharil* notes), there will surely be cases where there is considerable expense involved, and therefore *Rashba* takes the position that *bitul* of non-kosher dishes in kosher ones is not considered יש לו מתירין.

This analysis is based on the wording of *Rashba* in *Toras HaBayis HaAruch*, which is the one cited in *Beis Yosef's* main discussion of the matter (in YD 122). However, when *Rashba* summarizes this halacha in *Toras HaBayis HaKatzar*, he does not make this point. Rather, in that location, he stresses the loss involved in *kashering*, as if to say that this is the determining factor each time one considers whether a given case qualifies as יש לו מתירין. This is the version of *Rashba* cited by *Tur* and *Rema* (and *Beis Yosef* in YD 102). Thus, perhaps *Shulchan Aruch* favors the way the halacha is explained in the *Bayis HaAruch*, while *Maharil* and others are following the stricter approach given in the *Bayis HaKatzar*.[22]

---

[21] The same point can be seen later in *Rashba* when he discusses *Ramban's* application of the principle learned from *tevel* to the case of a non-kosher dish mixed with kosher ones. [The following quote is based on the version of *Beis Yosef* (and versions of *Toras HaBayis* that are corrected based on manuscripts) rather than how it is printed in the standard editions of *Toras HaBayis*].

והילכך אף כלי שנתערב באחרים...לא מיקרי דבר שיש לו מתירין כל שצריך להפסיד על הכשירן ואין הכשירן בא כדרכו בלא הפסד אחר אלא הרי הוא כיבש ביבש **וכל שנתערב אחד בין שנים בטל** ומשתמש בהן ואפילו לכתחילה

Why does he feel the need to give the example of a single non-kosher dish mixed into 2 kosher ones? Why was he not satisfied with just saying that the dishes can be *batel b'rov*? Seemingly, the point is to stress that even if there are very few dishes to *kasher* and the expense is minimal, the halacha still applies, because there are [other] situations where it will be very difficult and/or expensive to *kasher* them all.

[22] Alternatively, all might agree that every case is יש לו מתירין unless there is some expense involved in that specific *kashering*, and the disagreement revolves around the following issue: If the non-kosher dish had not gotten mixed into the others, the person would have been required to *kasher* it anyhow. Thus, he would have heated up the *hag'alah* water for that dish, and now [if the dish cannot be *batel*] he will be required to also immerse the other dishes in the boiling water. Once the water is heated up for this dish, there is <u>no</u> added expense to put in the remaining ones, and therefore (*Maharil* would say) there is no reason to view this as an "expense". But *Shulchan Aruch/Rashba* would argue that we should not compare the expense of *kashering* many dishes versus one dish, but rather we should compare the expense of *kashering* many dishes versus the choice to have <u>no</u> *kashering* at all if we would follow the general rule of *bitul b'rov*. In other words, if this is not a דבר שיש לו מתירין, the non-kosher dish is *batel* in the kosher ones, and no *kashering* at all is required. Thus, <u>all</u> *kashering* is "extra", and since there is expense (albeit minimal) to heat up water for that *kashering*, that is enough to dictate that the dish is not a יש לו מתירין.

In this context, see *Gr"a* 122:22, who says that the "loss" involved in *kashering* is that now you must *kasher* multiple utensils, while before the non-kosher utensil was mixed in, you could have just *kashered* one (i.e., the non-kosher one). Thus, he is viewing the judgement of loss/expense in the first manner suggested above as the explanation for *Maharil*. Additionally, *Shach* 102:8 discusses the

~ **Other factors**

Shach recommends following the strict approach of *Maharil*, that if the mixture of dishes can be *kashered* with minimal expense, a person should do so. At the same time, he says that in cases of *hefsed merubah* one may follow the lenient ruling and assume the non-kosher dish is *batel b'rov* in the other dishes. Seemingly, this means to say that in a case where being strict will result in a significant loss, even *Maharil* agrees that the non-kosher dish is not a דבר שיש לו מתירין. *Maharil* agrees with *Rashba's* principle that if a person must spend money to avoid the *issur*, that is not a יש לו מתירין, and just argued that *kashering* usually does not satisfy that criterion. But in cases where it does – such as if one non-kosher spoon got mixed into a caterers 500 kosher spoons, which will force the caterer to pay for hours of salary for a *Mashgiach* to *kasher* all 501 spoons[23] – he will agree that the spoon is *batel* and *kashering* is not required.

The same is also true if it is impossible to *kasher* the items, such as if they are *cheress*.[24] Since there is no way to *kasher* them, there is no question that *Maharil* [25] will agree that the dishes are not יש לו מתירין and are *batel*. This once occurred when a caterer served soup in 1,700 ceramic (*cheress*) bowls at a non-kosher venue, and when they packed up the dirty dishes

---

position of *Bach* (noted briefly in the upcoming text) that when one is not required to *kasher* (because the non-kosher dish is *batel*), one should nonetheless discard one dish since there is no loss to do so (ליכא פסידא). What does he mean "there is no loss"? How can there not be an expense to discard a pot? *Pri Megadim* ad loc. explains that the reason there is no loss is because before the non-kosher dish was mixed into the others, the person was anyhow going to have to discard it (since it is *cheress*), and therefore there is no loss to discard one now. Thus, *Shach* is comparing the current post-*bitul* status with that of what would have been had the non-kosher dish never gotten mixed in. Once again, this is consistent with the approach suggested for *Maharil*. [As noted in the coming text, *Shach* himself says that one should be *machmir* for *Maharil*].

On the other hand, some suggest that *ma'aser sheini* a דבר שיש לו מתירין since the mixture can be brought to be eaten in *Yerushalayim*, and *Rashba* rejects that line of reasoning (and instead suggests other reasons why it is יש לו מתירין) because the effort to bring the items to *Yerushalayim* is too much to qualify as a יש לו מתירין. The question on *Rashba* is that, before the *ma'aser sheini* got mixed into other food, the person would have had to travel to *Yerushalayim* with it anyhow, so why is *Rashba* certain that any extra effort is required to bring the entire mixture of foods? Seemingly the answer is that *Rashba* is comparing what happens if there is no *bitul* (due to יש לו מתירין) to what would happen if *bitul* would be allowed to proceed. If *bitul* would be allowed, the person would be excused from travelling to *Yerushalayim* altogether, since he has no more *ma'aser sheini* (as it was all *batel* in this food); if so, disallowing *bitul* forces him to make the trip, and that requires too much effort to be required. This explanation of *Rashba* is consistent with the approach suggested above for *Rashba/Shulchan Aruch*.

[23] See also *Chochmas Adam* 53:23 that one can also be lenient if there is a טורח גדול to *kasher* all the utensils, which would be appropriate in the case given in the text.
[24] See *Chok Yaakov* 447:44.
[25] Seemingly, in this case, *Ra'ah* (cited above in footnote 14) would agree that the non-kosher dish is *batel* since it is not possible to remove the absorbed non-kosher *ta'am* from it through *hag'alah*.

Bitul of Keilim

after the event, they found that there were 1,802 bowls! Clearly, 102 of the non-kosher bowls from the hotel got mixed into the 1,700 kosher ones, and there was no way to know which were the kosher ones and which were not. Since there is no way to *kasher* the *cheress* bowls, the 102 non-kosher ones are not considered a דבר שיש לו מתירין and are *batel b'rov* in the kosher ones. [Nonetheless, *Shach* rules that one should be *machmir* and not use all of the bowls; instead, in our example, 102 random bowls should be discarded].[26]

~ **Aino ben yomo**
We noted at the beginning of the chapter that our discussion will be about cases where a person can do an action to permit the use of the forbidden item. But *Shach* says that in a certain sense the case of a non-kosher dish that was mixed into kosher ones, is also an example of the classic cases of דבר שיש לו מתירין (discussed in Chapter 33) where the *heter* comes automatically with the passage of time. This is because *mid'oraisah*, 24 hours after non-kosher *ta'am* is absorbed into a utensil, the utensil can be used for kosher food without *kashering*. That means that without any action, if the person does not use the dishes (kosher and non-kosher) for 24 hours, they will all be permitted from a *d'oraisah* perspective. Of course, *mid'rabannan* utensils cannot be used without *kashering* even after 24 hours, but nonetheless, from a *d'oraisah* perspective the passage of time results in the dishes becoming permitted.

Based on this, *Shach* rules that even in cases where the non-kosher dish is suited for *bitul b'rov* since it is not a יש לו מתירין (as per the principles noted above), there is still a different type of יש לו מתירין which does apply: waiting 24 hours. Therefore, they cannot be used for 24 hours, after which time they may all be used without *kashering*. [*Chochmas Adam*[27] accepts this ruling].

However, *Tzlach*[28] argues that the concept of "waiting" for the *issur* to become *heter* is only appropriate for consumable items. For example, an egg laid on *Yom Tov* can only be eaten once, so " עד שתאכלנו באיסור אכלו בהיתר" says the person should wait to eat it after *Yom Tov* (when it will be

---

[26] See *Badei HaShulchan* 102:32 for details, and above in footnote 22.
[27] *Chochmas Adam* 53:23.
[28] *Tzlach*, *Pesachim* 9a, cited in *Pischei Teshuvah* 102:6. *Pischei Teshuvah* also records a question on *Shach* from *Rebbi Akiva Eiger* (1:27), which is also a similar question on the entire lenient position of *Rashba*. It is also noteworthy that *Rashba*, *Shulchan Aruch*, and the other *Poskim* who preceded *Shach* do not record the requirement to wait 24 hours before relying on *bitul*.

permitted) <u>instead</u> of on *Yom Tov* (when it is still *assur*). But this is not appropriate for reusable items, like a dish, which can be used now and again later. In those cases, the person wants to use it <u>both</u> during the time of *issur* (i.e., within 24 hours) and also during the time of *heter* (after 24 hours), and the fact that he can use it after 24 hours does not preclude him from also using it within 24 hours. As such, the "real" issue is whether he should be permitted to use it within 24 hours, and for that there is no עד שתאכלנו באיסור אכלו בהיתר since there is no way to use it "בהיתר" within 24 hours. Therefore, *Tzlach* says that there is no need to wait 24 hours before using the item.

~ **Pesach**

We have seen that there are cases where one can rely on *bitul* to permit the use of a set of kosher dishes into which a non-kosher dish was mixed. The general rule is that when a *ta'aruvos* occurs on *Pesach*, *bitul* is not effective (*issur mashehu*),[29] and *Shulchan Aruch*[30] favors the opinion that that strictness applies even when there is a *yavesh b'yavesh* mixture. At first glance, one would assume that a *chametz* dish which got mixed into *Pesach* dishes is an example of this, since the basis for permitting the mixture is *bitul b'rov* for *yavesh b'yavesh*. However, this case is somewhat more complicated since the dish is not inherently *chametz*, but just has an absorbed *ta'am* of *chametz*. *Mishnah Berurah*[31] cites a disagreement between the *Acharonim* whether one must be *machmir* in that case as well.

The preceding discussion relates to a *chametz* dish mixed into *Pesach* dishes <u>on</u> *Pesach*, when the strict rule of *issur mashehu* applies. Usually, *chumros* related to the *issur mashehu* do not apply any time before *Pesach*, even during the time on *Erev Pesach* when it is already forbidden to eat *chametz*.[32] However, *Mishnah Berurah*[33] says that our case is an exception, and a *chametz* dish which was mixed into *Pesach* dishes on *Erev Pesach* (after the time when *chametz* is forbidden), should not be used without *kashering*.[34] This is based on a combination of factors. Firstly, as we have seen, there are those who suggest that every mixture of non-kosher (or

---

[29] *Shulchan Aruch* OC 447:1.
[30] *Shulchan Aruch* OC 447:9, citing this as the standard opinion, with the lenient position listed just as ויש אומרים.
[31] *Mishnah Berurah* 447:93.
[32] *Shulchan Aruch* OC 447:2.
[33] *Mishnah Berurah* ibid., based on *Magen Avraham* 447:40 as per *Machatzis HaShekel* ad loc.
[34] In this context, it is worth noting that one may not perform *hag'alah* during *Pesach*, but may do so on *Erev Pesach*; see *Imrei Dovid*, *Kashering*, Chapter 58 (and there in footnote 4).

Bitul of Keilim

chametz) dishes into kosher (or Pesach) dishes is considered a דבר שיש לו מתירין since it is possible to kasher all the dishes. Secondly, we saw in Chapter 33 that some are of the opinion that chametz on Erev Pesach is a דבר שיש לו מתירין, and some of the logic behind Rema's rejection of that position does not apply when the chametz is absorbed into a utensil (as opposed to being a tangible piece of chametz).

Tevillas Keilim

The following is copied from Imrei Dovid, Tevillas Keilim, Chapter 11 see there for additional sources

One last question that has particular relevance to restaurants or other facilities is what to do if some flatware (for example) which did not have *tevillah* got mixed into the rest of the flatware that already had *tevillah*. Shulchan Aruch discusses a similar case of someone who has one non-kosher plate and it accidentally got mixed into a few kosher plates. Shulchan Aruch rules that that if there are more kosher plates than non-kosher ones, they can <u>all</u> be used without *kashering*. Although it would appear to be a *davar sheyesh lo matirim* to *kasher* all the plates, Shulchan Aruch believes the effort and cost required to *kasher* has the effect of saying that it is not a *davar sheyesh lo matirim* (since it is not "automatic"). Others, essentially agree with the principle of Shulchan Aruch – that if it is difficult to make the *issur* into *heter* then it is not a *davar sheyesh lo matirim* – but they disagree as to how to classify the effort to *kasher*; they consider it an insignificant effort and say that the dishes must be *kashered*.

Seemingly, these same principles and disagreement would apply to *tevillas keilim*; if the effort required to perform *tevillah* is minimal [by whatever definition one accepts], then it should be required as a form of *davar sheyesh lo matirim*, and *bitul* would not be effective, but if the effort is great, then the non-*toiveled* flatware should be *batel*. This would mean that if one fork which had no *tevillah* fell into 2 forks that did, the person would probably be required to perform *tevillah* because that does not require any significant effort, and therefore – due to the principle of a *davar sheyesh lo matirim* – it would not be *batel*. But if a restaurant had a non-*toiveled* fork fall into their box of 1,000 forks, they might not have to perform *tevillah* since that might be a significant effort that would be "too much" to retain the status of *davar sheyesh lo matirim*.

While this appears to be the simple understanding, there is an interesting *machlokes* in contemporary *Poskim* whether it is correct to say that *tevillas keilim* is a *davar sheyesh lo matirim*.

Minchas Shlomo[35] says that the principle – that when there is a *davar sheyesh lo matirim* one cannot rely on *safek* or *bitul* – only applies if there is some "outside" way to avoid the *safek*. For example, if there is an egg which might be *assur* to eat on *Yom Tov*, it is considered *yesh lo matirim* because you can wait to eat the egg until after *Yom Tov*, or (in the case noted earlier) you can *kasher* the utensil to remove the questionable *b'liah*. But if the way to avoid the *issur* is through doing the exact issue that you are unsure about, then *davar sheyesh lo matirim* does not require you to be *machmir*. Specifically, he addresses two cases and says the following:

- If a person is unsure whether a specific utensil requires *tevillah*, we do not say that it is a *"yesh lo matirim"* because you can just be *toveil* it – which (in contrast to *hag'alah*) is cheap and easy – for that would be saying that one should be *machmir* on the issue that the entire *safek* is about. That is not what is required by the principle of עד שתאכלנו באיסור, אכלו בהיתר because that principle only demands that the person wait or use some other "outside" means.

- If there is a *safek* whether *hafrashas challah* is required, there are many situations where *Shulchan Aruch* and others are lenient for *safek* as relates to *challas chutz la'aretz*. They say this due to the leniency of that *mitzvah*, even though it is easy and cheap to be *mafrish* a crumb to be *yotzeh* the *mitzvah*; even so, that is not included in the ...עד שתאכלנו באיסור because that is "internal" to the *safek* and not external.

In contrast, *Iggeros Moshe*[36] says that if a person has a glass dish made in a factory where one is unsure whether the owner is Jewish, then if it is very difficult to perform *tevillah* and you cannot determine who the owner is, you can be lenient and not perform *tevillah*. Here he is discussing something which is glass so its *mitzvah tevillah* cannot be more than a *mitzvah d'rabannan*, yet he is not saying that you should just be lenient and say *safek d'rabannan l'kulah* (since it is אי אפשר לברר). Instead, he says that it depends if it is very difficult. That is to say, if it is not too difficult then we will treat this as a *davar sheyesh lo matirim* and be *machmir* even though the question at hand is whether the dish needs *tevillah*, and *tevillah* is the possible "solution". This is disagreeing with *Minchas Shlomo*, and saying that even in cases such as ours, the principle of *davar sheyesh lo matirim* applies.

---

[35] *Minchas Shlomo* 2:68.
[36] *Iggeros Moshe* YD 2:40.

Part G

סימנים ק"ג-ק"ד

- Chapter 37 .... נותן טעם לפגם
- Chapter 38 .... הגדיל האיסור מדתו
- Chapter 39 .... לפגם Not and Not לשבח
- Chapter 40 .... בשר פוגם את השמן
- Chapter 41 .... אינו בן יומו
- Chapter 42 .... סתם כלים אינם בני יומן
- Chapter 43 .... Coatings
- Chapter 44 .... עכבר
- Chapter 45 .... Mitzvah Items
- Chapter 46 .... Bugs are נותן טעם לפגם

Chapter 37

נותן טעם לפגם

שולחן ערוך סימן ק"ג סעיף א
כל דבר שטעמו פגום אינו אוסר תערובתו, ואפילו אין
טעמו פגום מחמת עצמו שבפני עצמו הוא מוטעם
ומשובח אלא שפוגם תערובתו מותר. הגה: מיהו דברים
החשובים כבריה או כיוצא בה אם אין פגומים בעצמן אף על פי
שפוגמין התבשיל אינן בטלים אפילו באלף.

Rashba and Ran

Neveilah (an animal which died without *shechitah*) is not kosher and the *Torah*[1] says that it should be given to a גר תושב so that he can eat it. Why would the *Torah* bother to give instructions of what to do with non-kosher meat? The *Gemara*[2] answers that it teaches that the only time *neveilah* – or other non-kosher food – is forbidden is when it is suitable for a non-Jew to eat, but if it is inedible (נפסל מאכילה) then the food is permitted.

This rule applies to food which is itself inedible. However, there is another case, where non-kosher *ta'am* merely has a negative impact on kosher food, without rendering it inedible. That is known as נותן טעם לפגם and [the *Rishonim*[3] prove that] that is a case about which there is a *machlokes* in the

---

[1] *Devarim* 14:21.
[2] *Gemara*, *Avodah Zara* 67b. More on this derivation in the coming text.
[3] See *Rashba* (*Toras HaBayis* 4:1, page 19a, and *Responsa* 1:262), *Ran* (*Avodah Zara* 32a-b) who proves this from several cases that the *Gemara* refers to as נותן טעם לפגם, even though it is clear that people do eat those foods. For example, food cooked in an *aino ben yomo* pot (*Gemara*, *Avodah Zara* 75b/*Shulchan Aruch* 103:5), or oil and honey which absorbed *ta'am* from non-kosher meat (*Avodah Zara* 67a and 38b/*Shulchan Aruch* 103:4). This ruling is codified in *Shulchan Aruch* 103:2.

It is noteworthy that *Ra'ah* (*Bedek HaBayis* to *Toras HaBayis* ibid.) argues that נותן טעם לפגם only applies for cases where the *ta'am* is inedible, and he bases that on the question cited here in the coming text: how to understand the *Gemara* according to the other *Rishonim*. [He refutes the proofs noted in the previous paragraph by saying that the inedible טעם לפגם is not noticeable due to the pleasant tasting food it was diluted into]. *Chasam Sofer* YD 1:98 infers a similar position (regarding *ta'am* which is *aino ben yomo*) from *Tosfos*, *Avodah Zara* 76a, s.v., *bas*; the same inference can also be draw from *Rosh*, *Avodah Zara* 5:36.

Gemara:[4] *Rebbi Meir* says that the food becomes forbidden since it absorbed non-kosher *ta'am*, while *Rebbi Shimon* says the food remains permitted since the *ta'am* is לפגם. [The halacha follows the opinion of *Rebbi Shimon*].[5] What is surprising is that the *Gemara*[6] says that the source of *Rebbi Shimon's* position is the permissibility of inedible *issur* (noted above). That seems like an inappropriate leap: just because inedible *issur* is permitted, should not mean that *issur* which merely has a negative impact is also permitted?

One of those who addresses this question is *Rashba*,[7] who says that the standards for pure *issur* are different from those of *ta'am* of *issur*. Pure *issur* is defined as any mixture which contains at least 50% *issur*, and that mixture is forbidden unless it becomes inedible. But when there is less than 50% *issur*, the standard principles of *bitul* [operative in most halachos of the *Torah*] would indicate that the mixture is permitted, and the reason to forbid it is based on the concept of טעם כעיקר.[8] טעם כעיקר means that for food-related *issurim*, if you can taste the *issur*, it is not *batel*. In that context, we are only concerned with *ta'am* that is positive, but *ta'am* which has a negative effect on the mixture is not *ta'am* that we must be concerned with (כיון שנותן טעם לפגם כל שהוא בתערובתו מותר, לפי שאינו נותן טעם דאדרבה פוגם).

Ran[9] says that this might be a logical position but asks that the *Gemara* says that it is derived from the fact that inedible *issur* is permitted. How is *Rashba* answering that question? How does the permissibility of inedible *issur* teach that *ta'am* which has a negative impact does not "qualify" as *ta'am*? [See the footnote for suggestions of how *Rashba* might respond].[10]

---

[4] *Mishnah, Avodah Zara* 65b says that it is permitted, and *Gemara* 67b notes that other *Tana'im* disagree.
[5] *Gemara, Avodah Zara* 68b, codified in *Shulchan Aruch* 103:1 and 122:1.
[6] *Gemara, Avodah Zara* 67b-68a.
[7] *Rashba, Toras HaBayis* 4:1, page 19a.
[8] See Chapter 26.
[9] *Ran, Avodah Zara* 32b.
[10] *Rashba* does not appear to address this question, and *Ran* asks it after citing *Rashba*, implying that there is no readily apparent answer. The following are some suggestions.

Rabbi Nosson Dubin (*Hatza'as HaShulchan* 103:1 footnote 2) suggests that food has two potential values: nutrition (when it is absorbed by the stomach, הנאת מעיו), and taste (which is experienced in the mouth and throat, הנאת גרונו). Inedible food provides neither of these, and when the *Torah* says that inedible *neveilah* is permitted, the *Gemara* understood that to be saying that once it stops providing these values it is no longer "food" and therefore not forbidden. The *Gemara* extends that to mean that even if one of those is not present, that element of *issur* also does not apply. Therefore, if a food

Ran therefore argues with *Rashba* and says that the *Gemara* perceived a deeper meaning to the exclusion of inedible *neveilah*. That halacha teaches that eating-related *issurim* are only forbidden if the person enjoys or benefits from the food. But if the food is inedible, the person gains nothing by eating it, and that is why the prohibition falls off.[11] If so, the *Gemara* says that the same applies to the principle of טעם כעיקר. Forbidden *ta'am* only affects kosher food when that *ta'am* contributes something positive to it. But when it is נותן טעם לפגם, the *ta'am's* impact is negative and can therefore be ignored.

---

cannot provide a taste-value in a given case, its *ta'am*/taste is not forbidden and need not be considered. Thus, the permissibility of inedible food teaches us that "no value = no *issur*", and that is enough to say that טעם כעיקר does not apply in cases of נותן טעם לפגם. [In a sense, this means that *Rashba's* understanding (no value for *ta'am* = no *issur*) is not so different from that of *Ran* (no benefit from *ta'am* = no *issur*)].

One could also suggest an explanation based on a more careful reading of the *Gemara* (*Avodah Zara* 67b-68a). When it explains the *machlokes* regarding נותן טעם לפגם it says that the opinions are based on positions regarding inedible *issur* (אינו ראוי לאכילה). All agree that we can derive from the *posuk* of *neveilah* (i.e., that directs us to feed *neveilah* to a גר תושב) that inedible *issur* is permitted, and the *machlokes* revolves around which case that refers to. The one who says נותן טעם לפגם אסור holds that it refers to a case where the item was inedible before it became *issur*. For example, the animal was already inedible before it died and became a *neveilah*. If so, there is no source to permit something which became inedible after it was already *assur*. Those who argue that נותן טעם לפגם מותר take the position that obviously if the item was inedible before it was eligible for *issur*, it will never become *assur*. Therefore, the derivation is that even if it became inedible after it was already *assur* it can become permitted at that point.

Thus, the concept that an inedible item is permitted is not actually derived from *neveilah*; *neveilah* just teaches that what is already *assur* can change and become *mutar*, and the conceptual part – that inedible is different than edible – is something that appears to be logical. If so, when the *Gemara* says that אינו ראוי לאכילה is the source that נותן טעם לפגם is permitted, it means that now that we know that what is *assur* can become *mutar*, we can apply that to נותן טעם לפגם as well. That is all we can and need to derive from the permissibility of inedible *issur*. So how do we know the idea that נותן טעם לפגם is significant, if it is not derived from *neveilah*? The same way we know the concept that אינו ראוי לאכילה is permitted; as noted above, the *Gemara* assumes that concept is logical, and so too, the idea that נותן טעם לפגם is permitted is based on logic. And that is why *Rashba* says – based on what appears to be pure logic – that *ta'am* which is לפגם is not a *ta'am* (and the *Gemara's* association of this with inedible *issur* is essentially just for an important "side point").

Perhaps this is what *Pri Megadim* (MZ 103:1) means when he explains *Rashba* as follows:
והמתבאר מרשב"א...לדעתי כך הוא, דמנבילה גמרינן נותן טעם לפגם לאיסור בעין אף שהיה מושבח מעיקרא כל שאין ראויה לאכילת אדם כלל פקע איסורא, וע"י תערובת בהיתר שרי זה מן הסברא, דטעם כעיקר דלא בטיל מאחרי רבים האמור בסנהדרין יליף ממשרת או ממדין, וזה דוקא טעם מושבח, הא כל שנותן טעם קצת לפגם כזה לא אסרה תורה ומדין ביטול ברוב קאתינן עליה.

Pri Megadim's second explanation appears to say that, once we know that *neveilah* can lose its *issur* when it is not in its pristine state, we assume that טעם כעיקר has a similar point when it no longer applies, which is assumed to be when it is נותן טעם לפגם. His words are:
ואפשר נמי הא דאמרינן...נותן טעם לפגם יליף מנבילה, כולה מלתא כגמר מנבילה, כיון שמצינו חילוק בנבילה יש לנו לומר דטעם כעיקר לא אסרה תורה אלא במושבח גמור וכדאמרן

[11] *Ran* does not explain how the *Gemara* knows that this is the explanation for why inedible *issur* is permitted, and just says that this is what the *Gemara* must have understood. [The alternate and simpler explanation for why inedible *issur* is permitted is, as the *Gemara*, *Avodah Zara* 68a, says, that it is עפרא בעלמא, like "dirt", and no longer food].

Support for *Ran's* approach can be seen from the way the *Mishnah*[12] describes the opinion that נותן טעם לפגם is permitted, using the words "בהנאתו" (*that you derive pleasure from it*):

זה הכלל כל <u>שבהנאתו</u> בנותן טעם אסור
כל שאין <u>בהנאתו</u> בנותן טעם מותר

Ran concludes by noting that there is a potential practical difference between his understanding and that of *Rashba*. *Rashba* is clear that in every case where there is more *heter* than *issur*, נותן טעם לפגם permits the mixture. Non-kosher *ta'am* which has a negative impact is "not considered *ta'am*" and therefore since it comprises less than half of the mixture, the mixture is permitted. However, according to *Ran*, the only time non-kosher *ta'am* is ignored is when it provides no benefit. But in a case where the non-kosher item provides some other benefit which outweighs the negative taste it confers, then the mixture would indeed be forbidden.

In the coming chapter, we will describe the case which *Ran* constructs as an example of this difference of opinion, see how *Shulchan Aruch* rules, and also consider contemporary practical applications.[13] As part of that discussion, we will also see applications of several other principles regarding נותן טעם לפגם. The remainder of this chapter will note and reference points that are relevant to all cases of נותן טעם לפגם.

Details and examples

As already mentioned, a significant detail of נותן טעם לפגם is that it need not render the kosher food inedible, and just has to have a negative effect on it. This includes cases where the *issur* has a perfectly pleasant flavor, but that taste is not desirable when mixed into the kosher food.[14]

Rema[15] notes that the concept of *ta'am* is only relevant for standard *issurim* which are governed by the rules of *bitul b'shishim*. In those cases, if the *issur* is נותן טעם לפגם, it is *batel* even without *shishim*. However, for those situations – such as בריה, חתיכה הראויה להתכבד, or דבר שבמנין – where the *issur* cannot be *batel* even if there were no *ta'am*, *ta'am* clearly plays no role, and the mixture is forbidden even if the *issur* is נותן טעם לפגם.

---

[12] *Mishnah, Avodah Zara* 65b.
[13] See also footnote 16 for another difference between the opinions of *Rashba* and *Ran*.
[14] *Shulchan Aruch* 103:1.
[15] *Rema* 103:1 as per *Shach* 103:1.

Similarly, *Rema*[16] rules that נותן טעם לפגם is not a factor when *chametz* is mixed into food on *Pesach*, since *chametz* cannot be *batel* on *Pesach* (*assur b'mashehu*). In Chapter 46 we will discuss another possible application of this halacha when we consider how נותן טעם לפגם applies to insects (which are a common example of בריה).

By far, the most common example of נותן טעם לפגם is when a utensil is *aino ben yomo*, and that topic will be discussed in Chapter 41. Another everyday example of נותן טעם לפגם is soap. In Chapter 13 we spoke about how that relates to washing kosher and non-kosher (or meat and dairy) dishes in the same sink or dishwasher.[17]

Other relevant details and examples of the leniency of נותן טעם לפגם are:

- If someone is unsure whether the *issur* is נותן טעם לפגם, they should be *machmir* and assume that it is not.[18]

- Rav Schachter said that if a liquid has a pleasant taste but has a noxious odor, that also qualifies as a *"pegam"*. Additionally, Rav Belsky said if the liquid is poisonous or would make someone sick, it qualifies as a *"pegam"*, even if its taste is pleasant.[19]

---

[16] *Rema* OC 447:10. See *Beis Yosef* to that halacha, who cites this opinion from *Rashba* (*Responsa* 1:499), and *Pri Megadim* (MZ 103:1, end) points out that this is consistent with the opinion of *Rashba* noted here – that in all cases נותן טעם לפגם requires some level of *bitul* (i.e., *bitul b'rov*); since נותן טעם לפגם requires *bitul*, it is not applicable for *chametz* where *bitul* is not possible. In contrast, *Beis Yosef* cites a lenient opinion from *Rosh* (*Avodah Zara* 5:6) who says that נותן טעם לפגם means that there is no *issur* at all, in which case it is permitted even on *Pesach* since its permissibility does not require *bitul* at all. *Pri Megadim* says that this is reminiscent of *Ran* noted here, that *ta'am* which is לפגם it is not forbidden at all. Thus, *Rema's* strict position regarding נותן טעם לפגם for *Pesach* is consistent with his strict ruling cited here regarding בריה etc.

This raises a question that here in *Yoreh Deah*, *Shulchan Aruch* (103:2) cites both *Rashba* and *Ran* as possible positions, but in *Orach Chaim* (447:10) he [disagrees with *Rema* and] says that נותן טעם לפגם is permitted on *Pesach* which, as we have seen, is the opinion of *Rosh/Ran*. Why is he lenient for *Pesach* if here he considers *Rashba* as a legitimate position? *Rebbi Akiva Eiger* 1:166 suggests that since the *issur mashehu* for *chametz* is a *chumrah* (i.e., it is a position that not all *Rishonim* accept, see *Beis Yosef* at the beginning of OC 447, and *Darchei Moshe* OC 447:1), *Shulchan Aruch* chose to rely on *Rosh/Ran* for that halacha. [*Pri Megadim* (a) references *Minchas Kohen* (*Ta'aruvos* 1:9, end) who suggests a different reason why *chametz* is different, and (b) asks that *Levush* YD 103:2 accepts *Ran*, but *Levush* OC 447:10 says that one should follow *Rashba*. As relates to "b", *Pri Megadim* says ויש ליישב, and it may be that what he has in mind is that *Levush* is actually unsure about which position to follow and accordingly is choosing to be *machmir* in both cases].

[17] There we also referenced *Imrei Dovid*, *Alcoholic Beverages*, Chapter 11 which explained what "soap" is and offered other reasons why its use often does not pose a *kashrus* concern.

[18] See *Badei HaShulchan* (Biurim) 103:1 s.v. *v'aino*.

[19] See *Imrei Dovid*, *Kashering*, Chapter 64.

- *Shulchan Aruch*[20] discusses what to do if the *issur* is נותן טעם לפגם at certain parts of the process, but not at others. This is a rather unusual case, and we will therefore leave details for the coming chapter where we will consider an application where that set of halachos is relevant.

- We saw in Chapter 2 that if two components join to create a specific taste, and one of those would [on its own] be נותן טעם לפגם, those components more easily qualify as זה וזה גורם than if both contributed positive tastes.

- In Chapter 3, we considered the case of gum base made with non-kosher fatty acids and approached it from the position that חתיכה נעשית נבילה does not apply to an inedible item like gum base. From the perspective of our chapter, we can now add that the interaction between the fatty acids and gum base is likely נותן טעם לפגם, which is another reason to be lenient *b'dieved*.

- *Pegimah* of a steam system was discussed in Chapter 4.

   There, we also discussed *Chavos Da'as* 103:1 who differentiates between שלא כדרך אכילה and נפסל מאכילה.

- The *Gemara* says that the *ta'am* of meat into oil is לפגם; that halacha is codified in *Shulchan Aruch* 103:4, and in Chapter 40 we will consider if and when this applies in practice.

- One of the issues regarding coatings on new pots and pans is whether they are נותן טעם לפגם; see Chapter 43.

---

[20] *Shulchan Aruch* 103:2.

Chapter 38

הגדיל האיסור מדתו

שולחן ערוך סימן ק"ג סעיף ב

פגם זה אין צריך שיפגום לגמרי עד שיהא קץ לאכלו אלא אפילו פוגם קצת אינו אוסר תערובתו. ויש מי שאומר דהיינו דוקא כשנתערב איסור מועט עם היתר מרובה אבל איסור מרובה לתוך היתר מועט ואפילו מחצה על מחצה אין אומרים נותן טעם לפגם מותר עד שיפגום לגמרי שאינו ראוי למאכל אדם. ואם אין שם ממשות של איסור אלא טעמו בלבד אפילו איסור מרובה והיתר מועט מותר אם פוגם קצת.

ויש מי שחוכך (פי' מקוה להחמיר, ואוסר) לומר שאם הגדיל האיסור מדתו של היתר עד שהוא משביח יותר כשאוכלו בגודל מדתו ממה שהוא פוגם בהפסד טעמו אסור עד שיפסל מלאכול אדם.

במה דברים אמורים, שפוגם מתחילתו ועד סופו, אבל אם השביח ולבסוף פוגם או פוגם ולבסוף השביח, אסור. הגה: וי"א אף על גב דהאיסור נ"ט לפגם והמאכל מותר, מ"מ הקדרה אסורה ואם בשלו בה אח"כ תוך מעת לעת תבשיל שהאיסור הראשון נותן בו טעם לשבח, נאסר התבשיל השני אם לא היה בו ס' נגד האיסור הראשון. אבל אם נערו התבשיל הראשון בכף ותחבו אח"כ הכף לתבשיל שני שהוא ג"כ פוגם, לא נאסרה הקדרה. וכן בדבר שאין לו טעם כלל כגון היורה שמטיכין בו הדבש, אף על פי שיש שם רגלי הדבורים לא נאסרה היורה וכל כיוצא בזה.

In the previous chapter we saw a *machlokes* between *Rashba* and *Ran* regarding נותן טעם לפגם. *Ran* says that נותן טעם לפגם is permitted because the person does not benefit from the *issur*. However, in a case where the non-kosher item provides some other benefit which outweighs the negative taste it is contributing, then the mixture <u>will</u> be forbidden. In contrast, *Rashba* says that נותן טעם לפגם does not have the status of [forbidden] *ta'am* at all, and therefore it is always *batel* (assuming there is more *heter* than *issur*), regardless of the amount of benefit there is.

These two opinions are cited in *Shulchan Aruch*.¹ First he cites *Rashba* (ויש מי שאומר...) that it all depends on whether there is more *heter* than *issur*. Then he cites *Ran* (ויש מי שחוכך...) who rules that if there is so much *issur* that the person gains more from the bulk that the *issur* adds (הגדיל האיסור מדתו) than he loses from the negative taste it contributes, then one must be *machmir*. [The way this is recorded implies that one should follow the strict opinion].²

In this chapter we will see two examples where this issue is relevant.

Nutramigen

~ **Introduction**
Some infants are unable to digest any of the standard baby formulas and require a specialized formula where the protein is pre-digested. Two brands of that type of formula are Nutramigen and Alimentum. Both are produced by companies who have all their infant formulas certified as kosher (in the United States). However, these special formulas are not certified, because they contain porcine enzyme that digests the protein. Pigs are obviously not kosher, so there is no way to certify these products, but there are two important questions about these formulas: may infants use them, and must the company *kasher* their equipment after producing them? Related to that is the question of whether consumers who use the formula must keep them separate from their kosher foods. As we will see, these questions are connected to the *machlokes* between *Rashba* and *Ran*.

---

¹ *Shulchan Aruch* 103:2, as per *Taz* 103:4.
² *Shach* (הנהגת הוראות באיסור והיתר, printed after *Yoreh Deah* 242, point #5) says that when *Shulchan Aruch* cites two opinions, with the first one with no qualifiers (i.e., סתם) as if that is the standard halacha, and the second one as "יש אומרים", the halacha follows the first opinion. What about for cases like ours where he cites two opinions, and both are listed as יש אומרים (or something similar)? In some places *Pri Megadim* (כללים בהוראת איסור והיתר #2, and #4 (printed as introduction to *Orach Chaim*), and כללים #21 (printed after the פתיחה כוללת); see also OC MZ 449:1) says that this indicates that the halacha is undecided and one should be *machmir* for *d'oraisah* issues but can be lenient if it is only relevant for an *issur d'rabannan*. In other places (הנהגות הנשאל עם השואל 3:10, and also in OC MZ 193:5, 219:6, & 251:2), he says that this formulation indicates that the halacha follows the latter opinion cited. Perhaps the resolution to this apparent contradiction can be seen based on other places (i.e., עד שיבוא הכתוב השלישי ויכריע ביניהם), where he says (OC MZ 33:6) that in most cases this wording indicates that one should follow the second opinion (כי כן דרכו, יש אומרים ויש אומרים, דיעה בתרייתא רובא דרובא עיקר). In our case, the issue is one of a potential *issur d'oraisah* (i.e., טעם כעיקר דאורייתא, if it is not לפגם נותן טעם), and the second opinion (*Ran*) is the stricter one, so according to all versions of *Pri Megadim*, he is indicating that one should be *machmir*.

412 Chapter 38

~ **Whose taste**

As one might expect, pre-digested protein has an awful taste, which is to say that the porcine enzyme is a ripe candidate to qualify as נותן טעם לפגם. According to *Rashba*, since the non-kosher enzyme gives the formula a negative taste, it is *batel* like any other נותן טעם לפגם. But this case is one where *Ran* should argue because the enzyme's positive impact (i.e., digesting the protein) clearly outweighs the loss (i.e., the negative taste). Rav Schachter disagreed with this suggestion, based on a longstanding principle that decisions about halachic matters are made based on "average" people. For most people, there is no benefit to having predigested protein (since they can digest protein themselves), and the enzyme's effect is purely negative. Therefore, this is not a case where *Ran* would be *machmir*, even though the enzyme provides tremendous benefit for the babies who will consume this formula.

Based on this, Rav Schachter answered a second question on the underlying assumption that there is פגם here. Scientists believe that infants have an underdeveloped sense of taste and do not even notice the formula's negative taste! If so, perhaps this is not נותן טעם לפגם at all? The above point resolves this issue as well. Most people consider this taste to be putrid, and therefore it qualifies as נותן טעם לפגם, despite the fact that the babies who drink it are not bothered by the taste.

Rav Belsky agreed with the basic principle which Rav Schachter is suggesting — that halachic decisions are made based on the average person's perception — but argued that in this case, where the formula is being produced for a very specific audience, we must make judgements based on the intended consumers. For these babies, the benefit clearly outweighs the loss, and therefore *Ran* would say that the formula is forbidden. However, Rav Belsky said that since *Rashba* is lenient,[3] one can rely on that opinion in order to provide nutrition for these infants who are otherwise left with no good choices.

---

[3] One could question this position based on Rav Belsky's own line of reasoning. If we decide the enzyme's benefit based on the intended consumers' perception, we should also judge the enzyme's negative impact based on those same consumers. As noted earlier in the text, infants do not perceive the formula's bad taste, and if so, even *Rashba* should be *machmir* since there is no נותן טעם לפגם at all? In other words, according to Rav Belsky's logic, the second question noted in the previous text appears to be relevant once again. This requires further consideration.

~ **Other issues**

However, there are several other issues to resolve. One is that *Shulchan Aruch*[4] rules that in order to qualify as נותן טעם לפגם, the non-kosher item must cause פגם continuously. But if the non-kosher food contributes a positive taste when it is added, and only later does the taste becomes negative (השביח ולבסוף פוגם) (or vice versa), the mixture of kosher and non-kosher is forbidden. In fact, that is exactly what happens when the enzyme is added to protein. It takes many days before the enzymes is able to digest the protein, and it is only at that point that it is נותן טעם לפגם. If so, it appears to be "too late" for the mixture to qualify as נותן טעם לפגם.

A first answer to this question can be found in *Pri Megadim*,[5] who says that השביח ולבסוף פוגם is only a concern if both phases occur while the mixture is in the possession of a Jew. But if it happens to a non-Jew's food, and by the time the Jew receives it the non-kosher is already נותן טעם לפגם, one can be lenient. That is what occurs with the formula: the non-Jewish company produces it, and by the time the Jewish consumer purchases it, it is already at the נותן טעם לפגם phase; therefore, the enzyme is *batel*.

A second answer to this question is that this infant formula is produced in two stages: first the enzyme digests the protein, and then the digested protein is added to a standard mixture of other formula ingredients. Even if the digested formula is forbidden based on the *chumrah* of השביח ולבסוף פוגם, when that protein is added to the other ingredients, it is נותן טעם לפגם into them from the very first minute. Therefore, even if the protein is forbidden, the overall formula is permitted.

Rav Schachter said that this second answer will also resolve another question. The pig enzyme's effect on the protein seems dramatic enough to qualify as a *davar hama'amid*, and *Pri Megadim*[6] says that a *davar hama'amid* cannot be *batel* even when it is נותן טעם לפגם. [The logic is that נותן טעם לפגם is only relevant for *bitul* cases governed by the presence of *ta'am*, but since *davar hama'amid* prevents *bitul* even if there is no *ta'am*, נותן טעם לפגם is not relevant].[7] If so, the digested protein should be

---

[4] *Shulchan Aruch* 103:2.
[5] *Pri Megadim* SD 103:14 s.v., *v'hinei*, based on *Responsa Rema* 54. Rav Belsky and Rav Schachter accepted this ruling; however, see *Badei HaShulchan* (*Biurim*) 103:2 ד"ה ולבסוף, who suggests that others disagree with *Pri Megadim*.
[6] *Pri Megadim* ibid.
[7] See *Rema* 103:1 and below in Chapter 46.

forbidden since it has a non-kosher *ma'amid*? The answer is, as above, that this is a reason why the protein per se is forbidden, but the protein is not a *ma'amid* of the other ingredients, and therefore when it is added to them it can be *batel* since it is נותן טעם לפגם.[8]

~ **Kashering**
Equipment used for the enzyme and protein before (or both before and after) it becomes digested, requires *kashering*, since it absorbed pleasant *ta'am* from the non-kosher enzyme.[9] What about equipment that only comes into contact with the protein after it is digested (or with the digested protein after it is mixed into the other ingredients)? [This is relevant both to the manufacturing plant and to a home user whose child is drinking this formula]. According to *Rashba*, it surely does not require *kashering* since the protein is "kosher", and the same is true according to *Ran*, as per Rav Schachter's understanding.

One could speculate whether Rav Belsky would require *kashering* according to his understanding of how *Ran* would approach this case. Should we say that since *Ran* considers the formula to be non-kosher, the equipment needs to be *kashered* before it is used for kosher? Or should we say that the *ta'am* of this formula is נותן טעם לפגם into the equipment since it will surely ruin the taste of forthcoming food cooked there, and will provide no positive benefit (since the *ta'am* will not help predigest any future food)? If so, maybe no *kashering* is required?[10] This requires further consideration.

---

[8] In addition to the logic noted in the text to permit the formula for infants who need it, Rav Schachter referenced the overarching principle that one may always provide a child with items which are רביתיה (*the typical items required for the sustenance of a child*) (*Gemara, Yoma* 78b) as a reason to allow the formula's use.

[9] This is true regardless of the status of השביח ולבסוף פוגם (discussed earlier in the text) because the equipment absorbed *ta'am* during the time that the non-kosher was not לפגם, and one must *kasher* based on that absorption. [We noted previously that a *ma'amid* cannot be *batel* even if it is נותן טעם לפגם. That relates to whether one can eat the food/formula, but equipment must only be *kashered* if there was absorption of non-kosher *ta'am*, and from that perspective a *davar hama'amid* is irrelevant; see Chapter 1].

[10] When absorbed *ta'am* becomes *aino ben yomo*, it is נותן טעם לפגם, yet the גזירה אינו בן יומו אטו בן יומו dictates that one is not allowed to use an *aino ben yomo* pot without *kashering*. However, as we will see in Chapter 41, that גזירה only applies when at the time the *ta'am* was originally absorbed it was not נותן טעם לפגם, such as in a standard pot. But whenever the first absorption of *ta'am* is נותן טעם לפגם, the item is permitted to use or eat as-is. *Ran* (*Pesachim* 8b and *Chullin* 44a) describes this principle saying that if "תחלת בליעתו" was positive, then one must *kasher*, but if it was לפגם, then nothing is required. Therefore, the text suggests that in our case, where we know that the absorbed *ta'am* is (and will be) surely לפגם, *kashering* will not be required.

Carmine manufacturer

~ **B'lios**

We saw in Chapter 35 that carmine – a color made from cochineal insects – is *assur mid'oraisah*, and when it is mixed into other foods it cannot be *batel* since it provides color/חזותא.[11] For that reason, it would be forbidden to drink a beverage colored with carmine. But the equipment used to pasteurize that beverage does not require *kashering* because we only have to *kasher* when equipment has absorbed <u>*ta'am*</u> of *issur*. However, since the carmine is in tiny percentages which are not *nosein ta'am*, the pasteurizer can be used for kosher beverages without *kashering*.

The preceding leniency is for equipment used for foods that <u>contain</u> carmine. What about equipment used to blend carmine with other ingredients, to create the color profiles that other companies want? These companies are using carmine at relatively high percentages – as high as 30%[12] – and the carmine is often heated (since it does not dilute well in water at ambient temperature). Thus, the equipment has absorbed *ta'am* of carmine. At first glance, one would assume that it must be *kashered* before being used for processing kosher colors.

A simple reason to disagree with this is that bugs are assumed to be נותן טעם לפגם into all foods,[13] in which case there is no concern with their being נותן טעם. [This is only relevant to the status of the <u>equipment</u>, not to the food the carmine is used in; see the footnote].[14] However, what about according to *Ran*? The carmine is נותן טעם לפגם into the other ingredients, but clearly the color benefit it provides is more desirable than the negative taste.[15] If so, according to *Ran* that נותן טעם לפגם only applies

---

[11] See footnote 14.

[12] In calculating whether the carmine might happen to be *batel b'shishim* in a given case, it is worth bearing in mind that carmine has a low specific gravity, and a pound of carmine has more volume than a pound of water. Thus, to calculate if there is *bitul*, one must convert the formula from weight (which is the way companies typically measure ingredients) to volume (which is how *bitul* is calculated); see Chapter 20.

[13] See *Shulchan Aruch* 104:3 and Chapter 46.

[14] See *Rema* 103:1 and Chapter 46 that when considering items which are not *batel* even if they are not able to give *ta'am* (e.g., בריה, חזותא), the fact that the *issur* is נותן טעם לפגם is not relevant. Therefore, one cannot eat the food that contains carmine, since the carmine affects the food's color. However, as noted, *kashering* is dependent on *ta'am*, and therefore נותן טעם לפגם <u>is</u> relevant.

[15] The simplest way to know that the color benefit outweighs the negative taste is that people choose to use carmine color. Clearly, what they gain from the color is worth more than what they lose from its taste. From a "halachic" angle we can understand this because the carmine will eventually be used in tiny percentages where it cannot be *nosein ta'am* but can provide color; thus, the color benefit will be present in the final food, but the negative taste will not.

when/because the person has no benefit from the *issur*, but not when he gains from the *issur* (i.e., הגדיל מדתו), in this case should we say that [נותן טעם לפגם does not apply and] the carmine is not *batel*?

It appears that this rationale is not correct, because the question at hand is not whether one can use the carmine mixed into other ingredients, but rather if the equipment used to produce/blend it must be *kashered*. From that perspective, the carmine's "benefit" is completely meaningless, since the color is not "absorbed" into the tank-walls. Thus, as relates to *b'lios* and *kashering*, the carmine is only נותן טעם לפגם with no positive benefit. Accordingly, even according to *Ran*, there is no need to *kasher* the equipment that the carmine was produced on (assuming, as per *Rashba*, that the carmine is *batel b'rov* in the mixture).

~ **Inedible**

There is also aspect to consider: *Shulchan Aruch*[16] says that since insects are so disgusting, if an insect gets mixed into food, that food is permitted assuming the insect is *batel b'rov* (and that you remove as many pieces of insects as possible). What about according to *Ran*? *Beis Yosef*[17] says that *Ran* will agree with this halacha because:

> דבדברים הפגומים מעצמם כעכבר וכיוצא בו מודה להרשב"א ז"ל
> וטעם גדול יש לחלק ביניהם וק"ל

Ran agrees with Rashba for items which are inherently disgusting like rodents because there is a significant difference between this case and the one where Ran argues with Rashba, and it is easy to understand what that difference is

The *Acharonim* appear to have a subtle disagreement about the difference that *Beis Yosef* is referring to. One explanation comes from *Chasam Sofer*[18] and to understand it we must return to a point made at the beginning of Chapter 37. There we saw that *Rashba* and *Ran* are explaining how the *Gemara* derives the leniency of נותן טעם לפגם for edible items (which happen to give a negative taste into some other food) from the *Torah's* permissibility of inedible foods. There, *Ran* establishes a principle that *ta'am* is only forbidden when it provides benefit. But in cases where the forbidden item

---

The text assumes – as per the simple reading of *Ran* – that הגדיל מדתו is just one example of how a person might gain more from the *issur* than he loses from its negative taste, and that the same *chumrah* applies if the benefit is from the *issur's* color or some other factor. See *Badei HaShulchan* (*Biurim*) 103:2 ד"ה הגדיל.

[16] *Shulchan Aruch* 104:3.
[17] *Beis Yosef* to 104:3, cited in *Shach* 104:9.
[18] *Chasam Sofer* to *Shach* ibid.

הגדיל האיסור מדתו　　　　　　　　　　　　　　　　　　　**417**

is inherently inedible, the food's *ta'am* is permitted for a simpler reason,[19] and "benefit" is not relevant. Thus, when dealing with insects which are inherently disgusting, נותן טעם לפגם is permitted regardless of whether there is benefit (i.e., even in cases where it is הגדיל מדתו).[20] According to this explanation, we can say that even if the benefit of the carmine (i.e., its color) outweighs the negative effect of its taste, the carmine is still *batel* based on its being נותן טעם לפגם. Since insects are inherently inedible, *Ran's chumrah* in the case of הגדיל מדתו does not apply, and that would be a second reason why the equipment does not have to be *kashered*.

However, *Pri Chadash* and *Gr"a*[21] appear to have understood *Beis Yosef* differently. They say he means that when a forbidden food is inherently edible but happens to be נותן טעם לפגם into some other food, it is reasonable that one might benefit more from the *issur* (i.e., הגדיל מדתו) than he loses from the negative taste. The *issur* is tasty and edible, so it likely provides benefit to anything it is added to, and one might expect that sometimes that benefit will outweigh the negative interaction it has with the other ingredients. But when the *issur* is inherently putrid, it is not to be expected that you will get any benefit from it, so the entire discussion does not begin.

According to this latter explanation, *Ran* sees no halachic difference between the two types of נותן טעם לפגם, but rather it is a practical point that when the *issur* is inherently disgusting you are unlikely to have concerns of הגדיל מדתו. That is good for a standard case (as recorded in *Shulchan Aruch*), but in our example, it is not true. The carmine is inedible, but it nonetheless provides a huge benefit – color – that is quite valuable to users. If so, *Ran* would say that one must be *machmir* about הגדיל מדתו for the case of carmine, and the only reason to be lenient about *kashering* is for the reason noted earlier.

೧೦ ೦೩

We will briefly revisit some of these issues in Chapter 46, when we consider the נותן טעם לפגם status of certain insects.

---

[19] *Chasam Sofer* says that *ta'am* is permitted because טעם כעיקר דאורייתא is derived from the *Torah's* directive to *kasher* the utensils which the Jews obtained as booty in their war with *Midyan* (see *Gemara, Pesachim* 44b), and that directive is (*mid'oraisah*) not applicable for utensils which are *aino ben yomo* (i.e., נותן טעם לפגם).
[20] *Pri Megadim* MZ 103:1 (towards the end) references *Shach* ibid. and from his question (that insects are forbidden even if they are inedible, so they appear to be excluded from the "inedible" leniency) it appears that he understood *Shach* in the same manner as *Chasam Sofer*. [*Pri Megadim* says there is an answer to his question (ויש ליישב) and appears to accept *Beis Yosef/Shach's* ruling].
[21] *Pri Chadash* 104:10 and *Gr"a* 104:11 (end).

Chapter 39

Not לפגם and Not לשבח

שולחן ערוך סימן ק"ג סעיף ב

פגם זה אין צריך שיפגום לגמרי עד שיהא קץ לאכלו אלא אפילו פוגם קצת אינו אוסר תערובתו. ויש מי שאומר דהיינו דוקא כשנתערב איסור מועט עם היתר מרובה אבל איסור מרובה לתוך היתר מועט ואפילו מחצה על מחצה אין אומרים נותן טעם לפגם מותר עד שיפגום לגמרי שאינו ראוי למאכל אדם. ואם אין שם ממשות של איסור אלא טעמו בלבד אפילו איסור מרובה והיתר מועט מותר אם פוגם קצת.

ויש מי שחוכך (פי' מקוה להחמיר, ואוסר) לומר שאם הגדיל האיסור מדתו של היתר עד שהוא משביח יותר כשאוכלו בגודל מדתו ממה שהוא פוגם בהפסד טעמו אסור עד שיפסל מלאכול אדם.

במה דברים אמורים, שפוגם מתחלתו ועד סופו, אבל אם השביח ולבסוף פוגם או פוגם ולבסוף השביח, אסור. הגה: וי"א אף על גב דהאיסור נ"ט לפגם והמאכל מותר, מ"מ הקדרה אסורה ואם בשלו בה אח"כ תוך מעת לעת תבשיל שהאיסור הראשון נותן בו טעם לשבח, נאסר התבשיל השני אם לא היה בו ס' נגד האיסור הראשון. אבל אם נערו התבשיל הראשון בכף ותחבו אח"כ הכף לתבשיל שני שהוא ג"כ פוגם, לא נאסרה הקדרה. וכן דבר שאין לו טעם כלל כגון היורה שמטיכין בו הדבש, אף על פי שיש שם רגלי הדבורים לא נאסרה היורה וכל כיוצא בזה.

Bee legs

The first *siman* in *hilchos ta'aruvos* (*Yoreh Deah* 98) discusses the circumstances where the *ta'am* of a non-kosher food can be *batel* when it is mixed into kosher food. It is based on the assumption that טעם כעיקר – if one can taste the non-kosher food, then the mixture is forbidden – and there it details if/when one can make that determination by actually tasting the mixture or through a *bitul b'shishim* calculation that no taste is detectable. In contrast, the first halacha in this *siman* (*Yoreh Deah* 103) introduced the idea that if a forbidden food has a negative effect on the mixture (נותן טעם לפגם), then טעם כעיקר effectively does not apply and the mixture is permitted, even if the *issur* can be tasted. In this chapter, we will discuss a somewhat unusual case where the forbidden food has "no ta'am" and try to determine whether it is governed by the standard principles of טעם כעיקר and *bitul b'shishim*, or the leniency of a נותן טעם לפגם. [After clarifying the halacha, we will see practical applications].

Rema[1] seems to address this issue quite clearly when he says that bee legs are a דבר שאין בו טעם כלל and therefore, they do not affect the kosher status of a pot used to heat them (together with honey). Similarly, *Tosfos*[2] says that his understanding of the principle of סתם כלים אינם בני יומן (see Chapter 42) is partially based on the possibility that the forbidden item cooked in the pot was a דבר שאין נותן טעם. The clear implication is that if so, that food's "taste" cannot affect any kosher food subsequently put into that utensil. If so, *Pri Chadash*[3] wonders, why do *Beis Yosef*, *Rema*, and *Shach*[4] cite and accept the ruling of *Ohr Zaruah*[5] that *issur* which is לא לשבח ולא לפגם can affect the kosher status of other foods? *Pri Chadash* answers that this question is based on a mistaken assumption that foods which are אין בו טעם כלל are identical to those which are לא לשבח ולא לפגם. The former (אין בו טעם כלל) has absolutely no taste, and therefore there is no way it can affect the kosher status of any other food. In contrast, the latter (לא לשבח ולא לפגם) refers to foods which do have some taste and that taste would be detectable in a mixture. But the effect it has on the other food is "neutral" – neither לפגם nor not לשבח. Since its taste is detectable in the other food, the standard halachos of טעם כעיקר apply, and the leniency of נותן טעם לפגם does not.[6]

Pri Chadash is suggesting that the only time one need be *machmir* is when the *issur* has some taste (but that taste is not לשבח or לפגם in this food), and the following are two supports for that idea. Firstly, elsewhere *Rema*[7] discusses non-kosher wine that was mixed into another food and presents three scenarios – the wine is לשבח, "not לפגם", and לפגם – and rules that in

---

[1] *Rema* 103:2 (end).
[2] *Tosfos*, *Avodah Zara*, 38b ד"ה אי.
[3] *Pri Chadash* 103:2.
[4] *Beis Yosef* 103 (page 279), *Toras Chattas* (*Rema*) 85:22, and *Shach* 103:2.
[5] See below in footnote 8.
[6] In Chapter 37, we discussed the way *Rashba* and *Ran* understand the permissibility of an *issur* which is נותן טעם לפגם. *Rashba* says that *ta'am* which is לפגם is not considered (forbidden) *ta'am*. He can agree with the point made in the text that a *ta'am* which is neutral – not לפגם and not לשבח – remains forbidden, since it does not have the negative feature of being לפגם. However, it is not as clear if *Ran* can accept the text. *Ran* seems to stress that *ta'am* is only forbidden if a person benefits from it, which seemingly does not apply to a neutral *ta'am*. At the same time, *Ran* does note that נותן טעם לפגם bothers the person (מצטער עליו) and if that is the true criterion, then a neutral *ta'am* remains forbidden. This requires further consideration.
[7] *Rema* YD 134:13.

the first two cases the mixture is forbidden but in the third it is permitted. Clearly, wine has "taste" and is not אין בו טעם כלל, which is why *Rema* is *machmir* when the wine's effect on the other food is not לפגם (and not לשבח). Secondly, *Shach* supports the ruling of *Ohr Zaruah* from *Yerushalmi*[8] which uses the exact same phrase – הדא אמרה לא לשבח ולא לפגם אסור. The case that *Yerushalmi* bases the statement on (i.e., הדא אמרה) is one where olives of *terumah* were *kovush* with olives of *chullin*. As with the wine case of *Rema*, olives have a taste, so the ruling is specific to such a case where the *issur* has a taste but its effect on the taste of the next food is neither לפגם nor לשבח.[9]

A variation of *Pri Chadash's* answer is given by *Iggeros Moshe*[10] who says that the strictness is limited to cases of *min b'mino* where – it is almost axiomatic that – *ta'am* of the *issur* cannot affect the taste of the *heter*, since they taste exactly the same! Thus, this "strict" ruling is really just a detail within the general Rabbinic requirement that *min b'mino* requires

---

[8] *Yerushalmi, Terumos* 10:4.
  Sefer Ohr Zaruah was not widely distributed until it was printed in the 1800s and 1900s, and most rulings of *Ohr Zaruah* were cited either from the concise version of the *sefer's* conclusions, written by *Ohr Zaruah's* son, which is known as *Maharach Ohr Zaruah* (or *Piskei Ohr Zaruah*), or from rulings reported by *Ohr Zaruah's* students. The ruling noted in the text is an example of this, as the *Poskim* cite it from *Hago'os Sha'arei Durah* (85:15) and *Hago'os Ashri* (to *Rosh, Avodah Zara* 5:9) based on *Maharach Ohr Zaruah* (*Avodah Zara* 189). In these locations it briefly says that if it is לפגם ולא לשבח לא then it affects the other food. But now that we are privileged to have easy access to the full *Sefer Ohr Zaruah*, we can see that he himself (*Avodah Zara* 258-259) cites *Yerushalmi* as a proof to this position.
[9] What about *Shach's* other proof, from the halacha that although the *gid hanasheh* has no *ta'am* (as per *Gemara, Chullin,* 99b, and *Shulchan Aruch* YD 65:9), if a *gid hanasheh* dissolves into other food, that food must contain 60 times the volume of the *gid hanasheh* (*Shulchan Aruch* 100:2, end)? *Shach's* citation of this proof implies that even items with no *ta'am* also require *bitul b'shishim*. This seems contrary to the explanation of *Pri Chadash* that when there is no *ta'am* at all, all agree that *bitul b'shishim* is not necessary. Some suggest that although the *Gemara* says that *gid hanasheh* has "no *ta'am*", in truth that means that it has a very weak *ta'am*; see *Pri Megadim* MZ 100:5 (end), *Chavos Da'as* 100:2 (*Biurim*), and *Aruch HaShulchan* 102:19. [Support for this comes from the fact that some opinions in the *Gemara* say that *gid hanasheh* actually has *ta'am*. There cannot be a disagreement on an easily verifiable fact if the *gid hanasheh* has taste, and this indicates that there is some weak *ta'am* and the *machlokes* is whether that is "enough" to qualify as *ta'am* (*Chavos Da'as*)].
  Others answer that (a) *gid hanasheh* is similar enough to meat that it is like *min b'mino*, where lack of *ta'am* is not a factor (*Iggeros Moshe* YD 2:24), (b) the fact that the *Torah* forbade *gid hanasheh* despite its lack of *ta'am*, gives it special status as relates to these halachos (*Pri Chadash*), or (c) the case of *gid hanasheh* is where it was broken into tiny pieces which are not removable but are noticeable, which have a special status (*Dos Aish* 13, referenced in *Rebbi Akiva Eiger* to *Shach* 102:2; also see *Gilyon Maharsha* to *Shulchan Aruch*100:2) (for more on that special status, see *Imrei Dovid, Halachos of Insects,* Chapter 32 in the section titled "*Hopelessly Lost*").
[10] *Iggeros Moshe* YD 2:24. *Minchas Kohen* (*Ta'aruvos* 1:10) also considers this possibility.

bitul b'shishim even though there is no transfer of *ta'am*.[11] He sees support for this from the aforementioned *Yerushalmi* which, in fact, is discussing a case of *min b'mino* (olives in olives); if the strictness applied even to cases of *aino mino*, there is no way the *Yerushalmi* could have deduced that (and said הדא אמרה) from the case of *min b'mino*, which has a preexisting rule that *bitul b'shishim* is required even without transfer of *ta'am*.

What these two explanations – *Pri Chadash* and *Iggeros Moshe* – agree on is that if a non-kosher food with absolutely no taste is mixed into a kosher food that has taste (i.e., מין בשאינו מינו), the kosher food's status is not affected. This ruling is widely accepted.[12]

אין בו טעם כלל

How can we identify foods that have no taste at all, and are eligible for the leniency noted above? At first this seems like a foolish question: just bite into the food and it should be easy to tell if it has any taste.[13] But perhaps we can refine that answer somewhat and use that information to consider which foods qualify.

The following approach is speculative

Current scientific belief is that when we eat a food, our perception of the food's flavor is based on three factors: For most foods, the primary component is aroma, perceived in the nose either directly (orthonasal) entering our nostrils before the food gets into our mouth, or indirectly (retronasal) getting into the nasal cavity from the back of our throats as we chew the food. The second element is taste, which refers to 4 (or possibly

---

[11] *Shulchan Aruch* 98:2 as per *Taz* 98:3 and others. *Mid'oraisah*, *bitul b'rov* suffices for *min b'mino*, but *mid'rabannan* one is required to have *bitul b'shishim* so that people do not mistakenly think that *min b'mino* is also *batel b'rov* (גזירה מין במינו אטו מין בשאינו מינו). However, since *aino mino* is always judged by whether there is *ta'am*, there is no need to add extra strictness to cases where the *issur* provides little or no *ta'am*, since people know that these cases are being judged by the amount of *ta'am* they provide and will do the same for other *issurim* (*Iggeros Moshe* ibid).

[12] *Minchas Yaakov* 85:70, *Chochmas Adam* 54:4, and *Aruch HaShulchan* 103:19 (see also *Aruch HaShulchan* 103:9) accept *Pri Chadash*. See also *Dos Aish* 13 (and *Pri Chadash*) referenced in *Rebbi Akiva Eiger* to *Shach* ibid. Additionally, *Minchas Kohen* and *Chochmas Adam* ibid. believe that *Shach* per se is *machmir* even when the *issur* has no taste at all, but they personally disagree with his ruling.

The text notes the way the *Poskim* understand *Ohr Zaruah* et al. In addition to the proofs to this position, almost all of them note that from a logical perspective, they find it impossible to accept that if a forbidden item truly has no taste, it could forbid a different food that has taste. This is because *Shulchan Aruch* 98 makes it clear that if the *issur* provides no *ta'am*, the mixture is permitted. It therefore follows that if the *issur* has no *ta'am* then the mixture must surely be permitted.

[13] See Chapter 18, that a criterion for "tasting" is "a taste that an average person would detect"; see there also regarding whether one may rely on "testing" to determine if there is טעם in a given sample.

5) qualities we can detect with the tongue's tastebuds: sweet, sour, salty, bitter (and some add "umami" a meaty/savory taste). The final part is mouthfeel, which includes many things, such as chewiness, dryness, roughness, and smoothness, which are called trigeminal sensations perceived by pain nerves. For example, when someone bites into an apple, they taste the sweetness (and sometimes sourness), smell the fruity notes in the apple's hexyl acetate and butyl acetate, and feel the crunchiness; together, these three factors – aroma, taste, and mouthfeel – create the familiar apple "flavor".

Bearing in mind that aroma is the primary way we perceive a food's flavor, if we want to be accurate, we cannot translate the term אין בו טעם כלל as "it has no taste" since the word "taste" is reserved for the aspects of the food (sweet, sour, etc.) that are detected with the tongue. Thus, at a minimum, אין בו טעם כלל means the food that has no taste or aroma. What about mouthfeel? Is that included in "טעם"?

Let us consider that option, using beverage alcohol as an example. Scientists will say that it has all three elements of flavor noted above: it has a bitter (and sometimes sweet) taste, it typically contains aroma, and it also has pungent, burning, and astringent (drying) sensations. Most people would assume that the latter group of mouthfeel sensations are very much part of the טעם/flavor of alcohol, and presumably those are halachically included as well.

On the other hand, other parts of mouthfeel clearly seem not to be part of טעם. For example, some people's preference for al dente pasta or less viscous salsa are also examples of mouthfeel (unrelated to aroma or taste), but these factors seem intuitively unrelated to ta'am. Accordingly, we can understand that the *gid hanasheh* has no טעם, even though a person might find eating it to be chewy. Chewiness is an element of mouthfeel which is not part of טעם, just as the hardness of pasta and the smoothness of the salsa are not.

Perhaps the way to categorize these two types of mouthfeels is as follows: Only those aspects of mouthfeel which are uniquely detectable in the mouth (or nose or throat) are included in טעם, while those which are also measurable elsewhere in the body are not. For example, the cooling or stinging effect from mint or horseradish, respectively, is something that is only noticed when one chews them but cannot be discerned if you squeeze them between your fingers. Those are considered טעם, even though they are not aroma or taste. In contrast, the roughness, viscosity, or smoothness of a food can also be evaluated with one's hands or feet; those features are not unique to eating or to food, and therefore are not included in טעם.

There is another way of expressing the same difference between these types of mouthfeel. By and large, those which are only detectable in the mouth (or nose or throat) are because of a given chemical contained in the food (see footnote),[14] while those which can be identified in other parts of the body tend to be tactile (or have similar "physical") properties[15] of the food. While these terms – chemical and tactile – are less accurate than the description given in the previous paragraph (and are not even opposites of one another), they do have some advantages (see below) and for simplicity's sake, we will use them going forward.

Thus, if our analysis is correct, we can summarize as follows: a food is אין בו טעם כלל if it has no aroma, no taste, and no "chemical" mouthfeel, even if a person experiences certain elements of tactile mouthfeel when he consumes it.

Applications

At the beginning of the chapter, we saw that *Tosfos* says that the principle of סתם כלים אינם בני יומן is partially based on the possibility that the non-kosher item cooked in the food was one that does not give טעם. Clearly, then, this must be a somewhat reasonable possibility, and we should not

---

[14] In addition to mint and horseradish noted above (whose effects are created by menthol and allyl isothiocyanate), some other examples are: Szechuan pepper, chili pepper, and alcohol, whose numbing, sharp, and burning effects, respectively are created by hydro alpha sanshool, capsaicin, and ethanol contained in these foods. There are many more similar examples.

[15] Among the types of mouthfeel that fit into this category are chewiness, dryness, roughness, smoothness, crunchiness, and hardness (already noted in the text), and cohesiveness, creaminess, density, graininess, gumminess, heaviness, oily, and watery.

In fact, there is no food – or just about any other item – which would not present some sort of tactile mouthfeel if one were to chew it. This, itself, indicates that if there is such a thing as something which is אין בו טעם כלל, then (at least some of) these aspects do not qualify as טעם.

be surprised if a food item qualifies. *Rema* gives one example, bee legs,[16] and *Iggeros Moshe*[17] says that pure undiluted shellac[18] is another case.[19]

There are websites which claim that shark fin – a traditional food consumed in the Far East – has no flavor at all, and its role is to provide a gelatinous and chewy bite for people eating the eponymous soup. Since shark fin is not kosher, we have no way to independently verify this information. At the same time, other sites claim that foods as diverse as spinach, rice, chia, and flax seeds have no flavor, but simple taste-tests showed that they very much do. Thus, we must be cautious in accepting people's suggestions of which foods are flavorless.

There are three ingredients which *Mashgichim* have tasted and reported that – at least in some cases – they were אין בו טעם כלל: tofu, gelatin, and stearic acid (and some stearic compounds).[20] Each of these foods can potentially be *assur*[21] and also surely has a distinct tactile mouthfeel. But if they have no aroma, taste, or chemical-induced mouthfeel, they are unable to spread טעם to another food. Instead, if a non-kosher version of

---

[16] See below in footnote 20.

[17] *Iggeros Moshe* ibid.

[18] The *teshuvah* presents reasons why shellac is inherently permitted and adds that even if those lines of reasoning are incorrect, it will always be *batel b'rov* (and permitted) since it is sold diluted in alcohol (and it qualifies for *bitul b'rov* since it is אין בו טעם כלל, as noted in the text). [Pure shellac is solid at room temperature, and surely has tactile mouthfeel].

[19] Some point at two cases of dried out, non-kosher, meat which cannot affect the kosher status of other foods, as examples of this halacha. [The two cases are *Rema* 87:10 (end) regarding a non-kosher cow's stomach (קיבת נבילה), and the other is *Shach* YD 134:14 regarding dried meat mixed into saffron]. It is not clear if those are true examples of foods which are אין בו טעם כלל, or if they are just so dried out that they are inedible and no longer forbidden at all.

What about *gid hanasheh* which (as we have seen) the *Gemara* says has no טעם, and (see *Shulchan Aruch* 100:2) therefore its "b'lios" do not pose a concern? See footnote 9.

[20] Another potential item which is אין בו טעם כלל is waxes, as follows: How did *Rema* know that bee legs have no טעם? Bees are not kosher, so he could not have tasted the legs. Seemingly, since the bee leg is all "bone", he instinctively understood that it likely has no טעם, just like other bones are אין בו טעם כלל. The same appears to be true for waxes. As a rule, waxes are devoid of aroma or flavor (despite their having a very distinctive tactile mouthfeel), and therefore even without tasting the wax it may be easy to postulate that they have no טעם. [Beeswax is an exception in that it has a unique aroma].

Also see the see the article on Joulies by this author in *Journal of Halacha and Contemporary Society*, Volume 63.

[21] Tofu is made from soybeans, and if they grew during *shemittah* they would be forbidden as ספיחין, an *issur d'rabannan* on any vegetables grown during *shemittah*; for more on that see *Imrei Dovid, Shemittah*, Chapter 15. Gelatin and stearic acid can be made from animal bones, hides, and fat, and if they were they would be non-kosher (unless they were processed from kosher animals which had *shechitah*).

them is mixed into a kosher food,[22] the mixture is permitted assuming the *issur* is *batel b'rov*.[23] [In most cases, gelatin is a *davar hama'amid* (since it causes the food to "gel"), and for that reason it would not be *batel* even if it has no טעם].[24] In fact, in Chapter 43 we will see cases where this possibility is considered an important factor for a real-life issue.

However, the truth is that there have been cases where people tasted tofu and gelatin and thought that they did have טעם. Does the presence of flavor depend on the type of processing? Do some companies purify their ingredients more than others and does that explain why some have טעם and others do not? Or perhaps any flavor detected is so subtle that it does not even qualify as "טעם"[25] (and is not even noticed by others)? These questions require further consideration before one relies on the lenient assumption.

---

[22] The text refers to the status of the food *b'dieved* but does not condone purposely adding the *issur* to a kosher food. For example, uncertified stearic acid flakes (e.g., "Fry Away") should not be heated in a pot to remove grease (but if they were then, *b'dieved*, the pot would potentially remain kosher).
[23] These cases might well present a practical difference between the positions of *Pri Chadash* and *Iggeros Moshe* discussed earlier in the chapter. *Iggeros Moshe* said that a food with no טעם requires *bitul b'shishim* if it is mixed in *min b'mino*, and *bitul b'rov* is only relevant if it was mixed with *aino mino*. However, *Pri Chadash* (and many others) said that a food with no טעם is always *batel b'rov* seemingly even when it is *min b'mino*, so he would be lenient in all cases.
[24] Nonetheless, the lack of טעם means that the equipment used with that mixture will not require *kashering*, since *kashering* is only required to remove forbidden טעם.
[25] See above in footnote 9.

Chapter 40

בשר פוגם את השמן

שולחן ערוך סימן ק"ג סעיף ד
שמן ודבש של עובד כוכבים אף על פי שהם מבושלים
מותרים מפני שהבשר פוגם את השמן ומסריחו, וכן
לדבש. הגה: ויש אומרים דבשר אינו פוגם דבש עצמו, רק משקה
הנעשה מדבש, ובמקום שאין הפסד גדול יש להחמיר. בשר או חלב
ביין הוי לפגם ומותר.

This halacha[1] states that meat is נותן טעם לפגם into oil, and at first glance this would seem to permit purchasing vegetable oil which was produced on the same equipment as [non-kosher] animal fat or transported in ship holds which had previously carried animal fat. However, in practice, this is not the accepted halacha. The sources and details of this halacha, and the explanation why the proposed lenient application is not correct, can be found in *Imrei Dovid*, *Alcoholic Beverages*, Chapter 16, which focuses on *Shulchan Aruch* YD 114:7 (where this same halacha is noted). It is beyond the scope of this work to repeat that exposition of the five *Gemaros*, four opinions in *Rishonim*, and much technical information involved in the issue, but we will note several main points.

Shulchan Aruch is based on *Rambam's* interpretation of the relevant *Gemaros*, and in a *teshuvah*, *Rema* goes one step further, saying that it is well-known that the taste of pig fat is more disgusting than other items. *Shach*, however, argues that the halacha follows the opinion of *Rashi* that there is no source for assuming that the *b'liah* of meat is לפגם into oil. Some have suggested that although *Shulchan Aruch* takes a lenient approach, it is proper to be *machmir* for the opinion of *Shach* (*Rashi*) and forbid vegetable oil produced on equipment previously used for animal fat.

---

[1] *Shulchan Aruch* 103:4.

Based on several significant questions on the position of *Shach* (and even possible contradictions within *Shach* himself), *Minchas Yaakov* says that, even if one chooses to be *machmir* for the opinion of *Rashi/Shach*, it is only when one knows that fat was mixed into the oil, or the oil was processed on the same equipment as fat. But if a person has vegetable oil of unknown status, *Shach* agrees with *Rema* that one can purchase it and need not be concerned that it might have been processed on equipment used for animal fat.

In addition to the halachic rationale for being *machmir*, Rabbi Zushe Blech z"l raised a more practical point, best understood in light of *Beis Yosef* who asks an obvious question: how can anyone say that animal fat is לפגם into oil, when we find that people actually choose to make exactly such a mixture? If people purposely do it, does that not indicate that fat gives a positive taste to the oil?

Beis Yosef answers that the *Gemara* was referring to someone who puts plain fat into oil. However, if the fat is mixed with specific types of spices, it can give a positive taste into oil (and that is what chefs do when they mix fat into oil). In other words, fat into oil is only לפגם if it actually gives a negative taste, but if there is reason to think that in a specific case it will contribute a positive taste, then the *Gemara's* leniency does not apply.

The primary concern of uncertified vegetable oil is that it was "deodorized" in equipment used for animal fat. As its name implies, the process of deodorizing is a way to remove unwanted odors/tastes from the fat, leaving the oil with a much more neutral or pleasant taste. Thus, when the *Gemara* spoke of animal fat being לפגם into oil, it was referring to untreated animal fat which, as *Rema* stated in the *teshuvah*, is horribly putrid (מאוס הוא ביותר מכל שרצים שבעולם). In that case, the *Gemara* confidently stated that it is לפגם into oil. But when fat is deodorized, it loses that negative feature, and we must assume that it contributes positively to the oil. In this way, deodorized fat is like fat mixed with spices which *Beis Yosef* says is not לפגם into oil.

Thus, we can conclude that when a consumer purchases vegetable oil, they must be concerned that it was processed (deodorized) on the same equipment as animal fat. The reason *Shulchan Aruch* presents for assuming the fat is לפגם does not apply to the odor-free fat and oil which would be used on this equipment. Whether it applies to vegetable oil transported in ship holds would seem to depend on whether the oil is crude (i.e., in its raw, unprocessed state) or deodorized.

Chapter 41

אינו בן יומו

שולחן ערוך סימן ק"ג סעיף ה

כל קדרה שאינה בת יומא חשיבה טעמה לפגם ואינה אוסרת. ונקראת בת יומא כל זמן שלא שהתה מעת לעת אחר שנתבשל בה האיסור, וכיון שעבר עליה מעת לעת אחר שנתבשל בה האיסור אינה נקראת בת יומא. ואם בישל בה כשאינה בת יומא התבשיל מותר דהוי נותן טעם לפגם, והוא שתהיה מודחת שלא יהא שומן על פניה שאם לא הדיחה אוסר והרי היא כחתיכת איסור שלא נפגמה, ויש מתירין אפילו בישל בה קודם שהדיחה. הגה: ואם יש ס' נגד מה שדבוק עליו לכולי עלמא שרי מאחר דהקדירה אינה בת יומא, והכי נהוג.

General Halacha

The current halacha[1] teaches an important principle which is often relevant when there is some sort of mix-up in the kitchen, i.e., kosher is cooked in a non-kosher pot, or dairy food is microwaved on a *fleishig* plate. Namely, if the problematic utensil had not been used for non-kosher, etc., for 24 hours (i.e., it is *aino ben yomo*), any *b'lios* that come out of that utensil cannot affect the kosher status of other food, because at that point the *b'lios* are *nosein ta'am lifgam*.

This halacha – and many details of this entire *siman* in *Shulchan Aruch* – are repeated in *Yoreh Deah* 122, and there[2] it adds an important restriction: although *aino ben yomo* cannot affect food, *Chazal* were concerned that this leniency might inadvertently lead people to use utensils that are still <u>ben</u> yomo.[3] Therefore, they declared that,

---

[1] *Shulchan Aruch* 103:5.
[2] *Shulchan Aruch* 122:2.
[3] See Chapter 29, footnotes 11 and 12, that *Tur* 122:5 and *Bach* ad loc. disagree whether the concern is that (a) if you use this as an *aino ben yomo*, it might mistakenly lead you to use a <u>different</u> non-kosher utensil which is still *ben yomo* (*Tur*), or that (b) you might miscalculate and use <u>this</u> very item while it is still *ben yomo* (*Bach*).

l'chatchilah, one cannot use an *aino ben yomo* utensil without *kashering* (גזירה אינו בן יומו אטו בן יומו). This relegates the leniency of *aino ben yomo* to cases of *b'dieved*. *Tosfos*[4] explains that the גזירה אינו בן יומו אטו בן יומו applies to any item where the non-kosher *ta'am* was once viable and not *lifgam*; since it was once *ben yomo* in this utensil, it remains forbidden even when it becomes *aino ben yomo*. But when the *aino ben yomo b'lios* leave the utensil and transfer to food, that food is permitted since in that food the *ta'am* was always *lifgam*.

Calculation

The typical way a utensil becomes *aino ben yomo* is if 24 consecutive hours[5] pass between the time it was used for non-kosher before it is used for kosher. What if the utensil in question is a pot and during the 24-hour period it was not used for non-kosher but was used for something kosher? Does that prevent the *aino ben yomo* status from coming into effect?

One scenario where this would be relevant is if the pot was used for non-kosher at 9:00 AM on Sunday, and was then used to cook water (i.e., kosher pareve) from 10:00-10:30 AM. *Shulchan Aruch* and *Rema*[6] consider this in the context of *ChaNaN* (see Chapter 3); namely, the water cooked at 10:00 is (potentially) judged as being 100% non-kosher [based on *ChaNaN*] due to the non-kosher *ta'am* it absorbed from the pot. If so, the pot has absorbed fresh non-kosher *ta'am* at 10:00, and the 24-hour downtime clock restarts at that point. Accordingly, *Shulchan Aruch* – who is lenient regarding *ChaNaN* for most *issurim* – says this concern for *basar b'chalav*[7] where [*Shulchan Aruch* holds that] *ChaNaN* applies. However, *Rema* – who is *machmir* for *ChaNaN* for most *issurim* – says that one should generally be *machmir* and restart the 24-hour clock.

---

[4] *Tosfos*, *Avodah Zara* 76a s.v. *mikan*, cited in *Beis Yosef* 94:4. See also, above, in Chapter 38 footnote 10.

[5] Is the requirement 24 hours on a clock, or that it reaches the same point in the day as when the non-kosher was used? For example, if non-kosher was used at sunset on Tuesday which was at 6:23 PM, and then kosher was used on Wednesday at 6:22 PM, but sunset was at 6:21 PM. Is the pot *aino ben yomo*, since the non-kosher was used at sunset while the kosher was after sunset (a day later)? Or is it *ben yomo* since there was only 23 hours and 59 minutes between uses? See *Badei HaShulchan* (*Biurim*) 103:5 s.v. *kol*. [In practice, this issue would seem to be more practical when calculating the 72-hour period between *shechitah* and *melichah*, as in the scenario of "Barely missed the 72-hour deadline" in *Imrei Dovid, Meat and Poultry*, Chapter 35].

[6] *Shulchan Aruch/Rema* 103:7.

[7] See Chapter 3 footnote 5 for details on which cases that includes.

However, there are several caveats to that strict position. Firstly, *Rema* notes that his general opinion is that in cases of *hefsed* one can ignore *ChaNaN* for most *issurim* (other than *basar b'chalav*). Secondly, *Rema* notes there are specific situations where one can be lenient if the only concern is *ChaNaN* and the pot was completely unused for the entire night (לינת לילה). For more on that, see above in Chapter 3, footnote 20. Lastly, as noted in Chapter 3, there are *issurim* where all agree that there is no *ChaNaN*, including *chametz* before *Pesach* and kosher milk or kosher meat (not mixed together).

Any of these cases where *ChaNaN* does not apply brings us to a secondary issue. *Yad Yehuda*[8] suggests that during the time that water is cooking in the pot (i.e., from 10:00 to 10:30 in our example), the process of *pegimah*/degradation is paused and restarts once again at 10:30. But since the half hour is just a pause (rather than a break), the 24-hour clock resumes at 10:30 from where it left off, and at 9:30 AM on Monday it will be *aino ben yomo*. The 24 hours of "*aino ben yomo*" are from 9:00-10:00 on Sunday (1 hour), and from 10:30 on Sunday until 9:30 on Monday (23 hours), with a "pause" from 10:00 until 10:30 on Sunday when the pot was hot. *Yad Yehuda* notes that his position is contradicted by *Shach, K'raisi U'plaisi*, and others. The common practice is not to be *machmir* for this opinion. For more on this, see *Imrei Dovid, Kashering*, Chapter 63.

Another opinion which most *Poskim* reject is that of *Ma'amar Mordechai*,[9] who says that a container only becomes *aino ben yomo* if it is empty for 24 hours, but if there is liquid in the container, that stops (or pauses) the process. Therefore, if kosher food was put into a non-kosher container with liquid while the container was still *ben yomo*, the container will not become *aino ben yomo* even after 24 hours pass (as long as the liquid remains in the container).[10] *Mishnah Berurah*[11] records this position but appears to assume that the primary halacha is that one can be lenient. As

---

[8] *Yad Yehuda* 94:27 (*Aruch*).
[9] *Ma'amar Mordechai* OC 447:17.
[10] This suggestion is even stricter than that of *Yad Yehuda* noted above, for it posits that even if cold liquid – which causes no transfer of *ta'am* (before 24 hours pass) – is in the container, it prevents *pegimah*. Thus, it seems those who disagree with *Yad Yehuda* would surely disagree with *Ma'amar Mordechai*.
[11] See *Mishnah Berurah* 451:122 (cites *Ma'amar Mordechai* but says most are lenient), 447:39 (assumes the lenient position), and *Biur Halacha* 447:8 s.v. *im* (notes that many disagree with *Ma'amar Mordechai* but suggests being *machmir l'chatchilah* as relates to *kashering*).

with *Yad Yehuda*, the common practice is to be lenient on this issue. For more details and sources on this issue, see *Imrei Dovid* ibid.

Not effective b'dieved

There are several situations where the leniency of *aino ben yomo* does not apply, and the food which absorbed the *ta'am* is forbidden, even *b'dieved*:

- *Rema*[12] rules that one cannot be lenient about נותן טעם לפגם (and *aino ben yomo*) as relates to *ta'am* of *chametz* absorbed into food on *Pesach*.

- Although most absorbed tastes degrade when they remain absorbed in a utensil for 24 hours, that is not true of wine, since wine improves with age.[13] Accordingly, *aino ben yomo* is not a factor when the absorbed *ta'am* was non-kosher wine.[14]

- If the kosher food was *charif* when it was heated or cooked in the non-kosher pot, the food becomes non-kosher even if the pot was *aino ben yomo*, because the *davar charif* is מחליא ליה לשבח the *aino ben yomo ta'am*. For more on that, see Chapter 16.

---

[12] *Rema* OC 447:10. For more on that – including the lenient opinion of *Shulchan Aruch* and how this issue is tied to the *machlokes* between *Rashba* and *Ran* discussed in Chapter 37 – see Chapter 37 footnote 16.

[13] *Rema* YD 137:1 as per *Shach* 137:10.

[14] Ibid. *Shev Yaakov* 33, cited in *Pischei Teshuvah* 137:2, rules that in cases of *hefsed merubah* one can rely on those who say that the leniency of *aino ben yomo* applies when wine is absorbed into metal (as opposed to wood or ceramic).

Magen Avraham (447:25 (and) and 451:40 (end)) suggests that whisky has the same status as wine, since whisky also improves with age. [While this is technically true, it appears that whisky only improves when it is in a barrel, and it is the interaction between the whisky and barrel which drives the improvement, while wine inherently improves with age regardless of how it is stored (as long as it is not exposed to oxygen)]. There is also an implication in *Chasam Sofer* OC 120 to this effect, but *Pri Megadim* AA 451:25 questions such a position. *Mishnah Berurah* 451:122 notes that the leniency of *aino ben yomo* does not apply to a container that held whisky, but he connects this to the fact that experience shows that the container retains a (positive) taste of whisky. In other words, it is not because whisky is inherently like wine that "aging" does not ruin its taste, but rather that, on a practical level, we see that the taste remains viable. [See *Pri Megadim* AA 447:1, who may be based on this type of logic]. Therefore, he rules, based on *Gra"z* 451:63, that if the taste of *chametz* whisky is not detectable in the *Pesach* beverage, one may consume it; presumably, *Magen Avraham* would not have agreed with that exception. [See also *Mishnah Berurah* 451:120 regarding cleaning of whisky containers in preparation for *hag'alah*]. Thus, *Mishnah Berurah* appears to reject *Magen Avraham's* comparison of whisky to wine.

- *Pri Megadim*[15] says that if a person knowingly <u>chose</u> to cook kosher food in an *aino ben yomo* non-kosher pot, it is treated like someone who was מבטל איסור לכתחלה and he would not be allowed to eat the food cooked in that pot (just as one cannot eat a mixture created via ביטול איסור לכתחלה). For more on this, see Chapter 28, and particularly there in Point #9.

Rely on it l'chatchilah
Although the general halacha is that *aino ben yomo* is only permitted *b'dieved*, there are several applications where to some extent we may even rely on it *l'chatchilah*:[16]

~ Hag'alah
Hag'alah draws *ta'am* out of a utensil, and one way to avoid the *ta'am* immediately being reabsorbed is for the utensil to be *aino ben yomo* at the time of *kashering*. In this way, the *hag'alah* water is not affected by the *ta'am* being purged, which ipso facto means there is no non-kosher *ta'am* to be reabsorbed into the utensil.[17]

If the *aino ben yomo ta'am* will be reabsorbed into the utensil, why bother *kashering*? What is the value in removing the *ta'am* if it will go right back in? *Rashba*[18] answers, using a line of reasoning similar to the one cited from *Tosfos* at the beginning of the chapter. Since the *ta'am* absorbed in the utensil was originally *ben yomo*, the utensil cannot be used without removing that *ta'am*. But the *hag'alah* water <u>never</u> had viable *ta'am* in it, and from the perspective of the water it was always "*aino ben yomo*".

---

[15] *Pri Megadim* SD 99:7 (towards the end); see additional support to this position in *Rebbi Akiva Eiger* ad loc., and in *Badei HaShulchan* (*Biurim*) 103:5 s.v. *v'einah*.
    Pri Megadim references *Shach* 39:6, who also applies the fine imposed on someone who violates אין מבטלין איסור לכתחלה to cases other than the "traditional" one where *issur* is mixed into *heter*. *Shach* is commenting on *Shulchan Aruch* YD 39:6 who rules that if an animal's lungs were accidentally lost before being checked for טריפות, one may eat the meat and assume the animal was not a טריפה. To this, *Shach* says that if the person purposely discarded the lungs, the meat is forbidden to him just like our halacha which says it is the punishment for someone who violated ביטול איסור לכתחלה. In that case, no "*issur*" was diluted, yet conceptually it is like ביטול איסור לכתחלה because the person took steps to get around (potentially) forbidden food.
[16] What if the utensil is *aino ben yomo* and the *b'liah* will also be *batel b'shishim* in the kosher food? Can one use the utensil *l'chatchilah*? See *Badei HaShulchan* 103:62.
    See Chapter 11 Footnote 17 that one may not cook pareve food in an *aino ben yomo* dairy pot with intention to eat the food with meat. Although this is a case where there are two reasons to be lenient *b'dieved* – *aino ben yomo* and נ"ט בר נ"ט – both of those are not permitted *l'chatchilah* even if they occur simultaneously.
[17] For more on this, see *Imrei Dovid, Kashering*, Chapter 61.
[18] *Responsa Rashba* 1:262-263.

Therefore, גזירה אינו בן יומו אטו בן יומו does not apply to the water – or any utensil that absorbs *ta'am* from the water – and it remains kosher "*l'chatchilah*".[19]

~ **Waiting 12 months**
The following is copied and summarized from Imrei Dovid, Kashering, Chapter 60 see there for sources and more details

If a barrel used for *stam yayin* has been empty for 12 months, the absorbed wine dries up to the point that the barrel can be used for kosher wine without *kashering*.[20] Why is this halacha only stated regarding non-kosher wine and not for any other forbidden food? *Chacham Tzvi*[21] posits that it is based on a strict halacha regarding wine that does not apply to other forbidden foods.

For most forbidden foods, once *ta'am* has been absorbed for 24 hours, the *ta'am* is "*pagum*" and cannot affect food subsequently used in that utensil. But *Chazal* said that nonetheless, one cannot use an *aino ben yomo* utensil without *kashering*. Once *Chazal* instituted this requirement, the utensil remains "forbidden" (without *kashering*) even when 12 months have passed, and the absorbed taste has completely degraded. But wine is different, in that even when it is *aino ben yomo* it still has a positive effect on other foods. In a sense, the גזירה אינו בן יומו אטו בן יומו does not apply to those utensils. Accordingly, when they are 12 months old and the absorbed taste reaches the point of being completely inedible, one may use the utensil even without *kashering*.

Thus, it is the strict stance of *aino ben yomo* wine which leads to the lenient application for a wine barrel which is 12 months old. If so, *Chacham Tzvi* says, the same should apply to *chametz* on *Pesach*. It carries the strict halacha that *aino ben yomo* is forbidden, and therefore the halacha should also say that if the utensil has not been used for non-kosher for 12 months, then it can be used on *Pesach* without *kashering*. Although *Chacham Tzvi* finds this logic compelling, he says that one should rely on it only in cases where the utensil was already used for *Pesach* food, but he is unwilling to be lenient *l'chatchilah*.

Later *Acharonim* discuss the novel approach of *Chacham Tzvi*, and many disagreed with him but some were willing to (a) consider his position as a *tziruf* when there

---

[19] Nonetheless, *Rema* YD 121:2 rules that one should not use the *hag'alah* water. [See a similar ruling in somewhat different contexts, in *Rema* YD 94:5 as per *Shach* 94:19, *Rema* 95:3 as per *Shach* 95:14, *Rema* 135:12 as per *Shach* 135:29, and *Mishnah Berurah* 452:13 (end)]. Apparently, this is because if one were to use the water it would give the impression that they desire the non-kosher *ta'am* extracted during *kashering*, which would be akin to *bitul issur l'chatchilah*. This concern is specific to the water per se, but not to the utensil being *kashered* in that water.

[20] *Shulchan Aruch* YD 135:16.

[21] *Chacham Tzvi* 75 (and 80), cited in *Pischei Teshuvah* YD 122:3.

are other factors to be lenient, and (b) potentially apply this leniency to other *issurim* (where גזירה אינו בן יומו אטו בן יומו does apply). Any situation where one will consider being lenient based on *Chacham Tzvi* requires consultation with a qualified *Rav* who can weigh the appropriateness of applying that ruling to the given case.

~ **Other**

In Chapter 59 we will see that there are cases where a piece of equipment cannot be *kashered* and the need for its use is so critical, that one may "*l'chatchilah*" use it without *kashering* assuming it is *aino ben yomo*.

In Chapter 43, we will see a novel position of *Iggeros Moshe* to permit *aino ben yomo l'chatchilah* in very specific cases.

Chapter 42

סתם כלים אינם בני יומן

שולחן ערוך סימן קי״ג סעיף ה

כל קדרה שאינה בת יומא חשיבה טעמה לפגם ואינה אוסרת. ונקראת בת יומא כל זמן שלא שהתה מעת לעת אחר שנתבשל בה האיסור, וכיון שעבר עליה מעת לעת אחר שנתבשל בה האיסור אינה נקראת בת יומא. ואם בישל בה כשאינה בת יומא התבשיל מותר דהוי נותן טעם לפגם, והוא שתהיה מודחת שלא יהא שומן על פניה שאם לא הדיחה אוסר והרי היא כחתיכת איסור שלא נפגמה, ויש מתירין אפילו בישל בה קודם שהדיחה. הגה: ואם יש ס׳ נגד מה שדבוק עליו לכולי עלמא שרי מאחר דהקדירה אינה בת יומא, והכי נהוג.

Basic Halacha

In the previous chapter we noted that the halacha discussed here,[1] that *ta'am* which is *aino ben yomo* is considered לפגם and permitted *b'dieved*, is also recorded in *Yoreh Deah* 122:2, together with the caveat that due to the גזירה אינו בן יומו אטו בן יומו, one may not *l'chatchilah* use an *aino ben yomo* item without *kashering*. Both of those points are based on the *Gemara*, but there (122:6-7) it also adds another detail which is never clearly stated in the *Gemara*. Namely, if kosher food was cooked in a non-kosher utensil and we have no information about whether that utensil was used in the past 24 hours, we may assume that it was not.

This principle, סתם כלים אינם בני יומן, is a significant leniency, because it means that, unless we specifically know that a utensil was used for non-kosher in the past 24 hours, we can assume that *ta'am* coming out of the utensil will not affect other foods. As a result, when there is some mix-up in a kitchen and, for example, a *milchig* ladle was used to dish out a *fleishig*

---

[1] *Shulchan Aruch* 103:5.

soup, the soup remains kosher unless we have specific knowledge that the ladle had been used for dairy in the past 24 hours.[2] [3]

As noted, the *Gemara* never states this principle outright, but the *Rishonim* cite several places where the *Gemara* implicitly seems to assume it.[4] What is the basis for assuming סתם כלים have not been used in the previous 24 hours? *Rosh*[5] explains that it is based on a *sfek sfekah*: it might be that the utensil was not used in the past 24 hours, and even if it was, that food might be נותן טעם לפגם into the kosher food used in the utensil right now.[6] That is enough to permit the food *b'dieved*, but not *l'chatchilah*. *Shach*[7] says that the reason it cannot be relied on *l'chatchilah* is because of the גזירה אינו בן יומו אטו בן יומו. In other words, if we <u>knew</u> the utensil was *aino ben yomo* we would not be allowed (*l'chatchilah*) to use it without *kashering*, so how much more so should this be the rule when we are merely <u>assuming</u> (based on *sfek sfekah*) that it is *aino ben yomo*, (i.e., that we cannot use it *l'chatchilah*).

Kashering

This explanation for why one may not rely on סתם כלים אינם בני יומן *l'chatchilah* appears to lead to the following unexpected leniency: A basic rule is that one may not perform *hag'alah* unless the item being *kashered*

---

[2] Although the original "sources" for the principle of סתם כלים אינם בני יומן are from non-kosher utensils owned by non-Jews, it also applies to utensils owned by Jews (*Shulchan Aruch* 122:7). See reasons why some disagree with this in *Bach* 122:6, and below in footnote 17.
[3] Nonetheless, the ladle must be *kashered* since it has absorbed both *fleishig* and *milchig ta'am*, each of which renders it unusable for the other type.
[4] In fact, some *Rishonim* do not accept this principle at all, and find other explanations for the relevant *Gemaros*. See, for example, the lengthy discussion in *Beis Yosef* regarding the opinion of *Rambam* on this matter, and *Rebbi Akiva Eiger* to *Be'er HaGolah* 122:6.
[5] *Rosh*, *Avodah Zara*, 2:35, cited in *Tur*. This is the common understanding in the *Rishonim*, and *Shach* 122:4 just cites this as כתבו הפוסקים. However, see the coming footnote.
[6] The text notes the reason given by most *Rishonim*. However, see *Rebbi Akiva Eiger* in his gloss to *Rema* 87:6, who cites *Responsa Rashba* (1:497) who presents a slightly different version of the *sfek sfekah*, and *Rebbi Akiva Eiger* shows a practical difference between these explanations. See also *Tosfos*, *Avodah Zara*, 38b ד"ה אי cited in the beginning of Chapter 39.

One might wonder whether the possibility of the *b'lios* being classified as נותן טעם לפגם is relevant nowadays when we do not actually taste <u>any</u> *ta'am* from *b'lios*. This question is specific to the principle of סתם כלים and not to a case where we know the equipment is *aino ben yomo*. In the latter case we can be lenient because can be confident that any *ta'am* that comes out is לפגם. However, when saying סתם כלים, how can we be lenient based on the possibility that it is לפגם, when we are certain it is not? Perhaps this is why *Tur* 122:7 says that the *safek* is that the non-kosher might be לפגם if it itself – i.e., not its absorbed *ta'am* – was mixed into the kosher food (בעין שמא נשתמשו בו בדבר הפוגם). [Nonetheless, no source or logic is given why such a *safek* is relevant when the issue at hand is about absorbed *ta'am*].
[7] *Shach* 122:4. This also appears to be the logic of *Rashba*, *Toras HaBayis* 4:4 (38b-39a, *Aruch* and 38a-b, *Katzar*); see also *Responsa Rashba* 1:497 cited in *Beis Meir* in his gloss to *Shach* ibid.

is *aino ben yomo*,[8] and typically in a home or industrial setting, it is easy to determine whether the full 24 hours have passed to allow for *kashering*. [Accordingly, *kashering* should not be performed unless one is confident that the items are *aino ben yomo*]. But what about when someone comes to a hotel or Airbnb and wants to *kasher* the microwave or other utensils so they can use them? There is no reasonable way to determine if someone used the microwave etc., within the past 24 hours. Can the person *kasher* right away or must they wait till they can be sure the utensils are *aino ben yomo*?

Seemingly, we can be lenient based on the *Shach* cited above. He explained that the reason one may not rely on סתם כלים *l'chatchilah* is because doing so conflicts with the גזירה אינו בן יומו אטו בן יומו. However, that גזירה is only applicable for someone who wants to use the utensil for food preparation or similar uses, but it does not apply when *kashering*. Actually, as noted, we specifically rely on *aino ben yomo* when we choose to *kasher*. If so, when deciding if one can *kasher*, the principle of סתם כלים will apply, and therefore the person should be allowed to *kasher* the microwave in their hotel room right away.[9]

I shared these points with Rav Binyomin Weiss, and he showed me that *Zivchei Tzedek*[10] addresses this very question; although he does not use the logic noted above, he cites a proof from *Issur V'Heter*[11] that one can be lenient. Rav Weiss explained reasons why some might disagree with this (based on explanations that disagree with *Shach* noted above) but deferred to these *Poskim* who allowed it.

---

[8] See *Imrei Dovid, Kashering*, Chapter 58.
[9] We can come to the same conclusion from a different angle. *Pri Megadim* (SD 110 כללי ספק ספיקא המחודשים #7) says that there is a general rule that one may not deliberately choose to create a *sfek sfekah l'chatchilah* because doing so is a form of *bitul issur l'chatchilah*. When we discussed *bitul issur l'chatchilah* in Chapter 28, we saw that one notable exception is that it does not apply when the person is אין כוונתו לבטל. Seemingly, a person who is *kashering* qualifies as אין כוונתו לבטל because (a) his goal is to remove *ta'am* from the utensil rather than to somehow use it, and (b) any *ta'am* which is released goes into the *kashering* water, which will be discarded. Thus, if this is not an example of *bitul issur l'chatchilah*, it would be permitted to choose to create a *sfek sfekah*.
[10] *Zivchei Tzedek* YD 122:17 (and 21). *Zivchei Tzedek* was authored by Rav Abdallah Somech, a leader of the Bagdad Jewish community in the late 1800, who was also the Rebbi of the *Ben Ish Chai*.
[11] *Issur V'heter* 33:12. This is also cited in *Knesses HaGedolah* (*Tur*) 122:30.

Pesach

The principle of סתם כלים clearly does not apply on *Pesach* since we are *machmir* to forbid נותן טעם לפגם and *aino ben yomo* on *Pesach*.[12] That halacha per se only applies when *chametz* (or its *ta'am*) is mixed into food on *Pesach*, but if it occurs before *Pesach* – and even on *Erev Pesach* during the time when *chametz* is forbidden – one can be lenient.[13] Thus, if someone cooks *Pesach* food in a *chametz* pot that had not been used in 24 hours, the status of the food depends on when the cooking happened: if it was before *Pesach*, the food is permitted since the *chametz ta'am* was *aino ben yomo*, but if it was on *Pesach* the food is forbidden since *aino ben yomo* is not a cause for leniency.

The above is true regarding cases where we <u>know</u> that the utensil is *aino ben yomo*. However, *Rema*[14] rules that in a situation where we do not know if it was *ben yomo,* one may not eat that food on *Pesach*, even if the issue arose before *Pesach*. In other words, we cannot rely on סתם כלים אינם בני יומן in this case. Three possible reasons are given for this *chumrah*, and *Mishnah Berurah*[15] accepts the strictest of them, which is offered by *Magen Avraham*.[16] [The explanation of *Pri Chadash* will be noted in the coming section].[17] He says that since there is no clear *Gemara* source for the halacha of סתם כלים and there are even some *Rishonim* who do not accept it at all,[18] for *Pesach* we are *machmir* not to rely on it.

This has significant implications for situations when people mistakenly use a *chametz* utensil when preparing *Pesach* food (before *Pesach*). If they know that the utensil is *aino ben yomo*, the food is *b'dieved* still acceptable

---

[12] *Rema* OC 447:10.
[13] This is because the *chumros* regarding *bitul* of *chametz* do not begin until *Pesach* actually begins; see *Shulchan Aruch* OC 447:1-2.
[14] *Rema* OC 447:5.
[15] *Mishnah Berurah* 447:58.
[16] *Magen Avraham* 447:22 and *Gr"a* ad loc. ד"ה שהם.
[17] The third explanation is given by *Taz* OC 447:10. He cites *Darchei Moshe* YD 122:2, who says that some are *machmir* never to assume סתם כלים when the utensil is owned by a Jew. Since, for the Jew, we have a simple option to ask whether it was used for non-kosher during the previous 24 hours, and he is "fined/punished" (that the food is considered non-kosher) if he cannot remember. *Taz* says that although we generally reject this idea, *Rema* (in OC 447:5) is teaching that we should accept it for *Pesach*. People are particularly careful about avoiding *chametz* when preparing *Pesach* food, and any Jew who does not know the *chametz* status of a given utensil deserves to be penalized if he uses it with *Pesach* food. Thus, *Taz* is similar to *Magen Avraham* in that he sees *Rema's* ruling as specific to *Pesach*, but is more limited in that he says it only applies to a Jew's utensil and only for the <u>owner</u> of the utensil, and not to other people (see *Pri Megadim* to *Taz*).
[18] See footnote 4.

for use on *Pesach*. But if they do not know, the food is forbidden. [In some cases, there may be other considerations to permit the food].[19]

Factories

Previously, we saw that *Magen Avraham* understands that *Rema* is specifically *machmir* about סתם כלים as relates to *Pesach*. *Pri Chadash*[20] understands differently, that *Rema* is only *machmir* because he was discussing a specific type of pot (a מחבת) which is used so often (תשמישו תמיד) that it is inappropriate to assume it was אינו בן יומו.[21] Thus, *Rema's* ruling is not specific to *Pesach* and would apply equally if kosher food had been cooked in a non-kosher מחבת.

However, *Rema* gives no indication that there is something special about the מחבת he happens to be discussing, and the other *Poskim* do not understand *Rema* this way. But the point which *Pri Chadash* makes – that we cannot apply the principle of סתם כלים for a utensil which is תשמישו תמיד – is based on *Ran*,[22] and *Ran* is also cited in *Beis Yosef* in explaining the sources for סתם כלים אינם בני יומן.[23] Thus, the point which *Pri Chadash* makes remains valid, that in a situation where a given utensil is used frequently,

---

[19] For example, if the person used a *chametz* spoon to stir a pot of *Pesach* food, and they are sure that most of their *chametz* spoons are *aino ben yomo* from *chametz* use but are unsure whether all of them are. We cannot apply סתם כלים אינם בני יומן, since the issue is *chametz* (as per the text), but nonetheless we can assume that any *ben yomo* spoons are *batel b'rov* in the spoons which are *aino ben yomo* (or alternatively, that כל דפריש מרובא פריש allows us to assume that the person took an *aino ben yomo* spoon) and thereby permit the food for *Pesach* use. [See Chapters 61 and the end of Chapter 63 for details on if/when it is appropriate to rely on *bitul b'rov* of יבש ביבש and כל דפריש as relates to *chametz*].
[20] *Pri Chadash* to *Rema* OC 447:5.
[21] In other words, although there are still two legitimate *sfekos* – maybe it is *aino ben yomo* and maybe it is לפגם טעם נותן – the primary *safek* is that it is *aino ben yomo* as evidenced by the fact that this is referred to as סתם כלים אינם בני יומן rather than as "permitted based on *sfek sfekah*". Therefore, if the possibility of its being *aino ben yomo* is truly weak, the leniency does not apply. See also *Shach* 110, Rules of *Sfek Sfekah* #12, cited in *Rebbi Akiva Eiger's* gloss to *Shach* 122:4, who explains why the rules of *sfek sfekah* dictate that the primary *safek* must be the possibility that the item is *aino ben yomo*.
[22] *Ran*, *Avodah Zara* 14a.
[23] As noted at the beginning of the chapter, there is no *Gemara* which explicitly states the principle of סתם כלים אינם בני יומן, but rather it is deduced from many *Gemaros* that appear to be based on that idea. After citing many of those proofs, *Beis Yosef* (YD 122:6) considers that there is one *Gemara* (*Chullin* 8b) regarding non-kosher knives which implies that we do not say סתם כלים אינם בני יומן. To answer that question, he cites *Ran* who suggests that knives are תשמישו תדיר and that is why סתם כלים does not apply. *Ran* and *Beis Yosef* reject that answer, based on an alternate source which indicates that even knives can have סתם כלים (thus, it is not a feature of "knives" which negates the possibility of סתם כלים), but do not retract the idea that if a utensil is תשמישו תדיר then סתם כלים does not apply.
It is noteworthy that *Rosh* (*Avodah Zara* 2:35) says that סתם כלים applies even though the non-Jews likely use their utensils every day (ואע"ג דמסתמא העובד כוכבים משתמשים בכליהם בכל יום אפ"ה שרינן לנו משום ספיקא ספק דהוה). Although [*Tur* and] *Beis Yosef* references other parts of this *Rosh*, these words are not cited.

we cannot apply the principle of סתם כלים אינם בני יומן. For example, a person is given a baked apple made in a non-kosher restaurant; no ingredients were added to the apple, and there is no concern of *bishul akum* for apples (since they are edible raw), but the apple was baked in the restaurant's oven which is continuously used for baking non-kosher meat and poultry. The principle of סתם כלים אינם בני יומן does not apply in this case because the oven is תשמישו תמיד for non-kosher food, and it is unreasonable to assume that the oven was *aino ben yomo* when it was used to bake the apple.

However, it is not as clear that the same conclusion should apply to food made in an industrial factory. It is true that factories are תשמישו תמיד, and typically use every piece of equipment for many hours each day – and sometimes even 24 hours a day and 7 days a week. But at the same time, factories make many products, and it might well be reasonable to consider that their סתם כלים are *aino ben yomo* from non-kosher use. For example, if a kosher commercial bakery produces some pastries that contain dairy and others whose ingredients are all pareve. The company does not *kasher* between batches, and therefore all the products are labeled as "dairy". It is very unlikely that the dairy-free pastries were produced when the ovens had been idle for 24 hours (which likely only happens over the weekend, if at all). But it is very possible that they were baked when the oven was *aino ben yomo* from dairy production. Thus, one could argue that the principle of סתם כלים remains applicable even though the equipment is תשמישו תמיד in the literal sense. This issue requires further consideration. [Other reasons to be lenient are noted in the footnote].[24]

---

[24] The text considered being lenient for *b'lios* from the non-kosher or dairy equipment based on סתם כלים, but there are also other factors, including the following: (a) industrial batches of product are so large that any *ta'am* coming out of the equipment is likely *batel b'shishim* (see Chapter 20), (b) even if there is enough *ta'am* to forbid an entire batch, the "non-kosher" batch may well be *batel b'rov* in subsequent batches (see below in Chapter 61), (c) occasionally, the leniency of נ"ט בר נ"ט is relevant (see Chapter 11), and (d) in certain cases there is an added *safek* whether the food is made on shared equipment altogether.

Chapter 43

Coatings

שולחן ערוך סימן ק"ג סעיף ה

כל קדרה שאינה בת יומא חשיבה טעמה לפגם ואינה
אוסרת. ונקראת בת יומא כל זמן שלא שהתה מעת
לעת אחר שנתבשל בה האיסור, וכיון שעבר עליה מעת
לעת אחר שנתבשל בה האיסור אינה נקראת בת יומא.
ואם בישל בה כשאינה בת יומא התבשיל מותר דהוי
נותן טעם לפגם, והוא שתהיה מודחת שלא יהא שומן
על פניה שאם לא הדיחה אוסר והרי היא כחתיכת
איסור שלא נפגמה, ויש מתירין אפילו בישל בה קודם
שהדיחה. הגה: ואם יש ס' נגד מה שדבוק עליו לכולי עלמא שרי
מאחר דהקדירה אינה בת יומא, והכי נהוג.

This chapter will discuss the *kashrus* implications of the modern practice for producers to put imperceptible or barely noticeable coatings on kitchen utensils, foods, and pills. Those coatings tend to be made of fat or oil, or their derivatives, and that raises potential *kashrus* concerns.

Pots and Pans

The process of producing pots, pans (including disposable pans), and aluminum foil, involves rolling, pressing, scraping, buffing, and polishing. For example, after molten aluminum is cast, it is rolled repeatedly to attain the desired thickness, then it is pressed/stamped to form it into the shape of a pot or pan, rough edges are scraped off, after which it might be buffed and polished so that it shines. In many cases, the heat and friction which those processes generate would be damaging to the machinery or the metal, and therefore a lubricant is applied. In general, lubricants are made from oily substances, such as fat or wax, and it is not unusual for some of the ingredients to be non-kosher. In this section we will consider if that poses a concern for kosher consumers: can they use new pots and pans as-is, or must they *kasher* them beforehand? [Pre-seasoned cast iron pans have somewhat different issues and will be discussed separately below].

~ **Residue**

In the current halacha,[1] *Shulchan Aruch* discusses how to know when a utensil is *aino ben yomo* so that any *b'lios* are נותן טעם לפגם and permitted (*b'dieved*). One point he makes is that the generally accepted opinion is[2] that *aino ben yomo* only applies to <u>absorbed</u> *ta'am*, but not to residue that adheres to a utensil. Thus, an important issue we must consider is whether coatings applied by pot manufacturers are considered "residue" (for which *aino ben yomo* does not apply), or just absorbed *ta'am*.

The simple understanding seems to be that when the average consumer considers a pot or pan to be clean and free of oil, etc., any tiny bits of coating that remain are considered "absorbed" rather than "residue".[3] This is borne out in the *Poskim* (noted below) who present different arguments regarding the status and *kashering* method of pots smeared with oil, etc., by their manufacturers, and all seem to implicitly assume that the oil etc., is absorbed. We once discussed this question with Rav Schwartz regarding a pre-seasoned cast iron pan where the manufacturer not only greased it with oil, but also gave specific instructions not to wash it with soap in a manner that would remove the seasoning. Rav Schwartz rubbed his hand on the pan and was unable to feel any grease or oil, and based on that he ruled the seasoning had the lenient status of an absorbed *ta'am*.[4] Thus, even in this case, where the manufacturer specifically wants

---

[1] *Shulchan Aruch* 103:5.
[2] This is the first opinion cited in the current halacha and is cited without dissent in *Shulchan Aruch* 96:1 and 122:3; this position is also accepted by *Taz* 103:8, *Shach* 103:15, and many others.
[3] One indication for this assumption comes from the *Rishonim* which *Beis Yosef* (both in 103:5 and 122:3) cites regarding *aino ben yomo* for residue, who discuss the meaning of the word הדיח (washed) as used in a specific *Gemara* (*Avodah Zara* 75b). If it refers to a non-kosher pot being washed, then any non-kosher residue is considered "absorbed" and suitable to become *aino ben yomo* according to all. The implication is that standard "washing" qualifies, and anything remaining is considered an absorbed *b'liah*.
  Even if one were to consider this to be "residue" (rather than a *b'liah*), see (a) *Tuv Ta'am Vada'as* 1:182 (based on *Taz* YD 10:6) that all agree that certain very tiny residues become נותן טעם לפגם, and (b) *Minchas Yitzchok* 4:112 (Points 2-4) that even residue is נותן טעם לפגם after an extended time.
  In this context, it is noteworthy that American law (21CFR178.3910) provides a list of ingredients which can be included in lubricants that will be used for metal which will have food contact. The ingredients are divided into two groups, depending on what they will be used for. Group A is lubricants used for rolling metals, and the maximum amount of residue allowed is 0.015 mm per square inch. [For comparison, an average onion skin is about 5 times thicker, at about 0.08 mm thick]. Group B is lubricants used for stamping metal, and those can legally leave a residue which is as much as 0.2 mm thick per square inch, but people in the industry say that it is typically just 0.03-0.07 mm thick. [For comparison, standard copy paper (i.e., 20 lb. paper) is 0.1 mm thick].
[4] Rav Schwartz explained that when *Poskim* speak of *ta'am* being absorbed "in" the walls of a utensil, that includes anything undetectable that remains with/on the utensil. Therefore, it includes the grease that a person knows is there but cannot feel. For more on this, see *Imrei Dovid*, *Kashering*, Chapter 2.

some trace of the oil to remain with the pan, the fact that the seasoning is basically undetectable to the average person, gives it a status of a *b'liah* rather than tangible residue. This understanding will be the foundation of certain leniencies regarding these pots and pans.

~ Always aino ben yomo

The coating is put onto the pot or pan in the factory, which means that it will be *aino ben yomo* by the time a consumer uses it. In Chapter 41 we saw that although *aino ben yomo* is permitted *b'dieved*, the גזירה אינו בן יומו אטו בן יומו dictates that *l'chatchilah* one may not use a utensil which is *aino ben yomo* from a non-kosher *ta'am*. Earlier *Poskim* who discussed coatings on utensils seem to have assumed that the same applies in these types of cases, as is perfectly logical.

However, Rav Moshe Feinstein is quoted[5] as saying that גזירה אינו בן יומו אטו בן יומו only applies when it is at all possible that someone might use the utensil while it is still *ben yomo*. To avoid that mistake, you cannot use the utensil even when it is *aino ben yomo*. But in cases like ours, where it is impossible for a consumer to get the pot while it is still *ben yomo*, *Chazal* never forbade its use when it is *aino ben yomo*. According to this line of reasoning, regardless of what type of coating was put onto the pot, the pot is permitted and no *kashering* is required.

This is a novel understanding of גזירה אינו בן יומו אטו בן יומו and, as noted, those who directly discuss the question of non-kosher coatings on pans, etc., do not seem to agree with it. However, it is noteworthy that Rabbi Moshe Kaufman showed that Rav Moshe's line of reasoning can be inferred from *Shach* and *Gr"a*[6] in their discussions of a similar halacha, גזירה מין במינו אטו מין בשאינו מינו. [*Mid'oraisah*, מין במינו is *batel b'rov* since the *issur* does not affect the *heter's ta'am*, but *mid'rabannan* it must have *bitul b'shishim* to avoid confusing מין במינו with מין בשאינו מינו (where *bitul b'shishim* is required *mid'oraisah*)]. As relates to that, *Rema*[7] says that if a non-kosher utensil was dunked into two <u>different</u> pots of kosher food (one after the other), each pot must have enough *heter* in it to be *mevatel* the *b'lios*

---

[5] *Oholei Yeshurun*, Volume 1 Chapter 4 footnote 2 (who also cites many who implicitly disagree). Rav Fuerst says that he heard the same ruling from Rav Moshe, and Rabbi Moshe Kaufman (married to a great-granddaughter of Rav Moshe, and editor of many of the volumes of דברות משה printed posthumously) says that Rav Moshe's position on this matter is well known in the Feinstein family.
[6] *Gr"a* 98:20 and 94:9, referencing and explaining *Shach* 94:5.
[7] *Rema* 98:4 and 94:2.

b'shishim. But if the non-kosher utensil was dunked twice into the same pot, a second *bitul b'shishim* is not required. *Gr"a*[8] explains:

והטעם דהא אותו הבלוע הוי בקדירה מין במינו ובכה"ג אוקמוה אדאורייתא ברובא וכמ"ש הרא"ש בפרק ג"ה דמין במינו בס' גזירה אטו שאינו מינו משא"כ בכה"ג דליכא למיגזר דא"א באותו קדירה אלא במינו

In other words, since it is impossible to have מין בשאינו מינו in this situation (because the utensil is going back into the same pot again), there is no גזירה מין במינו אטו מין בשאינו מינו. This is similar to the idea Rav Moshe is saying – when it is impossible to use the non-kosher utensil as a *ben yomo*, there is no גזירה אינו בן יומו אטו בן יומו.[9]

Those who follow this approach would never be concerned about non-kosher coatings which manufacturers put onto pots, pans (or appliances). However, most do not subscribe to this novel way of thinking and therefore consider other reasons to be lenient.

~ עשוי להשתמש בשפע

In Chapter 29 we discussed the concept of כלי שעשוי להשתמש בו בשפע, a utensil which absorbed a small amount of non-kosher where we are confident that regardless of how the utensil is used, the *b'liah* will be *batel b'shishim* into the kosher food it is used with. There we saw that *Shulchan Aruch* accepts the view that such utensils can be used without *kashering*, but several *Acharonim* argued that one can only be lenient if the non-kosher will also be נותן טעם לפגם into the kosher food. Lastly, we considered whether those *Acharonim* would be lenient if the "פגם" were created as a result of the utensil being *aino ben yomo* and concluded with the lenient position of *Iggeros Moshe*, that מנהג מורי הוראה להתיר בשפע היתר דוקא לאחר מעת לעת.

The case we are discussing at present seems to be a perfect example of that halacha. There is so little coating used that any residue and *b'liah* will surely be *batel b'shishim* in the food cooked in that pot or pan; therefore, it qualifies as עשוי להשתמש בשפע. If one follows the approach of *Iggeros*

---

[8] This quote is from *Gr"a* 98:20.
[9] Rav Usher Anshel Eckstein directed me to *Rashba* (*Mishmeres HaBayis* 4:4 page 36a, cited in *Pri Megadim* OC AA 451:1 and YD SD 93:3) who says that as relates to *b'lios* of *chametz* after *Pesach* there is no גזירה אינו בן יומו אטו בן יומו since the *issur* of *chametz* is "finished" and there is no way to have that *issur* be *ben yomo* at this point. *Rashba* notes that his line of reasoning is specific to the unusual *issur* of *chametz* which does not apply anymore once *Pesach* ends, thus this is an *issur* which can never be *ben yomo* (anymore). Rav Moshe is extending this to include cases where the situation that raised the concern (a coating put on at the factory) will never apply as a *ben yomo*.

Moshe to be lenient for עשוי להשתמש בשפע when the item is *aino ben yomo*, that is another reason to permit the pot and pans regardless of the lubricants or coatings that might have been used during manufacture. Similar points are made by several *Poskim*,[10] and the fact that the grease is surely *batel* was confirmed by Rav Belsky through carefully measuring and testing the lubricants and pans at a specific pot manufacturing facility.[11]

~ אין כוונתו לבטל

Minchas Yitzchok[12] says that the minimal amount of *issur* is yet another reason to be lenient. Generally, it would be forbidden to allow even a tiny amount of *issur* to become mixed into kosher food (i.e., אין מבטלין איסור לכתחלה, see Chapter 28), but this case is an exception because the *issur*/coating was used in creating the pot rather than as an ingredient added to the food. He bases this on *Rivash*,[13] who says that such cases automatically qualify as אין כוונתו לבטל, since the *issur's* presence is not even remotely connected to the creation of the food. The *issur* was needed to create the pot/barrel; that means it is a step away from the food and therefore it is not a violation of אין מבטלין if some of it gets mixed into the kosher food.

Minchas Yitzchok notes that *Rivash* presents two reasons for leniency in the case he was addressing, and *Rema*[14] only cites the <u>other</u> reason, not this one. Nonetheless, *Minchas Yitzchok* says that this is a legitimate reason to be lenient and ignore the coating left on the pot or pan.[15]

~ **Other possible factors**
The above reasons will all seemingly apply for every standard pot or pan where there might be a non-kosher coating on it. [This does not include

---

[10] *Tuv Ta'am Vada'as* 1:182 suggests relying on עשוי להשתמש בשפע and also says that those who are *machmir* on that issue would agree in his case where there was no possibility of non-kosher *b'lios*, and the only concern was residue <u>on</u> the utensil. *Minchas Yitzchok* 4:112 Point 11 says that all agree that in this case one can rely on עשויה למשתמש בשפע because the person has no interest (and possibly even no knowledge) in the coating getting into his food, and therefore it qualifies as אין כוונתו לבטל. See Chapter 28 Point 16 where we cite *Poskim* who question such an approach. [Also see the coming text where we discuss other considerations related to אין כוונתו לבטל].
[11] See *Imrei Dovid, Kashering*, Chapter 2.
[12] *Minchas Yitzchok* 4:112 Point 9.
[13] *Rivash* 349.
[14] *Rema* 121:1.
[15] *Minchas Yitzchok* ibid. also suggests two alternate reasons why אין מבטלין איסור לכתחלה does not apply in this case: Firstly (Point 8), in the case he was addressing, the *issur* was inedible (see the coming text), and secondly (Point 11), אין מבטלין does not apply in cases where it is also a כלי שעשוי להשתמש בשפע (see footnote 10).

pre-seasoned cast iron pans; see below]. The following are other reasons to be lenient which might apply in some cases:

- The coatings are often inedible or נותן טעם לפגם due to the base oil (commonly made of kerosene or hexane) and/or the additives.[16]

- Some of the non-kosher additives may be functional but are אין בו טעם כלל, and we saw in Chapter 39 that ingredients like that cannot affect the status of kosher food or utensils.[17]

- It takes many steps to produce a pot or pan, and it is necessary (for annealing or other purposes) to heat the metal at different stages of that process. The heating typically qualifies as a *kashering*, which means that non-kosher lubricants, etc., applied before that point do not pose a *kashrus* concern for the end consumer.[18]

ଓଃ ଃଠ

If one were to disagree with any of the points noted above and choose to *kasher* the pans before using them, the proper method of *kashering* is *hag'alah* (or *libun kal* if that is easier). The rationale for this is explained in *Imrei Dovid*, *Kashering*, Chapter 2.[19]

Pre-seasoned cast iron pans

The previous section discussed lubricants and coatings put onto pots and pans as part of the manufacturing process. A related, but different, concern applies to traditional cast iron pans and skillets, which must be "seasoned" to prevent them from rusting and to give them non-stick properties. [This does not apply to ceramic/enameled cast iron, which has a separate coating on the cast iron]. Seasoning involves coating the metal with oil, fat, or butter, and then heating them in an oven for a few hours. Most consumers would rather avoid the hassle of seasoning their own pans and therefore purchase cast iron cookware that is "pre-seasoned" by the factory.

As above, the oil might be non-kosher and that raises the same *kashrus* concern. We have also seen that the seasoning is considered "absorbed" in the pan, rather than residue on its surface. Those who accept the ruling

---

[16] *Yabeah Omer* YD 6:10 (points 1-2) and *Minchas Yitzchok* ibid. Points 6-7. Rav Belsky (see *Imrei Dovid*, *Kashering*, Chapter 2) tasted the lubricant at one plant and confirmed this assumption.
[17] *Minchas Yitzchok* ibid. Point 6.
[18] *Minchas Yitzchok* ibid. Point 10 and Rav Belsky ibid.
[19] See also *Chazon Ish* OC 119:19 and *Har Tzvi* YD 110.

of Rav Moshe that there is no גזירה אינו בן יומו אטו בן יומו when the utensil will always be *aino ben yomo* by the time the consumer receives the pan, can be lenient about pre-seasoned cast iron pans and use them without *kashering*. However, the other reasons suggested for being lenient regarding standard pans, do not appear to apply to cast iron pans, as follows:

In the previous section the concern was lubricants added during processing. By their nature, these are not intended to remain in/on the metal when the consumer gets them, do not have to be edible, and are just there as a processing aid for the construction of the pot, etc. For that reason, we are confident that (a) this qualifies as an עשוי להשתמש בשפע, (b) the use as a processing aid provides a basis for assuming it is אין כוונתו לבטל, and (c) it is possible the heating/annealing will even *kasher* the pot. Additionally, the lubricant might be inedible or אין בו טעם כלל. In contrast, cast-iron pans are seasoned with edible food oils and fats which are surely intended to remain on/in the pan, and therefore the aforementioned reasons to be lenient will seemingly not apply.

For this reason, although many are lenient to permit using most new pots and pans without *kashering*, pre-seasoned cast iron pans require *hag'alah* (or *libun kal*, as above) before using them for the first time.

Styrofoam cups

Polystyrene, commonly known by the Styrofoam brand name, is used to create insulated cups and certain other containers and plates.[20] [For simplicity's sake, we will use the example of cups, but the same principles apply to other items made from Styrofoam]. It is produced by taking thousands of tiny "beads" of polystyrene filled with a volatile chemical (e.g., butane or pentane) and pouring them into a cup-shaped mold. The beads are then heated so that the chemical expands, puffing up the beads, and the beads fuse together. None of these components are kosher sensitive.

The *kashrus* concern is that in order to help get the finished cup out of the mold, manufacturers sprinkle a dusting of zinc stearate onto the beads before they are put into the mold. The largest manufacturer of these cups,

---

[20] Another use of Styrofoam is as "packing peanuts", and in recent years companies have created biodegradable packing peanuts (not made of Styrofoam) which present a possible *chametz* issue which is beyond the scope of this work.

Dart, says that the stearate portion of that molecule is made from animal fat (i.e., non-kosher), and that they have tried using vegetable-based zinc stearate (i.e., kosher), but it did not work satisfactorily. Thus, we are sure the powder is not kosher, and the question is if that means one cannot use Styrofoam cups.

There are several reasons to be lenient, most of which will be familiar from previous discussions in this chapter.

Firstly, there is just 1-2 pounds of zinc stearate for each 1,000 pounds of polystyrene, which means that the amount of zinc stearate in every cup is so miniscule that it is surely *batel* in any beverage that will be put into the cup. Thus, the three main reasons to be lenient regarding coatings on pots and pans – always *aino ben yomo*, עשוי להשתמש, and אין כוונתו לבטל [21]– also apply to Styrofoam cups.

Secondly, the melting point of zinc stearate is 266° F, and the molding process is often done at temperatures that are even higher (e.g., 280° F), which means that the zinc stearate likely melts and is chemically blended with the polystyrene. As a result, it adopts the inedible taste of the polystyrene and cannot affect the kosher status of anything else.[22]

Lastly, several Rabbis involved in *hashgachah* have tasted kosher varieties of zinc stearate and found that it is אין בו טעם כלל, which means, as we saw in Chapter 39, that it cannot affect the kosher status of other foods or *keilim*.

Fruits and vegetables

To maintain the moisture and improve the appearance of certain fruits and vegetables (e.g., apples, bell peppers, cucumbers, peaches, and tomatoes), a coating might be applied to them before they are shipped to the store.

---

[21] In this context, Rav Schachter suggested that the undetectable tiny bit of zinc stearate left on the beads might qualify as a utensil which was cleaned כדרך המכבדים, where it automatically qualifies as אין כוונתו לבטל; see *Imrei Dovid, Kashering*, Chapter 42.

[22] It was reported that when hot tea was put into a Styrofoam cup, there was a noticeable oily substance floating on the top. The person noticing this suspected this oily substance was the zinc stearate migrating into the tea, which would rate serious *kashrus* questions. However, as we have seen in the text (a) there is so little zinc stearate that there is no way it could be noticeable in the tea, and (b) the melting point of zinc stearate is much higher than any tea, and therefore it is basically impossible for it to melt and transfer into the tea. Rav Belsky suggested that the oily film was natural oils present in tea (or coffee) and would be seen regardless of which type of cup was used.

The functional part of the coating is a wax – typically carnauba wax or shellac – which is inherently kosher.[23] However, these waxes are solid at room temperature, and the only way to apply them onto produce is to first dilute them in water so that they can be sprayed on. In turn, that necessitates adding two other ingredients: alcohol, which will hasten the process of evaporating the water off the fruit (after the wax is applied), and an emulsifier so that the wax (which is not water soluble) can be mixed into the water.[24]

Generally, the alcohol used is isopropyl alcohol, which is not kosher-sensitive. However, there are those who use ethyl alcohol, which is typically *kitnios*, might be *chametz*, and on rare occasions can even be non-kosher. The emulsifier is even more sensitive, since it usually includes fatty acid components which can come from animal fat (and may also contain other components which are *chametz*-based). There are two other factors which make the emulsifier a more serious concern: firstly, the emulsifier serves as a *davar hama'amid* (since it allows the wax and water to remain in solution) and a *davar hama'amid* cannot be *batel*;[25] secondly, the emulsifier does not evaporate and will remain on the fruit.

> Since the emulsifier is the more serious concern, we will focus on that one; the logic presented for leniency applies equally to the alcohol and any other additives.

A first thought is that even if the wax is not kosher, one may eat the coated fruits and vegetables since the fruit surely has 60 times the volume of the wax,[26] and the wax is therefore *batel b'shishim*. However, the fault with this idea is the general principle that if one can remove the *issur* from the *ta'aruvos* they are required to do so and cannot rely on *bitul*.[27] One cannot merely wash off the wax, but the internet has several relatively simple do-

---

[23] Carnauba wax is exuded by the Brazilian palm tree. Shellac is secreted by the lac insects, and although it comes from non-kosher insects, it is generally considered kosher; for more on that, see *Imrei Dovid, Animal Products*, Chapter 11, and *Halachos of Insects*, Chapter 49.

[24] Other ingredients which might be added are (a) plasticizers, which make the coating tougher and also more flexible, and (b) thickeners. Both are potentially kosher-sensitive (fatty acids ("a") and whey ("b")), and the rationales presented in the text for being lenient would apply there as well.

[25] See Chapter 1 regarding *davar hama'amid* and whether it applies to emulsifiers.

[26] For perspective on how little wax there is per fruit, the claim is made that a pound of wax can coat 100,000 apples. While that may be an exaggeration, it gives an idea of how little wax is used per item.

[27] That principle, referred to as אפשר להסירו, was discussed in Chapter 24.

Coatings 451

it-yourself methods of removing it,[28] which means that we would not be entitled to rely on *bitul*.

Rav Belsky proposed a reason to consider the wax coating itself as kosher, even if it contains a non-kosher emulsifier. His logic is based on the fact mentioned earlier, that after the wax solution is sprayed onto the fruit, the water (and alcohol) evaporates. After that happens, the coating is 75-85% wax, with the remainder being the emulsifier and other minor ingredients. Accordingly, Rav Belsky applied a ruling he heard from Rav Yaakov Kaminetzky, that the only time *issur* must be *batel b'shishim* (to become permitted) is when the item in question is a "food" and the principle of טעם כעיקר applies.[29] But when *issur* is part of a non-food item – like wax – *bitul b'rov* suffices, just like with any other *Torah* halacha. Therefore, the emulsifier is *batel b'rov* and the fruit may be consumed. See the footnote for several challenges to this line of reasoning.[30]

---

[28] One that seems simple enough is to put the fruit in a pot of boiling water for 10 seconds, and then rub the fruit with a rough towel or cloth. Shellac and carnauba wax melt at 167° F and 187° F respectively, so putting them into boiling water (i.e., 212° F) will melt and loosen the wax, after which the rough cloth will wipe it off.

[29] Another example of where this ruling applies is for crayons. The main ingredient in crayons tends to be paraffin wax, an innocuous wax, and although some crayons contain kosher-sensitive ingredients such as stearic acid, those minor ingredients are *batel b'rov* in the inedible paraffin. Accordingly, there are no *kashrus* issues with melting crayons in a kosher oven.

[30] One question is that the original ruling of Rav Yaakov Kaminetzky was given regarding toothpaste (see Chapter 19 footnote 22) where we first noted this ruling) which, in his day, was primarily made from calcium carbonate (i.e., chalk), and since that is not an edible food item, Rav Yaakov said that non-kosher glycerin added to it is *batel b'rov* (and *bitul b'shishim* is not required). [Nowadays, calcium carbonate is rarely used in toothpaste]. In that case, the item which was going into the person's mouth was the inedible chalk mixed with some non-kosher glycerin, and the mixture is governed by *bitul b'rov*. That is quite different from our situation, where the person will not be consuming the wax as-is, but rather as part of an apple (or other fruit). The apple is obviously a food item, and the emulsifier-laden wax is becoming attached to and indistinguishable from it. Thus, Rav Belsky is seeing this as a *ta'aruvos* of *issur* into non-food wax, when it would seem more proper to view this as a *ta'aruvos* of *issur* and wax into an edible apple, where *bitul b'shishim* should be required.

Perhaps the answer is that if we insist on strictly seeing this as a *ta'aruvos* with the <u>apple</u>, then we can also leniently see it in the same light, and therefore permit the overall apple since the *issur* is *batel b'shishim*. Earlier in the text we rejected that possibility because one can potentially remove the wax from the fruit, and therefore it should not be treated as a "*ta'aruvos*". We now suggest that one cannot have it "both ways"; either the wax is part of the fruit, in which case it is *batel b'shishim*, or it is not part of the fruit, in which case the *issur* is *batel b'rov* in an inedible, non-food wax. Alternatively, we can suggest that the wax is *batel b'shishim* in the fruit, and one is not required to remove the wax, since were the wax to be removed it would (be an inedible hard wax and) itself be permitted based on Rav Yaakov's line of reasoning! [See a similar line of reasoning in Chapter 24, in the section on orange juice].

Maybe the emulsifier is *batel b'rov* in the inedible wax <u>before</u> it goes onto the fruit? This is incorrect, because at that point the majority of the mixture is edible water and alcohol, and seemingly not eligible

Medicine

It is generally assumed that medicinal tablets are permitted (regardless of what they are made of) since they are inedible.[31] However, there are several questions regarding coatings put on the outside of some pills, as follows:

The most common issue is that of magnesium stearate (and stearic acid), and this is how we addressed that issue in Chapter 24:

> Stearates (e.g., magnesium stearate) are added to medicinal tablets. From a scientific perspective, the stearates are known to migrate to the surface, where they assist the tablets in flowing smoothly through the equipment. But an average consumer cannot see or feel the stearates on the surface, and they cannot be "removed"; therefore, they do not qualify as "אפשר להסירו" and do not pose a *kashrus* concern (assuming they are *batel*, as is typical).

---

for Rav Yaakov's leniency. What about the fact that the wax solution (before it is sprayed on) has an unpleasant taste? Two reasons why this seemingly is not enough reason to be lenient are (a) נותן טעם לפגם seemingly cannot be a factor when the amount sprayed on is so minute that no one can taste it, and (b) we saw in Chapter 38 that when an additive's positive contribution (such as the wax's moisture retention qualities, etc.) outweighs the negative effects of its being נותן טעם לפגם, it is not *batel*.

A different question is that the logic noted in the text is not addressing the fact that the emulsifier is a *ma'amid* of the wax solution. This question was posed to Rav Belsky, and he responded that the emulsifier only serves a role (i.e., as a *ma'amid*) when the wax is in solution, but once the water evaporates and the wax hardens onto the fruit, the emulsifier's mission is complete. Thus, although the emulsifier is a *ma'amid* in the wax solution, it is not a *ma'amid* in the wax coating that is on the fruit, and the *chumrah* associated with *davar hama'amid* is no longer relevant. The question on this is that we saw in Chapter 1 that the classic cases of *davar hama'amid* are rennet which causes part of the milk to curdle into cheese, and yeast which causes grape juice (or other sugar) to ferment into wine (or other alcoholic beverages). In those cases, when the person is considering whether the cheese and wine are kosher, the *ma'amid* has already completed its role: the cheese has formed, and the juice became alcoholic. However, anyone looking at the cheese and wine can see the effect the *ma'amid* had, and since the *ma'amid* played such an important role it cannot be *batel*. The same is true here: the solid wax coating on a fruit can only be accomplished if the wax was first in solution, and that means the emulsifier performed its critical task. Thus, just as the non-kosher *ma'amid* is not *batel* in the cheese or wine, so too it is not *batel* in the wax, even though [in all three cases] there is no longer a need for the *ma'amid*.

Seemingly, a simpler answer to the questions posed to Rav Belsky would have been that when Rav Yaakov Kaminetzky said that *bitul b'shishim* is not required for non-foods, that means that non-foods are only governed by the basic halacha of *bitul b'rov*, and all the stricter requirements we are familiar with regarding food do not apply. Rav Yaakov said it regarding *bitul b'shishim*, but the same can be true about a *davar hama'amid*. Since the wax is a non-food item, *bitul b'rov* suffices even though the *issur*/emulsifier is a *davar hama'amid*. [See Chapter 1 where we discussed a similar issue of whether *davar hama'amid* is relevant for *issurim*, such as *kitnios* and *bishul akum*, which are *batel b'rov*].

The questions raised here on Rav Belsky's line of reasoning require further consideration.

[31] For more on this, see the article on medicine in *Sappirim* 16.

To that we can add that – as noted above regarding zinc stearate (in Styrofoam cups) – several *kashrus* professionals have tasted kosher magnesium stearate and believed it qualifies as אין בו טעם כלל, which would be another reason to ignore its presence.

In other cases, tablets might be coated with shellac, sweetener, or a flavor. As noted earlier, shellac (i.e., confectioner's glaze) is considered kosher from any source. The same is true of sweeteners, but it is noteworthy that some sweeteners are sensitive for *Pesach* since they are likely *kitnios* (and on rare occasions can be *chametz*). Once in a while, a flavor is listed in the ingredient panel of a tablet. Flavors are kosher-sensitive and, therefore, one should consult with a Rabbi about whether the person's medical condition warrants consuming a tablet which has a flavor of unknown status.

For further research

There are several other coating-related issues, most of which are assumed not to pose *kashrus* issues, but it would be worthwhile to review their status and ensure that the assumptions remain accurate. This includes:

- Paper
  The "sizing agents" added to paper as it is formed are assumed to be innocuous, *batel*, and/or inedible. Similarly, it is understood that the coatings put on parchment paper, cupcake holders, paper plates, and other paper products <u>after</u> they are formed (to make them grease resistant) do not pose a *kashrus* or *Pesach* concern, except for Quilon (and similar) coatings which require *hashgachah*.

- Plastic
  Plastic is inherently grease resistant and coatings are not required. However, there are those who have raised concerns that kosher-sensitive ingredients, such as glycerol monostearate, are added to serve as lubricants and release agents for the formed containers, etc. This is similar to the functionality of zinc stearate in Styrofoam cups, noted above, and many of the reasons to be lenient there would apply here as well.

- Appliances
  Oven manufacturers inform consumers that the interior of the appliances are coated with oil to protect the metal during transport, and that this oil will "burn off" during the first use of the

oven. Most assume that the oil used is mineral oil which does not pose a *kashrus* concern, but this is something that is worth clarifying.

- Others
  See *Imrei Dovid, Meat and Poultry*, Chapter 47, for a discussion of powder coating on netting and twine, ink used for marking meat, and possible coatings on artificial casings.

It would be appropriate that these assumptions and issues be investigated to confirm that they remain true and that advances in the industry do not raise new concerns.

Chapter 44

עכבר

שולחן ערוך סימן ק"ד סעיף א

עכברא דדברא נותן טעם לשבח הוא שהרי עולה על שלחן מלכים, אבל עכברא דמתא מספקא לן אם משביח בשכר וחומץ או אם הוא פוגם, ולפיכך אם נפל לשכר או לחומץ בצונן והסירו שלם אם לא שהה בתוכו מעת לעת מותר, אבל אם היה רותח או אפילו צונן ושהה בתוכו מעת לעת, בין שהסירו שלם בין שנחתך לחתיכות דקות ויכול לסננו במסננת בענין שלא ישאר ממנו בתוכו כלום, בין שנימוח בתוכו לגמרי ונעשה כולו משקה ולא נשתייר ממנו שום ממשות, ניתר על ידי שיהא ששים בהיתר כנגד העכבר. ואם נחתך לחתיכות דקות והוא בענין שאינו יכול לסננו כגון שנתערב השכר או החומץ במאכל עב, הכל אסור ואין שם ביטול דחיישינן שמא יפגע בממשו של איסור ולא ירגיש. הגה: ודוקא בשרץ יש לחוש אם נשאר שם שלא יוכל להוציאו אבל בשאר איסורין אין לחוש.

In previous chapters we discussed some of the relevant parts of this halacha (104:1):

- In Chapter 16 we identified the עכברא דדברא and עכברא דמתא, and recorded a *machlokes* between *Rashi* and *Tosfos* which relates to a larger question of whether the principle of מחליא ליה לשבח applies to foul-tasting foods or just to *aino ben yomo* absorbed *ta'am*.

- In Chapter 24 we discussed the principle of אפשר להסירו, that if it is possible to separate the *issur* from the *heter*, one generally cannot rely on *hilchos ta'aruvos* to permit the mixture. That included a fundamental disagreement as to the nature of that principle, and how it affects specific practical examples.

- *Rema's* limitation of this halacha to an עכבר – or other creatures which are part of the שמונה שרצים – is based on his understanding that עכבר is a specialized example of the rule that a בריה cannot be *batel*; see Chapter 30 footnote 3.

Chapter 45

Mitzvah Items

שולחן ערוך סימן ק"ד סעיף ב
אם נפל ליין ושמן או לשאר משקין פוגם בודאי ואין
צריך ס' לבטל פליטתו. הגה: ולפי זה אם נפל לשומן נמי דינא
הכי, ויש מחמירין בשומן ואפילו אם הוא קשה לפנינו, אם שפכו
מדי יום יום שומן בקדירה ויש לספק שמא העכבר היה שם כשעירו
עליו שומן רותח הכל אסור אפילו יש ס' בשומן נגד כל העכבר, ואם
לא עירו עליו או שעירו עליו וידוע שלא היה שם העכבר כשעירו עליו
והשומן בא לפנינו כשהוא קשה וכן נמצא העכבר עליו סגי ליה
בנטילת מקום ולא מחזקינן איסור שמא היה השומן רך כשנפל שם
דכבוש הוי כמבושל, דמותר מכח ספק ספיקא ספק שם נפל שם כשהיה
קשה ואם תמצא לומר כשהיה רך שמא נתקשה קודם שיעור
כבישה. ובמקום שהשומן מאוס לאכול אסור להדליק ג"כ בבית
הכנסת משום הקריבהו נא לפחתך. ובמקום הפסד גדול יש לסמוך
אדברי המקילין.

Rema[1] records that if something fell into oil rendering it repulsive for use in food or for cooking purposes, that oil should not be used for a *mitzvah*, since doing so is not respectful. Furthermore, *Rema* says that the oil should not be used to illuminate a *shul*, and *Pri Megadim*[2] says the same applies to candles/lamps used for *Chanukah*, *Yahrzeit*, or *Shabbos*. In all these cases, the oil would be used for a non-food purpose, where the fact that the oil has an undesirable taste is not relevant; nonetheless, since people would not want to cook with that oil, they also should not use it for a *mitzvah* purpose.

In this context, the *kashrus* of the oil is not particularly relevant,[3] and the criterion is whether the oil is disgusting. Apparently, this halacha is limited to food-grade oils which have become ruined to the point that no one would want to use them for their primary purpose (eating). In that case, it is disrespectful to decide that "it's not good enough for its primary purpose, so I will use it for the *mitzvah*". However, the same does not apply

---

[1] *Rema* 104:2. This halacha can also be found in *Shulchan Aruch* OC 154:12.
[2] *Pri Megadim* MZ 104:4, cited in *Mishnah Berurah* 154:20.
[3] See *Gr"a* 104:10.

to wax candles or paraffin oil, which are made from petroleum. No one would cook with or eat these items, but they are not "ruined" and are just inherently inedible. Thus, there is no lack of reverence for the *mitzvah* when we choose to use them for a *mitzvah* purpose.

This halacha is worth bearing in mind when *hashgachos* are called upon to certify non-food items.[4] In most of these cases, certification deals with the kosher status of the ingredients. We now see that when the item being certified is a candle or oil that will be used for *Chanukah*, *Yahrzeit*, or *Shabbos*, (or some other *mitzvah* purpose), there is an additional requirement that the ingredients not be unpleasant-tasting food items.

---

[4] For more on that topic, including the standards used for that certification, see *Imrei Dovid, Alcoholic Beverages*, Chapter 11 (end).

Chapter 46

Bugs are נותן טעם לפגם

שולחן ערוך סימן ק"ד סעיף ג
דברים המאוסים שנפשו של אדם קצה בהם כנמלים וזבובים ויתושים שכל אדם בודל מהם למיאוסן, אפילו נתערבו בתבשיל ונמחה גופן לתוכו אם ההיתר רבה עליו מותרים. ומכל מקום כל שאפשר לבדוק ולהעביר במסננת בודק ומסנן. (מיהו בחלא ושכר יש לחוש כמו בעכבר).

נפשו של אדם קצה מהם

Yoreh Deah 103 introduced the halachos of נותן טעם לפגם and branched out from there to discuss a common example of that halacha: אינו בן יומו. *Yoreh Deah* 104 continues that topic, with the first two halachos primarily about a specific set of cases the *Gemara*[1] discusses, having to do with a rodent/עכבר that falls into food, and which combination of rodent and food is נותן טעם לפגם.[2] When the *Gemara* discusses the different types of עכבר, it says that the one which is נותן טעם לפגם is revolting and avoided by people (מימאא מאיס ובדילי אינשי מיניה) (but another type is served as a delicacy).

Rashba[3] appears to pick up on the way that the *Gemara* describes the rodent which is נותן טעם לפגם and says that we can use this to identify other creatures that are also נותן טעם לפגם. In one place he says this applies to כל השרצים, and elsewhere he gives זבובים, נמלים, ויתושים (flies, ants, and mosquitoes) as examples. He classifies all these items using almost the exact words as the *Gemara* – דברים המאוסים שנפש האדם קצה בהם...שכל אדם בודל מהם למיאוסן, and says they are considered נותן טעם לפגם and their *ta'am*

---

[1] *Gemara, Avodah Zara* 68b-69a.
[2] Some elements of that *Gemara* were noted (in an ancillary way) in Chapter 16, in the section entitled "מחליא for foods".
[3] *Rashba, Toras HaBayis* 4:1 (*Aruch* page 20b, *Katzar* page 16b).

does not cause a mixture to become forbidden. These rulings are codified in our halacha and in *Yoreh Deah* 107.[4]

However, *Shach*[5] cites many who disagree with this and say that the decision whether a forbidden item is נותן טעם לפגם can only be made by tasting the *issur* or seeing the effect it has on the other foods. The fact that people are revolted by the idea of eating a fly, or some other insect, has nothing to do with whether the *ta'am* they give off is positive or negative. [What about the proof from the *Gemara*? See the footnote].[6] *Shach* favors the strict approach and says that one should be lenient only in cases of *hefsed merubah* or *sha'as hadchak*. However, it appears that the consensus[7] is to follow *Rema*[8] who, after noting the strict opinion, says that the common custom is to be lenient.

> This lenient stance is specific to determining which items are נותן טעם לפגם. But the decision that a food is considered inedible (נפסל מאכילה) to the point that prohibitions associated with it no longer apply, is only made based on <u>taste</u>, i.e., it spoils or becomes putrid to the point that no one can eat it.[9]

---

[4] *Shulchan Aruch* 104:3 and 107:2.
[5] *Shach* 107:7.
[6] Earlier we noted that the *Gemara* uses the term מימאס מאיס ובדילי אינשי מיניה to identify rodents as being נותן טעם לפגם and that this supports the position of *Rashba*. How will *Shach* and others respond to this proof? To answer this, we must look more carefully at the *Gemara*. The *Gemara's* full statement is:
אמר להו רב ששת בעלמא סבר רב נותן טעם לפגם מותר
והכא חידוש הוא דהא מימאס מאיס ובדילי אינשי מיניה ואפילו הכי אסריה רחמנא
הלכך נותן טעם לפגם נמי אסור
Tosfos (ad loc. ד"ה דהא) understands that the critical words (...מימאס מאיס) are connected with the words that <u>follow</u> it, ואפילו הכי אסריה רחמנא, meaning that insects are disgusting, and the *Torah* still forbade them. That indicates that נותן טעם לפגם is not a relevant consideration in this case. The clear implication is that, logically, we might assume that things which are disgusting should <u>not</u> be forbidden. That is consistent with *Rashba's* understanding, and the proof noted in the text.
However, *Rashi* (ad loc. ד"ה דהא) says that the words ...מימאס מאיס are the final part of the *Gemara's* <u>first</u> statement, חידוש הוא דהא מימאס מאיס ובדילי אינשי מיניה. He explains that this means that since people find insects to be disgusting, no one would ever eat one, so it is <u>unnecessary</u> for the *Torah* to forbid it. According to this reading, the term מימאס מאיס offers no proof that something which is disgusting is excluded from *issurim*. Presumably, *Shach* et al. will follow this approach to the words of the *Gemara*.
[7] In addition to *Shulchan Aruch* and *Rema* noted in the text, those who are lenient include *Taz* 84:15, *Minchas Yaakov* 46:28, *Pri Chadash* 84:32 and 107:7, *Pri Megadim* SD 107:7 (although he does say המחמיר תבא עליו ברכה), *Gr"a* 104:11, *Chochmas Adam* 54:14, and *Aruch HaShulchan* 104:15 and 107:14
[8] *Rema* 107:2.
[9] The previous text noted the ruling of *Rashba/Shulchan Aruch* that foods which are מאוס and נפשו של אדם קצה מהם are considered נותן טעם לפגם. How then are we to understand the discussion in the *Gemara* (*Bechoros* 7a, cited in *Shulchan Aruch* 81:1 & 5, see also *Imrei Dovid*, *Animal Products*, Chapter 14) whether urine from different animals is נפסל מאכילה (inedible) and therefore permitted? Is it not obvious that urine is מאוס and נפשו של אדם קצה מהם? This question is even more apparent on *Chazon Ish*

Cricket Powder

In recent years, manufacturers – especially in Europe – have begun adding crickets and other insects[10] into food as a source of protein. Crickets are not kosher, and at first glance one might assume that according to the lenient opinion cited above, their presence in a food would not be a *kashrus* concern. Most people are revolted by the idea of eating crickets, which means that they are נותן טעם לפגם, and as long as there is less than 50% cricket powder in the recipe, the crickets should be *batel* and the food should be kosher *b'dieved*.

But there are several reasons why this is not correct.

From a "halachic" angle, in Chapter 38 we discussed the opinion of *Ran* that when a food is נותן טעם לפגם but the person gains more from its presence than he loses from the negative taste it contributes (הגדיל מדתו), the *issur* is not *batel*. נותן טעם לפגם is only operative when/because the person gets no benefit from the *issur*, but if he benefits because the cricket powder adds protein to the mixture, it is not *batel*.[11] Clearly, the people producing this food believe that the benefit of the protein outweighs any negative association provided by the presence of crickets, otherwise, they would not add it!

That brings us to a more basic point. All the cases which the *Poskim* discuss of an insect being נותן טעם לפגם, are ones where the insects (or rodent)

YD 12:6 who comments on that *Gemara* and stresses that it clearly indicates that even if נפשו של אדם קצה from an item, the only way to decide if it is considered inedible is based on how it tastes. [In other words, someone who does not realize this is urine must taste it so he can give an unbiased assessment of whether it is even passably edible]. *Chazon Ish* is referencing the exact words of our halacha yet noting that the *Gemara* is saying that it is not the appropriate criterion. Is the *Gemara* a proof against *Rashba* and *Shulchan Aruch*?

The apparent answer is that there is a difference between נותן טעם לפגם (our halacha) and נפסל מאכילה (the other *Gemara*). To be considered נותן טעם לפגם, the taste must be "negative", and that can be based on physical criteria (e.g., taste) or emotional reasons (e.g., you find it revolting); regardless of the cause, if the taste is negative, it does not affect other foods. But נפסל מאכילה means that it is not edible, and that is dependent on the "reality" of whether it is possible to eat it or not. In fact, *Chazon Ish* says that passably edible foods are considered "edible". Food which is passably edible is likely "negative", and this highlights the point that the status of נפסל מאכילה is dependent on an objective status and does not depend on how good or desirable the item is for people.

[10] Some of the other insects which are currently legal are "lesser mealworms" and "migratory locust".
[11] There, in Chapter 38, we also saw a discussion whether the *chumrah* of הגדיל מדתו applies to insects.

The points made here in the text may also be relevant to the questions of (certain) homeopathic remedies and royal jelly (a bee product) being *batel* based on the idea that they are נותן טעם לפגם. For more on those items, see *Imrei Dovid, Animal Products*, Chapters 6 (homeopathic remedies) and 24 (with footnote 19) (royal jelly).

were accidentally present in the food. There, it is reasonable to say that since people are revolted by the idea of eating insects, the *issur* is נותן טעם לפגם. But in the case of cricket powder, the manufacturer is deliberately adding it to the recipe, and in amounts where it is not *batel b'shishim* and it (presumably) affects the taste of the food. That is the strongest evidence that people do not consider this to be נותן טעם לפגם and therefore cannot be included in the general leniency noted above.[12]

Moreover, if we probe a bit deeper, we may even have somewhat of a "source" for the proposition that crickets are not נותן טעם לפגם. Crickets have many similarities to grasshoppers,[13] and the *Torah*[14] is quite clear that certain grasshoppers are kosher and quite edible. Americans are not used to eating grasshoppers, but in other cultures this was – and is – common. [In fact, some *Sephardim* (who have a *mesorah* about which grasshoppers are kosher) consider them to be a delicacy, just as the *Gemara* says about certain rodents].[15] Thus, whether a given item is considered revolting and therefore נותן טעם לפגם, is very much a cultural issue. This means that as Europeans (and Americans?) become accustomed to the idea of eating crickets (from seeing more retail products that contain them, and hearing that they have a pleasant nutty taste, provide health benefits, etc.), crickets will slowly joins the list of forbidden foods that are not נותן טעם לפגם.

בריה

One of the common kashrus concerns raised by insects is that they are found in all types of fresh vegetables and some fruits. In almost every case, there are few enough insects that they would be batel b'shishim, and what prevents that bitul is (a) they might not be considered a ta'aruvos since they can be removed from the vegetable, and (b) if they

---

[12] This point is not relevant when the forbidden insect is put in at such tiny proportions that it is *batel b'shishim* and does not contribute *ta'am*. For example, carmine (see Chapters 35 and 38) is made from a forbidden insect, but very little of it is used in finished goods. Thus, the company's choice to add it to a product does not indicate that they do not consider it נותן טעם לפגם. [Nonetheless, as discussed in Chapter 35, it potentially is not *batel* since it is added to provide color/חזותא].

[13] Some of the differences are color (crickets are usually brown/black, while grasshoppers tend to be green), size (about 2 inches long for crickets, and about 4 inches for grasshoppers), and antenna length (longer for crickets). These relatively minor differences highlight that these creatures are actually not so different from one another.

[14] *Vayikra* 11:22.

[15] See also *Yam Shel Shlomo*, *Chullin* 7:49 (referenced in *Shach* ibid.) who says there may be a difference between ants (and other crawling insects) and flies and mosquitos (and other flying insects), as follows:

ומ"מ נ"ל שלא להקל שלא ידעינן איזה שרץ פוגם, על כן אין לנו אלא עכבר והדומה לו מן השרץ השורץ, אבל זבובים ויתושים מנין לנו שפוגמין שהן מין שרץ העוף ואינו מאוס כל כך

are whole, they cannot be batel since they are בריות. Those two issues were discussed in Chapters 24 and 30 respectively. Here we approach the latter issue (בריה) *from a different angle that is related to the negative taste associated with insects* (נותן טעם לפגם).

In Chapter 37 we saw that *Rema*[16] says that the concept of *ta'am* is only relevant for standard *issurim* which are governed by the rules of *bitul b'shishim*. In those cases, if the *issur* is נותן טעם לפגם, it is *batel* even without *shishim*. However, for those situations where the *issur* cannot be *batel* even if there is no *ta'am* – such as בריה, חתיכה הראויה להתכבד, or דבר שבמנין – *ta'am* clearly plays no role, and the mixture is forbidden if the *issur* is נותן טעם לפגם.[17] To this strict position, *Rema* adds one caveat: it is limited to נותן טעם לפגם cases where the *issur* is edible but happens to impart a negative taste into the kosher food. But if the *issur* is inherently disgusting (פגומים בעצמן), this *chumrah* does not apply.

This term "פגומים בעצמן" is somewhat vague. It certainly seems to indicate that the בריה etc. has some sort of intrinsic *pegam*, rather than just contributing a negative taste to the other food. How much of a *pegam* does the בריה have? And why is it different if it is פגום בעצמו or if it is just נותן טעם לפגם? The *Acharonim* have different ways to answer these questions.

Several *Acharonim*[18] understand *Rema* as referring to a בריה which became somewhat *pagum* but remains edible. The reason[19] why that makes a difference is because as soon as the *issur* is not in its finest form, it is no longer so prominent that it cannot be *batel*. Therefore, once it begins to intrinsically degrade, it can be *batel*, in which case נותן טעם לפגם is once again a factor.

Some[20] who take this approach say that there is one case where a minimal *pegam* is <u>not</u> enough to prevent *bitul*, and that is for flies, mosquitoes, and other insects, which are always inedible but yet are not *batel* when they are בריות. These have the strict status of בריה <u>despite</u> their being inedible,

---

[16] *Rema* 103:1 as per *Shach* 103:1.

[17] In Chapter 38 we discussed if and how this idea applies to Nutramigen.

[18] *Chavos Da'as* (*Chiddushim*) 103:3, and *Pri Megadim* MZ 103:2, based on *Taz* ad loc.

[19] See *Taz* ibid., and *Toras Chattas* 85:24.

[20] See *Gr"a* 103:2, who says *Rema* [cannot be referring to insects in their natural state (see below) and] that speaks of פגומים בעצמן means a whole non-kosher bird (i.e., a בריה) which rotted. He is consciously not choosing a case of an insect that spoiled, because he is of the opinion that such a case would not qualify.

and therefore if they spoil a bit, that does not diminish their standing at all. Others[21] argue that we only have a precedent to consider these insects as בריות when they are in their natural state, but once they degrade, we are entitled to remove that בריה status just as we would with any other בריה.

However, *Tzvi L'Tzadik*[22] goes one step beyond both these positions. He notes that *Rema* says that if the בריה is פגום בעצמו then נותן טעם לפגם applies and does not say that it must become פגום בעצמו. This means that any בריה which has an off-taste can be *batel* if it is נותן טעם לפגם – and that includes insects even in their natural state! Insects are inedible and פגומים בעצמן even without any spoilage, and therefore qualify for this leniency. Most *Poskim* disagree with this extension, and one simple reason is – as *Gr"a*[23] points out – that one of *Shulchan Aruch's* examples of a בריה which cannot be *batel* is תולעים, which includes insects that are inherently disgusting and considered inedible. Clearly, the leniency afforded to בריות which are פגומים בעצמן cannot extend to insects in their natural form.

Aruch HaShulchan[24] suggests and defends a position equivalent to *Tzvi L'Tzadik* as a (third) לימוד זכות for those who are not so careful about removing insects from produce before eating. They assume that since the insects are inherently repulsive, they do not have the status of בריות and can be *batel*. For details on that position and why most disagree, see *Imrei Dovid*, *Halachos of Insects*, Chapter 33.[25]

---

[21] *Chavos Da'as* ibid.
[22] *Tzvi L'Tzadik* to *Rema* ibid.
[23] *Gr"a* 103:2 based on *Shulchan Aruch* 100:4. *Gr"a* cites this proof from 100:4 which has the example of תולעים, and – despite his referencing 100:1 just a few words earlier – does not bring a proof from 100:1 where ants (נמלים) are an example of a בריה. Seemingly, ants would have provided a better proof since *Shulchan Aruch* 104:3 specifically notes that ants are disgusting and repulsive. Perhaps this relates to the fact that (as noted earlier in the chapter) some *Poskim* argue that ants etc. are not considered נותן טעם לפגם. [At the same time, there is also disagreement about תולעים being לפגם; see *Taz* 84:15 (who assumes they are), *Pri Chadash* 84:32 (who accepts this opinion, referencing *Toras Chattas* 46:8 supporting it), *Chavos Da'as* (*Chiddushim*) 104:9 (who cites different opinions and seems to accept the lenient position, and *Shach* 84:30 (who says that even those who say ants are לפגם might say that תולעים are not].
[24] *Aruch HaShulchan* 100:18.
[25] One aspect of the disagreement between those who leniently say that an insect is not a בריה (as relates to *bitul*) (*Tzvi L'Tzadik* and *Aruch HaShulchan*) and those who say it is a בריה – at least until it begins to spoil (*Chavos Da'as* et al.) – revolves around how to understand certain phrases in *Issur V'heter* 32:6 (the source of this halacha) and how it is recorded in *Toras Chattas* 85:24. [This is not noted in *Imrei Dovid* referenced in the text]. *Issur V'heter* speaks of a בריה שלימה מוסרחת...כגון נמלה, and in context it appears he is referring to an ant that (a) spoiled or rotted more than its natural

In contrast to these *Acharonim* who say that פגומים בעצמן refers to a בריה which became <u>somewhat</u> *pagum*, *Pri Chadash*[26] says that *Rema* is referring to בריות which became completely inedible. At that point, any *issur* which had applied to the food falls away, in which case *bitul* is obviously no longer required. Thus, according to this approach, בריה is <u>never</u> *batel* regardless of how much it spoils, even if it is נותן טעם לפגם. However, if the *issur* lifts, then there is essentially nothing to become "*batel*", and that is why the food is not affected.

---

repulsiveness, but (b) it is not yet so inedible that it becomes *heter*. Both of those points support the stricter understanding. *Toras Chattas* references *Issur V'heter* but writes it as follows: ...דאפילו בריה...אם הם פגומים בעצמם...הם בטלים שפיר דמאחר שהאיסור פגום בטל חשיבתייהו. The neutral way he describes this (פגומים בעצמם) (which he repeats in *Rema* 103:1) coupled with the explanation he gives (דמאחר שהאיסור פגום בטל חשיבתייהו) seems to include even insects in their natural (repulsive) state. That supports the lenient position. [Between these two phrases there is a parenthetical remark – פירוש שנסרחו ונפגמו אחר מותם קודם שנתערבו – which clearly points to *Toras Chattas* only being lenient if the insect rotted. However, *Pri Megadim* ibid. notes that that comment was added by "*Rav Pesachyah*" in the second edition of *Toras Chattas* (5388/1628) and is not from *Rema* (who died in 5332/1572)].

Aruch HaShulchan also notes that two extreme positions are logical, but not the compromise one suggested by many of those who are strict. One extreme position is that insects are considered בריות until they become completely inedible. The thinking is that the *Torah* forbade them even though they are repulsive, and therefore נותן טעם לפגם is irrelevant. The other extreme position (which he favors) is that their repulsiveness precludes them from having the important status of בריה, even if they are in their natural state. But he finds it hard to understand how becoming a bit <u>more</u> disgusting than they naturally are, can make a difference in their status.

[26] *Pri Chadash* 103:1.

Part H

סימן ק"ה

- **Chapter 47** .... B'liah Without Heat
- **Chapter 48** .... כבוש
- **Chapter 49** .... יד סולדת בו
- **Chapter 50** .... כלי ראשון וכלי שני
- **Chapter 51** .... דבר גוש
- **Chapter 52** .... תתאה גבר
- **Chapter 53** .... ניצוק חיבור
- **Chapter 54** .... מלח

Chapter 47

B'liah Without Heat

שולחן ערוך סימן ק״ה סעיף א
איסור שנשרה עם היתר מעת לעת בצונן מקרי כבוש והרי הוא כמבושל ונאסר כולו, אבל פחות מכאן בהדחה סגי. הגה: וכל מקום דאמרינן כבוש כמבושל אפילו מה שחוץ לכבישה אסור דעל ידי הכבישה שלמטה מפעפע למעלה כמו בבישול, ויש מקילין במה שבחוץ. וספק כבוש מלבד בבשר עם חלב דאזלינן לקולא דמן התורה אינו אסורה רק בבשול ממש.

ואם הוא כבוש בתוך ציר או בתוך חומץ אם שהה כדי שיתננו על האור וירתיח ויתחיל להתבשל הרי הוא כמבושל, ובפחות משיעור זה, לא נאסר אלא כדי קליפה. (ועי״ל סימן ע׳ מדין בשר שנפל לציר).

The general rule is that *ta'am* does not transfer without heat, and in coming chapters we will see more details of exactly which "heat" qualifies. *Yoreh Deah* 105 also notes some ways in which *ta'am* can transfer <u>without</u> heat, and those will also be discussed in the coming chapters.[1] In addition to those transfer methods, we saw in Chapters 14-15 that cutting or grinding certain foods causes some level of transfer (of *ta'am* or just residue) and to undo that necessitates certain steps (e.g., גרירה, שפשוף, נעיצה).

If none of the above apply, then – as stated in the current halacha[2] – all that is necessary is to rinse off the food or equipment. For example, if carrot was cut with a *fleishig* knife or soaked for an hour in a bowl of water together with non-kosher meat, the carrot is nevertheless considered kosher and pareve after it is rinsed to remove any meat that may have stuck onto it.

---

[1] See also *Imrei Dovid, Kashering*, Chapter 51, regarding the special case of a בית שאור and how that relates to using it for *Pesach*.
[2] *Shulchan Aruch* 105:1.

Chapter 48

כבוש

שולחן ערוך סימן ק״ה סעיף א

איסור שנשרה עם היתר מעת לעת בצונן מקרי כבוש והרי הוא כמבושל ונאסר כולו, אבל פחות מכאן בהדחה סגי. הגה: וכל מקום דאמרינן כבוש כמבושל אפילו מה שחוץ לכבישה אסור דעל ידי הכבישה שלמטה מפעפע למעלה כמו בבישול, ויש מקילין במה שבחוץ. וספק כבוש מלבד בבשר עם חלב דאזלינן לקולא דמן התורה אינו אסורה רק בבשול ממש.

ואם הוא כבוש בתוך ציר או בתוך חומץ אם שהה כדי שיתננו על האור וירתיח ויתחיל להתבשל הרי הוא כמבושל, ובפחות משיעור זה, לא נאסר אלא כדי קליפה. (ועי״ל סימן ע׳ מדין בשר שנפל לציר).

The most common way that *ta'am* transfers without heat is through a process known as *kovush* (steeping). The standard form of *kovush* takes 24 hours but there are also situations when it happens much more quickly. These two forms of *kovush* will be discussed below.[1]

Standard Kovush

> *The following text regarding standard kovush is from*
> *Imrei Dovid, Kashering, Chapter 27,*
> *where more details and sources are given*

Kovush is the term used to describe the transfer of *ta'am* which occurs when a liquid – or a mixture of solid and liquid – soaks someplace for some amount of time. [Generally, 24 hours is required; more on that below]. For example, if chicken soup sits in a container for a day, the container is now "*fleishig*" since it absorbed chicken taste from the soup. The halachos of *kovush* are discussed

---

[1] There are two other *kovush*-like processes which take 3 days:
- Raisins that soak in water for 3 days has the status of "wine" as relates to *kiddush* and *stam yayin*. For more on this see *Imrei Dovid, Alcoholic Beverages*, Chapter 34, footnote 17.
- There is a special set of halachos that is specific to wine which was stored in a container for at least 3 days, but not necessarily for 24 consecutive hours. See *Shulchan Aruch* YD 135:9, and briefly in *Imrei Dovid*, ibid. Chapter 48, footnote 12.

primarily in *Yoreh Deah* (*Shulchan Aruch* 105:1). The following are some highlights which have particular relevance to those involved in *hashgachah*:

~ **Liquid**

For purposes of these halachos, *Pri Megadim* defines a "liquid" as אם רך שהאיסור המונח בתוכו מתנענע ממקום למקום, כבוש מיקרי. Accordingly, honey, cream, oil, and liquified fat are considered liquids, but ice, congealed fat, and very thick honey are not.

~ **Movement**

Most assume that *kovush* can occur even if the liquid is moving around within the container. For example, if a tanker truck carries liquid animal fat, *ta'am* of that fat is absorbed into the tanker walls even though the liquid sloshes around within the tanker as it travels on the highway. However, that is true only if the <u>same</u> liquid is in the container for long enough to create *kovush* (and just happens to be moving around). But if different liquids are in contact with the container, there is no *kovush*. That means that if liquid is flowing through a pipe for an extended amount of time, there is no *kovush* since no single unit of liquid is in contact with the pipe for the required amount of time.

A practical example of this is the tanks used to store *chalav Yisroel* milk when it is being bottled at a factory that usually produces *chalav stam*. The storage tanks have absorbed *chalav stam* via *kovush*, and it is logistically very difficult to *kasher* those tanks. It is sometimes possible to process all the *chalav Yisroel* within 24 hours, thereby avoiding issues of its absorbing *ta'am* from the *chalav stam* tank. But if it must remain in the tank for 24 hours, some factories will avoid *kovush* by pumping the milk out of the tank within 24 hours, and then circulating it right back into the tank.

Rav Schachter viewed this process as if the milk circulating back into the tank is "new/different" milk than what was there originally, and therefore *kovush* is prevented.[2] In other words, this is similar to the case of liquid flowing through a

---

[2] According to this understanding, Rav Belsky and Rav Schachter agreed that *kovush* is prevented if <u>most</u> of the milk in the tank is "new" (circulated) before 24 hours have elapsed. How can one tell if most of the milk was circulated? One might think that if the tank holds 6,000 gallons and the pump operates at 50 gallons per minute, it would take 60 minutes to pump 3,000 gallons (50 * 60 = 3,000). But this is not accurate, because after the first 600 gallons of milk are circulated (for example), 10% of the milk being circulated will be "new" milk and only 90% will be the milk which "needs" to be moved.

To calculate how long the milk must be pumped in order to circulate half of the "old" milk, the author turned to Dr. Don Engelberg, Chairman of the Department of Physics at Queensboro Community College. [This occurred when the author worked for OU Kosher]. He created the following formula: **H** = **V** * .7 / **R**, where **H** is the hours of pumping needed, **V** is the initial volume of the tank (in gallons), and **R** is the flow rate of the pump (in gallons per hour).

pipe noted above. Rav Belsky did not accept this argument and said that instead we should view the tank together with the connected pipes and pumps as one large container, and that this case is akin to the tanker noted above: the same liquid is in the (expanded) "container" for 24 hours, and there is a concern of *kovush*. [The common practice in the *chalav Yisroel* industry is to be lenient on this matter].

~ Time

In general, it takes 24 consecutive hours for *kevishah* to occur. An exception to that rule is that if the forbidden liquid is so salty that it is similar to ציר (fish brine), the *ta'am* is absorbed in and out in just a few minutes. The amount of time is codified as כדי שיעמוד על האש וירתיח (*the time it takes to heat it on a fire*); there is some question exactly what that means, and it is generally accepted that it is somewhere between 6 and 18 minutes. Therefore, for example, when cheese is brined in a non-kosher brine tank, the tanks must be *kashered* or lined even if the cheese sits there for less than 24 hours, because *kovush* will happen in a few minutes.

Shulchan Aruch goes one step further and says that the quick-*kovush* of כדי שיעמוד על האש וירתיח also occurs when the liquid is something חריף/sharp, such as vinegar, but *Shach* argues that *kovush* for *charif* takes a full 24 hours. *Magen Avraham* says that one should adopt the strict position of *Shulchan Aruch* and resolves an apparent contradiction within that opinion by suggesting that even the *machmirim* adopt that position only when dealing with "strong vinegar" but would be lenient for "weak vinegar". *Mishnah Berurah* rejects *Magen Avraham* and rules that one can (leniently) assume that *kovush* for vinegar takes 24 hours. That is to say, one can be lenient even in the case of "strong vinegar" (i.e., the case where *Magen Avraham* was *machmir*).

Many American *hashgachos* have adopted this lenient position. Accordingly, the same set of bottling equipment can be used for both kosher and non-kosher vinegar, assuming the vinegar never remains in the equipment for 24 consecutive hours (e.g., it never remains there for a weekend when there is no production). Although the vinegar will invariably remain in the bottling tanks for more than 6-18 minutes, the assumption is that *kovush* takes 24 hours, and therefore *kovush* does not occur.

In general, in cases where *kovush* takes 24 hours to draw a *b'liah* out of a utensil, the status of the kosher food held in that utensil is not affected *b'dieved*, because

---

In our example, V = 6,000 and R = 3,000. If we insert those numbers into the formula, we can calculate that [Step 1] H = 6000 * 0.7 / 3000); [Step 2] H = 4200 / 3000; [Step 3] H = 1.4. This tells us that it will take 1.4 hours (84 minutes) for the majority of the milk in the tank to be "new" (circulated) and avoid *kovush*.

the *ta'am* is *aino ben yomo* by the time it comes out of the utensil. However, if the kosher food is *charif*, then another principle comes into play. Namely, the *charif* food "reinvigorates" the *aino ben yomo b'lios* and renders them "fresh" and once again forbidden (מחליא ליה לשבח).[3] Therefore, if the kosher food is *charif*, *kovush* takes 24 hours – but when that 24 hours is complete, the food is assur even *b'dieved*. [As relates to these halachos, it is irrelevant if the non-kosher products were *charif* or not].

~ **Depth**
When *kovush* occurs, the *ta'am* is generally absorbed through the entire thickness of the utensil. That is to say that if the utensil is a quarter of an inch thick, the entire thickness absorbs *ta'am*, and this must be borne in mind when considering (a) if those *b'lios* are *batel* into a food subsequently cooked in that utensil, and (b) how to *kasher* the utensil. However, the same is not true when only part of the container was *kovush*. In those cases, the part which was *kovush* absorbs fully, but the part which did not have contact with the liquid does not absorb. For example, if a barrel was 80% full of liquid, the other 20% of the barrel does not absorb *ta'am* via *kovush* unless the liquid qualifies as a דבר שמן (*fatty item*).

ଓଃ ଃଠ

~ **Kashering**
As noted, *kovush* generally causes *ta'am* to be absorbed through the entire thickness of the utensil. However, see *Imrei Dovid*, *Kashering*, Chapter 49, that this is not always the case. Briefly:

- *Shach*[4] shows that in four cases – *chametz* before *Pesach*, *stam yayin*, kosher meat, or kosher dairy[5] – we follow a more lenient opinion which states that *kovush* only causes *ta'am* to be absorbed into a thin layer, known as a כדי קליפה.[6]

- In the four lenient cases of *kovush*, the container can be *kashered* using a method known as *milui v'irui* (*filling and emptying*) (see there for details).

- *Milui v'irui* is insufficient to *kasher* a container which was used to hold a forbidden liquid that is not one of the four lenient ones noted above. However, what is required for those containers is not as clear.

---

[3] See *Imrei Dovid*, *Bitul and B'lios*, Chapter 16.
[4] *Shach* YD 135:33.
[5] What about *chalav stam*? See *Imrei Dovid*, *Kashering*, Chapter 49.
[6] For more on this see *Imrei Dovid*, *Alcoholic Beverages*, Chapter 48.

- *Shach* says that the container should be *kashered* with הגעלה גמורה; seemingly this means that it must undergo *hag'alah* at *roschin* temperatures in a *kli rishon*. While this might be practical in a home environment, it poses a particular challenge for commercial tanks designed for cold use only. However, there is reason to consider being lenient based on a combination of the following factors:
    o The tank will never be used for hot product which means that the kosher food stored in this tank will be permitted *b'dieved* since *kovush* takes 24 hours to extract *ta'am* and by that time the tank will be *aino ben yomo*.
    o In most cases, the physical dimensions of a tank dictate that any *ta'am* which leeches from the tank walls into the kosher food will be *batel b'shishim*, and it therefore qualifies as a כלי העשוי להשתמש בשפע (see Chapter 29).
    o The *Acharonim* disagree whether *kovush* can cause any absorption into a metal container.
    o *Pri Megadim*[7] makes two statements which, if combined, give the impression that when *kashering* after *kovush*, one can be satisfied with the water being just *yad soledes bo* (165-175° F).

In summary, tanks used to store non-kosher liquids are oftentimes too weak to undergo a full *kashering* with boiling water, and at first glance it appears that there is no way to *kasher* them if they absorbed via *kovush*. However, we have identified four possible reasons to be lenient and allow their use after doing "as much as one can", which might involve *kashering* with water that is 165-175° F.

For details on these points, see *Imrei Dovid, Kashering*, Chapter 49.

Fast Kovush

The above discussion applies to standard *kovush* which takes 24 hours, and we noted that if the liquid is particularly salty (ציר), *kovush* occurs in 6-18

---

[7] *Pri Megadim* OC MZ 451:9.

minutes. *Pri Megadim*[8] assumes that this concept – that *kovush* can occur more quickly for צִיר – is a *d'oraisah* principle, just like standard *kovush*; accordingly, if there is a *safek* regarding this type of *kovush* one must be *machmir*. However, there is a *machlokes* whether rapid *kevishah* only occurs between foods (in the presence of צִיר) or even causes *ta'am* to transfer into and out of utensils.[9] *Mishnah Berurah*[10] rules that one should follow the strict approach and assume *kovush* of צִיר affects *keilim* in a few minutes (just as with foods), but in cases of *hefsed* one can follow the lenient opinion which says that it takes 24 hours. [This is relevant for cases of *b'dieved*, when mistakes have already happened].

Shulchan Aruch[11] defines the amount of time for fast *kovush* to occur as:

שהה כדי שיתננו על האור וירתיח ויתחיל להתבשל

What is the logic for this amount of time for *kovush*? What are its parameters? This specification is not written in the *Gemara* but is rather taken from *Rosh*,[12] and a more careful reading of that source will shed light on the topic. The *Gemara*[13] says that salting meat after *shechitah* (to remove blood) must be performed in a perforated container (כלי מנוקב) so that the meat does not sit in the (non-kosher) blood that pools on the bottom of a non-perforated container. The *Rosh* adds that the *Geonim* said that if a person violated this requirement the meat is forbidden, but there is a *machlokes* when that applies: some say the meat is only forbidden if it remained in the non-perforated container for the entire *melichah* process

---

[8] *Rema* 105:1 says that if there is a *safek* regarding a standard *kovush* one should be *machmir*, except if the entire concern is that meat and milk were *kovush* together, since (as per *Shulchan Aruch* 87:1) meat and milk mixed together via *kovush* is only *assur mid'rabannan*. *Pri Megadim* MZ 105:1 says that this indicates that all other examples of (standard) *kovush* are a *safek d'oraisah*, and that indicates that the concept of *kovush* is itself a *d'oraisah*. He cites those who consider whether the same is true of the fast *kovush* which occurs with צִיר and concludes that since most *Poskim* do not raise such an issue, implicitly it means that they assume it is also *d'oraisah*.

See *Nodah B'yehudah* YD 1:26 (latter half of the *teshuvah*) who discusses whether *kovush* applies to all foods.

[9] *Pri Megadim* MZ 105:1 shows that many (including *Taz* YD 69:41, *Shach* 69:68, and *Toras Chattas* 85:1) are of the opinion that fast *kovush* of צִיר is only relevant for foods and not for utensils. [In this context, he notes a subtle difference between *Taz* and *Shach* whether this leniency only applies to *ta'am* coming out of the utensil (*Shach*) or if it is bi-directional (*Taz*)]. At the same time, he notes that *Drishah* 69:12 and *Magen Avraham* 447:16 (and *Plaisi* 69:18) argue that the fast *kovush* of צִיר causes *ta'am* to transfer into and out of utensils just as it does between foods.

[10] *Mishnah Berurah* 447:42 based on *Chayei Adam* 121:25 (but see *Chochmas Adam* 57:10, who says one should only be lenient if there is *hefsed merubah*).

[11] *Shulchan Aruch* 105:1.

[12] *Rosh, Chullin* 8:49.

[13] *Gemara, Chullin* 113a.

while *Rabbeinu Tam* says that if the meat was there for any amount of time, it becomes forbidden.

Rosh says that he disagrees with both of these opinions (אני אומר לא כדברי זה ולא כדברי זה) and offers a compromise,[14] based on a statement which the *Gemara* makes a few lines before the one cited above. It says that מליח כרותח וכבוש כמבושל, meaning that כבוש is like a full cooking (כמבושל) where the *ta'am* is absorbed through the entire food. However, מליח/salting is not as strong and is just treated like the foods were hot where the *ta'am* only transfers a bit; for this reason, the *Gemara* says that מליח is just כרותח, in contrast to כבוש which is כמבושל. The same principle applies when salted meat sits in blood in a non-perforated container. If it is there for just a few seconds, then that is "מליח", which only causes a transfer of non-kosher blood into a כדי קליפה of the meat. In order to make the entire piece of meat forbidden, the saltiness must create some sort of *kovush* (so that we can say כבוש כמבושל); this *kovush* happens much more quickly than 24 hours and is defined as:

ושיעור כבישה הוי כאילו נתנו על האור כדי שירתיח ויתחיל לבשל

It appears that he reasons as follows: The *Gemara* teaches that meat touching salty items is treated as if there is some heat (מליח כרותח). That "heat" is created by the salt (or ציר), which means that in a sense we are viewing the salt as if it were fire or some other heat source. It follows that the longer the meat contacts the salt the more the "fire's" heat can penetrate it, and in turn that would allow the *ta'am* to spread deeper and deeper into the meat. Therefore, if the meat is on/in the salt for long enough that had it been on a real fire it would have gotten hot, we will now judge the meat as if it were *kovush*. In a sense, this is like the way standard *kovush* works – after enough time soaking, the liquid penetrates the food or utensil. Here too, after the meat sits on or in the salt/ציר/fire for enough time, the "heat" penetrates the entire meat and *ta'am* transfers through all of it.

Darchei Teshuvah cites discussions in the *Acharonim* on some of the ambiguous points of *Rosh* (cited in *Shulchan Aruch*): in calculating the time

---

[14] *Rosh* does not explicitly state that his position is a compromise between the two *Rishonim* he had cited earlier, but that is the impression one gets from reading *Rosh*. Accordingly, it is understandable that the upper limit for כדי שיעמוד על האש וירתיח is 18 minutes, since that is the amount of time *melichah* takes (*Shulchan Aruch* YD 69:6 as per *Shach* 69:25); if *Rosh* is offering a position which is between the extremes cited beforehand, his opinion must be less than the 18 minutes suggested by the stricter opinion. See *Pri Chadash* 105:4.

it would take to heat up the meat or utensil, should we "imagine" a small fire or a large one,[15] as if the pot is covered or uncovered,[16] is it the time to heat the food or the water in which the food is cooking?[17] [18] Although those are (important) details, the overall point is that we are to treat the salt or ציר as if they are fire and estimate how much time it would take for that fire to heat up this item so that the *ta'am* can spread.[19]

---

[15] *Darchei Teshuvah* 69:296.

[16] Ibid.

[17] *Darchei Teshuvah* 69:295 and 105:42.

There is some indication from *Rosh's* words that he is referring to the heating of liquid – either the ציר or the (imaginary) water that the meat would be cooking in – since he says the time required is כדי שירתיח ויתחיל לבשל. What are the two times given: ירתיח and then יתחיל לבשל? This seems to imply that something is heating up plus something is starting to cook. This is what happens when food is cooked in a liquid: first the liquid gets very hot (ירתיח) and only as the food begins to cook does its internal temperature begin to slowly rise (יתחיל לבשל). In contrast, if meat is baked or broiled without liquid, the heating (ירתיח) and cooking (יתחיל לבשל) happen simultaneously.

[18] In addition to the technical questions noted in the text (and others found in *Darchei Teshuvah*), *Badei HaShulchan* 105:18-19 wonders how *Poskim* could specify that the time is 6 or 18 minutes: should the amount of time needed not fluctuate based on the size of the fire and ambient temperature?

[19] In a sense this is similar to the way Rav Schachter explained the reason *libun kal* is accomplished when the utensil reaches a certain level of heat on the "other side", i.e., the side which does not have contact with the fire (see *Imrei Dovid*, *Kashering*, Chapter 17). At that point, the heat has penetrated through the entire thickness of the utensil and is therefore judged to have accomplished its *kashering* role for all parts of the utensil.

But this highlights a question on the explanation given for *Rosh*. *Libun kal* is essentially a "leniency" in that it allows the non-kosher utensil to be used for kosher. Therefore, it makes sense not to consider it finished until heat has penetrated the entire utensil. However, absorption through (fast) *kovush* is a "strictness" in that it renders the utensil non-kosher. If so, we should say that if, for example, it takes 6 minutes for the salt to fully penetrate the utensil, then after 3 minutes (for example) we should assume that half the thickness of the utensil has absorbed non-kosher *ta'am*. Why then are there only two choices – כדי קליפה and full *b'liah* – and not some sort of gradations in between? Maybe that is why *Rosh* says *kovush* occurs when יתחיל לבשל because the "real" amount of time for *kovush* would be when the food is fully cooked, but once it begins to cook, we are already concerned that *ta'am* is being absorbed partway. This requires further consideration.

Chapter 49

יד סולדת בו

שולחן ערוך סימן ק"ה סעיף ב'
חום של כלי ראשון שהיד סולדת בו מבשל ואוסר כולו. אבל חום של כלי שני אינו מבשל, ויש אומרים שגם כן אינו מפליט ואינו מבליע, וי"א דמכל מקום הוא מפליט ומבליע ואוסר כדי קליפה. וראוי לחוש ליזהר בדבר לכתחלה (ועיי"ל סי' ס"ח סעיף י"ג) אבל בדיעבד מותר בלא קליפה ובהדחה בעלמא סגי. (ועיין לעיל סימן ס"ח וצ"ב וצ"ה נתבארו דיני כלי שני ועירוי).

Heat vs. Temperature

As relates to many halachos, the threshold of "hot", cooked, or some other status is reached when the item reaches "*yad soledes bo*". *Yad soledes bo* means that the item is so hot that a person touching it will pull his hand back because it is uncomfortable to touch/hold.[1] Some examples of where this *shiur* (criterion) is relevant are (a) *ta'am* transfers between foods if they are *yad soledes bo*,[2] (b) meat should not be put into water that is *yad soledes bo* before *melichah*,[3] (c) on *Shabbos*, one may not heat a liquid to the temperature of *yad soledes bo*,[4] (d) if a liquid reached *yad soledes bo*, it is considered "cooked" as relates to the principle of אין בישול אחר בישול,[5] (e) (according to some) wine is considered *mevushal* when it reaches *yad soledes bo*,[6] and (f) there is a form of *libun kal kashering* which requires

---

[1] As per *Rashi, Shabbos* 41b s.v. *soledes*, cited in *Sha'ar HaTziun* 318:19. This appears to be equivalent to the "withdrawal reflex", although there is discussion in the *Poskim* whether *yad soledes bo* refers to a level of heat which would cause someone to immediately pull back, or if it is just that the person cannot hold his hand there for an extended amount of time. See, for example, below in footnote 21.
[2] *Shulchan Aruch* 105:2 (our halacha).
[3] *Shulchan Aruch* YD 68:10-11.
[4] See, for example, *Shulchan Aruch* OC 318:14.
[5] See *Shulchan Aruch* OC 318:4. [Is it forbidden to heat it on *Shabbos* from *yad soledes bo* to a higher temperature? See *Imrei Dovid, Alcoholic Beverages*, Chapter 28 footnote 26].
[6] See *Imrei Dovid, Alcoholic Beverages*, Chapter 28.

that part of the metal reach the temperature of *yad soledes bo*.⁷ ⁸ In most cases, reaching *yad soledes bo* is a *chumrah*, while in the last three cases (ליבון קל, סתם יין, אין בישול אחר בישול) reaching *yad soledes bo* means that one can be lenient about a halachic issue.

Since the *shiur* is described as an amount of heat that one's hand can tolerate (*yad soledes bo*), one might think that it can easily be measured by placing your hand on the food or other item. But the *Gemara* implies⁹ that this is incorrect because people have different tolerances for heat, which means that one person might find the food to be too hot to handle while the next person would not. In turn, this leads many *Poskim* to discourage measuring *yad soledes bo* with a person's hand, and instead to be cautiously *machmir* for anything which might seem at all "hot".¹⁰ [The same is presumably also true when measuring the upper limits of *yad soledes bo* for the cases where that leads to a leniency].

---

⁷ See *Imrei Dovid*, *Kashering*, Chapter 17.
⁸ Other examples are (a) in certain cases, if one is *kashering* after *kovush*, the water need only be *yad soledes bo* (see *Imrei Dovid*, *Kashering*, Chapter 49), (b) oil is considered "cooked" as relates to being קבוע למעשרות when it is heated to *yad soledes bo* (*Rambam*, *Hil. Ma'asros*, 3:15), (c) one cannot use water which is *yad soledes bo* for *mayim acharonim* (*Shulchan Aruch* OC 181:3 as per *Mishnah Berurah* 181:8), and (d) some say that water which is *yad soledes bo* cannot be used for *netilas yadayim* (*Mishnah Berurah* 160:27).
⁹ *Gemara*, *Shabbos* 40b as per *Rashi* ד"ה והיכי, cited in *Mishnah Berurah* 318:89.

Since people have different levels of sensitivity to heat, the *Gemara* says that one should favor the more objective measure of כריסו של תינוק נכוית, which means the heat at which a [newborn - see *Pri Megadim* YD MZ 68:9] baby's stomach will become burned/scalded. We can imagine people testing items with their hands to see if they are *yad soledes bo*, but obviously no one will do the same with infant stomachs, so of what use is this measure of temperature? How will anyone know what level of heat qualifies as כריסו של תינוק נכוית to use in identifying "*yad soledes bo*"? Perhaps the answer is that (we will see in the coming footnote that) some *Acharonim* say that due to the ambiguity of what is considered *yad soledes bo*, one should *machmir* about anything which is at all "hot". In a similar vein, the *Gemara* might be saying that anyone bathing a newborn child will be particularly careful that the water is not too hot, because they want to avoid hurting the baby, and that is exactly how careful you should be about deciding which items are hot enough to be *yad soledes bo*. Just as you are afraid to bathe with water that might burn the baby, so too you should treat anything slightly hot as *yad soledes bo*. If so, כריסו של תינוק נכוית is not the "actual" criterion for the amount of heat but is rather a directive on how to apply the "actual" *shiur* of *yad soledes bo* (which is measured with one's hand).

Shulchan Aruch YD 105:2 cites the *shiur* as *yad soledes bo*, and in OC 318:14 adds that כריסו של תינוק נכוית.
¹⁰ See *Pischei Teshuvah* 105:7, *Darchei Teshuvah* 105:51, and the previous footnote. The *Poskim* cited there offer many possibilities of how to determine *yad soledes bo*, which we can divide them into three categories:
- Feel – try to touch the food (with hand or finger), see if you can hold the food in your hand for "some time", or (*Kaf HaChaim* OC 318:143) if it is too hot for people to eat or drink it.
- Heat – any food that has any warmth/heat (at least for *d'oraisah* issues) or is "חם היטב".
- Measure – estimate if כריסו של תינוק נכוית, if it is warmer than milk coming from a cow, or warmer than human saliva.

In the past century, as people have become more "scientific", the *Poskim* have offered opinions on an exact temperature which qualifies as *yad soledes bo*. Most did not want to determine that temperature by touching hot items since, as we have seen, that is too subjective. Rather, they found all sorts of places where *Chazal* describe something as hot, cold, cooked, etc., and then measured the exact temperature of that item. The range of sources used in this quest is quite breathtaking and includes citations from a wide array of *halachos*. We will cite the different opinions on this matter below, but for now will focus on the overall concept on which these *Poskim* are based on. They are assuming that *yad soledes bo* is at a certain temperature, and that it is equal for eggs, cows, ducks, water, milk, oil, and other items. For example, we know that milk expressed from a cow is at 40° C (104° F) which the *BeHaG* says is considered "cold", and therefore, Rav Shlomo Zalman Auerbach deduced that 40° C is below *yad soledes bo* for all items.[11]

While this assumption is perfectly logical, Rabbi Tzvi Aryeh Young pointed out that it does not appear to be accurate. The fault comes from the popular confusion of the terms, "heat" and "temperature", as we will demonstrate with the following examples: If a person enters a room that has been at 70° F for a few hours, he can assume that everything in the room (other than items with their own heat or cooling) will be at 70° F. Yet, if he puts one hand on a thick piece of metal that's in the room (e.g., a cast iron griddle) and another on a paperback book that is also there, he will notice that the metal feels much colder than the book. The griddle and book are both at the same temperature, but their "heat" is not equal. Physicists refer to the difference between the griddle and book as being based on "thermal conductivity", which describes how well a material conducts heat. The griddle has good thermal conductivity and therefore draws heat away from your hand very well, which makes it feel cold to the touch. In contrast, the book has poor thermal conductivity, does not pull heat from your hand as well, and therefore does not feel cold.

We can take the experiment one step further and place pieces of ice onto the book and griddle. Within a few seconds, the ice cube that is on the griddle will begin melting, while it will take a few minutes before any

---

[11] *BeHaG* (*Chullin, Perek Gid Hanasheh*), quoted in *Pischei Teshuvah* 108:8, and cited by Rav Shlomo Zalman Auerbach (*Noam*, Volume 6, and reprinted in *Minchas Shlomo* 1:91:8) as a proof to the temperature of *yad soledes bo*. [Rav Auerbach's actual position on this issue will be noted below in the text].

melting is seen for the one on the book. At first this seems counterintuitive. If the griddle feels colder, then the ice should melt <u>slower</u> on it than on the book? Thermal conductivity is once again the answer. Heat transfers more quickly to and from the metal griddle than the book, so the griddle's heat spreads to the ice cube relatively quickly and starts the melting process right away, while the transfer rate between the book and ice is slower and takes more time.

This indicates that temperature is not the most accurate way to measure how "hot" something is/feels. For our purposes it means that *yad soledes bo* – which is a measure of how hot an item <u>feels</u> – cannot be measured by temperature alone. In other words, the higher the temperature of any item, the hotter it will feel, but the temperature at which one item <u>feels</u> hot is not the same for all items. Therefore, the temperature of *yad soledes bo* for a cow might not be the same temperature as *yad soledes bo* for an egg, and the same for the other cases which *Chazal* discuss.

Physicists say that thermal conductivity is not the only factor that determines how hot an item is, and one must also consider each item's "specific heat capacity", which is the amount of energy it must absorb to increase its temperature.[12] If an item has a higher capacity, that means that it takes more energy for it to reach a high temperature than an item with a lower capacity. If these items are at the same temperature, the one with the higher specific heat capacity will feel hotter since it has more heat/energy to transfer into what it touches. Once again, this means that just because two items are at the same temperature, it does not mean that they will feel equally "hot", and *yad soledes bo* for one might not be *yad soledes bo* for the other.

We can demonstrate these two factors – thermal conductivity and specific heat capacity – using the cases of the primary *Gemara* on this topic. The one *Gemara*[13] which describes how hot something must be to qualify as

---

[12] A third factor is mass/density, and "thermal diffusivity" is a single number that combines these three factors. The formula for thermal diffusivity is $\alpha = K / (\rho * C_P)$, where α is thermal diffusivity, K is thermal conductivity (in watts per meter kelvin), ρ is density (in kilograms per cubic meter), and C_P is specific heat capacity (in joules per kelvin per kilogram).

[13] *Gemara*, *Shabbos* 40b, which is the source for our halacha (*Shulchan Aruch* 105:2), *Shulchan Aruch* OC 318:14, and other halachos.

yad soledes bo, is discussing two cases simultaneously: water and (olive) oil. Scientists describe their thermal properties as follows:

	Specific heat capacity	Thermal conductivity
Olive oil	1.97	0.170
Water	4.19	0.598

This means that if water and olive oil are at the same temperature, the water will feel hotter because (a) it has absorbed more than double the heat/energy to reach that temperature (i.e., it has a 4.19 specific heat capacity compared to 1.97), and (b) the water's heat transfers to one's hand at more than 3 times the speed of the oil's heat (i.e., it has a 0.598 thermal conductivity compared to 0.170).[14] [This author's experiments with hot water and oil at different temperatures demonstrate the veracity of these points]. Thus, when the *Gemara* speaks of *yad soledes bo* for water and oil, it surely did not have in mind that they would be considered "hot" at the same temperature. [Remember, thermometers were only invented 1,000 years after the *Gemara* was written!] Rather, when they reached a certain level of heat, where a person's hand would be unable to touch them, at that point they would halachically be considered hot, but those would not necessarily happen at the same temperature for each item.

All the above is essentially a question on the underlying idea of quantifying *yad soledes bo* as a temperature. It is theoretically possible to set an individual temperature of *yad soledes bo* for each specific material, such as water, since all water will always have the same thermal properties. But if we can prove that a duck is halachically considered "cold" when it is 45° C (113° F)[15] or that the white inside a whole egg does not undergo physical

---

[14] In fact, water has a higher specific heat capacity and thermal conductivity than many other foods. Accordingly, it is understandable that if a pot was used with non-kosher oil at (for example) 160° F, it can be *kashered* with water that is also 160° F (see *Imrei Dovid, Kashering*, Chapter 18), since the 160° F water is actually "hotter" than the oil. But it would be improper to *kasher* with 160° F oil (ignoring the concerns of *kashering* with *sha'ar mashkim*, see ibid. Chapter 69) if the pot had been used with meat cooking in 160° F water, since the oil is not as hot as the water was. In practice, this case is rare, and the more common scenario is that *hag'alah* is performed with water or with the same liquid as the forbidden item (e.g., כל יום נעשה גיעול לחבירו).

[15] *Noam/Minchas Shlomo* ibid. based on the *Poskim's* understanding of *Gemara, Chullin* 8b, that the area where *shechitah* takes place on the neck is not considered "hot", and an assumption that this also applies to ducks whose body temperature is 45° C. [The original, *Noam*, version says "doves" (יונים), but the later, *Minchas Shlomo* version says "ducks" (ברוז). It is not clear what the basis is for assuming such a high body temperature for ducks].

change until it reaches 58° C (136° F),[16] that does not mean that we can apply that temperature measure to milk or water. Ducks and eggs might feel cold at a temperature when milk or water feel hot or vice versa, and seemingly one should not draw conclusions from one material or food to the next.

We must conclude that although the halacha is determined by *Poskim* of each generation who use the tools and knowledge they have before them (אין לו לדיין אלא מה שעיניו רואות), the *Ribbono Shel Olam* makes sure that their well-intentioned decisions do not lead all of *Klal Yisroel* astray. Thus, although the actual temperature of *yad soledes bo* might be different for different foods and materials, the *Poskim's* measurements which have become widely accepted (see below) are at temperatures that qualify for all common materials. In this context, it is not a coincidence that the *shiur* of *yad soledes bo* – which is important for many halachos and should seemingly be easy for *Poskim* to quantify by merely touching foods – is one where there is a tremendous range of temperatures given, and sometimes even by the same *Posek* (depending on whether the high or low temperature is a *chumrah*). Once society "required" a temperature for *yad soledes bo*, the One Above made sure the *Poskim* would give temperatures which would suit people's needs regardless of which foods or materials they would apply it to.

Shiurim from Poskim

We saw at the beginning of the chapter that generally when an item becomes hotter than *yad soledes bo*, that causes a *"chumrah"* – such as it allows *ta'am* to transfer or the person heating up the liquid has violated *Shabbos* – but there are also cases where reaching *yad soledes bo* means that one can be lenient about a halachic issue (e.g., אין בישול אחר בישול). In truth, there is just one *shiur* of *yad soledes bo* and at that point both the *chumros* and *kulos* apply. But since we are unsure what *"yad soledes bo"* actually refers to, *Poskim* say that we should be strict in two different directions: for the cases where *yad soledes bo* is a *chumrah* we use a very low temperature, and for those cases where it leads to a *kulah* we use a very high temperature.

---

[16] See article by Professor Zev Lev in *Hama'ayan* 13:3 based on proofs from *Gemara, Shabbos* 38b, and other sources relating to the point when an egg is considered מגולגלת.

~ **Low end**

The following are the low temperatures given by *Poskim* for cases where a lower *yad soledes bo* leads to a *chumrah*:[17]

Fahrenheit	Celsius	Posek
104°	40°	*Chazon Ish*[18]
110°	43°	*Iggeros Moshe*[19]
113°	45°	Rav Shlomo Zalman Auerbach[20]
120°	49°	Rav Aharon Kotler[21]

In practice, many American *hashgachos* use the 120° F *shiur* given by Rav Aharon Kotler, while in *Eretz Yisroel* it is more common to follow the opinion of Rav Shlomo Zalman Auerbach.

~ **High end**

In general, few *Poskim* spoke about the high temperature of *yad soledes bo*, when that *shiur* is relevant.[22] One notable exception is *Iggeros Moshe*,

---

[17] The *Poskim* listed below who lived in *Eretz Yisroel*, gave their *shiurim* in degrees Celsius, while those who lived in the United States used Fahrenheit. In our listing, we convert the measures so that we can show the (rounded) Celsius and Fahrenheit number for each position.

[18] *Chazon Ish's* opinion as reported by *Shevet HaLevi* 7:131 (דכידוע דקצת יותר מארבעים מעלות אנו חוששין בו "ע ליד סולדת בו, וכן קבלתי מרבותי ומההגאון חזון איש ז). See also *Orchos Rabbeinu*, OC Volume 1 #192, and *Chut Shani*, Chapter 29, Footnote 7 (page 164) who both report that *Chazon Ish* thought that *yad soledes bo* was somewhere between 40-46° C (104-115° F) but in practice said that one should be *machmir* for anything above 40° C.

As noted previously in the text, the 40° C measurement is based on the temperature of milk as it drawn from a cow; see footnote 11.

[19] *Iggeros Moshe* OC 4:74 #3 in the *Bishul* section.

[20] *Shemiras Shabbos K'hilchaso* 1:1 based on the article by Rav Auerbach in *Noam*, Volume 6 (and reprinted in *Minchas Shlomo* 1:91:8).

[21] Opinion of Rav Aharon Kotler as reported by Rabbi Shimon Eider in *Halachos of Shabbos*, Volume 4 Chapter XIV Section A:3 footnote 19 (end), and Rav Heinemann, both of whom say that the determination was made by having people put their fingers into water at different temperatures. See also *Minchas Yitzchok*, *Likutim* #29, (first printed in *Tzefunos* 17) where his grandchildren report that he said that 49° C (120° F) is *yad soledes bo*, 47° C (117° F) is *safek yad soledes bo*, and 45° C (113° F) is surely not *yad soledes bo*. It notes that he arrived at these measures by seeing how long a person could keep their finger in the water: less than 15 seconds means the water is *yad nichvis bo* (see *Mishnah Berurah* 318:48, citing *Chayei Adam* 20:4, but see *Chazon Ish* OC 52:19), 15 seconds is *yad soledes bo*, 30 seconds is *safek yad soledes bo*, and 60 seconds is surely not *yad soledes bo*. This way of measuring is his interpretation of the words "*yad soledes bo*".

[22] *Minchas Yitzchok* 7:61:a and *Shevet HaLevi* 7:234:b discuss whether grape juice heated to *yad soledes bo* is enough to be considered *mevushal* as relates to סתם יין (see *Imrei Dovid*, *Alcoholic Beverages*, Chapter 28) (i.e., where the temperature is a leniency). The questions posed were regarding grape

but uncharacteristically, he does not give the same temperature in each *teshuvah* on the topic. In a *teshuvah* discussing אין בישול אחר בישול for *Shabbos*,[23] he says that 160° F (71° C) is unquestionably *yad soledes bo*. Yet in two *teshuvos* where he says that wine is *mevushal* for סתם יין when it reaches *yad soledes bo*, he rules that it should be measured as 165° F or 175° F (74° or 80° C).[24]

> Possibly we can resolve this apparent contradiction based on the difference between heat and temperature, as discussed at the beginning of the chapter. There we saw that water has a specific heat capacity of 4.19, which is somewhat more than grape juice and wine.[25] Thus, it is very possible that *Iggeros Moshe's* tests as relates to *hilchos Shabbos* were performed with plain water, where the heat of *yad soledes bo* is at a lower temperature (160° F), than when the same test was done with grape juice or wine to determine the heat of *yad soledes bo* for the halachos of סתם יין.

As unexpected as it is that *Iggeros Moshe* gives different *shiurim* in different *teshuvos*, the common practice is even more surprising. As relates to *hilchos Shabbos* where *Iggeros Moshe* says that 160° F is the *shiur*, people rely on this to (for example) permit putting milk into hot

---

juice heated to 140° F (60° C) and 122° F (50° C) respectively, and in each case the *Posek* assumed that the temperature given was surely *yad soledes bo*. [Some of the *Poskim* cited in the previous section (regarding the "low end") state with confidence that a specific temperature is "surely" *yad soledes bo*. However, it is not clear if they meant this even where that leads to a leniency, or just that at the given temperature one can confident in applying *yad soledes bo* as a *chumrah*].

The following is a test independently performed by Rav Yechiel Avraham Zilber (*Birur Halacha* OC 318:14 point 19 pages 174-175) and Professor Zev Lev (*Hama'ayan* 13:3). Eggs (in their shell) are a food that is halachically classified as *kalei habishul* (*easily cooked*) (*Gemara, Shabbos* 38b as per *Chazon Ish* OC 52:19) which should mean that putting them into water that is *yad soledes bo* should cause them to become cooked. However, in practice, eggs did not show any visible change until it was in water maintained at 70° C (158° F) for an extended amount of time. [Professor Lev saw minor changes at 58° C (136° F), but Rav Zilber did not]. This indicates that *yad soledes bo* is at approximately that temperature.

Other experiments or assessments performed by Rav Zilber to mimic measures given by the *Poskim* (see footnote 10) include: 63° C (145° F) is not enough to burn an infant's stomach (כריסו של תינוק נכווית) (ibid. point #16), a person can drink tea that is 58° C (136° F) without any special effort, and can sip a tea that is 67-77° C (153-171° F) (ibid. point 17), and people can keep their fingers in water that is 50° C (122° F) for 10 seconds, and at 54-56° C (129-133° F) they cannot keep them in for 5 seconds (ibid. point 18). It is noteworthy that in Point #20, Rav Zilber indicates that the lab thermometer used for these tests shows temperatures that are 2.5-3° C (3-5° F) lower than a standard home thermometer, which means that for average consumers the measured temperatures would be higher in each of these tests.

[23] *Iggeros Moshe* OC 4:74 #3 in the *Bishul* section (dated 1975).
[24] *Iggeros Moshe* YD 3:31 (dated 1966) – 165° F; *Iggeros Moshe* YD 2:52 (dated 1972) – 175° F.
[25] The specific heat capacity of grape juice varies depending on the specific type and concentration of the juice, and this author has seen measures between 3.43 and 3.85. For wine, an added factor is the percentage of ethanol/alcohol, whose specific heat capacity is 2.46.

coffee on *Shabbos*. If milk were not considered "already cooked", it would be forbidden to put it into hot coffee, and part of why it is permitted is because the milk was already pasteurized/cooked at the dairy factory.[26] Pasteurization is commonly done at 165° F, and therefore since we assume that 160° F is *yad soledes bo*, the milk was already "cooked" and אין בישול אחר בישול is relevant. For this halacha, we follow *Iggeros Moshe's* ruling that 160° F is considered *yad soledes bo*, which allows us to view the milk as "cooked".[27] But as relates to יין מבושל, *hashgachos* follow the other ruling of *Iggeros Moshe*, who said that it is not *mevushal* until 175° F.[28] Thus, just as *Iggeros Moshe* gives different temperatures for different halachos, we follow those different temperatures that he gave for each of those halachos.

---

[26] See *Mishnah Berurah* 318:39 (end) (מותר לתת לתוך הכוס הזה שהוא כלי שני חלב שנצטנן...).

[27] In the 2nd edition of *Shemiras Shabbos K'hilchaso* (5739), it cites *Iggeros Moshe's* 175° F (79.4° C) measure for *yad soledes bo* as relates to this application (Chapter 1 footnote 15), but in the 3rd edition (5770) it cites that *teshuvah* and the other one where he measures it as 160° F (71° C) (Chapter 1 footnote 17).

[28] Accordingly, grape juice or wine that was not pasteurized to that temperature will be labeled "not *mevushal*". It is worth bearing in mind that in many cases it has been pasteurized to a temperature that is well above the "low end" temperatures for *yad soledes bo* noted in the previous text. This means that the wine may indeed be *mevushal* and therefore does not have the "advantage" of non-*mevushal* wine which some prefer for *kiddush* (see *Shulchan Aruch* OC 272:8).

Chapter 50

כלי ראשון וכלי שני

שולחן ערוך סימן ק"ה סעיף ב'
חום של כלי ראשון שהיד סולדת בו מבשל ואוסר כולו. אבל חום של כלי שני אינו מבשל, ויש אומרים שגם כן אינו מפליט ואינו מבליע, וי"א דמכל מקום הוא מפליט ומבליע ואוסר כדי קליפה. וראוי לחוש ליזהר בדבר לכתחלה (ועיי"ל סי' ס"ח סעיף י"ג) אבל בדיעבד מותר בלא קליפה ובהדחה בעלמא סגי. (ועיין לעיל סימן ס"ח וצ"ב וצ"ה נתבארו דיני כלי שני ועירוי).

Basic halacha

In the previous chapter, we saw that for transfer of *ta'am* to happen based on heat, the items must be at least as hot as *yad soledes bo*. Additionally, the general rule is that *ta'am* can only transfer if the items are in a "*kli rishon*". Kli rishon literally means the "first/primary utensil" and refers to the original pot or pan in which food was cooked, even if the pot has already been removed from the fire.[1] In contrast, a *kli sheini* is a secondary utensil to which the food was transferred after removal from the *kli rishon*.[2]

Earlier *Poskim* had different opinions whether *ta'am* transfers in a *kli sheini* (and if it does, when and to what extent that occurs). *Shulchan Aruch* and

---

[1] See *Rema* 105:3; see also *Pri Chadash* 68:18 and *Pri Megadim* (MZ 68:9 ד"ה הדין הב') that even once it is removed from the fire the *kli rishon* status remains *mid'oraisah*.
    What if the *kli rishon* is on the fire but the contents have not yet reached *yad soledes bo*? A practical application of this is cheese vats which are heated by (very hot) steam but the content of the vat is carefully controlled to remain below *yad soledes bo*. See *Imrei Dovid*, *Animal Products*, Chapter 46 where this question was discussed and as relates to the overall question (on the fire but not *yad soledes*) one of the points made was:
    Shach 105:5 is personally inclined to be lenient but defers to others who are *machmir*. However, *Pri Megadim* ad loc. cites *Minchas Yaakov* 23:4 & 57:20 who says that this *chumrah* only applies as relates to the transfer of *ta'am* from the pot into food, but there is no need to be *machmir* about transfer from one food to another (מאוכל לאוכל), or from food into the pot (מאוכל לכלי).

[2] What if the food was cooked right over the fire with no pot and then placed onto a plate; is that plate the *kli rishon*? See the opinions cited in *Badei HaShulchan* 94:92 and *Biurim* ad loc.

Rema[3] say that *l'chatchilah* one should be *machmir* and assume *ta'am* will transfer in a *kli sheini*, but *b'dieved*[4] one can be lenient. While some later *Acharonim* disagree with that,[5] *Mishnah Berurah*[6] accepts this ruling, and *Chochmas Adam*[7] says that *b'dieved* one can be lenient if there is a *hefsed*.

Exceptions

Four notable exceptions to this general rule are:

- When there is the pressure of cutting or grinding a food, and that food is in a *kli sheini*, there is a transfer of *ta'am* into a כדי קליפה thickness of the food (see Chapter 15)[8]

- A דבר חריף that is in a *kli sheini* causes *b'lios* to transfer as if it were in a *kli rishon*.[9]

    Based on this, *Dayan Posen* zt"l suggested the following. Typically, the principle of כבולעו כך פולטו dictates that *hag'alah* can be accomplished by having the *hag'alah* water mimic the status (e.g., *kli rishon*, *kli sheini*) and temperature of the previous non-kosher product. However, this may be insufficient when *kashering* a factory which processed non-kosher vinegar. If the vinegar was (hot and) in a *kli sheini*, it has the status of *b'liah* in a *kli rishon*, and the *hag'alah* water must meet that standard rather than just be in a *kli sheini* like the vinegar was.

- The status of a hot דבר גוש (solid item) in a *kli sheini*, and how that potentially differs from a liquid, is related to the logic of דפנות מקררות discussed below. However, since that issue revolves around a statement of *Rema* in the coming halacha (YD 105:3), we will reserve our discussion on this for the next chapter.

---

[3] *Shulchan Aruch* 105:2 and *Rema* 68:10.
[4] As relates to *Pesach*, the ability to *kasher* a utensil which absorbed *chametz ta'am* through a *kli sheini* is treated as a "*l'chatchilah*", and one must *kasher* it before using it further (*Iggeros Moshe* YD 3:13).
[5] This includes *Yam Shel Shlomo*, *Chullin* 8:71 (full *b'liah* but not מפליט ומבליע כאחת), *Taz* 105:4 (follow *Yam Shel Shlomo* except in cases of *hefsed merubah*), and *Shach* 105:5 (absorbs *k'dei klipah* for *cheress* or food, but in cases of *hefsed merubah* one can be lenient). See also *Pri Megadim* MZ 105:4, *Pri Chadash* 105:5 (referencing his extensive comments in 68:18), and *Chavos Da'as* 105:10.

Chasam Sofer YD 95 (and *Pri Chadash* 68:18) say that those who are *machmir* regarding *kli sheini* would say the same if the food was in a *kli shlishi* or beyond; *Pischei Teshuvah* 94:7 cites this and says that the common practice among *Rabbonim* is not to be *machmir* beyond a *kli sheini*. See the same position in *Mishnah Berurah* (*Sha'ar HaTziun* 451:10, end) and *Shevet HaLevi* 8:181.
[6] *Mishnah Berurah* 447:25.
[7] *Chochmas Adam* 59:6.
[8] Particularly, see there in footnote 37.
[9] *Shach* 69:38. [However, since in truth the utensil was not on the fire, it can be *kashered* off the fire (in a *kli rishon*) (ibid)]. *Rema* 69:9 gives a similar ruling when the item is in brine in a *kli sheini*.

- *Rema*[10] rules that if food was put in a (hot) *kli sheini* which had previously been used for *chametz*, we should be *machmir* – even *b'dieved* – for the opinion that *kli sheini* can cause a full transfer of *ta'am*.[11] This *chumrah* is limited to mistakes which occurred on Pesach (rather than before *Pesach*).

דפנות מקררות

The following is copied from Imrei Dovid, Kashering, Chapter 18
see there for sources and more details

What is the difference between a *kli rishon* and a *kli sheini*? Should we not say that *ta'am* will transfer as long as the items are *yad soledes bo*? This question is posed by *Tosfos*, who answers:

ויש לומר לפי שכלי ראשון מתוך שעמד על האור דופנותיו חמין ומחזיק חומו זמן מרובה ולכך נתנו בו שיעור דכל זמן שהיד סולדת בו אסור

אבל כלי שני אף על גב דיד סולדת בו מותר שאין דופנותיו חמין והולך ומתקרר

That is to say that in a *kli rishon* the walls of the pot help heat the food, while in a *kli sheini* the walls cool down the water, and therefore even if the temperature is the same, the status of these two *keilim* is different. A *kli rishon* is the pot which was (or is) on the fire, so its walls are hot, while the *kli sheini's* walls are only heated by the food. Consequently, the walls of the *kli sheini* are actually drawing heat away from the food, and this is why the *b'liah* in a *kli sheini* is not the same as in a *kli rishon*.

Based on this, *Taz* says that logically it follows that if a person has a *kli sheini* which for some reason has no דפנות מקררות, then that *kli sheini* should have the status of a *kli rishon*. However, *Taz* says that one should only accept this logic when that results in a *chumrah*. In other words, if a *kli sheini* absorbed *ta'am* in a manner that had no דפנות מקררות, it cannot be *kashered* in standard *kli sheini*; examples of that will be discussed below.

But *Pri Megadim* and *Chavos Da'as* say that one should not rely on this idea when it results in a leniency. For example, if a pot absorbed *ta'am* as a *kli rishon*, then putting it into a hot *kli sheini* which has no דפנות מקררות is not enough to *kasher* the pot. *Pri Megadim* says the reason for this is that a utensil heated by hot water is not the same as when it gets heated through an actual fire. Therefore, if the *ta'am* was absorbed as a *kli rishon* – i.e., with a fire – then one must *kasher* it with water which was heated on a fire and cannot use water that attained its *kli rishon* status through heating with other water. Thus, he understands that the lack of

---

[10] *Rema* OC 447:3 and 451:1, as per *Mishnah Berurah* 447:26 and 451:11.
[11] In cases of great need where the utensil is also *aino ben yomo*, one can be lenient (*Mishnah Berurah* ibid. and *Sha'ar HaTziun* 447:20).

דפנות מקררות is what identifies something as a *kli rishon*, but even so, some types of *kli rishon* (heated by fire) are better than others (heated by water).

Chavos Da'as suggests an alternate reason. *Tosfos* says that in a *kli rishon* the walls are hot, and in a *kli sheini* they are not hot and instead are cooling. *Taz* is assuming that when the *kli sheini* is no longer cooling, it is upgraded to being a *kli rishon*, but in fact to become a *kli rishon* it must also be <u>adding</u> heat to the food or water. In a *kli rishon* (even one which is off the fire) the pot-walls are so hot that they continually make the water hotter, and that is what defines it as a *kli rishon*. But a *kli sheini* which does not have דפנות מקררות does not have the "weakness" of a *kli sheini* (i.e., walls that cool), but it also does not have the strength of a *kli rishon* (i.e., walls that heat), and therefore its status is in between those two.

ଓଃ ଔ

In *Imrei Dovid* ibid., Chapters 18-19, we discussed several examples where the stricter status of a *kli sheini* which does <u>not</u> have דפנות מקררות affects the way it is *kashered*. This included spray dryers, trailers, fillers, and other equipment where the metal becomes saturated with heat during standard use, and the *hag'alah* water must therefore flow for long enough to reach that same state.

An example that is relevant to home users is that of a ladle which is submerged into a pot of soup. It is not unusual that the ladle will get so hot from being submerged in the soup that it will no longer be cooling off the soup's temperature (i.e., not דפנות מקררות). In that case, it potentially has the elevated status akin to a *kli rishon*, and this must be borne in mind if the ladle ever requires *kashering*.[12] Additionally, it means that if soup is poured from the ladle into a bowl, the bowl has the status of עירוי כלי ראשון (discussed below) rather than עירוי כלי שני.[13] This elevated status also has effects on concerns of *bishul* as relates to *hilchos Shabbos*.[14]

Another case which seems somewhat of an exception to the general rule is that of a microwave oven. When food is cooked there, the "microwaves" heat up the food, which in turn causes the plate that the food is on to become hot. The plate surely acts to cool down and draw heat away from the food (דפנות מקררות), and it clearly does not contribute heat toward the food. At first glance, it seems to be a perfect candidate to be considered a

---

[12] See *Pri Megadim* OC MZ 451:9 and *Mishnah Berurah* 452:20. See also *Chochmas Adam* 59:3 and *Chazon Ish* OC 122:3 s.v., *seder*.
[13] See *Taz* 92:30, *Shach* 107:7, and *Chavos Da'as* 92:27 (*Biurim*).
[14] *Mishnah Berurah* 318:87. See also *Minchas Yitzchok* 5:127:3, based on *Mishnah Berurah* 318:45.

kli sheini as per *Tosfos'* line of reasoning. Yet, all contemporary *Poskim* seem to treat a plate or other utensil used in a microwave with the full strictness of a *kli rishon*. Apparently, the reason for this is that in the microwave the food (and plate) are becoming hotter and hotter as the oven operates. These are classic features of a *kli rishon*, even if the technical attribute of דפנות מקררות is present. For this reason, when food is heated in a microwave oven, the plate or other utensil used is given the status of a *kli rishon*.

עירוי כלי ראשון

Thus far, we have discussed transfers of *ta'am* in *kli rishon* and *kli sheini*; there is an intermediate designation between those two, עירוי כלי ראשון, which refers to a case where something hot is poured from a *kli rishon* into a *kli sheini*. Its status is somewhere between *kli rishon* (which is where the food is coming from) and *kli sheini* (where the food ends up), and the *b'liah* is a כדי קליפה [15] which is defined[16] as a thin layer which is nonetheless thick enough to be pulled off in one piece.

Once the "pouring" ends, the hot food is considered to be in a *kli sheini*, and the dividing line between עירוי כלי ראשון and *kli sheini* is called "נפסק הקילוח" which literally means "*the flow* (of hot food) *has been interrupted*". In Chapter 13 (in the section "עירוי כלי ראשון") we discussed (a) different opinions regarding the exact meaning of נפסק הקילוח, (b) whether it makes any difference if the *kli rishon* is on or off the fire when the liquid pours from it, and (c) how all these points relate to the issue of using the same sink to wash meat and dairy dishes.

Two other issues relevant to עירוי כלי ראשון are (d) that water flowing through pipes from a hot water tank to a sink is treated as עירוי כלי ראשון (and not as נפסק הקילוח), and (e) there is a *machlokes* whether עירוי כלי ראשון applies only to a meaningful "flow" of hot liquid or even includes cases where a bit of liquid is dripping from a *kli rishon* onto something else. These ideas were summarized in Chapter 9, based on the discussion in

---

[15] *Shulchan Aruch* and *Rema* 68:10; see also *Shulchan Aruch* 105:3.

Taz 95:12 says that the leniency of עירוי כלי ראשון applies only if happens <u>once</u>, but if there are multiple occurrences (within the same 24-hour period, *Pri Megadim* ad loc.) then *ta'am* transfers through the item's full thickness. See *Badei HaShulchan* (*Biurim*) (95:3 s.v. *she'balu*, and 98:3 s.v. *m'blias*), who cites *Pri Megadim* OC AA 452:2 and *Iggeros Moshe* YD 1:42:4 (towards the end) who question the logic of this position and rule that one need not be *machmir* for it.

[16] *Shach* 96:21.

Imrei Dovid, Meat and Poultry, Chapter 33, where it related to the issue of using a steam vacuum for animal carcasses at the slaughterhouse.

Tunnel Pasteurizer and Cooling Tunnel

Several of the points noted above come to play in the decision of whether one is required to *kasher* a tunnel pasteurizer and a cooling tunnel. First, we will explain how these operate, and then we will consider their status as a *kli rishon*, *kli sheini*, etc.

~ **The equipment**

When one pasteurizes food to prevent spoilage, the food container must also be sterilized. Two ways to do that are to either put the food in when it is hot, and that heat will be enough to decontaminate the container, or else, once the food is already in the container, the sealed container can be heated so that the food and container will simultaneously be sterilized. In both cases, the sterilization will only be successful if the product remains in the container above a certain temperature for a given amount of time (e.g., over 140° F for 15 minutes). One common method of doing this is to have the containers either pass through a cooling tunnel or a tunnel pasteurizer. Those two devices are quite similar, as follows:

The tunnel is a very long and wide piece of equipment – it can be 20 feet wide and 75 feet long – but it is not particularly tall. Rather, its interior might be just 12-16 inches tall, which is just a bit taller than the cans, bottles, or other containers that pass through it. Containers are on a belt that slowly moves through the tunnel, and water rains down on them during the entire time. However, the water is not the same temperature in all parts of the tunnel; rather, the tunnel is divided into "zones", and the water temperature changes from zone to zone.

In a cooling tunnel, the containers enter the tunnel very hot, and the water pouring down in the first zone of the tunnel will typically be just a bit cooler than the cans. For example, grape jelly might be filled into jars at 190° F and the water pouring onto the jars in the first zone might be 160° F. In each of the subsequent zones, the water will be progressively cooler, and the containers will typically exit the tunnel at just above ambient temperature. In this case, the hot jelly was in the jars for long enough – before and in the tunnel – to effect pasteurization, and the tunnel allows the jars to be cooled off somewhat for future handling.

A tunnel pasteurizer uses the same system in reverse. The containers enter the tunnel at ambient temperature and the water in the first zone may be just 100° F, but each of the other zones will be increasingly hotter (except for the final zone or zones which may serve to cool the containers before they exit the tunnel). In the tunnel pasteurizer, heating the product in the tunnel is what pasteurizes the container and product that is in it.

The water used for cooling or heating in these two systems is circulated and recycled in an ingenious manner, as can be seen in the accompanying illustration.

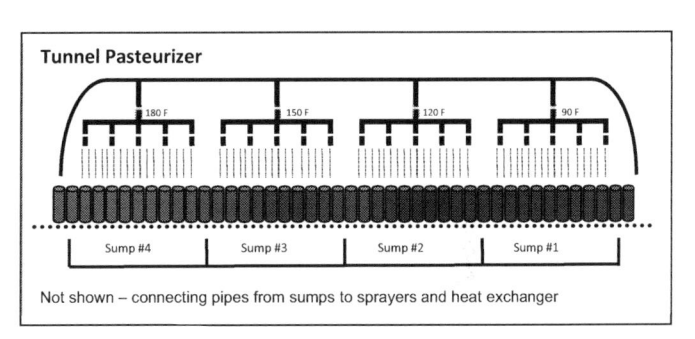

Tunnel Pasteurizer

180 F | 150 F | 120 F | 90 F

Sump #4 | Sump #3 | Sump #2 | Sump #1

Not shown – connecting pipes from sumps to sprayers and heat exchanger

The diagram shows a side view of a (see-through) tunnel pasteurizer with the cans moving from right to left through the tunnel's 4 zones. [From this perspective, only one row of cans is visible, but in truth the cans may be 10-20 deep]. The water coming out of the heat exchanger (not shown) at 180° F pours on the cans in Zone 4 and falls into a sump below the belt. During this phase, the cans get their final heating, and the water is cooled to 150° F. From the sump, the water is pumped to the top of Zone 3 (through a connection that is not shown in the diagram) where it once again rains down on the cans, heating the cans and cooling the water further. The process continues through the remaining zones, until the water has given up all of its heat into the cans and is ready for reheating (in the heat exchanger, not shown) and reuse. Thus, while the cans are slowly heated as they move from right to left, the water is slowly cooling as it moves from left to right. A certain amount of water remains on the cans and leaves the tunnel, but the vast majority of the water ends up being circulated again and again.

The exact same circulation system is used in a cooling tunnel, except that the water is cooled instead of heated, and the water gets progressively hotter while the cans are slowly cooling. This slow process is especially useful for hot glass bottles, which will break if they are "shocked" with very cold water.

~ **Transfer of Ta'am**

Although cooling tunnels and tunnel pasteurizers work in basically the same manner, the transfer of *ta'am* is quite different in these different systems. As we have seen, when hot food is in a *kli rishon*, *ta'am* transfers completely, but in cases of עירוי כלי ראשון the *b'liah* typically only transfers into a כדי קליפה. [As we will see in Chapter 52, there is also a further distinction between whether the hot product is on top/moving or bottom/stationary, with less *ta'am* transferring in the former case than in the latter].

In the case of a tunnel pasteurizer, it seems clear that *ta'am* transfers completely between the product, container, water, and belt. Although the hot water pouring onto the containers appears to be a mere עירוי כלי ראשון (or maybe even less), the fact that the water manages to heat the containers and their contents from ambient temperature to well over *yad soledes bo*, leaves us no real choice but to consider this as cooking in a *kli rishon*. Not only has the extended עירוי stopped the walls from cooling but it has even served as a catalyst for a thorough heating of the product, exactly as occurs in a *kli rishon*.[17] Thus, in the case of a tunnel pasteurizer, the water pouring down on the non-kosher containers absorbs *ta'am* and serves as a medium to transfer *ta'am* to the belt and other parts of the tunnel. [In many cases there are other factors which negate the need to *kasher*; see below].

As such, to use a non-kosher tunnel pasteurizer for kosher products, the water must be drained and replaced, the system must sit idle for 24 hours, and boiling water must be sprayed through the sprayers onto the entire system as the belt is in motion. Since there will be no containers passing through the tunnel, the water will stay quite hot from one zone to the next and it should be reasonably easy to accomplish this *kashering*.

On the other hand, it is much more difficult to claim that *ta'am* is transferred in a cooling tunnel. The food was put into the containers <u>after</u> it was heated or cooked in a kettle, which means that the containers enter the tunnel as a *kli sheini*. The water pouring down on the containers in the first zones might be above *yad soledes bo*, but it is <u>cooler</u> than the

---

[17] In a sense, this is similar to the point made above regarding a microwave; there, there are דפנות מקררות, but since the food gets progressively hotter in the microwave, it is treated as a *kli rishon*. Here too, the water is pouring from a *kli rishon*, but since it is heating the food a considerable amount, it seems appropriate to treat it as a *kli rishon*.

temperature of the cans and is specifically designed to cool them.[18] Thus, this is an example of עירוי כלי ראשון (onto a *kli sheini*) which can only cause transfer of *ta'am* to the depth of a כדי קליפה. Since the container is a כדי קליפה thick, עירוי cannot penetrate it, and no *ta'am* is transferred.[19]

Therefore, one is not required to replace the cooling tunnel's water or to *kasher* the chamber between non-kosher and kosher products. Nonetheless, some *hashgachos* insist that the water be changed before kosher product is processed.

~ **Additional Factors**

The above discussion assumes that the products in the containers were truly non-kosher, and accordingly considers whether *b'lios* transfer into the water and tunnel. In truth, the tunnels are very often used to process products and containers for which some of the following additional leniencies need to be factored in:

1. Although *Rema*[20] is *machmir l'chatchilah* to say that *ta'am* is absorbed into and out of glass, *Shulchan Aruch*[21] disagrees, and even *Rema* is lenient in cases of great need.[22]

2. It is generally accepted in the *kashrus* world that so little *ta'am* transfers through the walls of a container (or heat exchanger), that any *ta'am* of *stam yayin* would be *batel b'shishah* and can be ignored.[23]

3. Where the equipment is used for all-kosher items, but some are dairy, the dairy is often a relatively minor ingredient which might be *batel b'shishim* if we assume there is limited *b'liah* through the walls of a container (as in #2), and even more so if we take the position that חתיכה נעשית נבילה does not apply to *chalav stam*.[24]

---

[18] Similarly, it seems improper to view the entire container as a *davar gush* (discussed in the coming chapter) because the food was not cooked in that container; rather, we should view the liquid product sitting in the container as a classic *kli sheini*.

[19] Rav Schwartz added that even those who are *machmir* that there is full transfer of *ta'am* in a *kli sheini* could be lenient in this case, since it also requires assuming *ta'am* transfers through the walls of the container. Although we are generally *machmir* for that assumption (see Chapter 4), he did not think one needed to be *machmir* for that and *kli sheini* simultaneously.

[20] *Rema* OC 451:26.

[21] *Shulchan Aruch* OC 451:26.

[22] See *Mishnah Berurah* 451:155, and also see *Darchei Moshe* YD 135:4** (printed in the *Machon Yerushalayim* edition and based on *Darchei Moshe Ha'aruch*) and *Imrei Dovid, Kashering*, Chapter 56.

[23] See Chapter 4.

[24] For more on that, see Chapter 3 in the חלב סתם / איסור דרבנן section.

୧୦ ୡ

In Chapter 52 we will consider another piece of industrial equipment whose status is affected by the halachos discussed in this chapter.

These halachos also play an important role in understanding the acceptability of drinking coffee made at Starbucks. For more on that, see *Imrei Dovid, Alcoholic Beverages*, Chapter 2.

Chapter 51

דבר גוש

שולחן ערוך סימן ק"ה סעיף ג'

נפל איסור חם לתוך היתר חם דכלי ראשון או אפילו איסור צונן לתוך היתר חם, הכל אסור דתתאה גבר על העליון ומחממו עד שמפליט בתחתון. ואין צריך לומר דהיתר צונן לתוך איסור חם שהכל אסור, אבל אם העליון חם והתחתון צונן אינו אוסר אלא כדי קליפה אפילו אם העליון החם איסור.

הגה: וכל זה לא מיירי אלא בחום כלי ראשון כגון מיד שהסירו מן האש מניחו עם ההיתר, אבל אם כבר מונח בכלי שני ואחר כך מניח ההיתר אצלו או עליו אינו אוסר כלל דכלי שני אינו אוסר כמו שנתבאר. ואם הניחם זה אצל זה אם שניהם חמים מחום כלי ראשון הכל אסור, ואם האחד צונן ההיתר צריך קליפה במקום שנגע. איסור שהניחו בכלי היתר או להיפך אמרינן ביה גם כן דין תתאה גבר כמו בב' חתיכות, ועיין לעיל סימן צ"ד אם חתך בשר בסכין חולבת. אסור לערות מכלי שיש בו שומן כשר לנר דולק שיש בו חלב או שומן איסור ובדיעבד אין לחוש.

Halachos

In the previous chapter we saw that while full transfer of *ta'am* occurs in a *kli rishon*, there is little or no transfer in a *kli sheini*. We also saw that the difference between a *kli rishon* and a *kli sheini* is that in a *kli rishon* the "walls" of the utensil <u>heat</u> the food while in a *kli sheini* the walls are <u>cooling</u> the food (דפנות מקררות); since the walls are drawing heat away from the food, *ta'am* does not transfer even though the food is *yad soledes bo*.

This leads *Issur V'heter* and *Maharshal*[1] to suggest that דפנות מקררות only applies when the food is in a fluid form and has contact with the walls of the utensil. But if the food is solid (*davar gush*), most of it has no contact with the walls which means that there will be no דפנות מקררות and it will not downgrade to become a *kli sheini*. Therefore, if a *davar gush* is moved from the *kli rishon* to some other utensil, it retains its status of being in a

---

[1] *Issur V'heter* 36:7 and *Yam Shel Shlomo, Chullin* 7:44.

kli rishon even though it is not in the original cooking utensil (i.e., not in the "*kli rishon*").[2]

Many, including *Rema*,[3] do not accept this ruling, but *Mishnah Berurah*[4] follows the lead of *Shach*, *Magen Avraham*, and others,[5] who adopt the strict position. That said, in specific cases, particularly when there is a *hefsed merubah*, they agree that one may rely on *Rema*.[6]

Within the strict opinion there are several points that require clarification:

~ **What**
A solid piece of meat is clearly an example of a *davar gush*, and *Maharshal* says that the same is true of אורז ודוחן (rice and millet). The simple reading of this implies that a pot of rice is solid enough to qualify, but *Shach* – and even more clearly *Chochmas Adam*[7] – seem to have understood that *Maharshal* was referring to rice or millet cooked into a solid mass, possibly like a *kugel*. Only in that case is it a *davar gush*, but if it pours like a liquid, it is not considered a *davar gush*.[8]

---

[2] See *Shemiras Shabbos K'hilchaso* Chapter 1 footnote 169* who rules that the *davar gush* retains its status even if it is transferred multiple times, but see *Mishnah Berurah* 447:24 who seems somewhat unsure about that.
[3] See *Darchei Moshe* 105:4, *Rema* 94:7 and 105:3. See also *Taz* 94:14, who says to be *machmir* only in cases where someone cuts the solid item (so that there is דוחקא דסכינא together with the *davar gush*).
[4] *Mishnah Berurah* 447:24.
[5] *Shach* 105:8 and *Magen Avraham* 318:45. See also *Binas Adam* 48 (66), who says that the vast majority of *Poskim* follow this approach (והנה ממש כל האחרונים הסכימו לאיסור ורש"ל לדבדר גוש אפילו בכלי שני כיון דליכא דפנות המקררות מבשל לעולם); however, see more detail and nuance below in footnotes 6 and 14. Other *Poskim* will be noted below.
[6] See *Chasam Sofer* YD 95 (cited in *Pischei Teshuvah* 94:7), *Chochmas Adam* 60:12, and *Iggeros Moshe* YD 4:74 #5 in the *Bishul* section. *Chasam Sofer* says that (as noted in the previous chapter) *l'chatchilah* we are always *machmir* to assume *ta'am* transfers in a *kli sheini*, and therefore the questions regarding a *davar gush* are invariably for situations of *b'dieved*.
[7] *Shach* ibid. refers to the non-*gush* as צלולים; that word typically means "clear" or "transparent", and it could be that *Shach* means to say "watery". However, see *Chochmas Adam* ibid. who says that the אורז ודוחן which are considered *davar gush* must be כרוטב (המבושלים בישול עב שאינם נשפכים כרוטב) (*cooked so thick that they do not pour like gravy*).
[8] *Iggeros Moshe* ibid. describes the criterion for *davar gush* vs. non-*gush* as:
מסתבר שלא תלוי זה בדין אוכל או משקה לגבי טומאה, אלא באם הוא דבר הזב
או דבר שהוא חתיכה העומדת ומדובקת יחד אף בלא כלי המעמידן ומדבקן
שלכן יש להחשיבו כלח

Similarly, Rav Schachter said that דבר לח (i.e., non-*davar gush*) does not only include liquids and soups, but also includes items with the consistency of applesauce.

In a similar vein, Rav Schachter ruled that hot potato chips or corn chips falling onto a tumbler are not considered a *davar gush*, since they do not retain their heat at all, and quickly cool off.[9]

~ Mixture

Toras Ha'asham[10] says that if a solid piece of food is floating in liquid, such as meat or potatoes in a watery *cholent*, that does not qualify as a *davar gush*. The liquid portion has contact with the walls of the utensil, and therefore דפנות מקררות applies. In contrast, we can see that *Shach*[11] disagrees with this by the fact that he says that a fly mixed into liquid is treated as a *davar gush*; clearly, the solid fly retains its status as a *davar gush* even though it is mixed into liquid that touches the walls of the utensil.

~ Bishul

Can a *davar gush* in a *kli sheini* affect <u>bishul</u> or just the transfer of *ta'am*? *Magen Avraham*[12] says that just as a hot *davar gush* can transfer *ta'am* like a *kli rishon* (according to the strict opinion), so too it can create *bishul* like a *kli rishon*. This means that, for example, on *Shabbos* one should not place uncooked spices onto a hot piece of meat that is out of the *kli rishon*; the meat is a *davar gush* and will "cook" the spices, which is forbidden on *Shabbos*.

However, *Chavos Da'as*[13] argues that this is not true. Transfer of *ta'am* occurs if there are no דפנות מקררות, and therefore we must be strict regarding a *davar gush*. But for cooking/*bishul* to occur, we must meet a higher standard of <u>דפנות מחממות</u> – the walls of the utensil must be <u>heating</u> the food – as would be typical in a *kli rishon*. A *davar gush* that is out of the *kli rishon* does not satisfy that requirement, and therefore it cannot cook other foods.[14]

---

[9] It is not clear how this ruling can be reconciled with *Shach* cited below, who says that a fly is considered a *davar gush*. [Rav Schachter's approach seems quite logical, leaving us unsure how to understand *Shach*].

[10] *Toras Ha'asham* (by the author of *Tosfos Yom Tov*) to *Toras Chattas* 23:7 (ד"ה הכל אסור), cited in *Pischei Teshuvah* 94:7.

[11] *Shach* 105:8. [See above in footnote 9]. See also *Pri Megadim* MZ 107:2 who seems to have assumed this way as well.

[12] *Magen Avraham* 318:45. See below in footnote 14.

[13] *Chavos Da'as* 92:27 (*Biurim*).

[14] *Magen Avraham* is commenting on *Shulchan Aruch* OC 318:19, who says that one should not put oil on hot meat which is <u>on the fire</u> because that will cook the oil. The implication is that if the meat was

Mishnah Berurah[15] says that one should preferably follow the strict approach, but if someone already put the spices in, then *b'dieved* they may be lenient and eat the food. Similarly, *Iggeros Moshe*[16] says that when there are other reasons to permit the action, one may follow the lenient approach on this matter.[17]

~ **Kashering**

Even those who are *machmir* to treat a *davar gush* as if it were a *kli rishon*, agree that it does not have the status of a *kli rishon* which is on the fire. Therefore, a utensil which became non-kosher via a *davar gush* can be *kashered* in a *kli rishon* which is off the fire. For more on this, see *Imrei Dovid*, *Kashering*, Chapter 9.[18]

---

off the fire there would be no prohibition, because once the meat is in a *kli sheini* it cannot effect *bishul* on the oil. This would either be a rejection of the entire strict concept of *davar gush*, or at least saying that a *davar gush* cannot cook (even if it can create transfer of *ta'am*). Thus, *Magen Avraham's* statement that one cannot put oil onto the meat even if it is off the fire appears to be arguing with *Shulchan Aruch* rather than explaining it.

Chasam Sofer YD 95 (cited above in footnote 6) says that even if a *davar gush* can create *bishul* as relates to *hilchos Shabbos*, it would not create *bishul* as relates to *basar b'chalav*, since a hot piece of meat will create צלי (which, according to some opinions will only create *bishul mid'rabannan* for *basar b'chalav*). Binas Adam 48 (66) begins by stating (and proving) that just about all agree that a *davar gush* can cook, but then questions that. He appears to conclude that a *davar gush* can cook even after it has left the *kli rishon*, but that ability ends when it reaches the *kli sheini*, where דפנות מקררות comes into play (to some extent).

[15] *Mishnah Berurah* 318:65 and 118. In one situation, Rav Schachter ruled that one should be *machmir* not to allow spices to be put onto a hot *kneidel* sitting in soup on *Shabbos*: the *kneidel* is considered a *davar gush* (even though it is in a liquid, see previous text), and putting spices onto it is potentially considered a forbidden *bishul* (as noted in the text).

[16] *Iggeros Moshe* YD 4:74 #5 in the *Bishul* section.

[17] The specific case where he was lenient was to allow the placement of ketchup onto hot *davar gush*: not only is it a *chumrah* to assume a *davar gush* out of a *kli rishon* can "cook", but one must also assume (see *Rema* OC 318:15 as explained by *Iggeros Moshe* ibid. #2 and #5) that a forbidden *bishul* is possible on the precooked ketchup (i.e., יש בישול אחר בישול לח בדבר שנצטנן, see *Biur Halacha* 318:4 s.v. *yesh*).

[18] See there also in Chapter 40, footnote 7, regarding the use of *irui kli rishon* with an אבן מלובנת.

Chapter 52

תתאה גבר

שולחן ערוך סימן ק"ה סעיף ג'

נפל איסור חם לתוך היתר חם דכלי ראשון או אפילו איסור צונן לתוך היתר חם, הכל אסור דתתאה גבר על העליון ומחממו עד שמפליט בתחתון. ואין צריך לומר דהיתר צונן לתוך איסור חם שהכל אסור, אבל אם העליון חם והתחתון צונן אינו אוסר אלא כדי קליפה אפילו אם העליון החם איסור.

הגה: וכל זה לא מיירי אלא בחום כלי ראשון כגון מיד שהסירו מן האש מניחו עם ההיתר, אבל אם כבר מונח בכלי שני ואחר כך מניח ההיתר אצלו או עליו אינו אוסר כלל דכלי שני אינו אוסר כמו שנתבאר. ואם הניחם זה אצל זה אם שניהם חמים מחום כלי ראשון הכל אסור, ואם האחד צונן דהיתר צריך קליפה במקום שנגע. איסור שהניחו בכלי היתר או להיפך אמרינן ביה גם כן דין תתאה גבר כמו בב' חתיכות, ועיין לעיל סימן צ"ד אם חתך בשר בסכין חולבת. אסור לערות מכלי שיש בו שומן כשר לנר דולק שיש בו חלב או שומן איסור ובדיעבד אין לחוש.

Basics

In previous chapters we learned that *yad soledes bo* heat is required for *ta'am* to transfer, and in the current halacha[1] we are taught what to do if only one of the items is hot, but the other is not. For example, an ambient temperature potato is on top of a hot piece of meat. The rule is that hot/cold status is determined by whichever of the items is underneath. In our case it means that, since the bottom item (the meat) is hot, *ta'am* transfers between the meat and potato as if both of them were hot. This is known as תתאה גבר which literally means, "*the lower one overpowers the upper one*".

However, in the opposite case, if the hot meat was on top of the ambient temperature potato, the cold potato would be גבר so there would not be full transfer of *ta'am*. Nonetheless, the halacha says that it takes a moment for the cold item (the potato) to cool off the upper one (the meat) and that

---

[1] *Shulchan Aruch* 105:3. See also *Shulchan Aruch* 91:4 and *Rema* 92:7.

is enough time for *ta'am* to transfer into a thin layer of each food (כדי קליפה).[2] Thus, the *ta'am* transfers fully when the lower item is hot, and there is a minimal transfer when it is not *yad soledes bo*.

In this context, the halacha applies equally (a) if the *issur* is on top or on bottom,[3] (b) whether the items are foods or utensils,[4] and (c) regardless of whether the items are liquids or solids.[5] תתאה גבר applies when one of the items is <u>below</u> the other, but if they are side by side and one is not hot, there is a difference of opinion whether תתאה גבר applies.[6]

Tumbler

Badei HaShulchan[7] notes that the earlier *Poskim* give three subtly different explanations for <u>why</u> the lower item determines the status of the top one:

---

[2] Since *ta'am* only transfers into a כדי קליפה, if there is a barrier between the hot and cold items, there will not be a transfer of *ta'am* between the foods. This is common in a heat exchanger used for cooling; the hot product on one side of the heat exchanger's plates interacts with the cold water on the other side, but the *ta'am* cannot penetrate the כדי קליפה thickness of the plates. [This assumes either that the cooling water is considered the תתאה or that since both fluids are in motion they are considered to be "side by side" (see the coming text) and neither is the תתאה].

[3] *Shulchan Aruch* 105:3.

[4] *Rema* to *Shulchan Aruch* ibid. *Shach* 105:10 cites those who argue that *ta'am* transfers completely when hot food is put onto a cold utensil, because תתאה גבר only applies to foods, but *Shach* lists several proofs against this position and accepts the ruling of *Rema*.

[5] *Shulchan Aruch* 91:7. Within the halacha of תתאה גבר, *Shulchan Aruch* 105:4-6 differentiates between cases where there is liquid or the food is fatty/שמן and those where it is not, stating that there is more transfer in the former than in the latter. However, *Rema* 105:5 (and 105:9) says that our custom is to give the stricter status of שמן to just about all foods, due to our lack of skill to clearly identify which foods are not. [See *Shach* 105:16 for some exceptions and see *Sha'ar HaTziun* 461:57 regarding a *matzah kefulah* that touched another *Pesach matzah*].

One case where תתאה גבר does not apply is when the upper/hot one is still on the fire, because in that case the fire's heat counteracts the coldness coming from the lower item (*Shach* 92:33 as per *Dagul Mirivavah* and *Pri Megadim* ad loc).

[6] *Rema* 105:3 says that in such cases, neither is גבר and there is only a transfer of *ta'am* into a כדי קליפה. However, *Yam Shel Shlomo* (*Chullin* 8:70) argues that (a) no *ta'am* should transfer if the *issur* is cold, and (b) there should be full transfer if the *issur* is hot, but (c) one should not rely on this position as relates to leniency (i.e., "a" above). *Shach* 105:9 raises questions on *Yam Shel Shlomo*, but *Taz* 105:5 says that one should be *machmir* for *Yam Shel Shlomo*, except in cases of *hefsed merubah*, and *Chochmas Adam* 60:11 cites *Taz* on this matter.

The coming text will explain the logic for תתאה גבר. The first two reasons given there are from *Issur V'Heter* 29:1, and in the very next halacha (29:2) he records the leniency for cases where the foods are side by side, which is the source for *Rema* cited here in the text. The connection between these points is clear: since the reasons for תתאה גבר are specific to cases where one food is on <u>top</u> of the other, it makes no sense to apply it when they are side by side.

[7] *Badei HaShulchan* 91:25. The first two reasons are from *Issur V'Heter* 29:1 (שהעליון מפליט חום התחתון, וגם כח האש עולה תמיד), and the third is from *Rashba* (*Toras HaBayis* (*Aruch*) 4:1 page 3b), cited in *Shach* 91:23 (דכל שהוא במקומו הוא הגובר).

1. The pressure that the upper item exerts on the lower one expels the lower one's heat or coldness away from itself.
2. Heat rises.
3. Stationary items are more powerful than those which are in motion; therefore, the lower one – which was stationary – overpowers the upper one, which was in motion when it fell onto the lower one.

Let us see how these reasons apply to the case of a "tumbler".

A tumbler looks like a drum which is open on both ends and is turned on its side with a slight downward incline. Product continuously falls into the inside of the upper end of the tumbler, and as the tumbler rotates, the food is slowly conveyed to the lower opening and eventually falls out of the tumbler. As the food passes through the tumbler, liquid or powdered seasoning sprays down, so that the food becomes coated with seasoning. Tumblers are commonly used to season potato chips, corn chips, French fries, and similar foods where the factory will cook/fry all chips, etc., plain and then apply salt and different seasonings (e.g., barbecue or sour cream flavors) per batch in the tumbler. Thus, the plain chips etc. produced in the factory may be kosher and pareve, but if some seasonings used for the tumbler are non-kosher or dairy, we must consider whether the tumbler's kosher status is affected by them.

An important part of the question is that generally the chips, etc., reach the tumbler shortly after they are fried/cooked and in many cases, they are still *yad soledes bo* at that point. [This varies from factory to factory and must be assessed in each case]. Another issue to consider is that we saw in the previous chapter that potato chips and corn chips are too thin to be considered a דבר גוש. This means that after the chips travel from the fryer to the tumbler on one or more belts, the tumbler is merely a כלי שני (or even less) where, as noted in Chapter 50, the possibility of *ta'am* transferring (and the potential need to *kasher*) is minimized. However, the same is not true of a tumbler used for French fries, potato wedges, or other

---

Shach 92:36 (second answer) relies on the logic of *Rashba* to explain a ruling of *Rema* 92:7. However, see *Pri Chadash* 92:24, who says that if so, there will almost never be a case of hot and cold which are side by side where we would apply the ruling (noted in the text) that תתאה גבר does not apply, since invariably one of the items will have been there first (and thus be stationary).

larger/thicker foods, which qualify as a דבר גוש and might retain full ability to transfer *ta'am* even in a כלי שני.

The part of the issue which is relevant to this chapter is that even if the chips etc. are hot, the tumbler itself is typically not *yad soledes bo*, and seemingly this is an instance where תתאה גבר should play a role. Clearly, that is accurate according to the first two reasons given above for the principle of תתאה גבר: heat rises on its own or the pressure of the תתאה expels temperature from the lower one. Both of those apply in this case, because the chips fall onto/into the tumbler and basically stay in the bottom half of the device as it rotates. Thus, the chips are always above the metal (i.e., the tumbler).

It is not as clear if the third line of reasoning applies. It stated that it is not the physical location of the תתאה which dictates that it is גבר, but rather that it is stationary and can therefore "overpower" the hot or cold temperature of the moving/dropping other item. But what about this case, where the "תתאה" is fixed in place but is constantly in motion as it rotates? Does such a device have the status of a stationary תתאה, or should we give the tumbler and chips equal standing (since both are moving) and treat this more like a case of items which are side by side where there is no תתאה? This requires further consideration.[8]

However, further analysis shows that תתאה גבר does not play a significant role in the status of a tumbler. That is because even if תתאה גבר dictates that there cannot be a <u>complete</u> transfer of *ta'am* between the (lower) cold tumbler and the (upper) hot chips, we have seen that nonetheless there is a transfer of a כדי קליפה of *ta'am*. This means that the chips etc. will become non-kosher or dairy (especially for chips which themselves are only a כדי קליפה thick), and the tumbler itself will require *kashering* even if all it absorbed was a כדי קליפה of *ta'am*.[9] Thus, the question whether the

---

[8] In this context, it is noteworthy that in the original sources (*Rashba*, cited in *Shach*) the third reason is cited to explain why תתאה גבר applies even when meat falls into milk (see *Rashba* and *Shulchan Aruch* 91:7). The milk is considered תתאה and stationary even though the [meat becomes submerged in the milk and the] milk moves somewhat when the meat falls into it. Thus, even according to this line of reasoning, the תתאה does not have to be perfectly stationary for the entire time it is contact with the upper item. Nonetheless, the question posed in the text is that the tumbler is <u>constantly</u> in motion and might therefore not qualify as "stationary" (and תתאה).

[9] See *Pri Megadim* SD 105:5, who makes the point that when that when we are <u>confident</u> (i.e., based on a *Gemara* source) that a utensil absorbed כדי קליפה, we cannot *kasher* that utensil with *irui kli rishon*,

tumbler and the food that passes through it have a full transfer of *ta'am* or not (i.e., if and how תתאה גבר applies) is moot.[10]

Heat sealer

A heat sealer stamps down on the cover of a container and uses heat to bond the cover onto the container. Often, there is no liquid between the sealer and cover, and in those cases the principle of אין הבלוע יוצא מכלי לכלי בלי רוטב (see Chapter 7) dictates that *ta'am* cannot transfer from the container into the sealer; therefore, the sealer can be used for both non-kosher and kosher without *kashering* between uses.

In other cases, such as if there is steam coming out of the sealer, there will be liquid between the cover and sealer. That would be a situation where תתאה גבר comes into play. The hot sealer is contacting the ambient temperature container, and *ta'am* can only transfer to/from a כדי קליפה. Since the cover is a כדי קליפה thick, that effectively means that *ta'am* cannot transfer between the sealer and food inside the container. Accordingly, even in this case, the sealer can be used for both non-kosher and kosher without *kashering*.

Shrink tunnel

The following is a practical application of principles regarding תתאה גבר
It is taken from Imrei Dovid, Meat and Poultry, Chapter 46
See there for additional sources and details

Some meat leaves the packing house as whole forequarters, but most of the time it has been cut to smaller sizes and is packaged in Cryovac bags. The meat is put into a bag, the bag is sealed, after which the bag is heated until it shrinks and snugly encases the meat. Heating the bag is done by passing the bag (with the

---

since it is just a *chumrah* to assume that *irui* affects a כדי קליפה of the utensil. Our case would seem to be another example of that principle; the *Gemara* is clear that when the lower item is cold, *ta'am* is absorbed into it כדי קליפה, and therefore one cannot *kasher* the tumbler (or other equipment where this applies) with a mere *irui kli rishon*.

[10] Furthermore, most cases are like the one described in the earlier text, where all the chips are kosher and pareve before they reach the tumbler, and it is just the seasonings which are sometimes dairy or non-kosher. Thus, the interaction between the hot (kosher) chips and the cold tumbler is insignificant, since there is no forbidden *ta'am* that might pass between them. In almost every case, the seasoning is at ambient temperature when it is sprayed on so the only case where hot touches cold and one is non-kosher is when the seasoning hits the chips. Those chips are obviously not kosher. The issue would therefore be limited to cases where the seasoning itself gets (physically) heated by the chips and then hits the walls of the tumbler. Another case would be if the factory previously fried their chips etc. in non-kosher animal fat such that the tumbler was in contact with not non-kosher, and now the factory will be switching to kosher vegetable oil and a decision is being made whether to *kasher* the tumbler one time as part of the changeover.

meat inside it) either through (a) a tunnel (or chamber) where hot water pours down on the bags, or (b) a bath filled with hot water. Since the meat is cold, and the bag and meat spend just a few seconds in the shrink tunnel, the meat does not reach *yad soledes bo* during this process.

The shrink tunnel becomes non-kosher when it is used to process non-kosher meat. The question we must consider is whether it must be *kashered* before it is used for kosher meat.

Hot tunnel
At first glance, it would appear that when the bag and meat are heated by passing through a hot tunnel ("a" above), the interaction between the bagged meat and the shrink tunnel is an example of *irui kli rishon* (hot water hitting a cold package) where the *b'liah* is not more than a כדי קליפה. If that were true, no בליעות would pass through the bag [which is a כדי קליפה thick], and therefore even though the tunnel is not kosher, it can be used for kosher meat without *kashering*.

However, a good argument could be made that the interaction should not be viewed as just being *irui kli rishon*. Rather, the interior chamber of the tunnel should have the same status as the headspace in a pot where בליעות are considered to have occurred in a כלי ראשון (הבל הקדירה) rather than as עירוי כלי ראשון. As *Shulchan Aruch*[11] states, כסוי של ברזל שמכסים בו הקדירה, צריך הגעלה כיון שמזיע בכל שעה מחום הקדירה. Here too, the chamber is constantly filled with steam and is basically the headspace of the "pot". If, in fact, the chamber has the status of a כלי ראשון, then the need for *kashering* is seemingly more significant. The counterargument would be that the chamber is different than the headspace of a pot in that the chamber (a) is significantly larger, and (b) has openings on both sides through which the meat passes in and out. The final decision whether the tunnel/chamber should have the status of the headspace of a pot, may well depend on the specific device in use.

Hot bath
The situations where the bagged meat is submerged in a bath of hot water ("b" above) would appear to be a simple example of צונן לתוך חם (*a cold object falling onto a hot one*), where we rule that תתאה גבר and בליעות spread through the entire thickness of the upper/cold object. In this case, that could potentially mean that the cold meat absorbs *ta'am* in this type of shrink tunnel. In fact, the application of that principle to our case depends on a *machlokes* between the *Acharonim*.

Aruch HaShulchan[12] suggests that even in cases of צונן לתוך חם, if one is sure that the upper/cold object did not becomes יד סולדת בו, *ta'am* transfers only minimally (כדי קליפה). According to this opinion, once again we would say that the עיקר הדין

---
[11] *Shulchan Aruch* OC 451:14.
[12] *Aruch HaShulchan* 91:11-12.

is that no *kashering* is required for this type of shrink tunnel because the meat does not get hot. However, it appears that most *Poskim* implicitly follow the ruling of *Chavos Da'as*[13] – that the principle of תתאה גבר applies even if the upper item did not get hot at all. Accordingly, the tunnel truly requires *kashering*.

Layers

Upon further consideration, it may be that even where the tunnel is a כלי ראשון, there is no requirement for *kashering*, for the following reason. *Chavos Da'as* explains that תתאה גבר does not mean that if the lower item is hot then the upper one will reach יד סולדת בו.[14] Rather, it means that in spite of the upper one not reaching the standard temperature at which transfer of *ta'am* occurs (יד סולדת בו), the lower item is able to create a נתינת טעם. Based on this explanation, *Chavos Da'as* notes that if one were to stack two pieces of cold, kosher meat on top of a piece of hot, non-kosher meat, only the lower piece of kosher meat would be affected. The hot piece transfers *ta'am* into the lower kosher piece due to the principle of תתאה גבר, but that transfer does not result in the lower piece becoming hot; therefore, the lower "kosher" piece does not serve as a "תתאה גבר" for the upper piece of kosher meat.

It may well be that the bagged meat is equivalent to this latter example of *Chavos Da'as*, in that the bag and meat are basically two different layers. תתאה גבר may rule that the layer which has contact with the non-kosher tunnel-water (i.e., the bag) is rendered non-kosher due to that contact, but that layer/bag is not hot enough to serve as its own "תתאה גבר" for the layer/meat which is above it. If so, the bag would serve as a buffer between the non-kosher hot water and the cold kosher meat.

The fault with this line of reasoning is that data from the company which produces the bags indicates that the bags themselves reach temperatures that are well above *yad soledes bo*. This is because the specifications say that to reach the desired shrink-percentage, the bags must be heated to approximately 190° F. Thus, in the case of the shrink tunnel, the middle layer (the bag) is hot, and is therefore not like the middle layer that *Chavos Da'as* was discussing. When the hot bag comes in contact with the cold meat, *ta'am* transfers into the meat due to תתאה גבר – with the <u>bag</u> serving as the תתאה – even though the meat does not get hot.

---

[13] *Chavos Da'as* (Biurim) 91:5.
[14] Based on the point made in the text, *Chavos Da'as* explains why, as relates to *hilchos Shabbos*, a person who puts considerable amounts of cold water into a small amount of hot water does not violate the *issur* of בישול בשבת (see *Shulchan Aruch* OC 318:12); the water will not get hot, and therefore there is no violation of בישול בשבת.

Conclusion

In summary, shrink tunnels require a full *kashering*, especially if they are the "hot bath" style, and serious consideration should be given as to whether to allow *kashering* as a *ben yomo* which relies on the use of a דבר הפוגם.

Before (*kashering* and) use for kosher meat, all water must be drained from the tunnel and the entire chamber must be thoroughly cleaned. In this context, it is noteworthy that the "hot tunnel" devices are easier to *kasher* for two reasons: they are easier to clean, and it tends to be easier to get them to *kashering* temperatures as compared to a "hot bath" machine which commonly has controls that prevent making the water too hot.

In cases where *kashering* the heating tunnel is not possible, some will choose to not use the tunnel and instead create a "homemade" hot bath by filling a kettle or tank with hot water and manually dunking each bag of meat into it.

Chapter 53

ניצוק חיבור

שולחן ערוך סימן קי"ה סעיף ג'

נפל איסור חם לתוך היתר חם דכלי ראשון או אפילו איסור צונן לתוך היתר חם, הכל אסור דתתאה גבר על העליון ומחממו עד שמפליט בתחתון. ואין צריך לומר דהיתר צונן לתוך איסור חם שהכל אסור, אבל אם העליון חם והתחתון צונן אינו אוסר אלא כדי קליפה אפילו אם העליון החם איסור.

הגה: וכל זה לא מיירי אלא בחום כלי ראשון כגון מיד שהסירו מן האש מניחו עם ההיתר, אבל אם כבר מונח בכלי שני ואחר כך מניח ההיתר אצלו או עליו אינו אוסר כלל דכלי שני אינו אוסר כמו שנתבאר. ואם הניחם זה אצל זה אם שניהם חמים מחום כלי ראשון הכל אסור, ואם האחד צונן וההיתר צריך קליפה במקום שנגע. איסור שהניחו בכלי היתר או להיפך אמרינן ביה גם כן דין תתאה גבר כמו בבי חתיכות, ועיין לעיל סימן צ"ד אם חתך בשר בסכין חולבת. אסור לערות מכלי שיש בו שומן כשר לנר דולק שיש בו חלב או שומן איסור ובדיעבד אין לחוש.

At the end of the current halacha, *Rema*[1] says that *l'chatchilah* one should not pour from a container of kosher animal fat into a burning candle made of *chailev*[2] or animal fat from a non-kosher animal, but *b'dieved* if this occurred, any residual fat in the container remains kosher. This halacha is based on a set of *Mishnayos* in *Machshirin*,[3] as cited in *Mordechai*.[4]

The *Mishnayos* are discussing a case where someone poured *tahor* liquid from one container into *tamei* liquid in a second container, and the issue is whether the liquid in the upper container becomes *tamei* as a result. The general rule is[5] that it depends on the temperature of the liquids: If the upper one is hot, then it is not *tamei*, and the same is true if both are cold/ambient, but if the upper one is cold and the lower one is hot then

---

[1] *Rema* 105:3.
[2] I.e., fats which are forbidden even if they come from a kosher animal that underwent *shechitah*.
[3] *Machshirin* 5:9-11.
[4] *Mordechai, Chullin* 715.
[5] See *Mishnah, Machshirin* 5:9, as per *Gemara, Nazir* 50b, that an exception occurs with two kinds of honey (דבש הזיפין והצפחת) where a type of ניצוק חיבור occurs regardless of the temperatures of the items.

the liquid that remains in the upper container becomes *tamei*. The reason for this is - similar to the concept of תתאה גבר [6] discussed in the previous chapter – that when the lower one is hot, heat rises from it through the column of liquid. The rising heat creates a ניצוק חיבור – *connection through pouring* – between the lower (*tamei*) liquid and the upper liquid, and the upper liquid therefore becomes *tamei*.[7]

Mordechai concludes that the same concern applies when kosher liquid is poured into non-kosher, and therefore one should not pour kosher oil (i.e., ambient liquid) into a lit candle (i.e., hot) made of non-kosher materials.

> The coming explanation is based on Terumas HaDeshen, referenced in Gr"a,[8] and appears to be the simplest way to understand this halacha. Pri Megadim seems to have a different approach, as will be noted in footnote 10.

At first glance, the *kashrus* application which *Mordechai* is suggesting seems to be identical to the halacha of *zei'ah* which *Shulchan Aruch* 92:8 records (and which we discussed in Chapter 6). There it states that if steam rising from a hot pot of milk comes in contact with a *fleishig* pot, the *fleishig* pot absorbs dairy *ta'am* and becomes not kosher. This seems similar:

---

[6] *Taz* 105:6 specifically uses the term תתאה גבר in this context, and the other *Poskim* similarly appear to have assumed this. This is also why *Rema* cites this halacha at the end of 105:3, which is all about תתאה גבר.

[7] *Mishnah, Machshirin* 5:11 takes this halacha one step further, providing a case where the *tumah* will travel <u>downwards</u>. In a simple case where *tamei* was poured into *tahor*, it is obvious that the liquid in the lower container would become *tamei* since the *tamei* liquid is pouring into it. Therefore, the *Mishnah* describes a case where the woman who is *tamei* is stirring a (hot) pot filled with liquid that is *tamei*. No liquid is pouring into the (lower) pot, but under the right circumstances (i.e., her hands become moist from the condensate of rising steam) there is a ניצוק חיבור connection – with hot below and cold/ambient on top – and that connection causes a <u>downward</u> spread of *tumah* into the pot.

The case given in this *Mishnah* is specific to *tumah* where the person's hand has a "status" (i.e., *tumah*) that can transfer to the pot of food below. At first glance, this would not be relevant to kosher and non-kosher, which is probably why that possibility is not cited in *Yoreh Deah*. [As relates to *tumah*, it is recorded in *Rambam, Hil. Tumas Ochlin*, 7:3]. However, there appears to be a contemporary *kashrus* case where this comes up: The *Ashkenazic* custom is not to *kasher* (or use) glass, and therefore when someone *kashers* a microwave oven, the glass tray must be discarded. What about the glass "window" in the door? *Zei'ah* is not a concern since any condensation which forms on the door can only drip <u>downwards</u> which means it will not come into contact with the kosher food. But, seemingly, ניצוק חיבור is a concern (*l'chatchilah*) since hot steam escaping from the food contacts the door and condenses on it. This is exactly like the case of the *Mishnah*: there, ניצוק חיבור causes her hand's *tamei* status to go downwards to the pot, and here the door's non-kosher (i.e., un-*kashered*) status should pass down through the steam to the kosher food in the microwave. Does this mean that *l'chatchilah* one cannot use a microwave even after it is *kashered*? Perhaps, since ניצוק חיבור is only forbidden *l'chatchilah* (as relates to non-kosher and kosher), it is not necessary to be concerned with it when dealing with glass that was *kashered*, since even *Ashkenazim* are only *machmir l'chatchilah* not to *kasher* glass (see *Imrei Dovid, Kashering*, Chapter 56).

[8] *Terumas HaDeshen* 2:103 cited in *Gr"a* 105:21. See also *Minchas Yaakov* 23:12.

vapors rising from the hot non-kosher wax in the candle affect the kosher fat pouring into it. However, this cannot be the case which our halacha is discussing because if it was, then why does *Rema* rule that the fat in the upper container is permitted *b'dieved*? If *zei'ah* reaches the upper container, then – just like in *Shulchan Aruch* 92:8 – it should become non-kosher?

This indicates that in our case there is no concern of *zei'ah*. The simple reason for that is that, as noted in Chapter 6, *zei'ah* only poses an issue when the vapor is *yad soledes bo* at the time it comes into contact with the upper food or container. If, however, the containers are far enough apart, the vapors will have cooled by the time they reach the upper container and cannot transfer *ta'am* via the "*zei'ah*" effect. *Mordechai* is teaching even when *zei'ah* is not a concern, under the right circumstances – when the lower is hot and the upper is cold, and there is a flow of liquid[9] between them – *ta'am* can still transfer through ניצוק חיבור.[10]

---

[9] In fact, *Responsa Maharil* 190 (218) points out that, since ניצוק חיבור is limited to <u>liquids</u>, that is why *Mordechai* specifically chose a case where liquid is being poured, instead of a simple case of a kosher container passing over the burning candle (which would be akin to the case in *Shulchan Aruch* 92:8), or where powders or solids are being poured. In those cases, ניצוק חיבור would not apply, and if *zei'ah* were not a concern, the food in the upper container would remain kosher. Only in cases of liquids is there ניצוק חיבור, and that is why that type of cases was picked.

[10] The understanding of *Mordechai* presented in the text can be seen clearly in *Terumas HaDeshen*, who was asked three questions: (a) as relates to *zei'ah* in a case of meat hanging above cooking milk ((i.e., *Shulchan Aruch* 92:8), how far above the milk can the meat be, (b) is *Mordechai's* ruling only in the cases of ניצוק חיבור as outlined in the *Mishnayos* in *Machshirin*, or does it apply in all cases, and (c) how close does the upper container have to be to the lower one, to qualify for the *chumrah* of *Mordechai*? His response to "a" is that the vapor must be *yad soledes bo* when it contacts the meat. As relates to "b" and "c", he [essentially argues with *Mordechai* and] says that ניצוק חיבור only applies to issues that depend on touching (*stam yayin* (see the coming footnote) and *tumah*) but not to interactions between non-kosher and kosher. Thus, it is clear that he views these two concepts – *zei'ah* and ניצוק חיבור – as very different from one another.

In contrast, *Pri Megadim* (*Hanhagos Issur V'heter* 2:37 and MZ 105:6) appears to have understood that *Mordechai's* halacha is just another example of *zei'ah* rising up from the lower container and spreading *ta'am* into the upper one. [He sees them as so identical, that (in *Hanhagos Issur V'heter* he says that) according to a position he considers that the *Mishnayos* in *Machshirim* do not apply when the lower item is solid, that indicates that *zei'ah* would not apply to such cases]. He finds support to this position in *Shach* 105:11, who describes ניצוק חיבור (in our halacha) using the term "הבל", which is a term we associate with *zei'ah* (see Chapter 57). Another potential support can be seen from the halacha of ניצוק חיבור as relates to non-kosher wine; for more on that see footnote 11.

On the other hand, *Pri Megadim* does not explain why *Rema* is lenient *b'dieved* and why the case is specific to <u>pouring</u> (rather than just a kosher item above a non-kosher one). Perhaps, the answer to these questions is that [*Pri Megadim* understood that] even *Mordechai* held that by the letter of the law neither ניצוק חיבור nor *zei'ah* apply, but *l'chatchilah* we expand ניצוק חיבור to apply to non-kosher and kosher (see *Issur V'Heter* 29:6 (end) cited in *Darchei Moshe* 105:6), using the existing structure of *zei'ah*

This is *Mordechai's* opinion, which equates the transfer of *ta'am* to the transfer of *tumah*. But *Terumas HaDeshen* and others disagree and say that the *Mishnayos* are limited to *tumah*[11] because *tumah* transfers when items touch each other. Therefore, ניצוק חיבור can create a bond between the liquids where *tumah* can pass from one to the other. But touching alone does not cause *ta'am* to transfer, and for that there must be heat; since none of the candle's heat reaches the upper container, it remains kosher. *Rema's* ruling is therefore understood to be saying that *l'chatchilah* one should be *machmir* for *Mordechai* that *ta'am* can also transfer via ניצוק חיבור, but *b'dieved* we accept the ruling of most *Rishonim* that ניצוק חיבור is only relevant for *tumah* but not for transfer of *ta'am*.

ଔ ୭

A practical example of the halacha of ניצוק חיבור is that a person should not pour oil into a pot of hot *fleishig cholent* or *milchig* soup. If the vapor/*zei'ah* rising out of the *cholent* or soup is *yad soledes bo* when it reaches the oil container, then the oil remaining in the container will be *fleishig* or *milchig* respectively. If the container is high enough above the pot so that the vapor hitting it is not *yad soledes bo*, then the remaining oil is permitted

---

(which does apply to some cases of non-kosher and kosher). In a sense, it is a Rabbinic version of *zei'ah* (*l'chatchilah*) for cases that meet the requirements of ניצוק חיבור.

Pri Megadim also questions his own position, asking that if ניצוק is based on *zei'ah*-like concerns, then it should also apply when both containers are hot, yet the *Mishnah* is clear that it only applies when the lower one is hot and the upper one is cold. He does not offer an answer for this question. [Bearing this in mind, it is somewhat surprising that *Pri Megadim* OC AA 444:4, cited in *Sha'ar HaTziun* 444:4, basically says that because of ניצוק חיבור one should not pour hot *Pesach* food from a *Pesach* pot to a *chametz* dish, since the *chametz ta'am* will spread to the pot. There it is an example of hot food pouring into a hot (or cold) dish, and ניצוק חיבור does not apply in that case, so it is not clear why he forbids it].

The text follows the approach of *Terumas HaDeshen*.

[11] *Terumas HaDeshen* actually says that ניצוק חיבור applies to *tumah* and non-kosher wine. The case of *tumah* is the one listed in *Mishnayos Machshirin*, as described in the text. *Shulchan Aruch* YD 126 discusses ניצוק חיבור as relates to non-kosher wine, and specifically to those types of wine which would become forbidden if a non-Jew touched them (see *Shulchan Aruch* 126:1 as per *Shach* 126:9). However, the halacha there is presented that ניצוק חיבור tells use to view the non-kosher wine in the lower container as if it is mixed into the kosher wine in the upper container, to the point that (*Rema* 126:5) if there is relatively little wine in the lower container it can be *batel b'shishim* in the upper wine (and the upper wine remains kosher). This seems consistent with the understanding of *Pri Megadim*, discussed in footnote 10, rather than the approach noted in the text. This needs further consideration.

A question that both approaches must resolve is why the halachos of ניצוק חיבור as relates to wine make no mention of the limitation that it only applies if the lower container is hot and the upper one is cold. This indicates that that type of ניצוק חיבור is somehow different than the one in *Mishnayos Machshirin*, and this might offer a possible resolution for how those who disagree with *Pri Megadim* will reply to the proof noted in the previous paragraph.

For details on how ניצוק חיבור is addressed at certified wine tastings where non-*mevushal* wine is served, see *Imrei Dovid, Alcoholic Beverages*, Chapter 42, footnote 59.

b'dieved. Nonetheless, *l'chatchilah* one should avoid doing this, and be *machmir* to assume that *ta'am* transfers through ניצוק חיבור.

However, this *chumrah* to avoid ניצוק חיבור *l'chatchilah* even when the vapor hitting the oil is not *yad soledes bo*, is limited to cases where liquids are being poured, but not if someone was pouring spices or other solids into the *cholent* or soup.

Chapter 54

מלח

שולחן ערוך סימן ק"ה סעיפים ט-י"ד

The last several *halachos* in *Yoreh Deah* 105 discuss two topics which we have dealt with elsewhere, and this chapter will just reference those locations for further study.

מליח כרותח

The following is from *Imrei Dovid*, *Kashering*, Chapter 26 (see there for sources and more details):

> This halacha[1] is based on details which are given in *Yoreh Deah*[2] where it says that when there is food with a high level of saltiness, the salt can effect a transfer of *ta'am* even if there is no heat. However, this functions only to create *b'lios* <u>from</u> the [forbidden] salty food into the other food (regardless of whether that second food is salty). However, if the *issur* is not salty, then *b'lios* are not drawn out of another food even if the permitted food is salty. An extension of that halacha is that salting/*melichah* can cause *ta'am* to be absorbed <u>into</u> a utensil (i.e., from the salty one into the non-salty one) but never <u>out of</u> a utensil. This is because the utensil is always viewed as being "non-salty", so *ta'am* can never come out of the utensil via a salty food.
>
> Although this is the basic halacha, *Rema* in *Yoreh Deah* says that *l'chatchilah* one should be *machmir* and not use a non-kosher container to salt kosher meat, because there are those who argue that salty food <u>can</u> draw *ta'am* out of a utensil. That ruling of *Rema* is essentially repeated in our halacha which says that utensils in which meat was salted during the year should not be used *l'chatchilah* for salting meat for *Pesach* (unless they are *kashered*). There were *b'lios* all year long, and *l'chatchilah* one must assume that the salting of *Pesach* meat will draw out those *b'lios*.

---

[1] *Shulchan Aruch* OC 451:10.
[2] *Shulchan Aruch* YD 105:12, and earlier halachos in that *Siman*.

The following is from *Imrei Dovid*, *Animal Products*, Chapter 50 (see there for sources and more details):

> *Rema*[3] says that *l'chatchilah* one may not use a non-Jew's cheese-mold for kosher cheese (without *kashering*) due to a concern that the salting of the cheese will draw non-kosher *ta'am* from the mold into the kosher cheese. This concern is based on the principle of מליח כרותח which says that when foods are being salted (מליח), *ta'am* can transfer from the food as if the food was hot (כרותח). *B'dieved*, this is not a concern because the halacha is that מליח can only transfer *ta'am* from the food into the mold but not from the mold back into other food; but *l'chatchilah* we are *machmir* that *ta'am* transfers in both directions.
>
> It seems that in the days of *Rema* the dry salting was done when the cheese was already in the mold such that this was a real concern, but nowadays this is not at all common. Rather, it is now common to do dry salting on the finishing table 10-30 minutes before the cheese is put into the mold. With this manner of salting there is no issue because מליח כרותח only applies when such a significant amount of salt is added that the food it renders the food inedible (אינו נאכל מחמת מולחו).[4] Clearly, that much salt is not being added in this case, since all of the salt added remains in the finished product which is obviously still "edible".[5]

---

[3] *Rema* YD 105:12.
[4] See *Shulchan Aruch* YD 105:9.
[5] What about the fact that *Rema* YD 91:5 says that we no longer consider ourselves qualified to decide if a food is אינו נאכל מחמת מולחו, and instead apply the principle of מליח כרותח even if a smaller amount of salt was used? It seems that this incorrect in our case for the following reasons:

- *Yad Yehudah* 91:20 (*Aruch*), cited in *Darchei Teshuvah* 91:43, says that even *Rema* is only *machmir* if there is a <u>significant</u> salty taste to the food (אם עכ"פ נרגש בו הרבה מלח) such that it may be borderline אינו נאכל מחמת מולחו. But if there is a tiny amount of salt where no "judgment" is required to decide that it edible, even *Rema* is lenient (וגם אין להחמיר בזה מחמת מליח אנו בקיאים דבזה בודאי לא שייך בקיאות כלל). Our case, where the relatively small amount of salt added is widely considered an improvement to the cheese's flavor, seems to be a situation where *Rema* would be lenient.
- The salt does not remain <u>on</u> the cheese's surface as in the case described by *Rema* (regarding cheese molds) and *Shulchan Aruch*, but rather is immediately mixed <u>into</u> the curd. Accordingly, it seems reasonable to view the salt as an ingredient (about 0.5% of the cheese by weight) rather than as something applied to the cheese for *melichah*-purposes. [In contrast, there is approximately 4.5% salt used when *melichah* is performed on (sides of) beef, and about 7-14% salt when the same is done for lamb or chicken. The pieces of lamb and chicken are smaller than sides-of-beef, and therefore the former two have a larger surface area per pound of meat than the latter case].
- *Badei HaShulchan* 91:52 says that one does not have to be *machmir* for *Rema* (and be concerned that all salting might qualify as אינו נאכל מחמת מולחו) in cases where there is another meaningful reason to be lenient. This would seemingly apply in our case where, as noted, even if the salting is able to "push" (non-kosher) cheese-*ta'am* into the equipment, the letter of the law is that it is unable to "pull" cheese-*ta'am* from the equipment back into the (kosher) cheese. Although *l'chatchilah* we are *machmir* to assume *melichah* can also transfer *ta'am* <u>from</u> the utensil (as noted above), it would seem that one need not be *machmir* for both that concern and the concern that

See also above in Chapter 48.

מלח הבלוע מדם

The final halacha in *Yoreh Deah* 105 records the principle of מלח הבלוע מדם. It states that if a kosher מילתא דעבידא לטעמא (such as salt/מלח) absorbed non-kosher *ta'am* from a food which is not עבידא לטעמא (such as from blood/דם), and then became mixed into another food, the mixture is permitted if the מילתא דעבידא לטעמא is *batel b'shishim*. Although the general rule is that מילתא דעבידא לטעמא is not *batel b'shishim*, here *bitul* is appropriate since the מילתא דעבידא לטעמא is inherently kosher and is only not acceptable for use due to an absorption of something which is not עבידא לטעמא. In that case, the מילתא דעבידא לטעמא can be *batel b'shishim*.

This concept, and its significant relevance to the topic of "flavors" and whether they can be *batel*, is discussed at length in Chapter 26.

---

all salting is אינו נאכל מחמת מולחו. [This line of reasoning would not apply if the kosher cheese was hotter than *yad soledes bo*].

- Lastly, it is worth noting that *Rema* says that in cases of *hefsed merubah* one can trust their own judgment that a given food is אינו נאכל מחמת מולחו, and in certain cases a requirement to *kasher* the tables and molds (or have specially dedicated kosher equipment) would qualify as a *hefsed merubah*.

Part I

סימנים ק"ו-ק"ט

- **Chapter 55** .... Surface Propagations
- **Chapter 56** .... Keilim Used For Safek Issur
- **Chapter 57** .... ריחא
- **Chapter 58** .... Milk and Meat Cooking Side by Side
- **Chapter 59** .... מרדה
- **Chapter 60** .... Cigtrus and Air Up
- **Chapter 61** .... יבש ביבש

Chapter 55

Surface Propagations

אפשר לסוחטו

שולחן ערוך סימן ק"ז סעיף א
חתיכה שבלעה איסור ואין בה ס' לבטלו שנפלה לקדרה אינה אוסרת אלא לפי חשבון איסור שבה, שאם יש במה שבקדרה מצורף עם החתיכה עצמה ששים כנגד איסור הבלוע בה מותר מה שבקדרה, אבל החתיכה עצמה אסורה לפי שאיסור שבה אינו נפלט ממנה לגמרי (וכן עיקר ודלא כמו שכתב לעיל סימן צ"ב דאף אותה חתיכה מותרת). מה שאין כן בדבר הנבלל ונימוח שאם נפל דם וכיוצא בו לתוך רוטב של היתר ואסרו מחמת מיעוטו ואח"כ נתרבה הרוטב של היתר עד שיש בין כולו ס' לבטל הדם כולו מותר, שהכל נבלל ונתערב.

הגה: ולפי מה שנוהגין לומר בכל האיסורים חתיכה נעשית נבלה אין חלוק בין דבר לח לדבר יבש אלא לענין זה דאם הנאסר כבר הוא דבר יבש ויש ס' כנגדו החתיכה הנאסרת תחלה נשארת באיסורה וצריך להסירה משום אם מכירה, ואם אינו מכירה בטילה אם אינה חתיכה הראויה להתכבד, ואם הוא דבר לח הכל מותר מאחר דאיכא ס' נגד מה שנאסרה תחילה. ועיין לעיל סימן צ"ב וצ"ט.

Introduction

Microbiologists use several methods to propagate the microorganisms which will later be used in food production. This chapter will focus on the methods and applications where the microorganism grows on <u>top of</u> a substrate.[1]

---

[1] In contrast, a common method (or stage) of propagating a microorganism involves introducing it into a liquid broth (e.g., glucose) which the microorganism either feeds on to replicate itself or converts to something new. For example, yeast added to grape juice will convert the juice's sugar into alcohol. There, it is assumed that if the base material (e.g., glucose, grape juice) is not kosher or not kosher for *Pesach*, then the finished item has that same status.

One example of this is Koji Fermentation (common in Japan) where microorganisms grow on the surface of wheat bran.[2] [The same is done elsewhere with rice, breadcrumbs, or other substrates]. The bran itself does not appear to change during the process, but rather, a "mold" grows on the bran's surface, and this mold is the desirable product. In this case, the question is whether the microorganism is considered *chametz* since it grew on a *chametz* substrate. The same question applies if a scientist rubs an innocuous sample onto a Petri dish so he can watch it grow. If the nutrients in the Petri dish are non-kosher (e.g., animal protein), does that mean that the microorganisms that grow on the surface of that Petri dish are also not kosher? Here again, the microorganisms grow on top of the Petri dish, and the substrate shows no indication of having been affected or participating in the growth.

The question also applies in the opposite manner. What if the substrate is innocuous, but the original sample was from a non-kosher source? Two examples of this are cordyceps[3] and "artificial" meat. Sample cells are taken from an insect or animal and are propagated on a Petri dish to start the process of creating cordyceps and artificial meat, respectively. What is the status of these growths if the original contents of the Petri dishes were innocuous? Should we say that the "mold" growing on the dish is a product of the innocuous Petri dish components? Or do they retain the forbidden status of the original cell samples?

Our discussion will be divided into two parts:

1. The inherent status of the finished microorganism.
2. The status of the (finished) microorganism if some of the forbidden substrate was temporarily mixed into it and later removed.

Part 1
INHERENT STATUS

There are several possible reasons why a microorganism which grows on a non-kosher substrate should itself be non-kosher. From the perspective of the substrate, the microorganism might be viewed as (a) an expansion, (b)

---

[2] Wheat bran is assumed to be *chametz*. See *Mishnah Berurah* 465:1 and the discussion in *Imrei Dovid, Kashering*, Chapter 53.
   A well-known product which is believed to be produced using Koji fermentation is the lactase enzyme which is used to create lactose-free milk (e.g., Lactaid).
[3] See *Sappirim* Volume 30, available at www.Sappirim.com.

a growth, (c) a *yotzeh* (*excretion*), or (d) something that drew all its nourishment from a forbidden item (נתפטמה כל ימיו). Are any of those reasons to forbid the microorganism? Does it depend whether the substrate was איסורי אכילה (*items forbidden to eat*) or איסורי הנאה (*items from which it is even forbidden to get benefit*)? These possibilities will be considered in the coming paragraphs.

גידולים

The first two choices noted above – that the microorganism is an "expansion" or a growth of the forbidden substrate – appear to be equivalent to an issue which applies anytime a forbidden seed or plant grows. For example, what happens if someone plants an onion or wheat kernel which is *tevel* or *ma'aser sheini*? What is the status of the onions or wheat that grow from that plant (a.k.a. גידולים)?

The general halacha is that anything which grows is permitted, even if the item planted is something that does not disintegrate as part of the growing process (אין זרעו כלה).[4] *Chazon Ish*[5] explains that this is because the growth is considered to be something "new" (פנים חדשות באו לכאן) and essentially unrelated to the original. Therefore, based on this logic, even if we view the microorganism as an expansion or growth from the substrate,[6] it would be permitted.

> Even where גידולים are permitted, it is *assur l'chatchilah* to plant a forbidden seed, etc., based on the assumption that the growth will be permitted.[7] In turn, [if microorganisms growing on a non-kosher (or *chametz*) substrate are treated like the גידולים of that substrate],[8] it might be inappropriate for a *hashgachah* to certify a company doing exactly that.

---

[4] See the sources cited in the coming paragraph, who essentially make this point when discussing each of the exceptions. See also *Rambam, Hil. Me'ilah* 5:11, and *Tosfos, Bava Metziah* 80a ד"ה גידולי.

[5] *Chazon Ish, Shevi'is* 8:1 as per *Derech Emunah, Hil. Ma'aser Sheini* 6:109.

[6] It is not clear that it is reasonable to compare a microorganism "growing" on a substrate to the growth of a wheat kernel. When one plants wheat, it is clear that the kernel "replicates" itself to become a stalk filled with more wheat kernels, and in that sense, the resulting stalk is clearly an "expansion" of the original. That is not true of the microorganism, which in no way seems to have come from the substrate – they are not physically intertwined, and the two parts bear no resemblance to one another. Thus, even if גידולים are forbidden, it might well be that the microorganisms would not have the status of גידולים of the substrate. Nonetheless, the text continues with the possibility that it would be considered גידולים for the point drawn from *Tosfos* in the coming text, where the difference between גידולים and fermentations seems not to be relevant.

[7] See many of the sources cited in the coming paragraph.

[8] See footnote 6.

There are quite a few exceptions to this rule that גידולים are permitted, including: *terumah* (גידולי תרומה),[9] *tevel*,[10] and *ma'aser sheini* or *bikkurim* that have arrived in *Yerushalayim*.[11] One other exception which is potentially more relevant to us is *arlah*. *Tosfos*[12] explains that גידולי ערלה have a stricter status than other גידולים because *arlah* is *assur b'hana'ah*. The גידולים are not considered "ערלה" (just as other גידולים do not have the status of the seed they were grown from), but since the growth originates from the ערלה, someone who partakes in the fruit/growth is benefitting from the ערלה. In the actual case of ערלה, the halacha is that the גידולים are permitted due to the principle of זה וזה גורם since the plant comes from both the forbidden seed and the permitted soil.[13] But *Tosfos* has taught us a principle that [in cases where זה וזה גורם does not apply] גידולים of *issurei hana'ah* are forbidden as a form of prohibited *hana'ah*.

This principle would appear to be relevant to us in cases where the substrate was *issurei hana'ah*, such as if it were made of בשר בחלב, which is *assur b'hana'ah*. Whether *chametz* qualifies as *issurei hana'ah* in this context will be discussed below.

יוצא

The general rule is that the יוצא/excretion of an animal has the same status as the animal itself (כל היוצא מן הטמא טמא).[14] The most common examples of this rule are eggs and milk; if they come from a non-kosher bird or animal they are not kosher, and if they come from a kosher species, they are permitted.[15] If the microorganism's relationship to the substrate is that of a יוצא, then if the substrate was non-kosher or *chametz*, the microorganism would also be forbidden.

---

[9] *Rambam, Hil. Terumos* 11:21, based on *Gemara, Shabbos* 17b, that גידולי תרומה are *mid'oraisah* considered *chullin* but *Chazal* forbade them because they were concerned that *Kohanim* might save תרומה טמאה to plant it (if גידולי תרומה were permitted), and in the interim would mistakenly end up eating it.

[10] See *Rambam, Hil. Ma'aser* 6:6, that גידולי טבל are forbidden if the טבל was a type which is אין זרעו כלה, because טבל is seen as containing the future *terumah* and *terumas ma'aser*, such that it has the concern raised in the previous footnote regarding גידולי תרומה.

[11] *Rambam, Hil. Ma'aser Sheini* 6:15 (*ma'aser sheini*) and *Hil. Bikkurim* 4:15 (*bikkurim*).

[12] *Tosfos, Avodah Zara* 48b s.v. *v'Rabannan* and 49a s.v. *v'im*.

[13] *Shulchan Aruch* YD 294:12; see Chapter 2.

[14] *Gemara, Bechoros* 5b, as codified in *Shulchan Aruch* YD 81:1. [See *Imrei Dovid, Animal Products*, Chapter 1].

[15] Ibid.

However, there are two potential reasons why this rationale might not be applicable in this instance. The first is that *Acharonim*[16] disagree whether the principle of יוצא applies only to the excretions of living objects (e.g., animals, birds, fish), or even to plants. Rav Schachter[17] favored the approach that it does not apply to plant material. Therefore, יוצא would potentially be a reason to forbid a microorganism that grew on נבילה (non-kosher meat) since meat is from a living animal, but not if the substrate was forbidden because it was *chametz*, *stam yayin*, or other forbidden "plant" materials.

A more fundamental reason why יוצא is not a concern in most cases is that the inedible excretions of non-kosher animals, etc., are classified as פירשא (*excrement*) and are permitted.[18] In this context, the determination whether an excretion should be treated as יוצא or פירשא depends on its edibility at the time it is excreted or separates from the non-kosher animal. If at that point it is not edible, it is permitted, even if at some later point it will be processed and become edible.[19] In most cases, the microorganism growing on the substrate qualifies as inedible/פירשא as it is has the texture and appearance of moldy fuzz. [Of course, this would have to be evaluated on a case-by-case basis].

נתפטמה כל ימיה

Rema[20] rules that if the only food which an animal ever ate (נתפטמה כל ימיה) was something which is forbidden, that animal, in turn, is itself forbidden. *Shach*[21] argues that this halacha applies only if the food which it ate (its entire life) was something which is *issurei hana'ah*, but if it was just *issurei*

---

[16] *Minchas Boruch* (OC 41:2, and also in *Nachlas Boruch* #7) assumes that יוצא מן הטמא טמא also applies to byproducts of plants, saying:

...מי פירות אע"ג דלא הוה פרי אלא זיעה בעלמא מ"מ הא מקרא דבת היענה ילפינן לכל איסורין שבתורה דאוכל היוצא מן האיסור אע"ג דלא הוה גוף האיסור מ"מ אסור מן התורה

In contrast, *Kehillos Yaakov* (*Avodah Zara* #20) argues that יוצא does not apply to plants (דבדבר שאינו בעל חי לא מצינו שהיוצא ממנו אסור), he cites proofs for that position and suggests that this underlies the position of *Tosfos*, *Avodah Zara* 49a s.v. *v'im*, cited above. *Keren Orah* (*Nedarim* 47b) agrees with this idea, based in part on the fact (noted in the previous text) that גידולים are permitted. He says:

גידולי הפירות והצמחים לא באו לכלל זה דיוצא מן הטמא טמא משום דהגידולין הם בריה חדשה ועיקר גדילתן הוא מן הארץ והאויר, ולא דמו לולד טריפה שמתגדלת בבטן אמה הטריפה ומשום הכי גידולי איסור בכל גוונא מותרין מהתורה בכל האיסורין.

See also below from Rav Schachter.

[17] Point 11 of Rav Schachter's article on enzymes in *Mesorah*, Volume 1. He says:

דלא שייך כל העניין של יוצא מן האסור אלא בציור דומיא דחלב וביצה מבע"ח האסור, מפני שגדל באיסור

[18] For more on the status and criteria of פירשא, see *Shulchan Aruch* YD 81:3-4 and *Imrei Dovid, Animal Products*, Chapter 10.

[19] For more on this see *Iggeros Moshe* YD 2:24 (discussing shellac), *Imrei Dovid, Animal Products*, Chapter 11, and *Imrei Dovid, Halachos of Insects*, Chapter 49.

[20] *Rema* YD 60:1.

[21] *Shach* 60:5.

achilah, then the animal is permitted. Rav Schachter[22] said that the halacha follows *Shach* in this regard, and we will continue based on that assumption.

We can see from the halacha of נתפטמה כל ימיה, that although the animal's growth is only an indirect benefit one receives from the food which it ate, that is enough to be deemed (forbidden) *hana'ah* to make the animal *assur*. Rav Schachter said this is comparable to the halacha that bread is forbidden if it was baked in a fire fueled by wood that is *issurei hana'ah* (e.g., *avodah zara*).[23] There is no direct benefit from the wood, but the fact that it was used to bake a loaf of bread (יש שבח עצים בפת) or that the forbidden food provided nourishment for an animal's entire life is so significant, that eating the bread or the animal is considered having *hana'ah* from the fuel or food.

However, he also noted that the halacha of יש שבח עצים בפת has its own limitations, such as if the baking was done using coals that were already nearly extinguished (גחלים עוממות) (made from forbidden wood).[24] In that case, the connection between the *issurei hana'ah* and the benefit which the person receives (i.e., eating the bread) is much more tenuous, and the bread is permitted.

In our case, the microorganism is not an "animal", and it did not "eat" the substrate. But if its entire growth is from the substrate, should this be viewed as similar to נתפטמה כל ימיה or יש שבח עצים בפת? Rav Schachter said the answer to that question depends on how the growth of the microorganism is used. In some cases, the microorganism that grows is the actual desired item (and in turn, is what the consumer will eat). That case is treated like נתפטמה כל ימיה and is forbidden. But in most cases, the microorganism is merely a stepping-stone used to create other useful chemicals that have a food use. An example of this is if *aspergillus niger* was grown and used as the enzyme to convert glucose into citric acid. The growth itself is not the eventual food item, and the extra step between *issur* (the substrate) and the food (microorganism to enzyme to food) means that it is permitted, much as bread baked on גחלים עוממות.

---

[22] See *Mesorah* ibid. footnote 9.
[23] See *Gemara, Pesachim* 27a, codified in *Shulchan Aruch* YD 142:4 & 6.
[24] Ibid.

However, Rav Schachter himself questioned this conclusion. The typical form of *issurei hana'ah* which we might encounter in a substrate is *chametz*, and *chametz* has a particular *chumrah* that if *chametz* was used as a fuel to bake food <u>on</u> Pesach, that food is forbidden even if the *chametz* fuel was in a state of גחלים עוממות.[25] This means that since *chametz* on Pesach is *assur b'mashehu*, even the slightest connection to benefitting from *chametz* is enough to render the food forbidden. Therefore, although a גחלים עוממות connection is generally not enough to be considered *hana'ah*, on Pesach it is. If so, should we not say that the microorganism grown on *chametz* [and anything made from it] may <u>not</u> be eaten on Pesach?

Rav Schachter answered that the *chumrah* is limited to cases where the baking actually occurred <u>on</u> Pesach when *chametz* is [*assur b'mashehu* and is] *assur b'hana'ah*. But if the baking occurred before Pesach, when it is perfectly permitted to have benefit from *chametz*, the standard rules of יש שבח עצים בפת apply, and the items created with גחלים עוממות (or, in our case, the microorganisms created) are permitted. On an industrial level, the microorganism consumed on Pesach will have been grown well before Pesach, and therefore one can be lenient as per the standard rules of גחלים עוממות.

This idea – that the benefit that one has <u>on</u> Pesach from *chametz* functionality which occurred <u>before</u> Pesach is not viewed as "*hana'ah* on Pesach" – is echoed by *Nishmas Adam*[26] when discussing milk from cows which ate *chametz*. In Chapter 2 we saw that some are concerned that if one drinks milk from such a cow on Pesach, they are having *hana'ah* from *chametz*. One of *Nishmas Adam's* questions on that position is that the milk should only be forbidden if the cow's entire life it had only eaten *issurei hana'ah* (as per *Rema/Shach* above), which is impossible, since the *chametz* it ate before Pesach was not *issurei hana'ah*![27] This is the same point which Rav Schachter is making – that *chametz* playing a role before Pesach does not have the *chumros* of *issurei hana'ah* on Pesach, even though the milk or microorganism is being consumed on Pesach.

---

[25] See *Shulchan Aruch* OC 445:2 as per *Mishnah Berurah* 445:12.
[26] *Nishmas Adam, Hilchos Pesach* #9. This also appears to be the position of *Iggeros Moshe* OC 1:147:5, who is also discussing milk from cows which ate *chametz* and says: בחמץ בפסח הוא לעולם זה וזה גורם אף שאכלה רק חמץ מחמת האכילה דקודם פסח.
[27] Although it is possible that a calf was born on Pesach and only ate *chametz* for the first few days of its life, it would not produce milk until it gave birth and obviously that cannot happen before Pesach ends.

Some of the other *Poskim* who are *machmir* regarding milk from cows which ate *chametz* on *Pesach* might implicitly disagree with *Nishmas Adam's* view on this issue. [But some are *machmir* because they assume the milk is only associated with what the cow ate during the most recent 24-hour period,[28] and therefore are not expressing an opinion regarding *chametz* that the cow ate before *Pesach*].

Part 2
SEPARATION

אפשר לסוחטו

We have seen that there are situations when the "mold" (i.e., the finished microorganism) is permitted even though it grew on a substrate of *chametz* or *issur*. However, the common way the microorganism is isolated from the substrate involves first mixing the microorganism and substrate together, and then using mechanical (or other) methods to separate them. [Other methods do not involve any mixing of substrate with the microorganism; see footnote].[29] For example, when a Koji fermentation is finished, the spores might be washed off the wheat bran and then the mixture of bran and spores will be filtered and purified until there is a pure microorganism without any trace of substrate. Does that mean that we can ignore the fact that it was temporarily mixed with the forbidden substrate before separation occurred?

This appears to be an example of the halacha of אפשר לסוחטו, and we will review some details of that halacha before seeing how it applies to our case.

An example of אפשר לסוחטו would be if 1 cubic inch of blood (i.e., non-kosher) was absorbed into a piece of kosher meat (Piece #1) which has a volume of 10 cubic inches. The blood is not *batel b'shishim*, so Piece #1 is forbidden. Piece #1 was then cooked in a pot with 10 other pieces of kosher meat (Pieces #2-11) such that there is now enough kosher meat to

---

[28] See *Iggeros Moshe* ibid. who says דאפשר שהחלב בא רק מאכילת אותו היום, and *Pri Megadim* (OC AA 448:10 (end) and YD SD 60:5), cited in *Mishnah Berurah* 448:33 (end).

[29] For example, in one factory, the microorganism is covered with a mesh that is so fine that none of the substrate can pass through it, but the microorganism can. Then a vacuum hose is placed on top of the mesh, which sucks all the microorganism out without any of the substrate. In that case, there is never a mixture of substrate with microorganism, and the issue discussed in this part of the chapter is moot.

be *mevatel* the original blood. The *Gemara*[30] cites a *machlokes* whether one can assume that the *issur* left Piece #1 and spread to Pieces #2-11 (אפשר לסוחטו/*it is possible to squeeze out the non-kosher ta'am*). The halacha follows the strict opinion that אפשר לסוחטו אסור,[31] and therefore Piece #1 remains forbidden.

Rashba[32] explains that although it may well be that the non-kosher *ta'am* has, in fact, spread to Pieces #2-11 and the taste of the non-kosher can no longer be detected in Piece #1, nonetheless Piece #1 remains forbidden since a *mashehu* of the original blood remains. This is reflected in *Shulchan Aruch*,[33] who says אבל החתיכה עצמה אסורה לפי שאיסור שבה אינו נפלט ממנה לגמרי.

At first glance, it appears that since אפשר לסוחטו is אסור, the microorganism should remain forbidden even after the substrate is separated. Although the forbidden component is no longer present, the status of the microorganism cannot change from *assur* to *mutar*.

No ta'am left

However, if we probe a bit deeper into *Rashba's* point, we may find a reason to permit the microorganism. Does *Rashba* mean to say that Piece #1 remains forbidden <u>because</u> there is a trace of the blood's *ta'am* in it? Or does he mean that *Chazal* declared that once Piece #1 became forbidden, it can never lose that status? In other words, what would be the halacha if 100% of the non-kosher *ta'am* was taken out of Piece #1? Would it become permitted since there is not even a *mashehu* of *ta'am* left in it? Or would it remain forbidden since it was once *assur* to eat?

---

[30] *Gemara, Chullin* 108a-109a.
[31] *Shulchan Aruch* 106:1. *Rema* raises the point that *Shulchan Aruch* 92:4 appears to be lenient, but see *Shach* 92:11 who suggests an answer.
[32] *Rashba* (*Toras HaBayis HaAruch* 4:1, page 8a) says that the strict opinion assumes that enough non-kosher *ta'am* remains in the original *heter*. If so, *Beis Yosef* asks why not have a non-Jew taste the original piece to see if it is true? *Beis Yosef* answers, based on other statements of *Rashba* (*Toras HaBayis HaKatzar* 4:1, page 6b, *Responsa Rashba* 1:495, and מיוחסות 151), who says that even if the non-kosher *ta'am* spreads evenly to all the pieces, the original one remains forbidden. *Pri Megadim* SD 92:11 understands that the latter *Rashba* disagrees with the former and reflects *Rashba's* rejection of his original line of reasoning. In contrast, *Rebbi Akiva Eiger* (to *Shulchan Aruch* 106:1) says that these two opinions are consistent with one another; typically, most *ta'am* remains in the original piece, but even if it spread evenly, the first piece remains forbidden.
[33] *Shulchan Aruch* 106:1, as per the inference drawn by *Badei HaShulchan* 106:4.

We can bring a proof for the lenient position from the way a *Gemara* is explained by *Tosfos*.[34] The case is that a piece of meat is being *kashered* over the fire and the process appears to be just about completed. A person wants to put a pan underneath the meat to catch the (kosher) fat dripping off, but obviously does not want any (non-kosher) blood mixed into his fat. The *Gemara* says that he should put תרי גללי דמלחא (*two rock-hard*[35] *pieces of salt*) into the pan, which will attract any blood that drips in and separate it from the fat. On this, *Tosfos* asks that if אפשר לסוחטו is אסור, the fat should remain forbidden? It became forbidden when blood was mixed into it, so even after the תרי גללי דמלחא remove the blood, the fat should remain *assur*? *Tosfos* answers that in the times of the *Gemara*, they knew how to put in just the right amount (and type) of salt which would remove <u>all traces</u> of blood from the fat.[36] In other words, אפשר לסוחטו is only forbidden if some small amount of *issur* remains in the item, but if there is absolutely none left, then all agree that the item returns to its original permitted state. *Pri Megadim*[37] independently comes to the same conclusion.

This is directly relevant to our case. Our technology is undoubtedly more capable than that of תרי גללי דמלחא, and we are confident that the recovered microorganism is pure with no trace of substrate. *Tosfos* is teaching that in such a case, there is no concern of אפשר לסוחטו אסור and the microorganism is permitted.

It is noteworthy that *Rashba* has a different understanding of the *Gemara's* leniency regarding תרי גללי דמלחא, according to which there is no proof from this *Gemara* to our question.[38]

---

[34] *Gemara*, *Chullin* 112a-b as per *Tosfos*, *Chullin* 112a s.v. *trei*.
[35] See *Sefer HaAruch* s.v. גלל #4 says (דמלחא) גללי means חזק כאבן (*rock hard*).
[36] *Tosfos* notes that in subsequent generations this scientific knowledge was lost, and therefore one cannot rely on the תרי גללי דמלחא method anymore.
[37] *Pri Megadim* SD 106:2 says ומיהו אם בא אליהו ואמר שנפלט לגמרי היה מותר אלא שאין במציאות.
[38] *Rashba*, *Chullin* 112a says that there are enough ספיקות (doubts) whether there is any concern of blood in the fat (maybe all blood drained from the meat before the pan was put there, even if a bit of blood dripped in it might be *batel b'shishim*, in many cases the blood would not be more than *assur mid'rabannan*). Therefore, one should use תרי גללי דמלחא to get out as much blood as possible, but (a) there is no claim that this method will be foolproof, and (b) *b'dieved* the fat would be permitted even if תרי גללי דמלחא were not added. If the fat is not forbidden <u>before</u> the תרי גללי דמלחא are added, there clearly cannot be אפשר לסוחטו to say it should "remain" forbidden after the blood is removed.

לח בלח

Another detail of אפשר לסוחטו is that *Shulchan Aruch*[39] tells us that it is not forbidden when the mixture is לח בלח (*two liquids mixed together*). Why should that case be more lenient? Why would we not say that since the original דבר לח became forbidden, it retains that status even if it is diluted? *Badei HaShulchan* provides two possible explanations (see the footnote).[40] It appears that in cases such as ours, where the *issur* is <u>removed</u> from the mixture – in contrast to the case of *Shulchan Aruch*, where the *issur* is merely being diluted by adding more *heter* – at least one of those explanations would apply even if the mixture was not לח בלח.[41] Thus, this is another potential reason to say that אפשר לסוחטו does not apply in this case.

חנ"נ

The above point regarding לח בלח leads directly to a question relative to much of what has been written in this section. Just after *Shulchan Aruch* says that one can be lenient about אפשר לסוחטו in cases of לח בלח, *Rema* notes that this leniency is not relevant to *Ashkenazim*. Although אפשר לסוחטו does not apply, *Ashkenazim*[42] are *machmir* that חתיכה נעשית נבילה (חנ"נ) <u>does</u> apply [for all *issurim*] even in cases of לח בלח. Thus, even if we can present a good argument for not being concerned for אפשר לסוחטו, we must still forbid the mixture based on the principle of חנ"נ.

Consequently, we must say that generally אפשר לסוחטו tells us the forbidden (original) piece of meat (Piece #1, above) remains *assur*, even after it was mixed into the other pieces (Pieces #2-11) to the point that there is no longer any *ta'am* of blood in Piece #1. But אפשר לסוחטו only

---

[39] *Shulchan Aruch* 106:1.

[40] *Badei HaShulchan* 106:10 explains that a לח בלח mixture is different than a לח ביבש in two ways: Firstly, liquids mix thoroughly such that after the second dilution there is an equal amount of *ta'am* in the original liquid as in the newly added liquid. It therefore does not make sense to give the original liquid a stricter status than the overall mixture. [He bases this on *Pri Megadim* SD 106:1]. Secondly, in a לח ביבש mixture the *heter*/יבש <u>absorbs</u> *issur* and becomes inherently (and permanently) forbidden. But when liquids mix (לח בלח) one can no longer distinguish between the *heter* and *issur* (and therefore one cannot eat them) but the *heter* retains its inherently permitted status. Therefore, once more *heter* is added and the ratios change, there is not enough *issur* left to confound the *heter* and the mixture is permitted. [He bases this on *Beis Yosef* 92 (discussing *ChaNaN*); *Rashba*, *Chullin* 112a makes a similar point when discussing the *Gemara* of תרי גללי דמלחא].

[41] Namely, when the forbidden component is extracted from the mixture, it is extracted equally from all parts; therefore, the first reason noted in the previous footnote would say that we can be lenient just as with a לח בלח mixture. *Badei HaShulchan* ibid. rules that one can leniently rely on the first reason (in the case he constructs).

[42] *Rema* 92:4.

relates to Piece #1. As far as the other pieces (Pieces #2-11), they have no *ta'am* of blood and are permitted, since Piece #1 only contains 1 cubic inch of blood and that is not enough to be *nosein ta'am* into Pieces #2-11. But for those who are *machmir* for חנ"נ, Piece #1 is not viewed as containing just 1 cubic inch of blood. Rather it is נעשית נבילה and is henceforth treated as being 100% blood (i.e., 10 cubic inches of blood). If so, when it is mixed into Pieces #2-11, those pieces do not have enough volume to be *mevatel* 10 cubic inches of *issur*, so they also become forbidden.

Does this mean that even if we are correct that אפשר לסוחטו does not apply in the case of the microorganism separated from the substrate – because there is no *ta'am* left at all, or it is like לח בלח – we must still forbid it based on חנ"נ?

While this point is accurate, it does not necessarily mean that we must be *machmir* in all cases. That is because there are many leniencies associated with חנ"נ which are particularly relevant here. חנ"נ does not apply to *chametz* before *Pesach*,[43] such that if the only issue with the substrate is that it is *chametz* (e.g., wheat bran, breadcrumbs), we can ignore חנ"נ and just consider if אפשר לסוחטו applies. Similarly, since חנ"נ is a Rabbinic stringency, it only applies if we are sure there was *issur* mixed in. But in cases of *safek issur*, there are many situations when we are not *machmir* for חנ"נ.[44] Thus, unless we are sure the substrate included forbidden ingredients, we may not have to be concerned for חנ"נ.[45] Lastly, there is a general principle that in cases of הפסד מרובה one can be lenient about חנ"נ בשאר איסורים,[46] and there may be cases where there is a great need for the particular microorganism which would justify being lenient.[47]

---

[43] See above in Chapter 3, in the *chametz* section.
[44] See details in Chapter 3 in the *safek issur* sections.
[45] Additionally, see the ידיעת התערובת section of Chapter 3 that there may not be a need to be *machmir* for חנ"נ in cases such as ours, where there is no ידיעת התערובת.
[46] *Rema* 92:4.
[47] In this context it is worth bearing in mind that microorganisms are typically used in small proportions in food, such that it is only a Rabbinic principle of *ma'amid* that prevents them from being *batel b'shishim*. In turn, if the microorganism is only forbidden based on חנ"נ (rather than being inherently *assur*), it may be that *ma'amid* is not a concern altogether; see the איסור דרבנן section of Chapter 3.

Chapter 56

Keilim Used For Safek Issur

שולחן ערוך סימן ק"ז סעיף א

המבשל ביצים הרבה בקליפתן לא יוציאם מהמים שנתבשלו בהם עד שיצטננו או יתן עליהם מים צוננים לצננם ואחר כך יוציאם, משום דחיישינן שמא ימצא באחת מהן אפרוח ואם היה מוציא מהם קודם שיצטננו שמא היתה נשאר אותה שיש בה אפרוח עם האחרונות והיתה אוסרתן לפי שלא היה נשאר שם ששים לבטלה. הגה: ואם לא עשה כן אלא עירה אותן לקערה ונמצא אחת מהן טרפה יש אוסרין הכל דחיישינן שמא הטרפה נשאר לבסוף ולא היה ששים בקדרה לבטל ונאסר מה שבקדרה וחוזר ואוסר כל מה שבקערה. וכן בדגים קטנים שנמצא דג טמא בקערה ולא עירה כולם בפעם אחת אל תוך הקערה דאז יש לחוש שמא נשאר האיסור לבסוף, ויש מתירין בכל עני דלא מחזיקין איסור לומר דנשאר האיסור בלא ס', וכן עיקר. ואפילו לדעת האוסרים אין לאסור הכלים שנתבשלו בו דמעמידין הכלי על חזקתו.

At the end of the current halacha, *Rema*[1] describes a case where there is a question whether a food is forbidden, and due to that possibility, the food cannot be eaten; however, since the pot has a חזקת היתר it is permitted to use the pot in the future without *kashering*. At first glance, this seems to be saying that whenever there is a question about the *kashrus* of a food, a utensil used with it remains kosher due to its חזקת היתר, even though we are *machmir* about eating the food itself. If that were true, it would be a significant *heter* which would apply in many situations.

In fact, this is not at all what *Rema* intends to imply, and to understand why, we need to probe a bit into the case that *Rema* was discussing. A person cooked more than 61 eggs in a pot and later discovered that one of them was not kosher (since it was found to contain a chick). The non-kosher egg will be discarded, but what is the status of the other eggs?

---

[1] *Rema* 107:1.

Before any eggs are removed from the pot, the *b'lios* from the non-kosher egg spread evenly to the other eggs and will be *batel b'shishim* in those eggs.² However, if batches of eggs are poured from the pot while they are still hot, some of them will become non-kosher, for the following reason: If the non-kosher one is in an early batch, eggs in that batch will be non-kosher, since in that batch there are not enough eggs for *bitul b'shishim* of the non-kosher egg's *ta'am*. And if the non-kosher egg is in the final batch, then the eggs in that batch will be non-kosher for the same reason (there are not enough of them for *bitul b'shishim* of the non-kosher *ta'am*). Therefore, one should cool all the eggs to a temperature below *yad soledes bo* before removing them from the pot.³ This way there will never be a time when a hot non-kosher egg is with less than 61 other eggs.

What if someone did not wait for the eggs to cool down, and poured them out in batches (as above) but does not know which batch of eggs the non-kosher one was in? *Rema* cites two opinions on the matter: some say that all of the eggs are forbidden, but others argue that they are all permitted. [*Rema* favors the lenient opinion, but others disagree in specific cases].⁴ In that context, *Rema* says that even those who forbid the eggs, would permit the use of the pot without *kashering* due to the pot's חזקת היתר.

Maharil ⁵ explains that really there is strong basis for permitting all the eggs, because for each one there is only a *safek* whether it was one of the forbidden ones (and that *safek* is countered by its חזקת היתר). The primary reason to be *machmir* is because the average person will not understand how the eggs can all be permitted when the non-kosher egg must have come out in one of the batches and at least affected that batch. Therefore, to avoid giving a ruling that will encourage mockery of the halacha (משום חוכא ואטלולא), we are *machmir* not to eat any of these eggs. This issue does not apply to the status of the pot since it is very possible and understandable that the pot has no non-kosher *b'lios* – which would have happened if the non-kosher egg came out in the first batch. Accordingly, *Rema* says that as relates to the pot, we can follow the letter of the law and rely on חזקת היתר to maintain the pot's kosher status.

---

² See *Shulchan Aruch* 98:7. See *Imrei Dovid, Animal Products*, Chapter 30, that in most cases, there is actually no need for there to be 61 eggs to create the *bitul*; *Shulchan Aruch* here appears to be referring to cases where 61 eggs are required.
³ *Shulchan Aruch* 107:1.
⁴ See *Badei HaShulchan* 107:15, summarizing the opinions of *Taz* 107:4-5 and *Shach* 107:1.
⁵ *Responsa Maharil* 151 (162), referenced in *Shach* 107:2.

Thus, this is a very specific case where the food is treated as non-kosher for a "non-halachic" reason (משום חוכא ואטלולא) that does not apply to the pot, so the pot can remain kosher due to חזקת היתר.

In contrast, in the typical case where there is a question about the kosher status of a food and the halacha requires us to be *machmir*, that strict status applies equally to the pot it was cooked in. The same rationale for forbidding the food (e.g., ספק דאורייתא לחומרא) applies equally to the pot,[6] which must be *kashered* before it is used for kosher food.[7]

---

[6] If the food was forbidden based on ספק דאורייתא לחומרא, can we wait for the pot to be *aino ben yomo* so that any *ta'am* absorbed will be downgraded to a mere *issur d'rabannan*, and then be lenient regarding its kosher status since ספק דרבנן לקולא? This is an example of the principle of נתגלגל, that when an *issur d'oraisah* becomes converted to an *issur d'rabannan*, we generally do not apply the leniency of ספק דרבנן לקולא (*Pri Megadim* SD 107:2). For more on the principle of נתגלגל, see Chapter 65.

[7] Another case where the food is deemed non-kosher, but the pot can be used without *kashering*, is when there are special reasons to be lenient regarding the pot that did not apply to the original food. A prime example of that is when we are no longer sure which pot was used with the non-kosher; the food is forbidden, but the non-kosher pot is potentially *batel* in the other kosher pots that the person owns. For more on that, see Chapter 36.

Chapter 57

ריחא

שולחן ערוך סימן ק"ח סעיף א

אין צולין בשר כשרה עם בשר נבילה או של בהמה טמאה בתנור א' ואף על פי שאין נוגעים זה בזה, ואם צלאן הרי זה מותר ואפילו היתה האסורה שמינה הרבה והמותרת רזה, ואם התנור גדול שמחזיק י"ב עשרונים ופיו פתוח מותר לצלותם בו ובלבד שלא יגעו זה בזה, ואם אחד מהם מכוסה בקערה או בבצק וכיוצא בו מותר לצלותם אפילו בתנור קטן ופיו סתום: הגה וה"ה לבשר עם חלב נמי דינא הכי. ונהגין להחמיר לכתחילה אפילו בתנור גדול ובדיעבד להקל אפילו בתנור קטן.

ואם אפה פת עם בשר אסור לאכלו עם חלב אם יש לו פת אחר, וכן אם עובד כוכבים אפה פת עם איסור אסור לקנות אותו אם יש פת אחר דכל זה מקרי לכתחילה, אבל אם אין לו פת אחר בריוח מותר בשניהם דזה מקרי לענין זה דיעבד.

יי"א דאין מתירין ריחא אפילו בדיעבד אלא אם כן התנור פתוח קצת מן הצד או למעלה במקום שהעשן יוצא, ובמקום הפסד אין להחמיר בדיעבד אפילו סתום לגמרי, ואם האיסור דבר חריף וכל שכן אם ההיתר דבר חריף ריחא מילתא היא ואפילו בדיעבד אסור אם שניהם מגולים אבל אם אחד מהם מכוסה אפילו בבצק בעלמא מותר.

אם אפו או צלו איסור והיתר תחת מחבת אחת מגולין אסור אפילו בדיעבד, וה"ה אם אפו בכה"ג פת עם בשר אסור לאכלו בחלב, אבל בזה אחר זה אין לחוש אלא אם כן הזיע המחבת משניהם דאז אסור אפילו בזה אחר זה אם היו שניהם מגולין דהוי ככיסוי של קדרה כדלעיל סימן צ"ג.

יי"א דכל מקום דאמרינן ריחא מלתא ואוסר בדיעבד היינו דוקא דליכא ששים מן ההיתר נגד האיסור אבל בדאיכא ששים מן ההיתר אפי' בכל מה שבתנור מבטל האיסור, ולצורך הפסד יש לנהוג כן. יי"א דאיסור האוסר במשהו כגון חמץ בפסח ריחא מלתא ואוסר אפילו בדיעבד אם התנור קטן והוא סתום והאיסור מגולין תוך התנור, ויש אומרים שאין לחלק, ובמקום הפסד יש לסמוך אדברי המקילין, ועיין לקמן סוף סימן קי"ח אם יש להחמיר לכתחילה לשפות ב' קדירות וא' מהן של איסור על הכירה או לצלות איסור אצל היתר.

Different types of vapors

In Chapter 6, we discussed the concept of *ta'am* transferring via זיעה/vapors rising from typical moist or liquidy foods – as described in *Yoreh Deah* 92:8 – quoting part of *Imrei Dovid*, *Kashering*, Chapter 36.

However, there are also two other forms of vapor-like transfers which have different halachos than זיעה; they are הבל הקדירה (literally: vapor/cloud of the pot)[1] and ריחא (literally: aroma or fragrance).[2] The following is an overview of those topics, based on *Imrei Dovid*, ibid., Chapters 36-37. See there for more details and sources.

~ הבל הקדירה

There is a type of steam vapor known as הבל הקדירה whose status is <u>stronger</u> than that of זיעה. This is understood to be because the pot cover basically seals the steam inside the pot, and there is a relatively small amount of space between the top of the food and the pot cover, such that a "cloud" of vapor forms in that head space. As a result, the vapor is given a higher status called הבל הקדירה, which results in our treating the pot cover as if it absorbed the vapor as a true *kli rishon*. This is in contrast to זיעה which comes into contact with utensils, which we have seen is treated as *irui kli rishon*. Accordingly, the pot cover must be *kashered* as a *kli rishon* and not with *irui kli rishon*.

On an industrial level, this applies to a covered kettle. In most cases, the kettle is full enough that the buildup of steam above the top of the product qualifies as הבל הקדירה, and therefore the cover of the kettle must be *kashered* as a *kli rishon*.

~ ריחא

In addition to הבל הקדירה which causes <u>more</u> *b'liah* than זיעה, there is another type of vapor which creates <u>less</u> *b'liah* than זיעה. That is the vapor which is emitted by a dry product. It is referred to as ריחא and carries so little *ta'am* that if ריחא from a non-kosher food spread to a kosher food, the kosher food *b'dieved* remains permitted to eat. At the same time, ריחא does carry some *ta'am*, and therefore *l'chatchilah* one may not bake (dry) non-kosher and kosher items simultaneously.

~ Pesach

If a transfer of *chametz*-ריחא happened <u>on</u> Pesach, the Pesach food becomes forbidden. This is because even the tiniest amount of *chametz* cannot be *batel* <u>on</u> Pesach (חמץ אסור במשהו), and therefore the tiny amount of *ta'am* transferred through ריחא is enough to forbid the food.[3]

There is a well-known halacha that absorbed non-kosher *ta'am* which is *aino ben yomo*, will *b'dieved* not affect the status of kosher food. There is a *machlokes* whether that leniency applies to *chametz ta'am* absorbed into Pesach food <u>on</u> Pesach; *Shulchan Aruch* is lenient, and *Rema* is machmir. According to *Rema*, if a *chametz* cover was placed onto a pot in which (non-*chametz*) food was cooking on

---

[1] A primary location where that is discussed is *Shulchan Aruch* OC 451:14.
[2] This is the focus of the current halacha, *Shulchan Aruch* YD 108:1-2, and 97:3.
[3] *Rema* OC 447:1 and YD 108:1; see also *Mishnah Berurah* 447:13. In cases of *hefsed merubah*, one can be lenient even on *Pesach* (ibid).

Pesach, that food becomes forbidden to use on *Pesach* even if the pot cover had not been used for *chametz* in the previous 24 hours.

In fact, this situation unfortunately occurs too often when someone's *chametz* dishes are not properly put away before *Pesach* and they mistakenly use a *chametz* utensil during *Pesach* cooking. According to *Rema*, the *Pesach* food is forbidden even if the *chametz* utensil was *aino ben yomo*.

ריחא Details

~ Exceptions

We saw that the general rule is that *l'chatchilah* one must avoid forbidden ריחא, but *b'dieved* it will not affect the *kashrus* of other food. Some exceptions are:

- If the food is covered, that prevents vapors from escaping and obviates the concern even from a *l'chatchilah* perspective.[4] Similarly, ריחא is only a concern (*l'chatchilah*) if the permitted and forbidden foods are cooking simultaneously. However, once the forbidden food is removed from the oven, *l'chatchilah* one may put kosher food into that oven and there is no need to be concerned for absorbed ריחא.[5] [As noted, this is limited to cases where the only concern is ריחא; in many cases one must also be concerned for זיעה which does affect equipment as well].[6] Both leniencies noted here apply even on *Pesach*.[7]

---

[4] *Shulchan Aruch* 97:3 and *Rema* 108:1.

[5] *Rema* 108:1 as per *Shach* 108:12.

[6] *Pri Megadim* (OC AA 447:4 towards the end) shows some conceptual differences between זיעה and ריחא. He says:

גם ב' קדירות זה על גבי זה ותחתונה מגולה זיעה כממש,
כבסימן צ"ב סעיף ח' ביורה דעה ולקמן תנ"א במ"א ל',
ואסור אף בדיעבד שנבלע בקדירה עליונה ומשם לתבשיל,
וריחא הוא בזה אצל זה.

One source he cites is *Magen Avraham* 451:30, who provides two reasons why *Shulchan Aruch* OC 451:15 says that the cover of a baking pan must be *kashered* with *libun*. One reason given is that the cover is מזיעה מהבל החררה, which supports *Pri Megadim's* classification of זיעה (at least in such a confined place) as equivalent to an extension of the food (זיעה כממש), and that is why it affects what it comes in contact with (while ריחא does not). Another source he references is *Yoreh Deah* 92:8 which describes זיעה as rising upwards. He appears to be saying that זיעה only goes vertically, in contrast to ריחא, which he says spreads in all directions (וריחא הוא בזה אצל זה). [See a related issue in Chapter 53 footnote 7].

[7] *Mishnah Berurah* 447:13, based on the general rule provided by *Rema* OC 447:1 and YD 108:1 that we are only *machmir* on *Pesach* in cases where there is at least a *mashehu* of *ta'am* passing through the ריחא, but if there is absolutely no transfer, then all agree that the food is permitted.

- If the permitted[8] food is a דבר חריף (see Chapter 14), it becomes forbidden even *b'dieved*.[9] Although we saw above that if the food is covered there is generally no concern of ריחא even *l'chatchilah*, *Shach*[10] says that when dealing with a דבר חריף one should *l'chatchilah* not rely on the fact that the food is covered (but *b'dieved* the food will be permitted).

- The *Acharonim* suggest that if foods are in the oven together for many hours – such as a *cholent* cooking overnight on *Shabbos* – the ריחא may have a stricter status, somewhat akin to הבל הקדירה noted above.[11]

~ **Large vs. small oven**

Regarding ריחא, there is much discussion in the *Poskim* about the difference between (a) whether one is dealing with a "large oven chamber" or a "small oven" (defined below) and (b) whether that chamber is completely enclosed with no exhaust vent, has an exhaust vent but is otherwise enclosed, or is fully open on top. Nowadays, these opinions are rarely relevant since (almost) all of our devices have exhaust vents and the consensus is that in such a case – regardless of whether the chamber is large or small – we will avoid ריחא *l'chatchilah*[12] but permit it *b'dieved*.[13] As

---

[8] *Rema* 108:1 says that the same applies if the *issur* (or *chametz*) is a דבר חריף. [In Chapter 14 we saw many examples of דבר חריף, and *Magen Avraham* 447:4 (end) says that borscht (fermented from wheat bran) is an example of *chametz* which is *charif*]. However, *Chok Yaakov* 447:10 argues that one need only be *machmir* if the permitted food was *charif*. *Sha'ar HaTziun* 447:6 cites both opinions – including that *Gra"z* 447:11 agrees with *Rema*, and *Mekor Chaim* 447:6 (*Chiddushim*) accepts *Chok Yaakov* – without offering a ruling.

[9] *Rema* 108:1. This is true even if it occurs in a "large" oven (defined below) (*Sha'ar HaTziun* 447:7).

[10] *Shach* 108:10 as per *Pri Megadim* and *Rebbi Akiva Eiger* ad loc.

[11] See *Magen Avraham* 447:13 and others cited towards the end of *Mishnah Berurah* 447:13.

[12] In this context, *Rema* notes that if a person has bread (for example) which absorbed ריחא of meat, they cannot eat that bread with dairy. At first glance, one might think that this *chumrah* is based on a concern for those *Rishonim* who follow the opinion in the *Gemara* (*Pesachim* 76b) that ריחא is forbidden even *b'dieved*. In fact, the source of this halacha is *Rif* (*Chullin* 32a) who rules that ריחא is permitted *b'dieved* (i.e., ריחא לאו מילתא), and must reconcile that with a statement in the *Gemara* (*Pesachim* ibid.) that bread baked with meat cannot be eaten with *kutach* (a dairy dish). If ריחא לאו מילתא, why is that forbidden? *Rif* answers that this teaches that (a) even those who say ריחא לאו מילתא agree that it is *l'chatchilah* forbidden, and (b) the choice to use this bread with dairy is itself a form of "*l'chatchilah*" (since it could be eaten with meat or pareve foods instead). [*Ran* ad loc. disagrees with both points]. *Rema* is a codification of that ruling.

[13] The simple reading of *Shulchan Aruch* and *Rema* implies that there is disagreement if there is a *l'chatchilah* concern of ריחא in a large chamber. This is because (a) *Shulchan Aruch* 97:3 says that in a large oven one can be lenient *l'chatchilah*, (b) *Shulchan Aruch* 108:1 says that one can be lenient *l'chatchilah* if it is a large chamber which has an "opening" (פיו פתוח) (see *Taz* 108:2), and to this, *Rema* comments that (c) we are *machmir l'chatchilah* even for a large chamber, and (d) some take a strict

relates to ריחא of *chametz* on[14] *Pesach*, the halacha is stricter, and there the size of the chamber makes a difference: in a large oven with a vent the food is permitted *b'dieved* (like year round),[15] and without a vent it is only permitted in cases of *hefsed merubah*,[16] while in a small oven (with or without a vent) the food is only permitted in cases of *hefsed merubah*.[17]

One notable exception is that many full-sized "hot boxes"[18] qualify as a "large oven" and do <u>not</u> have an exhaust vent. In that case, the food would

---

stand even *b'dieved* unless there is an exhaust vent to the chamber. However, *Shach* 108:3 (as per *Pri Megadim* ad loc.) (cited in *Mishnah Berurah* 447:13 with *Sha'ar HaTziun* 447:8) says that all these opinions agree that the only time one can be lenient *l'chatchilah* for a large chamber is when it is <u>fully</u> open on top (hence, rulings "a" and "b" above), but if there is merely an exhaust vent, it is only permitted *b'dieved* (hence, "c" and "d")s.

As relates to a small chamber, if there is a vent, the food is permitted *b'dieved*, and if there is no vent, it is only permitted in cases of *hefsed merubah* (*Rema* 108:1 as per *Shach* 108:8).

[14] This *chumrah* is an outgrowth of the *issur mashehu* (i.e., that *chametz* cannot be *batel b'shishim*). The *issur mashehu* is limited to cases where *chametz* interacts with food <u>on</u> *Pesach* (*Shulchan Aruch* OC 447:1), but if it happened beforehand – and even if it happened on *Erev Pesach* at a time when it is forbidden to eat *chametz* (ibid. 447:2) – the halacha is not stricter than for year-round. Therefore, if a question of ריחא of *chametz* arises before *Pesach*, the status *b'dieved* is the same as would be for any other *issur*.

[15] *Pri Megadim* SD 108:14.

[16] Ibid.

[17] *Rema* 108:1 rules that for *Pesach*, if the oven is small and it is פי סתום one should be *machmir* except in cases of *hefsed* (i.e., *hefsed merubah* – *Pri Megadim* AA 447:4, *Mishnah Berurah* 447:13). *Magen Avraham* 447:4 understands that in this context, פי פתוח refers to a chamber which at least has an exhaust vent but if there was no vent then *Rema* would not be lenient even in cases of *hefsed merubah*. However, *Mishnah Berurah* rules in favor of those who are lenient (if there is a *hefsed merubah*) even if the small oven has no vent.

Mordechai, *Pesachim* 570 rules that there is no ריחא from bread to *Pesach* matzos. *Darchei Moshe* 108:1 seems to have understood that *Mordechai* based his ruling on the opinion that ריחא is permitted *b'dieved* on *Pesach*. According to this approach, we would reject *Mordechai's* leniency regarding *matzah* since we rule that ריחא is forbidden on *Pesach*. However, *Taz* 108:1, *Shach* 108:15 (as per *Pri Megadim* ad loc.; see also *Shach* 108:1), and *Aruch HaShulchan* 108:15 understand that the rationale for *Mordechai* is that ריחא is only possible if at least one of the foods is somewhat fatty or moist but bread and *matzah* are both so dry that there is absolutely no ריחא; if so, we could be lenient even on *Pesach*. This ruling is reflected in *Shulchan Aruch/Rema* OC 461:5 as per *Taz* OC 447:3, and *Magen Avraham* 461:9, which are the basis for *Mishnah Berurah* 461:22.

In this context, *Pri Megadim* (SD 108:18a) adds that since *Rema* 105:5 rules that we are unqualified to determine which foods are considered "dry", we must limit this leniency to foods such as bread and *matzah* which are unquestionably dry. [Bread made with oil or fat is also considered dry (*Mishnah Berurah* ibid.)]. Hence, the leniency is limited to cases, such as the one given by *Shulchan Aruch/Rema* ibid., of bread baked together with *Pesach matzah*. Accordingly, nowadays – when almost no one bakes *Pesach matzah* at home – this leniency would almost never apply.

[18] Caterers use "hot boxes" as a way to keep large quantities of food hot and ready to serve. The standard hot boxes are insulated and have a heater on bottom. They are typically used to warm up food or maintain the temperature of food that is already hot, and it would be counterproductive to have exhaust vents since that would allow heat to escape.

only be permitted in cases of *hefsed merubah* – whether the issue arose for *Pesach* or year-round.[19]

How does one define a "large oven"? *Shulchan Aruch*[20] says that it is one that can hold all the *matzos* which would be produced by 12 "*esronim*"[21] of flour, and the *Poskim* say that this is equivalent to about 60[22] cubic *tephachim*.[23] The issue which is less clear is which part of the oven is it that must hold this volume of *matzah*, and there are three opinions:

1. The most lenient is *Yad Eliyahu*[24] who says that an oven is "large" if that much *matzah* can fit into the entire interior <u>airspace</u> of the chamber.

2. The middle opinion is that of *K'raisi U'plaisi*[25] (and favored by *Chochmas Adam*)[26] that we imagine the four <u>walls</u> of the oven are

---

In contrast, there are other hot boxes which are most often used for <u>cooking</u> food. In general, they are not insulated and do not have heaters; instead, "Sternos" (disposable canisters of chafing fuel) are put into the bottom of the chamber, and this cooks the food. In order to get proper circulation of the heat (so that the food on bottom does not burn and the food on top is hot enough to cook), there will often be ventilation holes near the top of the chamber. The hot air escaping through the vents creates the desired flow of heat from bottom (i.e., where the Sternos are) throughout the chamber.

[19] *Pri Megadim* SD 108:3 (end) says that in a large oven with no vent the food is only permitted in cases of *hefsed merubah*. Then in SD 108:14 he notes that although we generally treat ריחא of *chametz* on *Pesach* as one step stricter than year-round (which might lead one to think that the food should be forbidden even if there is a *hefsed merubah*), in this case the status is the same since some *Poskim* are *b'dieved* lenient year-round for a large oven with no vent (even without *hefsed merubah*).

[20] *Shulchan Aruch* 97:3 and 108:1.

[21] One *esaron* is the minimum amount of flour from which one must be *mafrish challah* (*Shach* 97:5).

[22] The opinions on this matter revolve around determining the thickness of the *lechem hapanim*, each of which was made of 2 *esronim* of flour (*Vayikra* 24:5). The text follows the positions of *Kesef Mishnah* (*Hil. Temidim U'musafim* 5:9) and *Tifferes Yisroel* (*Chomer Bakodesh*/Introduction to *Kodashim* 2:49 and 2:51) who respectively prove – based on the *shiur challah* – that the *lechem hapanim* were 0.75 or 0.85 of an *etzbah* thick. Accordingly, the volume of 12 *esronim* is 56.25 or 63.75 cubic *tephachim*. [There are four *etzbo'os* in a *tephach*].

These positions are in stark contrast to *Binas Adam* 62 (81) who calculates – based on the simple reading of *Gemara*, *Beitzah* 22b, that the *lechem hapanim* were one *tephach* thick – that the volume of 12 *esronim* is 300 cubic *tephachim*. According to *Binas Adam*, the common ovens used nowadays would not be considered "large" according to any of the three ways of measuring that (noted in the coming text).

[23] There are three standard opinions of how many of inches there are in [an *etzbah* and] a *tephach*. [For more on that, see *Imrei Dovid*, *Hafrashas Challah*, Chapter 12]. This potentially plays a role in determining whether certain chambers are considered "large", but the text does not detail this information since, in practice, they all agree about the status of the common ovens used nowadays. See below in footnotes 27 and 30.

[24] *Responsa Yad Eliyahu* 25, cited (and rejected) by *Pri Megadim* 97:5. [*Yad Eliyahu* was printed in 1712, about 15 years before *Pri Megadim* was born].

[25] *K'raisi U'plaisi* 108:4 (*K'raisi*) & 108:3 (*Plaisi*).

[26] *Chochmas Adam* 62:1.

covered with *matzos* which are each a *tephach* thick; an oven is "large" if those *matzos* would total 12 *esronim*.

According to these first two opinions, a standard home oven is big enough to qualify as "large".[27]

3. *Pri Chadash* and others[28] take the strictest approach, saying that the oven must be so sizeable that 12 *esronim* of *tephach*-thick *matzos* could fit onto the <u>floor</u> of the oven; *Pri Megadim*[29] accepts this opinion. This approach would maintain that the typical home oven is only about 60%[30] of the size required to be considered "large" and should therefore be classified as "small". [All would agree that a microwave or toaster oven is "small"].

~ **Other discussions**

We noted previously that since a bit of *ta'am* transfers even with ריחא, that is a reason to forbid ריחא in cases where the *issur* is not suitable for *bitul b'shishim*, such as *chametz* on *Pesach*.[31] See Chapter 12 footnote 27, for a discussion for how that relates to the question of whether *bitul b'shishim* is effective for mixtures of fish and meat.

---

[27] Calculations in this footnote will use the measure of 3.54 inches per *tephach*, which is the opinion of *Iggeros Moshe* OC 1:136 (and *Kol Dodi* 2:6). Similar results would be true according to Rav Avrohom Chaim Na'ah and *Chazon Ish*, who respectively hold that a *tephach* is 3.15 or 3.78 inches.

12 *esronim* have a volume of 2,499-2,832 cubic inches according to the opinions of *Kesef Mishneh* and *Tifferes Yisroel* noted above in footnote 22. [It is 13,327 cubic inches according to *Binas Adam*]. The interior measurements of a standard home oven are approximately 17 inches high, 25 inches wide, and 19 inches deep. According to *Yad Eliyahu* that all 8,075 cubic inches of the oven's interior airspace (17 * 25 * 19 = 8,075) count towards the 12-*esronim* measure, the oven is clearly "large". According to *K'raisi U'plaisi*, we can calculate that 4,445 cubic inches of the oven count towards the required amount, which is still well above the amount required for the oven to be considered "large". [This calculation takes into consideration that *matzos* lining the walls will overlap near the corners of the oven].

[28] *Pri Chadash*, *Kuntress Acharon* to YD 97; *Soless Lemincha* to 35:1 (6) (author's addendums to *Minchas Yaakov*); and *Chavas Da'as* (*Biurim*) 108 (point #10 of the summary).

[29] *Pri Megadim* SD 97:5.

[30] See above in footnote 27 that 12 *esronim* have a volume of 2,499-2,832 cubic inches. According to *Iggeros Moshe* ibid., a *tephach*-thick layer of *matzah* on the floor of the oven (i.e., the opinion of *Pri Chadash*) would have a volume of 1,682 cubic inches (25 * 19 * 3.54 = 1,682) which is 67% or 59% of the amount required for a "large" oven according to *Kesef Mishneh* and *Tifferes Yisroel* respectively. [According to Rav AC Na'ah, it would be 85% or 75%, and according to *Chazon Ish* it would be 59% or 52%].

[31] In light of the fact that we are *machmir* for *mashehu* on *Pesach*, what might be the rationale for the opinion that ריחא is <u>permitted</u> (*b'dieved*) even on *Pesach*? *Beis Meir* 447:1 s.v. *u'bidin* and *Mishnah Berurah* 447:10 say that this opinion holds that although we are *machmir* to forbid a *mashehu* of actual (or absorbed) *chametz*, that *chumrah* does not apply to a *mashehu* which just came from ריחא. These *Poskim* do not clarify exactly what the difference is between these different types of *mashehu*.

In Chapter 19 (and particularly in footnote 8) we saw that *Rema's* position forbidding ריחא *l'chatchilah* is the basis for his explanation of why it is forbidden to taste *issur* even if one does not swallow it.

Below in Chapter 60 we will see examples of cases where the person specifically wants the ריחא of *issur* to affect a food, leading to a stricter halacha.

Chapter 58

Meat and Milk Cooking Side by Side

שולחן ערוך סימן ק"ח סעיף א

אין צולין בשר כשרה עם בשר נבילה או של בהמה טמאה בתנור א' ואף על פי שאין נוגעים זה בזה, ואם צלאן הרי זה מותר ואפילו היתה האסורה שמינה הרבה והמותרת רזה, ואם התנור גדול שמחזיק י"ב עשרונים ופיו פתוח מותר לצלותם בו ובלבד שלא יגעו זה בזה, ואם אחד מהם מכוסה בקערה או בבצק וכיוצא בו מותר לצלותם אפילו בתנור קטן ופיו סתום: הגה וה"ה לבשר עם חלב נמי דינא הכי. ונהגין להחמיר לכתחלה אפילו בתנור גדול ובדיעבד להקל אפילו בתנור קטן.

ואם אפה פת עם בשר אסור לאכלו עם חלב אם יש לו פת אחר, וכן אם עובד כוכבים אפה פת עם ישראל אסור לקנות אותו פת יש פת אחר דכל זה מקרי לכתחלה, אבל אם אין לו פת אחר בריוח מותר בשניהם דזה מקרי לענין זה דיעבד.

י"א דאין מתירין ריחא אפילו בדיעבד אלא אם כן התנור פתוח קצת מן הצד או למעלה במקום שהעשן יוצא, ובמקום הפסד אין להחמיר בדיעבד אפילו סתום לגמרי, ואם האיסור דבר חריף וכל שכן אם ההיתר דבר חריף ריחא מילתא היא ואפילו בדיעבד אסור אם שניהם מגולים אבל אם אחד מהם מכוסה אפילו בבצק בעלמא מותר.

אם אפו או צלו איסור והיתר תחת מחבת אחת מגולין אסור אפילו בדיעבד, וה"ה אם אפו בכה"ג פת עם בשר אסור לאכלו בחלב, אבל בזה אחר זה אין לחוש אלא אם כן הזיע המחבת משניהם דאז אסור אפילו בזה אחר זה אם היו שניהם מגולין דהוי ככיסוי של קדרה כדלעיל סימן צ"ג.

י"א דכל מקום דאמרינן ריחא מלתא ואוסר בדיעבד היינו דוקא דליכא ששים מן ההיתר נגד האיסור אבל בדאיכא ששים מן ההיתר אפי' בכל מה שבתנור מבטל האיסור, ולצורך הפסד יש לנהוג כן. י"א דאיסור האוסר במשהו כגון חמץ בפסח ריחא מלתא ואוסר אפילו בדיעבד אם התנור קטן והוא סתום והאיסור וההיתר מגולין תוך התנור, ויש אומרים שאין לחלק, ובמקום הפסד יש לסמוך אדברי המקילין, ועיין לקמן סוף סימן קי"ח אם יש להחמיר לכתחלה לשפות ב' קדירות וא' מהן של איסור על הכירה או לצלות איסור אצל היתר.

At the very end of this halacha, *Rema*[1] references his ruling in YD 108:11 regarding two pots cooking side by side on the same stovetop, when one

---

[1] *Rema* 108:1.

pot contains permitted food and the other is filled with *issur*. When we look at that halacha, we see that *Shulchan Aruch* says that this is totally permitted, while *Rema* rules that *l'chatchilah* one should avoid it. The *Acharonim* disagree as to the reason for *Rema's chumrah*, and that issue revolves around the following questions/proofs:

Yoreh Deah 118 is a *siman* which is all about when one needs to be concerned that a non-Jew switched his non-kosher food for your kosher food.[2] The fact that *Rema* is in that *siman* (118:11) implies that the concern is that the non-Jew whose pot has the non-kosher food, might take advantage of the proximity of the two pots to switch some food. This idea is also borne out in the wording of *Shulchan Aruch* 118:11, which stresses this point. On the other hand, *Shulchan Aruch* also briefly notes that one need not be concerned that this food might spray from the non-kosher pot to the kosher one. Which of these concerns is *Rema* saying to avoid *l'chatchilah*?

Taz[3] says that *Rema* is concerned that the non-Jew might switch some non-kosher meat for kosher – i.e., the primary issue which *Yoreh Deah* 118 discusses. Accordingly, *Taz* says that if there is no non-Jew involved, and it is just that a Jew has one pot of kosher meat and another of kosher dairy, it is perfectly acceptable to have them cooking side by side. There is no concern of "switching" (and *Rema* agrees with *Shulchan Aruch* that there is no concern of "spritzing") and therefore it is permitted.[4]

There is support for *Taz's* approach from the words of *Darchei Moshe*,[5] who cites those who are *machmir l'chatchilah*, and then records that *Issur V'heter*[6] says one can be lenient (and permit pots side by side) if a Jew stays and watches the pots. According to *Taz*, this is perfectly understandable:

---

[2] For example, the halachos before and after 118:11 are about leaving a non-Jew alone in one's home together with kosher food.
[3] *Taz* 118:12.
[4] *Taz's* makes this point using the words, " ולפי זה אי הוי שתי קדירות של ישראל, אחת של בשר ואחת של חלב, אין", and the word "ישראל" in that phrase implies that he is referring to the case noted in the text: both pots are filled with kosher food, where one is dairy and the other is meat. However, see *Pri Megadim* SD 108:3 describes the case where *Taz* is lenient as "והם שני מינים", which seems to include even cases where one is kosher and the other is not kosher, but the type of food cooking in one pot is so different from what is in the other pot that there is no concern someone might switch the foods.
[5] *Darchei Moshe* 118:11.
[6] *Issur V'Heter* 22:3.

a Jew watching the pots ensures that the non-Jew will not put any non-kosher food into the kosher pot, and that is why it is permitted *l'chatchilah*.

At the same time, *Darchei Moshe* twice references the discussion in *Yoreh Deah* 108. What connection does the halacha of ריחא have to do with whether one should be concerned that a non-Jew might replace kosher food with non-kosher? For that matter, according to *Taz*, why does *Rema* in 108 reference the discussion in *Yoreh Deah* 118? While both halachos relate to pots of food where one is kosher and the other is not, there seems to be no meaningful connection between them?

These points support *Shach's*[7] understanding of *Rema* 118. He sees the reason *Rema* says not to allow non-kosher and kosher pots to be adjacent to one another is because food might spray from one pot to the other (i.e., the reason which *Shulchan Aruch* briefly discounts). Just as *Rema* 108 says that *l'chatchilah* one must avoid transfer of *ta'am* via ריחא – even though by the letter of the law that it is not a concern – so too one must avoid any possibility that non-kosher food will spritz onto kosher, even though it is so uncommon that the letter of the law is that there is no need to be concerned about that possibility.

Shach says that one can deduce a proof for this understanding of *Rema* from the very words of *Rema*, who says that *l'chatchilah* one should not allow two pieces of meat – one kosher and the other non-kosher – to broil next to one another, and one should <u>even</u> (אפילו) be *machmir* if the meats are cooking in pots. If the concern is that food might spritz from the non-kosher to the kosher, then it logical that this concern is much greater when food is broiling without being enclosed than when it is in a pot. Therefore, *Rema* says that <u>even</u> when it is in a pot one should be *machmir*. On the other hand, according to *Taz*, the word "even" is inappropriate, since the

---

[7] *Shach* 118:36 (and 37).
    It is noteworthy that although *Pri Chadash* 118:38 accepts *Taz's* understanding of *Rema* 118:11, he says – based on *Rema* 95:6 – that one should <u>also</u> avoid pots cooking side by side due to a concern that food will spray from one to the other. Thus, even if *Rema* 118 is not focusing on that point, that idea can be deduced from a different ruling of *Rema*. In a somewhat similar vein, *Gr"a* 118:35 and *Aruch HaShulchan* 118:34 say that pots should not be put side by side due to <u>both</u> reasons (*Taz*/switching and *Shach*/spraying).
    Chochmas Adam 70:10 records *Shach's* concern (ומכל מקום יזהר שלא יתזו ניצוצות), but then gives a general statement to avoid pots being on the same stovetop side by side (ולכתחילה יש ליזהר שלא לשפות שתי קדירות זו אצל זו), which might be understood as broadening the concern even to cases where spraying is not relevant (e.g., if the pot is covered).

possibility that the non-Jew might switch the kosher for non-kosher is not affected by whether the food is in or out of a pot.[8]

According to *Shach*, the only concern is that food might spray from one pot to the next, and therefore he leniently rules that the pots can be placed side by side if they are covered.[9] Once they are covered, there is no way for food to spray from one to the other, and even *Rema* would agree that it is permitted. [And since the Jew is present – or even *yotzeh v'nichnas* – there is no concern that the non-Jew will switch some of the kosher food for non-kosher].[10] However, *Shach's* opinion leads to a *chumrah* in cases where a person wants to cook dairy and meat side by side. *Taz* said that it is permitted since (a) both are kosher and (b) there is no non-kosher (or non-Jew) to make a "switch". On the other hand, *Shach's* concern that food might spray from one pot to the other is just as relevant to (kosher) meat and dairy as it is to non-kosher and kosher. Therefore, *Shach* would say that *l'chatchilah* one may not have meat and dairy cooking in adjacent pots, unless (as noted above) the pots are covered.[11]

For most people, it is rather uncommon to have non-kosher food cooking anywhere near their kosher food, and therefore the case where *Taz* is *machmir* is not so relevant. But it might be relevant if a kosher caterer is preparing for an event in a non-kosher venue, and one of the venue's chefs wants to cook food at the same time that the kosher food is being made. *Taz* would say that this is forbidden because of a concern that one of the non-Jews might switch some non-kosher food for kosher. [Truth be told, every reputable *hashgachah* – even if they were not familiar with this *Taz* – would never allow such a setup].

---

[8] Presumably, *Taz* would respond to this point by saying that it is easier to (quickly) switch foods that are exposed than those which are inside a pot.
[9] If one pot is dairy and the other is meat (a case discussed below), clearly both pots must be covered to prevent spraying in either direction. What if one pot is filled with non-kosher food and the other has kosher food (the case of *Shulchan Aruch*)? Which of the pots must be covered? See *Chelkas Binyamin* (*Tziunim*) 118:236.
[10] See the end of *Shach* 118:37, based on *Rema* 118:12, who says *yotzeh v'nichnas* is acceptable. How will *Taz* reconcile his understanding of *Rema* 118:11 (that *l'chatchilah* there is a concern of switching) with *Rema* 118:12, who says that *yotzeh v'nichnas* suffices? Presumably, he would say that *yotzeh v'nichnas* – or even a Jew standing right near the pots – is ineffective in 118:11, since the pots are so close to one another that it will just take a second to move meat from one pot to the other. In that case, even with a Jew present, we are *l'chatchilah* concerned for a mishap.
[11] *Shulchan Aruch* structures the case as one where a Jew and non-Jew put pots on the fire side by side and says that even so it is permitted. According to *Shach*, one could question why *Rema* did not stress that his *chumrah* applies even in cases of pots of kosher meat and milk.

However, *Shach's* understanding of *Rema* is quite relevant for any consumer who has just one stovetop which is used for both meat and dairy. In Chapter 7 we discussed why it is permissible to use the same grates for both meat and dairy,[12] and here we are noting that, nonetheless, *l'chatchilah* one should not cook meat and dairy <u>simultaneously</u> on adjacent burners. If/when the pots are uncovered, food might spray from one pot to the other, and therefore, the pots must be far enough apart[13] that there is no realistic possibility of food which sprays from one pot might reach the other one. For example, on most stovetops there are two burners on the right side and two on the left; *Shach* would say that if the pot on the front right burner is cooking dairy, a pot of meat should not be put onto the back right burner, but it is probably acceptable to put a pot of meat on the front left burner since it is so far away from the front right burner that food cannot spray from one to the other. The exact determination of what is "too close" and what is "far enough away" depends on the size of the stovetop, how full the pots are, and similar factors which vary depending on the situation.

In this context, it is worth noting that *Rema's* concern is just on the level of *l'chatchilah*, but he agrees that if the pots were cooked side by side, the food remains kosher *b'dieved*.

---

[12] Similarly, it is permitted to use the same grate for non-kosher and kosher, but, as noted in Chapter 7, for *Pesach* we are *machmir* only to use grates that were *kashered* from *chametz* use.

[13] This logical point – that if the pots are far enough apart there is no concern of spritzing – is noted in *Pri Megadim* SD 108:3, who says that *Shach* is lenient if the pots are מרוחקין from one another.

Meat and Milk Cooking Side by Side

Chapter 59

מרדה

שולחן ערוך סימן ק"ח סעיף ג
אם יש שמנונית של איסור על המרדה שקורין פאלי"א,
אסור ליתן עליה היתר כל היום, מיהו כשאינה בת
יומא מותר להשתמש בה משום דאי אפשר בענין אחר.
הגה: כל זמן שהיא בת יומא לא מהני בה הגעלה ולא קליפה בכלי
אומנות.

This halacha[1] refers to a time when Jews were forced to bake their bread in non-Jews' ovens but could not afford to have their own מדרה (a wooden tool used to remove the bread from the oven), and it was impossible to kasher the non-kosher מרדה. *Shulchan Aruch* rules that due to the dire need to have bread, the Jews can use a non-kosher מדרה (without kashering) as long as it is *aino ben yomo*. We no longer face this type of situation where we are forced to rely on the *b'dieved* of using an *aino ben yomo* מרדה to obtain bread. But there were those who suggested that the same concept might justify using non-kosher spray dryers, ship holds, and glass-line reactors, without a proper *kashering*, assuming they are *aino ben yomo*. For more on those cases, see *Imrei Dovid*, *Kashering*, Chapters 15, 47, and 56.

---

[1] *Shulchan Aruch* 108:3.

Chapter 60

Cigtrus and Air Up

שולחן ערוך סימן ק"ח סעיף ה
מותר לשאוף בפיו ריח יין נסך דרך נקב שבחבית לידע
אם הוא טוב. הגה: אבל אסור לטועמו אף על פי שאינו בולעו.
ואסור לזלף יין נסך שאסור בהנאה, אבל מותר לזלף סתם יינם
דמותר בהנאה.

Vapors

The current halacha[1] states that it is permitted to put one's mouth over the opening in a barrel filled with non-kosher wine (*yayin nesech*) and inhale wine vapors to assess if the wine is good. This halacha records the opinion of *Rava*, and the *Gemara*[2] which states that it is based on *Rava's* opinion that ריחא לאו מילתא, meaning that although the wine is not kosher, the vapors rising from it are insignificant. This statement by itself is understandable, but several questions are raised based on other *Gemaros* and halachos:

Firstly, *Abaye* disagrees with *Rava* in this *Gemara*. Many *Rishonim* discuss the relationship between this *machlokes* and the disagreement between *Rav* and *Levi* in a different *Gemara*.[3] In an earlier halacha, *Shulchan Aruch* (108:1) assumes that the two disagreements are connected and accepts the lenient opinion of *Levi*, which is consistent with his lenient ruling here as per *Rava*. But what about *Rema*, who is *machmir l'chatchilah* regarding the issues in 108:1? Why does he not record the same *chumrah* in our halacha?

---

[1] *Shulchan Aruch* 108:5.
[2] *Gemara, Avodah Zara* 66b.
[3] *Gemara, Pesachim* 76b.

Secondly, *Shach*[4] asks that if *Rava* believes that vapors rising from non-kosher wine do not have non-kosher status, then that should apply in all cases. If so, why does the ensuing *Gemara*[5] say that if bread is placed on top of a barrel of non-kosher wine, it can become forbidden (under specific circumstances) because it absorbs wine vapors? If vapors are truly "nothing", then the bread should remain kosher? And why does *Shulchan Aruch* (108:4) record the strict halacha regarding bread on a wine barrel, if in the very next halacha (108:5) he accepts *Rava* who permits inhaling wine vapors?

The answer to these questions can be found in *Tosfos*,[6] which *Shach* references. *Tosfos* says that *Rava's* leniency is specific to this case because inhaling wine vapors directly into one's body is harmful (שאני הכא שהריח מזיק לו לפי שנכנס בגופו), but the vapors are not harmful when absorbed into bread (108:4) or other foods (108:1), and that is why one must be more *machmir* in those cases. Several *Acharonim*[7] accept this understanding (or a similar one)[8] which essentially limits the leniency of our halacha to the very specific case noted and would not allow one to extrapolate a similar position in other cases.[9]

The strictness of this position is directly relevant to the phenomenon of artisan coffee companies putting their raw beans into empty wine barrels in order to absorb aroma from the wine before roasting. If the wine is not kosher, the beans (and the coffee made from them) will be forbidden. In this case, the vapors do not pose any danger, and therefore, this is an example where all agree that one must be strict.[10]

---

[4] *Shach* 108:21.
[5] *Gemara*, *Avodah Zara* 66b-67a.
[6] *Tosfos*, *Avodah Zara* 66b s.v. *Rava*.
[7] See *Pri Megadim* (SD 108:24 and 26), and *Responsa Maharik* 133 (towards the end) referenced in *Gilyon HaShas* to *Tosfos* ibid. *Shiltei Giborim*, *Avodah Zara* 32a-b, suggests an alternate reason why inhaling wine vapor is different, (because the taste is not so strong and the person is just assessing the wine rather than trying to enjoy the taste); *Emunas Shmuel* 45 (cited partially in *Pischei Teshuvah* 108:5) disagrees with this point if one smells the vapor with their nose, but agrees that these factors are relevant (and one can be lenient) when inhaling through the mouth. [*Emunas Shmuel* was a contemporary of *Shach*]. See also *Minchas Yaakov* 35:38.
[8] See the previous footnote.
[9] See also *Shach* 108:22, that although *Shulchan Aruch* 108:4 cites a case of *yayin nesech*, the same halacha applies if the forbidden food is a food that is not *assur b'hana'ah*.
[10] For more details, see (a) *Imrei Dovid*, *Alcoholic Beverages*, Chapter 12 (regarding the possibility that the wine is נותן טעם לפגם into the coffee beans) and (b) above in Chapter 7 (regarding the status of other coffee roasted on the same equipment as the wine-infused beans).

Cigtrus

The above discussion is also relevant to a consumer product, called "Cigtrus", which is an "aromatic inhaler" intended to help people overcome their smoking addiction. It is a thin tube, about 3-4 inches long, shaped somewhat like a vape pen, with a small hole on each end. Inside the tube there is a piece of cotton saturated with citrus oils and other flavorful liquids. When someone sucks one side of the tube, vapors rising from the cotton/oils give a pleasant taste into their mouth.

In a certain sense, inhaling flavor from a Cigtrus is like inhaling from a cigarette or e-cigarette (vape pen).[11] But there is no tobacco, no nicotine, no addictive ingredients, no heat or flame, no electricity, no visible vapors, and no exhaling. The person using the Cigtrus gets a taste in their mouth, but there is no smoke (as would be with a cigarette) and no droplets of liquid (as would be with an e-cigarette), and there is nothing for the user to exhale (as would be with cigarettes or e-cigarettes).

A respected *Posek* ruled that one may use Cigtrus even without knowledge that the oils and liquids in it are kosher. He argued that just as our halacha permits a person to inhale non-kosher wine vapors, so too one may inhale Cigtrus vapors, even if the product is not certified kosher. However, we have seen that there is strong basis for assuming that our halacha is limited to a very specific case where the vapors are not being inhaled for pleasure and are damaging to the person. But there is no reason to think the Cigtrus vapors are at all damaging or have any negative affect on the user. Therefore, it appears that since we are generally *machmir* – at least *l'chatchilah* – to avoid ריחא/vapors of *issur*, one should not use Cigtrus or similar products unless they are certified kosher.

Suitability for hashgachah

Many *hashgachos*, including cRc Kosher, will not certify recreational marijuana,[12] cigarettes, or e-cigarettes because they do not want to

---

[11] See Chapter 19 regarding the kosher status of e-cigarettes.

[12] Regarding (recreational) marijuana, Rav Reiss wrote the following (which is part of a statement signed by him, Rav Fuerst, and Rav Zucker):

Recreational marijuana use is אסור על פי הלכה as is clearly delineated by Rav Moshe Feinstein in אגרות משה יו"ד ג:לה. Additionally, accordingly to experts with whom we have consulted, the data is clear that there are long-term health consequences, risk of addiction, and increased danger of permanent cognitive impairment. Therapists attest to the harm that marijuana use has wrought upon families and relationships, with users becoming less conscientious about their personal behavior רחמנא ליצלן.

promote or condone the use of marijuana or of smoking. What about Cigtrus? It is designed to look somewhat like an e-cigarette, but it has no fire, no electricity, no nicotine, no tobacco, no marijuana, and really is just a form of "aromatherapy" which is essential oils mixed with flavors. It seems quite clear that this is no more a cigarette than a candy cigarette that children blow on. There was therefore some support at the cRc for certifying this type of product, but the final decision was not to get involved with it. Anyone who looks carefully at this product will see that it is not a cigarette by any stretch of the imagination, but casual viewers might not understand that and will be left with the impression that we condone smoking.

Air Up Water Bottle

An invention which raises similar issues to Cigtrus is the Air Up water bottle. This is a specially designed water bottle where the cover/mouthpiece forms an (almost) airtight seal with the water bottle. On the top of the mouthpiece, the user inserts a round "flavor pod" that fits snugly around the center part of the mouthpiece (which itself encircles the straw). As a result of these tight-fitting parts, when the person sips water from the bottle, it pulls air through a tiny hole in the flavor pod, where it passes over a flavor-infused cotton-like material, and the air then exits through a series of other small holes and gets sucked into the flow of water going up the straw. Thus, the person sipping from the bottle sucks in water with fragrance mixed into it (and the presence of the air creates a gurgling sound). In the person's mouth, the fragrance separates from the liquid and goes up the person's pharynx (back of their throat) to the nose where the scent is detected. The net result of this is that – since much of how we "taste" is through smell – the person perceives the water as having cherry, orange, lemon, or other taste that the flavor pod is made to mimic.

This mental impairment is devastating to our divine mission in this world, 'וכו ולעשות לשמור וללמד ללמוד. Teenagers and young adults are at heightened risk of cognitive damage from regular use of marijuana, and are more likely to experiment, depending upon their susceptibility to social pressures.
  Unlike the ritual use of wine or alcohol, there is no tradition of using such substances under any circumstances, and no consideration of 'ד פתאים שומר.
  ...It goes without saying that processed marijuana products, such as marijuana brownies, or any extraction of marijuana oils from the plant, present a wide range of routine kashrus problems, and in the absence of reliable kosher certification are obviously prohibited independent of the concerns articulated by Rav Moshe zt"l in his teshuva. While certification may be appropriate for medical marijuana prescribed by a doctor to alleviate terrible pain, we pray that there not be a regular need for such prescriptions. If a person's condition does warrant such a prescription, an appropriate שאלה can of course be asked.

The perceived taste in the water is much more subtle than in the Cigtrus; nonetheless, it is quite noticeable, and of course, that is exactly why customers purchase the water bottle and flavor pods. Accordingly, it seems comparable to the Cigtrus and the vapors absorbed into bread, which we have seen should be avoided unless one knows that they are made from kosher ingredients.

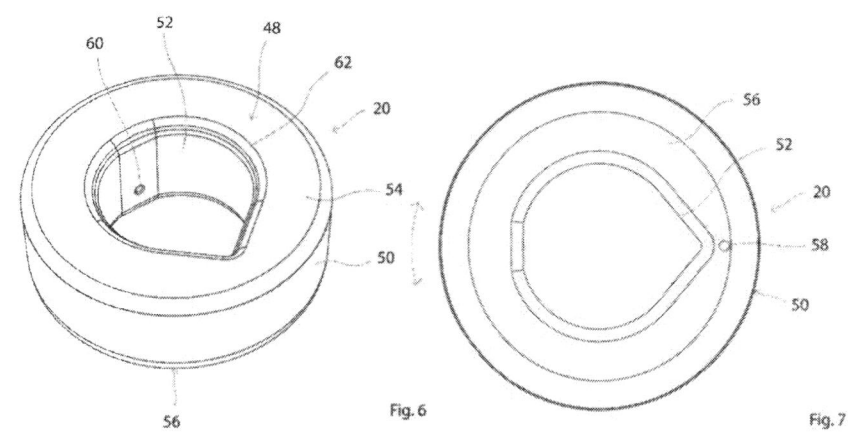

**Diagrams from one of the Air Up patents,
showing two of the holes (#58 & #60) in the flavor pod**
other holes are in the mouthpiece and straw

Chapter 61

יבש ביבש

> **שולחן ערוך סימן ק"ט סעיף א'**
> חתיכה שאינה ראויה להתכבד שנתערבה באחרות מין במינו יבש ביבש (דהיינו שאין נבלל והאיסור עומד בעצמו אלא שנתערב ואינו מכירו) חד בתרי, בטיל, ומותר לאכלן אדם אחד כל אחת בפני עצמה אבל לא יאכל שלשתם יחד, ויש מי שאוסר לאכלם אדם אחד אפילו זה אחר זה.
>
> הגה: וכן יש לנהוג לכתחלה. ויש מחמירין להשליך אחד או ליתן לא"י, ואינו אלא חומרא בעלמא. וכל זה כשנתערב במינו אבל שלא במינו ואינו מכירו אפילו יבש ביבש צריך ששים. ואין חילוק בכל זה בין אם האיסור מדרבנן או מדאורייתא. וע"ל סימן קכ"ב אם נתערבו כלים ביחד.

ביטול ברוב

The general halacha is that if *issur* and *heter* are mixed together, the status of the mixture is determined by whichever of them there is more of.[1] A significant exception to that principle, known as *bitul b'rov*, is that when dealing with food-related *issurim*, the mixture is forbidden anytime one can <u>taste</u> the *issur* component. Accordingly, forbidden foods typically require *bitul b'shishim* to be permitted, since at that level of dilution it will be impossible to taste the *issur*. We have discussed that concept many times in this work (see, for example, Chapter 26), and the focus of this chapter will be on the food-related cases where *bitul b'rov* remains effective.

For several food-related *issurim*, *bitul b'rov* is sufficient due to the nature of the *issur*. In these cases, *Chazal* deemed it sufficient to forbid the item itself but not its *ta'am*; therefore, it is treated like a non-food *issur* and if there is more *heter* than *issur*, the mixture is permitted. Some examples

---

[1] *Shulchan Aruch* 109:1 uses the term חד בתרי בטיל (following the lead of *Gemara, Gittin* 54b, see *Gr"a* 109:4) which leads some to say that there must be twice as much *heter* as *issur*, but it is generally accepted that the requirement is merely that there be more *heter* than *issur* (i.e., *bitul b'rov*); see *Shach* 109:6, *Pri Megadim* ad loc., and *Pischei Teshuvah* 109:1.

of this are *pas akum*, *bishul akum*, *kitnios*, and foods forbidden due to *maris ayin*.[2]

However, the broadest situation where *bitul b'rov* suffices is when the *issur* and *heter* meet two criteria: they are מין במינו rather than מין בשאינו מינו, and the *ta'aroves* qualifies as יבש ביבש. As noted in Chapter 21, the term מין במינו is generally assumed to refer to foods that have similar taste, such that it would be impossible to detect the *issur's* taste in the mixture. Since the *issur* cannot be tasted, it makes sense that *bitul b'shishim* (i.e., the point when taste is no longer noticeable) is not required. יבש ביבש (literally: dry in dry) is how we designate situations where the *issur* and *heter* remain distinct entities even though there is a *ta'aroves* (*Rema* 109:1). For example, if there are 3 pieces of meat and we know that one of them is a *neveilah* (i.e., did not have *shechitah*) but we cannot tell which one it is. Each piece remains distinct and the three have not blended into one amalgam (such as would happen if non-kosher wine was mixed into kosher wine), and the mixture is therefore designated a יבש ביבש *ta'aroves*. Here again, we are confident that the permitted items do not carry any of the *issur's* taste, and therefore *bitul b'shishim* should not be required.

Another example of יבש ביבש is if wheat kernels that had become *chametz* (as a result of getting wet) were mixed into kernels that were not *chametz*. It is impossible to identify and remove the *chametz* kernels since they look just like the non-*chametz* ones, and therefore this qualifies as a *ta'aroves*. However, since each kernel is distinct, this is considered יבש ביבש. What if all the kernels were ground into flour? Once that happens, all the flour fuses into one compound where it is impossible to distinguish one bit of flour from the next. Accordingly, most *Poskim* assume that mixtures of very fine powders (a.k.a. קמח בקמח) are not considered יבש ביבש (and are instead designated as לח בלח).[3] [More on *Pesach* below].

---

[2] *Shulchan Aruch* YD 112:14 (*pas akum*), *Shach* 112:23 (*bishul akum*) (see *Imrei Dovid*, *Pas Yisroel and Bishul Yisroel*, Chapter 20), *Rema* 115:1 (end) (*chemas akum*), *Mishnah Berurah* 453:9 (*kitnios*) (see above in Chapter 1, and in *Imrei Dovid* ibid., Chapter 21), *Shulchan Aruch* YD 87:4 and *Shach* 66:11 (*maris ayin*). Some say that *bitul b'rov* also applies to חמץ שעבר עליו הפסח (see Chapter 21) and *gevinas akum* (see *Issur V'Heter* 47:7 cited in *Shach* 115:17, discussed in *Imrei Dovid*, *Animal Products*, Chapter 43).

Two other cases where *bitul b'rov* is effective for a food-related *issur* is when the *issur* is נותן טעם לפגם (see Chapter 37) or is mixed into a non-food item (see Chapter 43, footnote 30).

[3] See *Shach* YD 109:3, *Taz* OC 453:2, *Magen Avraham* 453:6 & 498:28, *Chok Yaakov* 498:28, and *Mishnah Berurah* 447:32; but also see *Pri Megadim* SD 109:3 and *Mishnah Berurah* 453:17, who say that a בעל נפש should be *machmir* (where appropriate).

As noted, logically, *bitul b'shishim* is only required if the mixture is מין בשאינו מינו, where it is possible that the *issur's* taste will be detectable in the *heter*, and not in cases of מין במינו. Furthermore, it makes sense that *bitul b'shishim* is only necessary when *ta'am* transfers from the *issur* to the *heter*, such as if two liquids were mixed together (i.e., לח בלח) or the foods were cooked together. Based on these points, *mid'oraisah*, *bitul b'shishim* is only required if the mixture is <u>both</u> מין בשאינו מינו and לח בלח (and, in this context, absorbed *ta'am* is also considered "לח").[4] However, *Chazal* were concerned that being lenient in cases of מין במינו or יבש ביבש might lead to mistakes, and therefore said that *bitul b'shishim* is required if only <u>one</u> of those conditions is true. More specifically:

- If people rely on *bitul b'rov* for mixtures of מין בשאינו מינו which are יבש ביבש, they might subsequently cook the items together thereby converting it to a לח בלח mixture (which requires *bitul b'shishim mid'oraisah*).

- If they rely on *bitul b'rov* for mixtures of לח בלח which are מין במינו, they might mistakenly think that they can do the same when they have a *ta'aroves* which is מין בשאינו מינו (which requires *bitul b'shishim mid'oraisah*).

To avoid these concerns, *Chazal* forbade mixtures that are <u>either</u> מין בשאינו מינו (even if it is יבש ביבש) or לח בלח (even if it is מין במינו). The only case that they left with the original leniency that allowed for *bitul b'rov*, is in cases where <u>both</u> positive factors applied: it is מין במינו and also יבש ביבש.[5]

In Chapter 3 we noted that the criteria for יבש ביבש are different as relates to חתיכה נעשית נבילה from the halacha discussed here in the text.

[4] Since the criteria for יבש ביבש are that the two items remain distinct and there is no *ta'am* of the *issurim* the *heter*, it is obvious that in this context *ta'am* per se – whether it transfers directly from one food to the next or does so after being absorbed in the walls of a pot – is "לח". This is clearly noted in *Shulchan Aruch* 109:2, which states that a יבש ביבש mixture which is cooked has the stricter status of לח בלח, where *bitul b'rov* is insufficient.

[5] The *Gemara* does not clearly state the points made in the text – and, in fact, *Beis Yosef* 109:1 cites *Rishonim* who disagree with some of the rulings noted here. The text is based on *Shulchan Aruch* 109:1 (לח בלח מין), *Rema* ad loc. (יבש ביבש מין בשאינו מינו), and *Shulchan Aruch/Rema* 98:1 (יבש ביבש מין במינו) (בשאינו מינו ומין במינו) and the explanations given are most clearly and succinctly noted in *Ran, Chullin* 36a ד"ה גרסינן בגמרא, cited in *Shach* 109:9.

In the case of יבש ביבש which is also מין במינו , *Chazal* were lenient because even if a mistake was made (and the foods were cooked, or someone mistakenly thought the same halacha applied to מין בשאינו מינו), the mixture would be permitted *mid'oraisah* (*Ran*), and it would be a גזירה לגזירה to forbid יבש ביבש מין במינו out of concern that a double mistake might happened and people would permit לח בלח מין בשאינו מינו (*Pri Megadim, Sha'ar HaTa'aruvos* 2:1).

The examples given above – of meat or wheat kernels – meet both of these requirements: they are מין במינו and יבש ביבש, and therefore *bitul b'rov* is enough to permit the mixture.

Pesach

Mid'oraisah, chametz is *batel b'shishim* just like any other forbidden item.[6] However, *mid'rabannan*, any *chametz* which is mixed into food <u>on</u> *Pesach* is not *batel* regardless of how little *chametz* is in the mixture; this is known as "*issur mashehu*".[7] *Rosh*[8] says that this *chumrah* is limited to cases where *bitul* would otherwise – meaning, not on *Pesach* – depend on the absence of *ta'am*. In those cases, *Chazal* said that even the tiniest bit of *chametz ta'am* must be avoided, and therefore it is *assur b'mashehu*. However, if the mixture is יבש ביבש and מין במינו, where *bitul b'rov* suffices and there is no need to nullify the *ta'am* (i.e., there is no requirement of *bitul b'shishim*), *issur mashehu* does not apply and *bitul b'rov* is enough even if the *ta'aroves* was created on *Pesach*.

Rif[9] approaches this in an opposite manner: he says that *bitul b'rov* is only appropriate where there is an overarching concern of non-kosher *ta'am*, and therefore, in a case where *ta'am* is not an issue – i.e., יבש ביבש which is מין במינו – we can permit the *ta'aroves* with just *bitul b'rov*. However, when a food such as *chametz*, is *assur b'mashehu*, that means that *ta'am* is not a factor. If so, there is no difference between יבש ביבש and לח בלח (or between מין במינו and מין בשאינו מינו), and the *issur mashehu* applies in every situation.

Shulchan Aruch[10] cites both of these opinions and does so in a manner[11] indicating that the halacha primarily follows the strict opinion of *Rif*. Later

---

Mid'rabannan, one may not eat <u>all</u> the items at once, since if you did that, you would surely be eating *issur* (*Shulchan Aruch* 109:1 as per *Shach* 109:7). [See the question that *Badei HaShulchan* (*Biurim*) 91:5 s.v. *rak*, page 133, raises based on this halacha]. Nonetheless, if, for example, there was one non-kosher item and 2 kosher ones, you may eat two of the items at the same time (and the other one at a different time) and are not required to assume that the *issur* is with the majority (i.e., the two pieces that you are eating) (*Pri Megadim* ad loc).

[6] See *Mishnah Berurah* 447:1.
[7] *Shulchan Aruch* OC 447:1.
[8] *Rosh, Avodah Zara* 5:30.
[9] *Rif, Avodah Zara* 37a as per *Beis Yosef* OC 447:9.
[10] *Shulchan Aruch* OC 447:9.
[11] I.e., *Shulchan Aruch* first states the opinion of *Rif* in a definitive manner and only adds the opinion of *Rosh* as "יש אומרים"; this indicates that he favored the first opinion (הלכה כדיעה א' בסתם) (*Pri Megadim* MZ 447:16).

Acharonim accept this ruling.[12] Thus, in the case noted above of *chametz* kernels that were mixed into non-*chametz* kernels, the kernels are not permitted even though it is an example of יבש ביבש and מין במינו.

The general rule is that *issur mashehu* applies only when *chametz* is mixed into other food on Pesach, but if the *ta'aruvos* was created before Pesach – and even if it occurred on *Erev Pesach* after midday[13] – the standard rules of *bitul* apply. Therefore, if *chametz* was *batel* before *Pesach*, it remains permitted and one can eat that food on *Pesach*.[14] That seems to mean that even according to *Rif/Shulchan Aruch*, we must only be *machmir* if the mixture occurred on *Pesach*.[15] However, the apparent issue with that is the halacha that if a mixture is יבש ביבש, even if the *chametz* was *batel* before *Pesach* (and may be eaten on *Erev Pesach*),[16] once *Pesach* begins the *chametz* is חוזר וניעור (*reawakened*), and the mixture is forbidden.[17]

Thus, at first glance, the leniency of יבש ביבש seems to have almost no application for *Pesach* since it only permits the food on *Erev Pesach* for the few hours when *chametz* is forbidden but before the *issur mashehu* (which only applies on *Pesach* itself) coupled with the principle of חוזר וניעור (for יבש ביבש) comes into play. However, see the footnote for two scenarios where one can be lenient.[18]

---

[12] See, for example, *Magen Avraham* 447:40, citing *Toras Chattas* 39:6, *Pri Megadim* 447:15-16, and *Mishnah Berurah* 447:95. However, see *Chazon Ish* OC 119:2 (end) that this only applies to someone who wants to eat from the mixture on *Pesach*, but one can be lenient and have benefit from it.

[13] *Shulchan Aruch* OC 447:2.

[14] *Shulchan Aruch* OC 447:4.

[15] See *Taz* OC 447:15 and *Magen Avraham* 447:40.

[16] See *Shulchan Aruch* OC 447:2.

[17] *Rema* OC 447:4.

[18] One case where one may be lenient and even eat from the יבש ביבש on *Pesach* is where enough of the mixture was eaten or destroyed that is possible that all the *chametz* is gone. If that happens, one is entitled to "assume" that that is exactly what happened even though the actual possibility of its happening is quite small (*Magen Avraham* 467:4, cited in *Mishnah Berurah* 447:95, based on *Shulchan Aruch* YD 110:7). This is an example of the principle of תולין בדרבנן, which is a leniency rooted in the fact that *issur mashehu* is, itself, only *assur mid'rabannan*. For more on the principle of תולין בדרבנן see *Imrei Dovid, Alcoholic Beverages*, Chapter 20. [In recording this detail in 447, *Magen Avraham* (447:40) seems to say all the items must be eaten (or destroyed) before *Pesach* (צריך לאכול כולם), but *Pri Megadim* and *Rebbi Akiva Eiger*, ad loc., direct the reader to *Magen Avraham* 467:4, who clarifies that it is enough to eat just enough to raise the possibility that all the *chametz* is gone (ונאכל אחד מהם), and this is how the ruling is recorded in *Mishnah Berurah*, ibid.]

A second leniency can be gleaned from *Shulchan Aruch* 109:2, who is not discussing *chametz*. His case is that someone has a mixture which is יבש ביבש (and מין במינו) which is therefore permitted, but he wants to cook the entire mixture. If he does that, it will become לח בלח (since *ta'am* that spreads during cooking is considered לח), which will require *bitul b'shishim*, at which point the mixture will

B'lios

The examples we have discussed thus far were cases where the *issur* and *heter* were essentially identical – *neveilah* meat and kosher meat, or *chametz* wheat kernels and non-*chametz* wheat kernels – and it is clear that the mixture qualifies as מין במינו. What about if it was a case of non-kosher meat, but rather than *neveilah*, it was meat that had *shechitah* but was not salted? The simple reading of *Shulchan Aruch*[19] is that this is considered מין במינו, since at the end of the day it is non-kosher meat mixed into kosher meat. However, *Shach*[20] says that this cannot possibly be true since it is the <u>blood</u>, not the meat, which is not kosher, and the blood is not מין במינו with the kosher pieces of meat. Many *Acharonim*[21] accept the general premise of *Shach* and find ways to explain that *Shulchan Aruch* also agrees to the basic idea.[22]

At first glance, this appears to be quite relevant to many practical cases where people consider relying on *bitul b'rov* for מין במינו יבש ביבש. One example of this is the use of a cut lemon at a non-kosher restaurant.[23] We saw in Chapter 16 that some of the slices might be considered non-kosher, but they are *batel b'rov* in the majority of slices which are kosher [See

---

become forbidden since there is not enough *heter* in the mixture for *bitul b'shishim*. *Shulchan Aruch* rules that before he cooks the mixture, he can add *heter* to it, so that there will be enough *heter* to accomplish the *bitul b'shishim*. Why is that not a violation of איסור לכתחילה מבטלין אין? *Shach* (109:13, based on *Ran, Avodah Zara* 36a) answers that at the time *heter* is added the mixture is *permitted* (since at that point it qualifies for *bitul b'rov*), and therefore the person is not being מבטל איסור. The same line of reasoning is valid for *chametz* wheat kernels mixed into non-*chametz* kernels before *Pesach*. At that point, the mixture is permitted since the *issur mashehu* does not begin until *Pesach* starts. Therefore, at that point the person can add more non-*chametz* kernels (and it is not considered ביטול איסור לכתחילה, as per *Shach*) and then grind the kernels into flour. As flour, the *chametz* kernels are *batel b'shishim* and, since a mixture of flour is considered לח בלח, the *chametz* will not be חוזר וניעור when *Pesach* starts (since חוזר וניעור only applies to mixtures which are יבש ביבש). Thus, by adding non-*chametz* kernels and grinding them all into flour before *Pesach*, it will be permitted to eat *matzos* made with this flour even once *Pesach* starts. [See *Mishnah Berurah* 453:20 that many do not agree with this line of reasoning. See also above in Chapter 12 footnote 33].

[19] *Shulchan Aruch* YD 69:14. *Rema* appears to agree with this; see also *Toras Chattas* 2:2-3 cited in *Shach* 69:17.
[20] *Shach* 69:57.
[21] See *Minchas Yaakov* 2:6, *Pri Chadash* 6:48, *Pri Megadim* MZ 109:2, *Chavos Da'as* 69:20 (*Biurim*), *Aruch HaShulchan* 69:82, and many others.
[22] Some of the answers given are: (a) *Shulchan Aruch* is only lenient in the specific case he was discussing where it is merely a *chumrah* to say the meat was not properly salted (*Shach* ibid., *Gr"a* 69:54); (b) when dealing with an *issur d'rabannan* (such as in the specific case of blood under discussion), יבש ביבש is *batel b'rov* even if it is מין בשאינו מינו (according to *Shach* 109:9, which *Rema* 109:1 disagrees with) (*Nekudos HaKesef* to *Shach*); and (c) the blood remaining in the meat tastes similar enough to meat to qualify as מין במינו (*Chavos Da'as* ibid.).
[23] A similar issue relates to the purchase of raw fish, fruit, or vegetables that are already cut at a non-kosher store (see Chapter 15).

Rema 96:4]. In turn, that is based on an assumption that the non-kosher lemons are מין במינו with the kosher lemons. Is this consistent with *Shach*? The lemons per se are kosher and it is the absorbed non-kosher *ta'am* which is the concern; if so, this should be a *ta'aroves* which is מין בשאינו מינו (non-kosher *ta'am* absorbed into lemons, which is mixed into kosher lemons) just like the case of unsalted meat, and require *bitul b'shishim*? The same point can be made regarding the status of commercially produced foods labeled "DE", where one reason to consider them pareve is that the packages which absorbed dairy *ta'am* are *batel b'rov* in those which did not (see Chapter 11).[24]

In these types of cases, it is generally assumed that one can be lenient and assume the non-kosher (or dairy) is *batel b'rov* in the kosher. Rav Schachter said that this is correct and gave two reasons why even *Shach* would agree. Firstly, on a simple level, although the halacha indicates that lemons cut with a *treif* knife (or food cooked on dairy equipment) will absorb *ta'am*, in practice we do not notice any difference in taste. Thus, although we would forbid any individual slice cut with the non-kosher knife, realistically we "know" they all taste alike, and therefore we consider the *ta'aruvos* to be מין במינו. In other words, מין במינו is determined by foods that <u>actually</u> taste alike, and the lemons qualify for that.

Rav Schachter's second reason to be lenient is based on the logic for why מין בשאינו מינו is forbidden when it is יבש ביבש. As noted earlier, no *ta'am* transfers when the mixture is יבש ביבש, and the reason to require *bitul b'shishim* is out of concern that the person might choose to cook (or heat) all parts of the mixture together. If that were to happen, non-kosher *ta'am* would transfer to the kosher food, and to avoid that possibility, *Chazal* said that יבש ביבש requires *bitul b'shishim* (for מין בשאינו מינו) so that the *ta'am* would be *batel* even if the person did cook them together. However, Rav Schachter argued that when there is no chance at all that the items in question will be cooked together, there is no reason to forbid a יבש ביבש

---

[24] A third case which is not like the two presented in the text, is when a company mistakenly used a non-kosher ingredient in some of their products and there is no way to know which specific product it was used in. For example, some fruit punch was made with non-kosher grape juice instead of kosher grape juice. In that case, the kosher fruit punch tastes exactly the same as the non-kosher fruit punch, so the bottles of fruit punch clearly qualify as מין במינו. This is different than the lemon or "DE" food noted in the text, where the one that is truly non-kosher or dairy is halachically assumed to taste different than the kosher/pareve ones.

mixture even if they are מין בשאינו מינו.²⁵ This is exactly what happens when dealing with multiple lemon slices or hundreds of packages of food prepared commercially. It is possible that some parts of the *ta'aroves* will be cooked (or heated), but there is no foreseeable way that all parts will be cooked together. Therefore, even if it is considered מין בשאינו מינו, the non-kosher ones can be *batel b'rov* in the kosher items.

৪০ ○৪

Elsewhere we discussed the following cases which are potential examples of *bitul b'rov* for יבש ביבש which is מין במינו: bourbon which includes *chametz* that was owned by a Jew over *Pesach* (Chapter 21), a utensil used for non-kosher which was mixed into kosher utensils (Chapter 36), and a drum or bottle filled with non-kosher food that became mixed into other containers which are holding kosher food (Chapter 62).

This chapter focused on *issur* and *heter* which are currently mixed together. However, in cases where one of the items separated from the mixture, there may be alternate considerations, as discussed below in Chapter 63.

---

[25] See *Tzvi L'Tzadik* (to *Shach* ibid.) who makes a similar point in his third answer. See also *Minchas Yaakov* ibid. who appears to theoretically agree with this idea, but just notes that in his case it is possible all the pieces of meat will be heated together (even though they will surely not be cooked together since they are already cooked); that possibility does not exist in the cases noted in the text.

Part J

סימן ק"י

- Chapter 62 ....דבר שבמנין
- Chapter 63 ....כל קבוע, כל דפריש
- Chapter 64 ....Kashrus Scandals
- Chapter 65 ....נתגלגל
- Chapter 66 ....Papain

Chapter 62

דבר שבמנין

שולחן ערוך סימן ק"י סעיף א

דבר חשוב אוסר במינו בכל שהוא, והם ז' דברים ואלו הם: אגוזי פרך ורמוני בדן וחביות סתומות וחלפות תרדין וקלחי כרוב ודלעת יונית וככרות של בעל הבית. וכן בעלי חיים חשובים הם ואינם בטלים. אבל שאר דברים אף על פי שדרכן למנות הרי אלו עולים בשיעורן. הגה: ויש אומרים דכל דבר שבמנין, דהיינו שדרכו למנותו תמיד, אינו בטל, וכן נוהגין. הא דדבר חשוב אינו בטיל אינו אלא מדרבנן ואזלינן בספיקו לקולא.

כל דבר שהוא חשוב אצל בני מקום מהמקומות, כגון אגוזי פרך ורמוני בדן בארץ ישראל באותם הזמנים, הוא אוסר בכל שהוא, לפי חשיבותו באותו מקום ובאותו זמן, ולא הוזכרו אלו אלא לפי שהן אוסרים בכל שהן בכל מקום. וה"ה בכל כיוצא בהן, בשאר מקומות.

An underlying assumption of הלכות תערובות is that if a forbidden item is insignificant, its presence in a mixture can be ignored, and therefore it is "*batel*". Typically, significance is measured by the volume of issur and whether it affects the taste of the mixture. However, we have seen that there are times when the *issur* is either inherently important or plays a noteworthy role in the mixture, and therefore is not suited for *bitul*. In previous chapters we explored five examples of that idea,[1] and in this chapter we will see the final ones.

This halacha,[2] and several that follow, discuss a general category called "דבר חשוב", which is to say something that is prominent and, therefore, cannot be *batel*. For example, the *Gemara*[3] says that a living animal is חשוב and cannot be *batel*. The most relevant example of a דבר חשוב is the one

---

[1] See Chapters 1 (דבר המעמיד), 30 (בריה), 31 (חתיכה הראויה להתכבד), 33, (דבר שיש לו מתירין), and 35 (חזותא).
[2] *Shulchan Aruch* 110:1.
[3] *Gemara, Zevachim* 73a; see *Shulchan Aruch* 110:1, 2 & 6.

known as a דבר שבמנין, *something which is counted*; *Shulchan Aruch* provides many details of that halacha, and that will be our focus.

What qualifies

The *Mishnah* and *Gemara*[4] cite three primary opinions as to which items qualify[5] as a דבר שבמנין:

1. *Rebbi Akiva* .... there are only 7 items which are so valuable that they qualify as a דבר שבמנין.
2. *Rebbi Yochanan* ..... items which are <u>always</u> sold by "number" cannot be *batel* (את שדרכו לימנות).
3. *Reish Lakish*............ items which are <u>ever</u> sold by "number" cannot be *batel* (כל שדרכו לימנות).

Shulchan Aruch[6] accepts the (most-lenient) opinion of *Rebbi Akiva*. Most of the 7 items are not relevant to us, but one[7] is: חביות גדולות (large containers), which includes a 55- gallon drum or a tote.[8] Therefore, if a drum filled with animal-based glycerin (i.e., something which is inherently forbidden)[9] was mixed into drums of vegetable glycerin, all the drums would be forbidden, since the non-kosher drum is a דבר שבמנין which cannot be *batel*. A retail-sized container of animal fat or a bottle of *stam*

---

[4] *Mishnah*, Arlah 3:7 as per *Gemara*, Beitzah 3b.
[5] In previous chapters we saw that for דבר שיש לו מתירין it is only not *batel* in cases of מין במינו, but for the other items which cannot be *batel* (חתיכה הראויה להתכבד, בריה, מעמיד, and חזותא) the rule applies even for מין בשאינו מינו. As relates to דבר שבמנין, *Shulchan Aruch* 110:1 says that it is specific to cases of מין במינו, but *Shach* 110:1 (based on *Toras Chattas* 40:6 and *Rema* 101:6) and others say that in truth it even applies for מין בשאינו מינו and *Shulchan Aruch* said מין במינו since it is almost impossible to have a practical case of מין בשאינו מינו where one cannot easily tell which is the *issur* and which is the *heter*.
[6] *Shulchan Aruch* 110:1. *Beis Yosef* also notes that were one to argue that the halacha does not follow *Rebbi Akiva* (as some *Rishonim* do), he would favor *Rebbi Yochanan* as compared to *Reish Lakish*.
[7] Another one of the 7 which could possibly be relevant is a homemade loaf of bread (ככרות של בעל הבית) (and see *Shach* 110:6 that nowadays it may also include commercially produced loaves). [בעלי חיים are a דבר שבמנין which are not *batel* even according to *Shulchan Aruch* and are not included in the 7 דבר שבמנין].
[8] Although people do consider the volume of the drum (hence the name, "55-gallon" drum), that is overshadowed by the fact that it is counted and sold by the "drum" (i.e., by the number of units) and therefore it is considered a דבר שבמנין (Rav Belsky).
[9] As with most other items which cannot be *batel*, the strict status of דבר שבמנין only applies to thing which are אסור מחמת עצמו (inherently forbidden) (*Toras Chattas* 42:2, and *Magen Avraham* 447:40 cited in *Sha'ar HaTziun* 447:147-148). See *Meat and Poultry*, Chapter 35 footnote 25, that a piece of meat which was not salted is therefore not considered a דבר שבמנין (or a חתיכה הראויה להתכבד) since the meat is inherently permitted and it is an outside item (i.e., the blood) which is forbidden.

yayin wine[10] is not a "large" container and would not be considered a דבר שבמנין, according to this opinion.

Rema accepts the opinion of *Rebbi Yochanan*, that any item which is <u>always</u> sold by the number is considered a דבר שבמנין. For example, in the United States eggs are always sold by the dozen (or 30 to a tray), and therefore they qualify. Therefore, if a chicken which is a טריפה lays an egg, that egg is not kosher, and if it gets mixed into other eggs, the entire batch of eggs is forbidden.[11] However, even *Rema* agrees that a retail-sized container or bottle of food is not a דבר שבמנין (and he specifically notes this elsewhere).[12] Although people do usually count containers and might say "I need to buy 2 boxes of cereal", the container is really just a premeasured amount/weight of food and a convenient way to package and purchase that amount.[13] [Things sold by weight do <u>not</u> qualify as a דבר שבמנין].[14] Thus, the "count" is no indication of its being a דבר חשוב or a דבר שבמנין, and it can be *batel*.

---

[10] See *Rema* YD 134:2 cited below.

[11] *Shulchan Aruch* YD 86:3. Why does *Shulchan Aruch* list that as a דבר שבמנין if we have seen here that he holds that דבר שבמנין is limited to 7 specific items (of which eggs are not one of them)? See *Imrei Dovid*, *Animal Products*, Chapter 28 footnote 20.

[12] See *Rema* YD 134:2.

Gemara, *Zevachim* 74a, says that in general, a ring used in an *avodah zara* service cannot be *batel*. *Rambam* (*Hil. Avodah Zara* 7:10) and *Shulchan Aruch* (YD 140:1) understand that this is a special strictness that תקרובת עבודה זרה (items used in the worship of an *avodah zara*) can never be *batel*. Accordingly, they would rule that <u>any</u> sized container of יין נסך (wine poured for an *avodah zara*) cannot be *batel* in other containers; in fact, that is what *Shulchan Aruch* YD 134:2 says. Thus, when *Rema* comments that the ruling is specific to <u>large</u> containers which qualify as a דבר שבמנין, he is not explaining *Shulchan Aruch*, but is rather arguing. *Rema* is following the lead of *Tosfos*, *Yevamos* 81b s.v. *Rebbi Yochanan* (and others) who say that there is no special *chumrah* regarding תקרובת עבודה זרה, and the reason why the ring used for *avodah zara* cannot be *batel* is because it is a דבר שבמנין. Therefore, only a large container (which is a דבר שבמנין) cannot be *batel*, but a smaller one can. *Shach* 110:5 accepts the ruling of *Rema*.

This was once relevant when a company was found to be selling water into which they poured a small amount of water that had been used in idolatrous service. [They would recite a prayer over water (which had been mixed with some salt), dedicate it to their deity, after which this תקרובת עבודה זרה water would be added to a large vat of regular water to be sold as "miraculous" water. See *Shulchan Aruch* YD 139:3, that this situation is relatively easily classified as תקרובת עבודה זרה since (a) water and salt are used in the *Beis Hamikdash*, (b) water has a role in that religion's service, and (c) potentially the pouring qualifies as a זריקה המשתברת]. As per *Rema*, the תקרובת עבודה זרה water can be *batel* in the rest of the water (but, obviously, it would be improper to certify such water as kosher).

[13] The proof to this is that the same food might be sold in 3 different package sizes, indicating that the container per se is of no significance, and is just a convenience for all parties involved.

[14] *Terumas HaDeshen* 103 cited by *Darchei Moshe* 110:2 (and many others).

Lastly, *Shach*[15] cites many who are *machmir* for *Reish Lakish*, and *Taz*[16] says that one should follow that (most-strict) opinion except במקום הפסד. In contrast, *Chochmas Adam and Aruch HaShulchan*[17] accept the opinion of *Rema* (*Rebbi Yochanan*).

Meat

Several cases related to meat illustrate the difference between the stricter opinion of *Reish Lakish* and the more moderate position of *Rebbi Yochanan*.

Slaughterhouses are careful to mark any animal which is a נבילה or a טריפה, and at the point when the carcass is cut into pieces, all pieces will be marked accordingly. However, sometimes a mistake happens and after a שחיטה goes bad, they may forget to mark the carcass as a נבילה. Similarly, it can happen that after the animal's lungs are checked and it is deemed kosher (i.e., not a טריפה), it is discovered that there is a סימן טריפה in some other [unexpected] part of the animal (e.g., a meningeal worm found in the brain when the sheep's head is cut open for מליחה,[18] or a hole in the טרפש).[19] By that time, the non-kosher animal (or parts thereof) have been mixed in with the rest of the kosher animals and there is no way to determine which is the non-kosher one.

At certain early[20] stages of processing, the non-kosher carcasses are just referred to by "number", meaning that the slaughterhouse will note, for

---

[15] *Shach* 110:9.
[16] *Taz* 110:1. *Pri Megadim* ad loc. explains that *Taz* means to say that במקום הפסד one can rely on *Rebbi Yochanan/Rema* (as opposed to *Rebbi Akiva/Shulchan Aruch*).
[17] *Chochmas Adam* 53:16 cites only *Rema/Rebbi Yochanan* and does not even note the dissenting opinion. *Aruch HaShulchan* 110:1-2 & 5 says that most *Poskim* follow *Rebbi Yochanan*, and that someone who relies on this הפסד במקום ובפרט לסמוך מה על לו יש.
[18] See *Imrei Dovid, Meat and Poultry*, Chapter 23.
[19] This latter case is the subject of *Chasam Sofer* YD 91. See *Chaver Ben Chaim* (a *talmid* of *Chasam Sofer*) volume 3 page 38b (commenting on this *teshuvah*) who reports the situation that led to that *teshuvah*, as follows:

מעשה זה דכירנא, כי בעת ההיא יצקתי מים על ידי מרן זצוק"ל ונמצא מחט בטרפשא דכבדא בבית השוחט הממונה התו' הרה"ר איצק וואלף ע"ה, כי היה אז גם בפ"ב המנהג שלקחו השוחטים מכל הכשרות טרפשא דכבדא, ולא נודע מאיזה בהמה הי' הטרפשא הזה, והבד"ץ שהיו גאונים מפורסמים לא רצו להורות בתערובת זאת אף כי מרן הי' לשאוף אויר צח בעת ההיא בקהל ראקענדארף עד בא תשובתו זאת.

[20] In this context it is noteworthy that *Shach* 101:7 says that if the animal's hide is still on (or a bird's feathers have not yet been removed), it automatically does not qualify as a דבר שבמנין, thus the "early stage" noted in the text must be after that point. In other words, at the stages when the animal cannot qualify as חתיכה הראויה להתכבד (even according to *Rema* 101:3) (see Chapter 31, noted briefly in the coming text), it also cannot be considered a דבר שבמנין. [*Shach* notes that *Darchei Moshe* 40:3 argues that it can be a דבר שבמנין even when the hide is still on; *Shach* and *Pri Megadim* ad loc. cite many *Poskim* who disagree with that position].

example, that they have 137 kosher forequarters. However, once the meat is ready for sale, it is referred to in two ways: by weight and by count. This means the slaughterhouse might fill an order for 45 beef livers, 28 skirt steaks, and 22 tails, all of which are "numbers", but that order will be billed based on weight. Thus, *Reish Lakish* would be *machmir* and consider this a דבר שבמנין since the sale is <u>sometimes</u> calculated by a number, while *Rebbi Yochanan* would allow *bitul* since it is not <u>always</u> measured that way. [As noted, even *Taz* says that one can follow the leniency of *Rebbi Yochanan/Rema* in cases of הפסד; seemingly, these types of mistakes would often affect many carcasses and thus qualify as a הפסד].

A similar issue would also apply to a homeowner who somehow had non-kosher meat or poultry mixed into their kosher items. Certain cuts of meat, such as a roast, are purchased based on weight or size (both of which do not qualify as a דבר שבמנין). Others are based on a combination of count and weight, such as when they buy a package of chicken bottoms or rib steaks; the consumer wants 4 bottoms or 2 steaks, but the transaction also depends on the weight of the meat.

These examples are theoretical and only touch on one element of the issue: are they considered a דבר שבמנין. In the coming two chapters, we will see the [unfortunate] very real applications where these halachos come into play. There we will also be introduced to the concepts of כל קבוע and כל דפריש מרובא פריש and כמחצה על מחצה, which are particularly relevant to these cases.

At this juncture it is also worth noting that many of the cases involving non-kosher meat are subject not only to considerations of דבר שבמנין but also might be considered a חתיכה הראויה להתכבד. That concept was discussed in Chapter 31; the following is a brief quote from that chapter:

> Does the piece of meat (or other food) have to be fit for honored guests as-is, or does even it include pieces that will only be ראויה להתכבד when they are cooked or otherwise prepared? *Shulchan Aruch* rules like the former position, and therefore meat which is raw or too large to serve respectably, is not considered ראויה להתכבד and can be *batel*. But *Rema* argues that if all that is required is some small amount of preparation, the meat is considered ראויה להתכבד. This includes meat which requires *melichah*, dividing into serving-sized pieces, or cooking. For example, a forequarter of beef is a חתיכה הראויה להתכבד which cannot be *batel* even though it cannot be served to guests without being salted, cut up, and cooked. However, if significant effort is

needed to prepare the meat – such as removing the hide from an animal or removing the feathers from a chicken – then it is not ראויה להתכבד.

☙ ❧

The principle that a דבר שבמנין cannot be *batel* is not limited to food items. We can see this in the ruling of *Rema*[21] that candles which were (partially) used for the *Chanukah menorah*, cannot be *batel* into other (unused) candles because, during *Chanukah*, people count their candles to know how many they should use for the *mitzvah*. Thus, as a דבר שבמנין, they cannot be *batel*. The following case is another example where the principle of דבר שבמנין was applied to a non-food item.

Sefer Torah

Approximately 200 years ago, several *Gedolim* exchanged letters[22] regarding applying the principle of דבר שבמנין to a specific non-food case, and as we will see parts of the question relate to a *machlokes* that has food relevance. A *sefer Torah* was found to have a mistake which rendered it *passul*, but with time the community forgot which was the *passul sefer Torah*. They checked all their *Torahs* and could not find any mistakes, and the community wondered if the *passul sefer Torah* could be *batel b'rov* in the other *sefer Torahs* that they had. Some parts of the discussion relate to the permissibility of using a non-kosher *sefer Torah* when a person has no other choice; those issues are beyond the scope of this work and will not be considered. What we will focus on is the two elements of the question which are connected to *hilchos ta'aruvos*.

The first is directly related to our halacha: *Chasam Sofer* and *Maharam Shick*[23] said that the *sefer Torah* is a דבר חשוב and for that reason it should not be *batel*. The mistake in the *sefer Torah* renders the entire *Torah passul*, and therefore it is considered אסור מחמת עצמו and subject to the strictness of דבר חשוב which cannot be *batel*. *Binyan Tzion*[24] argued that, although the entire *Torah* is *passul*, it should not be viewed as אסור מחמת עצמו. When milk gets mixed into meat, the meat becomes permanently

---

[21] *Rema* OC 673:1 as per *Mishnah Berurah* 673:22.
[22] The original (strict) ruling in the case was given by *Chasam Sofer* YD 277. *Binyan Tzion* 13 disagreed and based himself to a great extent on *Responsa Yad Eliyahu* 88. [*Yad Eliyahu* was authored by a Rav from Poland and Lithuania, and was printed in 1712, approximately 125 years before the others cited here]. *Maharam Shick* YD 282 wrote to the *Binyan Tzion* to defend the position of his *Rebbi*, the *Chasam Sofer*, and *Binyan Tzion* responded to that letter in *teshuvah* #14.
[23] *Chasam Sofer* and *Maharam Shick* ibid.
[24] *Binyan Tzion* in both *teshuvos*, ibid., but with more detail at the end of the latter *teshuvah*.

assur even if one could possibly remove the milk (אפשר לסוחטו אסור),[25] but the same is not true for the *sefer Torah*. If someone finds the mistake and corrects it, the *Torah* will revert to its kosher status. That indicates that it is not inherently *passul*, and therefore does not qualify as אסור מחמת עצמו.[26] Therefore, the single *passul sefer Torah* is *batel b'rov* in the other *sifrei Torah* that the community owns.[27]

The other argument *Chasam Sofer* raises is that since the mistake can be found and corrected, there is no *ta'aruvos* at all, and *bitul* is not an option. We discussed this issue in Chapter 24, and there we saw that the *Poskim* disagree whether that concept (אפשר להסירו) is a *d'oraisah* or *d'rabannan*. If it is a *d'oraisah*, that means that it applies no matter how difficult it is to find the *issur* or mistake, and that is the position which *Chasam Sofer* and *Maharam Shick* appear to espouse in this case. In contrast, *Binyan Tzion*[28] is quite clear that he considers that to be a *d'rabannan* principle, similar to דבר שיש לו מתירין; if you can remove the *issur* or find the mistake, you are Rabbinically obligated to do that and not rely on *bitul*. But in a case like this, where the people made every effort to find the mistake and were unsuccessful, they fulfilled the obligation *Chazal* had in mind. Therefore, at this point, they may rely on *bitul*.[29]

---

[25] See Chapter 24 and Part 2 of Chapter 55.

[26] Contemporary *Poskim* disagreed about a similar question, in *hilchos muktzeh*. If something *muktzeh* is purposely placed onto a table (or anything else), and remains there when *Shabbos* starts, the table is *muktzeh* for that entire *Shabbos* even if the *muktzeh* is removed; the table is referred to as a בסיס לדבר האסור. There was a *simcha* at a catering hall and some people lit *neiros Shabbos* on chairs, rendering those chairs a בסיס. After the candles went out they were removed, and the chairs were moved around so that no one can tell which chairs were a בסיס (and *muktzeh*). *Chut Shani* (Rav Nissim Karelitz) (*Shabbos*, Volume 3, page 156) ruled that the forbidden chairs are אסור מחמת עצמו, as evidenced by the fact that they remain *muktzeh* even after the candles are removed, and therefore qualify as a דבר שבמנין which cannot be *batel*. Accordingly, all the chairs in the catering hall are treated as *muktzeh* and cannot be moved. In contrast, *Mishnas Yosef* (Rav Yosef Liberman) 5:76:4 said that since there is nothing inherently "*muktzeh*" about the chairs, and they are just affected by an outside object (i.e., the candles), they are not אסור מחמת עצמו and can be *batel*. [There were other factors within *hilchos muktzeh* which were relevant to the question at hand, but those are not pertinent to our discussion].

[27] *Yad Eliyahu* ibid. adds that if the community only has 3 *sifrei Torah* and it comes a *Shabbos* when they must use all three (i.e., שבת ראש חודש טבת or שבת ראש חודש ניסן) they may have קריאת התורה from all 3 *sifrei Torah* even though they know that one is surely *passul*.

[28] *Binyan Tzion*, second *teshuvah*.

[29] Both arguments noted in the text regarding a *sefer Torah* should seemingly also apply if a garment that contains *shatnez* was mixed into other *shatnez*-free garments; garments are sold by the piece so they qualify as a דבר שבמנין but (a) the *shatnez* can be removed from the garment just as the mistake can be corrected in the *Torah*, and (b) if one looks carefully enough they can discover the one garment that contains *shatnez*.

Chapter 63

כל קבוע, כל דפריש

שולחן ערוך סימן ק״י סעיף ג

ט׳ חנויות מוכרות בשר שחוטה ואחת מוכרת בשר נבילה ולקח מאחת מהן ואין ידוע מאיזה מהן לקח הרי זה אסור שכל קבוע כמחצה על מחצה דמי, אבל בשר הנמצא בשוק או ביד עובד כוכבים מותר כיון שרוב החנויות מוכרות בשר שחוטה דכל דפריש מרובא פריש. זהו דין תורה, אבל חכמים אסרוהו אף על פי שכל השוחטים וכל המוכרים ישראל.

הגה: ועיין לעיל סימן ס״ג. והא דאמרינן כל דפריש מרובא פריש היינו שלא פירש לפנינו, אבל אם פירש לפנינו או שראוה כשהא״י לקחו הוי כאילו לקחו משם בידו.

קבוע דאורייתא

The bulk of *hilchos ta'aruvos* is about situations where there is a *ta'aruvos*, meaning non-kosher and kosher have gotten mixed in a way that one cannot tell which is the *heter* and which is the *issur*. The halacha is not the same in all cases, but the starting point is that one cannot distinguish the forbidden items and separate them from the permitted ones. However, a separate set of halachos applies in certain cases where the status of the different items is clear, but there is nonetheless a *safek*. We will begin with the *Gemara's* source for this issue, which is known as קבוע ("designated").

The background to this issue is that the *Chachomim* are of the opinion that a person is liable for murder if he (a) intends to kill one Jew and instead kills a different Jew, or if he (b) shoots an arrow into a crowd of Jews with the intention of killing one of them (with no specific victim in mind) and, in fact, kills a Jew, but is not liable if he (c) intends to kill a non-Jew and ends up killing a Jew. [In this context, "liable" refers to whether a *Beis Din* can punish the person for what he did; it does not imply that *Hashem* will not hold him responsible for his actions]. With this in mind, the *Gemara*[1] records that there is a verse which teaches that the person is not liable in a variation of case "b", where the crowd of people had many Jews and some non-Jews (and the person who ends up being killed is a Jew). One might imagine that הולכין אחר הרוב (*we always follow the majority*) should dictate that since most of the people are Jewish this should have the same status as case "b", and the person should be liable. The verse teaches us that this is not true, and it is based on a new principle called כל קבוע כמחצה על מחצה.

That principle, כל קבוע כמחצה על מחצה, means that whenever the permitted and forbidden items are clearly designated (קבוע) – such as in this case, where it is obvious which people in the crowd are Jewish and which are not – we treat them as an equal mixture (כמחצה על מחצה, literally *like half and half*) and do not follow the majority. Therefore, since the crowd of people is halachically viewed as being half Jews and half non-Jews, the murderer is not liable since he did not specifically intend to kill a Jew.

This is the source for the halacha of כל קבוע, and a different *Gemara*[2] applies it to a case which is the basis for the current halacha (*Shulchan Aruch* 110:3). Namely, that of a city which has 9 kosher butcher shops and one non-kosher store, and someone purchased meat from one of the stores but cannot remember which one he went into. Here again, the principle of כל קבוע כמצחה על מחצה dictates that we can<u>not</u> assume the person went into a kosher store (which is what הולכין אחר הרוב would have indicated). The kosher and non-kosher stores are clearly identifiable as to their status, and therefore the *safek* revolving around the קבוע stores is treated as if there are an equal number of kosher and non-kosher butchers. Accordingly, the meat is forbidden since from a halachic perspective there is an equal *safek* whether the meat was bought in a kosher store or not.

But this *Gemara* adds one more detail, which is also recorded in the current halacha: כל קבוע כמחצה על מחצה is limited to cases where the *safek* arises at the place where the קבוע is. For example, in our case, the question is which store did the person walk into. But if the story had been different and a person found a piece of meat in the street with no indication which store it came from, there כל קבוע does not apply. The question is not which store

---

[1] *Gemara*, *Sanhedrin*, 79a as per *Rashi* ad loc.
[2] *Gemara*, *Chullin* 95a, and elsewhere.

the person went into, but rather which store did the meat <u>leave</u> from, and in that case, we apply a second principle known as כל דפריש מרובא פריש, which means that an item which separated itself from a group of items (כל דפריש) is assumed to have come from the majority of those items. This means that we may assume the meat came from one of the 9 kosher butcher shops and ignore the possibility it came from the one non-kosher store. [*Mid'rabannan*, there is a special stringency that is specific to cases of non-kosher meat, (*Shulchan Aruch*) but for all other cases the principle of כל דפריש is in effect].

What these two cases of כל קבוע have in common is that there is no question regarding the inherent status of the subjects – Jews and non-Jews or kosher and non-kosher butcher shops. *Bitul* cannot possibly say that the non-Jews in the crowd are actually Jewish, or that the non-kosher butcher shop is kosher, since it is plainly obvious that this is not true. The question at hand is rather how an outside force acted on those קבוע items: whom did the murderer intend to shoot, or which store did the person walk into. This is very different from a standard *ta'aruvos* where the items are thoroughly mixed or look identical and no one can identify which is the non-kosher one. In those cases, *bitul* can potentially rule that the relatively minor non-kosher component is nullified and is subsumed into the larger kosher group.

The above is an explanation of the standard case of כל קבוע כמחצה על מחצה, which the *Poskim* refer to as "קבוע מדאורייתא".[3]

קבוע דרבנן

However, the *Poskim* tell us that there is another type of case which does not match that of קבוע דאורייתא, but nonetheless has a very similar halacha, and the source of this is a third *Gemara*.[4] It is discussing a case where an animal that is not suited for a *korban* is mixed with many other animals which are intended as *korbanos*. The forbidden animal cannot be *batel* because it is a living being and is therefore too important or significant to be "*batel*" (בעלי חיים חשיבי ולא בטילי).[5] So, why not just take one animal from the group and bring it as a *korban*, based on the principle of כל דפריש

---

[3] The terminology (קבוע דאורייתא, קבוע דרבנן) and explanation of the halachos noted in the text are based on *Binas Adam*, *Sha'ar Hakavuah*, #1, which can also be found in *Taz* 110:3 and *Shach* 110:22, based on the *Rishonim's* explanation of *Gemara*, *Zevachim* 73a-b discussed below.
[4] *Gemara*, *Zevachim* 73a-b.
[5] The principle that living items cannot be *batel* is codified in *Shulchan Aruch* 110:1.

מרובא פריש (which would say that one which was taken came from the majority which are suitable for *korbanos*)? The *Gemara* answers that this is a case of קבוע, and actively taking one from the קבוע does not qualify for כל דפריש.

How is this a case of קבוע? If people could tell which animal is the one that is not suited to be a *korban,* they would obviously just pull it out of the group. So, the entire discussion assumes that there is no way to tell which animal is which. If so, how is this a case of קבוע? Did we not see above that קבוע is specific to cases where the *issur* and *heter* are clearly identifiable?

This indicates[6] that when *Chazal* said that certain items cannot be *batel* – such as דבר שיש לו מתירין, or דבר שבמנין, חתיכה הראויה להתכבד, בעלי חיים – they structured the rule to be like that of כל קבוע כמחצה על מחצה. Just like in cases of קבוע where the inherent status cannot be changed, the *safek* is viewed as being impossible to determine, so too when the mixture contains a component that *mid'rabannan* cannot be *batel*, the mixture/*safek* is viewed as if it is קבוע and its status remains unresolved (and therefore forbidden). Thus, these cases where *bitul* is ineffective *mid'rabannan* can be referred to as קבוע מדרבנן: a Rabbinic form of the principle of כל קבוע כמחצה על מחצה.

In the previous chapter we saw that a drum of (non-kosher) animal-based glycerin qualifies as a דבר שבמנין, and similarly, a forequarter of beef is considered a חתיכה הראויה להתכבד, and both cannot be *batel*. Therefore, if it was discovered that a drum delivered to a factory was not kosher or that one of the animals is a טריפה but there is no way to identify the non-kosher drum or forequarter, all the drums or forequarters that are in the factory are forbidden. This is an example of a קבוע דרבנן.

כל דפריש

We have seen that the *Gemara* says that it is not considered כל דפריש if a person takes an animal from the קבוע דרבנן; this is reflected in *Rema* in the current halacha.[7] However, the *Gemara* subsequently suggests a way that the person can cause some of the animals to disperse in a way that would qualify as כל דפריש, and wonders whether the person should do that in order to permit the animals as a *korban*. To this the *Gemara* answers that

---

[6] See footnote 3.
[7] *Rema* 110:3.

Chazal specifically forbade this because they were concerned that, if כל דפריש was permitted, people would end up just removing an animal from the state of קבוע which (as we have seen) is not permitted. In other words, cases which qualify as כל דפריש are technically not included in כל קבוע, but in practice one cannot rely on that.

How can this be reconciled with the case of the city with 9 kosher butcher shops, where the *Gemara* says that כל דפריש is effective, and the meat is permitted? Why is כל דפריש acceptable in that case but not in the case of *korbanos*? There are two primary answers in the *Rishonim*.[8] *Rashba*[9] says that the only cases where כל דפריש is ineffective is where the person <u>deliberately</u> caused the situation to change from קבוע to כל דפריש. In that case, *Chazal* were concerned that if the person is taking such an active role, he might mistakenly choose to take an animal directly from the קבוע in ways that (as we have seen) do not qualify as כל דפריש. But the case of 9 butcher shops is one where the people innocently purchased the meat (i.e., created the כל דפריש) without any knowledge of the significance of what they were doing. In that case, the leniency of כל דפריש remains in effect, and the meat is permitted.

In contrast, *Rosh*[10] says that *Chazal* only restricted כל דפריש when there is a realistic concern the person might take from the קבוע. That makes sense when discussing a קבוע דרבנן (such as in the case of *korbanos*) where the permitted and forbidden animals are all intermingled and there is no obvious *issur*. But in a קבוע דאורייתא (such as in the case of 9 kosher butcher shops) where the non-kosher items are readily identifiable, there is no

---

[8] *Tosfos* offers a third answer (not cited as widely by the *Poskim*) that the Rabbinic restriction on כל דפריש only applies to cases of *kodashim* (and ones with a concern of *Avodah Zara*), but not to other potential *issurim*.

[9] *Rashba, Toras HaBayis* 4:2 page 30a.

Rav Henkin (*Kol Torah* Journal, *Nissan* 5722 (as reprinted in *Yeshurun* 21), *Teshuvos Ivrah* 38b and 39a) has a novel position that a person choosing to purchase an item that is already separated from the group can sometimes be considered "taking from the קבוע" (and not qualify as כל דפריש), since the person should have been more discerning in what he chose to purchase. The specific case he is discussing is that of canned tuna, where no one verified the *kashrus* of the fish before they were packaged; for more on that, see *Imrei Dovid, Alcoholic Beverages*, Chapter 19. [Rav Henkin does acknowledge that eggs or milk available for retail sale (where no one verified that the fish or animal that produced them was from a kosher species) does qualify for כל דפריש. In turn, this is based on *Rema* 110:6 (end)].

If the entire mixture disperses, each of the items is permitted (*Rema* 110:6 and *Shach* 110:35). If just one of the items was destroyed or eaten, the remaining items remain forbidden, but there is a special leniency (for קבוע דרבנן) that one may eat any <u>two</u> (or more) of the remaining items simultaneously (*Shulchan Aruch* 110:7), but one person should not eat <u>all</u> of them (*Rema* ad loc).

[10] *Rosh, Chullin* 7:20-21 with further details added in *Responsa Rosh* 20:17.

reason to be concerned that a religious person will consciously choose to buy meat from that store. Therefore, in that case כל דפריש remains effective and the meat is permitted.[11]

Rosh adds that there is a second case where – for a somewhat counterintuitive reason – Chazal would not have forbidden כל דפריש. As noted, the Gemara says that כל דפריש cannot be relied upon when there is a concern that leniency might mistakenly lead people to think they can take items directly from the קבוע. But what if the item was separated from the group/קבוע <u>before</u> anyone realized that there was *issur* mixed into it? At that point, there would be no reason not to take more items from the group, since everything is believed to be kosher. If so, since the whole reason to forbid כל דפריש is because it might encourage people to take from the קבוע, in this case where there is no such concern (since it is "permitted" to take from the קבוע), items that qualify for כל דפריש remain permitted.[12]

Shulchan Aruch[13] follows the approach of *Rashba*, ruling that כל דפריש permits the items whether it is a case of קבוע דאורייתא or קבוע דרבנן, and the only situation where one must be *machmir* is if the person intentionally took the item from the group.[14] In *Toras Chattas*,[15] *Rema* records both *Rashba* and *Rosh* and says that it is good to be *machmir* for the opinion of *Rosh*. However, *Pri Megadim*[16] says that the fact that in *Shulchan Aruch*, *Rema* does not disagree with *Shulchan Aruch*'s citation of *Rashba*, indicates that *Rema's* final ruling is to accept that position. In contrast, *Taz* and

---

[11] Thus, a mixture which is forbidden *mid'rabannan* (i.e., קבוע דרבנן) has an added (Rabbinic) restriction that כל דפריש is ineffective, but a mixture which is *assur mid'oraisah* (i.e., קבוע דאורייתא) has a more lenient status in that כל דפריש can permit the food.

[12] Should we be concerned that if we permit כל דפריש for animals separated from the group when it was "permitted" to take from the קבוע, that might lead people to take animals from the group after we realize that it includes some forbidden animals? There is no Gemara source for such a concern (and people realize that what is permitted before the issue is discovered, is different from how one should act after it comes to light that forbidden animals are in the group), and therefore כל דפריש remains effective (Rosh).

What if some people knew of the קבוע דרבנן mixture, but the person who removed this item did not? *Pri Megadim* SD 110:33 raises this question and seems inclined to be *machmir*. [See footnote 8 in Chapter 64].

[13] *Shulchan Aruch* 110:6.

[14] Similarly, one must be *machmir* if the person was observed taking the item from the group; see *Taz* 110:3 and *Shach* 110:22.

[15] *Toras Chattas* 43:1. However, in *Simanei Toras Chattas*, he cites only the opinion of *Rosh*.

[16] *Pri Megadim* MZ 110:6. Among other things, he notes that *Rema's* glosses to *Shulchan Aruch* were written <u>after</u> he wrote *Toras Chattas*, and therefore are considered more authoritative. For more on that, see Point #9 of *Pri Megadim's* כללים בהוראת איסור והיתר (printed as part of his introduction to *Yoreh Deah*).

Shach[17] cite *Rosh* in a manner that indicates that they accept his ruling. *Chochmas Adam* and other later *Acharonim*[18] accept the decision of *Minchas Yaakov* that one should be *machmir* for *Rosh*, except in cases of *hefsed merubah*.

Let us now apply these opinions to the scenarios noted above, where at 10:00 AM it was discovered that a drum of glycerin or a forequarter is not kosher, but no one can identify the specific drum or forequarter. All drums (or forequarters) in the facility are considered קבוע דרבנן and are forbidden. We have now learned that any drum that was removed from the factory before 10:00 AM is permitted based on כל דפריש,[19] [and drums taken out at any time with intent to separate them from the group are forbidden]. But drums innocently shipped from the factory after 10:00 AM are subject to the disagreement noted above: *Rashba* would permit them since they were not removed on purpose, while *Rosh* will say that they are forbidden since they were taken out after the קבוע דרבנן issue was discovered.

What is considered פריש

The case noted above, where a drum was taken out of the factory, is a simple example of כל דפריש, but *Poskim* note that there are other cases which also qualify. One such case is that if any of the items are permanently changed (שינוי), they are considered to have separated from the group.[20] For example, if one of the forequarters noted above had been

---

[17] *Taz* 110:6 and *Shach* 100:36.

[18] *Chochmas Adam* 63:5 and *Rebbi Akiva Eiger* to *Shach* 110:36, citing *Minchas Yaakov* 43:3. As relates to the strict position of *Taz* and *Shach*, *Pri Megadim* SD 110:32 suggests that there might be more reason to be lenient if the קבוע דרבנן is based on the forbidden item being a דבר שיש לו מתירין (as opposed to a חתיכה הראויה להתכבד, or בעל חי, דבר שבמנין).

[19] See also *Shulchan Aruch* 110:5.

The same applies to the case of forequarters noted earlier, where some meat from a day's שחיטה is permitted while other meat is forbidden. This gives rise to a question of what is the halacha if half of an animal has already left the slaughterhouse (so that it is permitted) while the other half is still there (such that it is forbidden)? Can it possibly be that half of the animal is permitted and the other half is forbidden? If not, should both halves be permitted or forbidden? *Pischei Teshuvah* 110:4 cites many *Acharonim* who discuss this question; see also *Chazon Ish* YD 37:17.

Shulchan Aruch notes that there are situations where even if the meat is not a חתיכה הראויה להתכבד (or some other type which is not suitable for ביטול), all meat which remains in the slaughterhouse is forbidden. However, see *Shach* 110:31, who limits this *chumrah* to cases where the meat is at a butcher store or other location where the public at large comes to purchase meat. But in venues with a much more limited clientele, the status of the meat depends on the standard rules noted in the text. Modern slaughterhouses qualify for this latter status, and therefore that *chumrah* does not apply.

[20] *Binas Adam*, *Sha'ar Hakavuah* #10; see also *Taz* 101:14 (and *Pri Megadim* ad loc. who refers to it as "קצת כפירש").

cut into smaller retail cuts [before 10:00 when people found out about the תערובות], that would be enough to qualify it for כל דפריש.[21]

A somewhat more contentious question is whether something can be considered פירש if no change happened and it separated somewhat from the other items, yet it is still in the same store or basic location where the others are. This issue is discussed by *Chochmas Adam*, *Chasam Sofer*, and *Beis Yitzchok*,[22] and all agree that it is not considered פירש if the item is moved away from the group in a temporary manner. Two examples of this are (1) if the תערובות is a group of live animals walking together and one happens to walk a few steps ahead of the others or lags a bit behind, and (2) if someone picks up one of the pieces of meat to decide if he should buy it. The animal is just temporarily away from the group, and the customer might put this piece down when he sees a more desirable one, so these are surely not considered פירש and retain their status of קבוע.

What if the separation is permanent but the item in question is still in the same home or store? *Chochmas Adam* says that if the item has truly separated from the group, it qualifies as פירש regardless of whether it has left the room.[23] *Beis Yitzchok* discusses a case of קבוע דאורייתא, such as separate stores which sell kosher and non-kosher meat, and argues that it is not logical that a piece can be considered פירש if it is still in the store. Even though it is not near the other pieces, it is obvious that it came from this store, and is still part of the קבוע even though it is not proximate to them.

Chasam Sofer is convinced that כל דפריש applies even if the meat has not left the house or store where the rest of the pieces of meat are, but there is a significant difference between his case and those of the previously mentioned *Poskim*. As noted, they were discussing cases of קבוע דאורייתא, while *Chasam Sofer's* case is one of קבוע דרבנן: 5 geese were slaughtered, and it turned out that one was a טריפה, but no one knows which one it was. In קבוע דרבנן cases, the logic of *Beis Yitzchok* does not apply, and he might well agree that as long as one piece of meat etc. has meaningfully

---

[21] *Binas Adam* ibid.
[22] *Binas Adam*, *Sha'ar Hakavuah* #9 (cited in *Darchei Teshuvah* 110:64), *Chasam Sofer* YD 99 (cited in *Pischei Teshuvah* 110:4 and *Darchei Teshuvah* ibid), and *Beis Yitzchok*, *Sha'ar Hakavuah* #9 (cited in *Darchei Teshuvah* ibid. and 110:96). [*Binas Adam* and *Chasam Sofer* were contemporaries, while *Beis Yitzchok* lived approximately 100 years later].
[23] He further says that even if a piece of meat falls onto the floor of a store, it is considered פירש, since that is not part of the typical flow of business.

separated from the others it qualifies for כל דפריש, even if it is still in the store with them.[24]

For example: owners of a store realize that some of the meat they bought was non-kosher, but they cannot identify the problematic pieces. Assuming the meat is a חתיכה הראויה להתכבד, it cannot be *batel*, and all the meat in the store's walk-in refrigerator is considered non-kosher. What if some meat has been moved into the refrigerated display case in the front of the store where customers can choose what they want to buy? That meat has permanently separated from the group [since stores rarely bring meat back from the display case to the walk-in refrigerator], and therefore *Chochmas Adam* and *Chasam Sofer* would surely say that כל דפריש applies even though that meat is still in the store. We have also suggested that in this example of קבוע דרבנן, even *Beis Yitzchok* would agree to leniently apply כל דפריש.

The halachos of קבוע *and* פירש *are very relevant when a significant kashrus scandal occurs, as will be considered in the coming chapter*

Pesach

One common case where the possibility of כל דפריש arises is that of *chametz*. Namely, in the United States, there are ingredients which some companies make from *chametz* (e.g., wheat), but most produce them from *kitnios* (e.g., corn). A good example of this is white distilled vinegar. There is at least one producer who uses wheat as the starting material, but the vast majority of manufacturers produce it from corn. Are consumers who have white distilled vinegar in their house (or a condiment made with vinegar) required to dispose of it (or sell it) before *Pesach* to avoid the prohibition against owning *chametz*? Or can they rely on כל דפריש to assume that their vinegar is from the majority that is just *kitnios*? [It is permitted to own *kitnios* on *Pesach*].[25] Similarly, what if a medicine includes "starch" and there is no way to determine if it is wheat starch (*chametz*) or corn starch (*kitnios*)? If a person is sick enough that he is permitted to eat *kitnios* on *Pesach* (but may not eat *chametz*), can he rely on כל דפריש to take this medicine?

---

[24] See a similar point in *Yad Yehudah* 110:21 (*Katzar*) and 110:32 (*Katzar*).
[25] *Rema* OC 453:1.

This seems like a simple case which qualifies for כל דפריש, and to understand the possible concern we turn to a *Gemara* in *Pesachim*.[26] The *Gemara* relates that there was one pile of *chametz* and several piles of non-*chametz*, and a rodent took a piece from one of the piles and brought it into a house. The *Gemara* explains that in the cases which qualify for כל דפריש, one can leniently assume the rodent took non-*chametz*. *Tosfos*[27] says that the intent of the *Gemara* is that the food which the rodent took may be eaten on *Pesach*. According to *Tosfos*, the *Gemara* is clearly stating that כל דפריש permits a person to eat possible *chametz* just as it would for any other possible *issur*. However, most *Rishonim*[28] follow the lead of *Rashi*,[29] who understands the *Gemara* as referring to a situation where this happened on *Erev Pesach*, and no one knows where the rodent put the food. The *Gemara's* point is that one may assume the rodent brought non-*chametz* into the house and there is no need to repeat *bedikas chametz* to find the potential *chametz*.

According to *Rashi*, the *Gemara* is ruling on the *mitzvah d'rabannan* of *bedikas chametz* [and the potential prohibition of owning *chametz* after *bitul*] and not commenting on whether כל דפריש permits consumption of potential *chametz*. Nonetheless, several *Acharonim*[30] say that there is no logical reason to think כל דפריש should not be effective in this case just as it is when considering eating possible *neveilah* or other *issurim*. Just as כל דפריש clearly allows one to be lenient regarding all other potentially forbidden foods, the same applies to *chametz*.

However, *Chok Yaakov*[31] says that due to the strictness of eating *chametz*, one should be *machmir* and not rely on כל דפריש to eat a food that might be *chametz*; this ruling is cited by *Mishnah Berurah*.[32] [More on his reason below]. At first glance, this ruling would seem to indicate that one should

---

[26] *Gemara, Pesachim* 9b.
[27] *Tosfos* ad loc. ד"ה היינו.
[28] This includes *Rambam* (*Hil. Chametz U'matzah* 2:11), *Tur* (OC 439, where *Tosfos* is not even cited), and *Shulchan Aruch* (OC 439:1).
[29] *Rashi* ad loc. ד"ה ואתא.
[30] *Pri Chadash* 439:6, *Elyah Rabbah* 439:3, *Minchas Kohen* (*Sefer HaTa'aruvos* 3:5) cited by *Chok Yaakov* noted in the coming text, and *Chazon Ish* OC 119:6 ד"ה ולפ"ז.
[31] *Chok Yaakov* 439:6. See also *Mekor Chaim* 439:3 (*Chiddushim*).
[32] *Mishnah Berurah* 439:6. He cites this ruling from *Chok Yosef* 439:5 who says אבל באכילה אסור ולא כדעת ר"י דלדליה מותר אף באכילה, אחרונים "ולא כדעת ר"י" refers to the opinion of *Tosfos* (noted earlier) which is stated in the name of ר"י. Seemingly, *Chok Yosef* understood that since the halacha follows *Rashi's* interpretation of the *Gemara*, that indicates that כל דפריש is not sufficient to permit eating the food; in other words, following *Rashi* is to the exclusion of [the halacha stated in] *Tosfos*. Others apparently understood (as noted in the text) that this is not a foregone conclusion.

be *machmir* regarding the medicine case noted above and not allow the *choleh* to assume his medicine is made from *kitnios* (corn starch). However, at the same time we must consider *Maharsham*,[33] who asks that *Chok Yaakov* seems to be contradicted by a later halacha in *Shulchan Aruch*[34] which says that on *Pesach* one may eat a food based on the majority/*rov* that it is not *chametz*. An apparent answer to this question can be seen by looking more carefully at how *Chok Yaakov* explains why one should be *machmir*. He says:

נראה לי דאין לסמוך על קולא זו להלכה
באסור חמץ דחמיר לענין ביטול יותר משאר אסורים

He is saying that not relying on כל דפריש is another example of how one must be extra strict regarding *bitul* of *chametz* as compared to *bitul* of other *issurim*. The halacha is clear[35] that that strictness – which states that even the slightest amount of *chametz* cannot be *batel* (חמץ אסור במשהו) – only applies if the *chametz* is mixed into other foods on *Pesach*, but if it happens <u>beforehand</u>, the standard rules of *bitul* apply. Thus, it is reasonable to say that *Chok Yaakov* is only suggesting one be strict when the possible *chametz* separated from the other foods on *Pesach*. But if the separation occurred before, he would agree that one may eat the food on *Pesach*.[36] The case of *Shulchan Aruch* which *Maharsham* cites is an example of that;[37] clearly, it is one where the issue occurred before *Pesach*, and for that reason *Chok Yaakov* would agree that the standard principles of *bitul* (*rov*, כל דפריש, etc.) apply.

---

[33] *Da'as Torah* (*Maharsham*) to *Shulchan Aruch* OC 439:1 (ד"ה ואם פירש).

[34] *Shulchan Aruch* OC 467:4; see *Mishnah Berurah* 467:15.

[35] See *Shulchan Aruch* OC 447:1-2.

[36] Support for this idea can also be seen from the following: *Beis Yosef* OC 513:6 cites *Ran* (*Beitzah* 3b), who questions whether כל דפריש is effective for a דבר שיש לו מתירין. His reason to be strict is that כיון דקיימא לן אפילו באלף לא בטל, which is to say – as noted here in the text – that it is the inability to be *batel* which suggests that כל דפריש is ineffective. *Chok Yaakov* would be suggesting a similar line of reasoning for *chametz* which is also unable to be *batel* <u>on</u> *Pesach*. *Beis Meir* (to *Rema* OC 447:5, cited in part in *Biur Halacha* ad loc. ד"ה שמבשלין), discusses *Ran* and notes that even *Ran* would be lenient if כל דפריש occurred before *Pesach*. Presumably, this is based on the logic noted in the text.

In this context, it is noteworthy that *Magen Avraham* 513:13 appears to accept *Ran's* position, but *Tzlach* (*Beitzah* 10b ד"ה שנים) brings a strong proof against it from *Shulchan Aruch* YD 16:12; however, see *Pischei Teshuvah* YD 16:6, who suggests a response to this proof. See also *Pischei Teshuvah* 102:1 and *Darchei Teshuvah* 102:11 who cite many prominent *Poskim* who are lenient on this issue (and some who are *machmir*). If *Chok Yaakov* is essentially an extension of *Ran*, then those who do not accept *Ran* would also permit כל דפריש for *chametz*.

[37] That case of *Shulchan Aruch* is where rain that fell onto grain while it was still in the fields (שנה שרבו גשמים וירדו על ערימות שבשדות), which, of course, happened well before *Pesach*.

If this analysis is correct,[38] then in the typical case where the possible *chametz* (e.g., the starch in our example of medicine) separated from the group (i.e., from all manufacturers of starch) well before *Pesach*, all would agree that it is permitted for the *choleh* to assume it is *kitnios* and not *chametz*.

---

[38] According to the point made in the text, there may be just a minimal disagreement between *Chok Yaakov* and the other *Poskim* cited above in footnote 30.

Chapter 64

Kashrus Scandals

שולחן ערוך סימן ק"י סעיף ה

מי שלקח בשר ממקולין (פי' בית המטבחיים) ואפילו חתיכה הראויה להתכבד ונמצאת טרפה במקולין ולא נודעו חתיכות הטריפה ואינו יודע מאיזו לקח, כל מה שלקחו מהמקולין קודם שנמצאת הטרפה מותר, שלא נפל הספק בקבוע אלא לאחר שפירש וכיון שהרוב כשר מותר, אבל ליקח מכאן ואילך אסור, ואפילו חתיכה שאינה ראויה להתכבד שאין הכל בקיאין בזה ויטעו בין ראויה להתכבד לשאינה ראויה.

In the previous chapter we discussed cases which resemble those noted in the *Poskim*, where someone discovered that an item believed to be kosher was not. For example, it was determined that an animal is a טריפה after it had already been declared kosher and mixed with other carcasses. Those types of *shailos* have a relatively limited scope and are dealt with by whoever is responsible for *hashgachah* at the slaughterhouse or other facility where the issue arises.

But in recent years, these halachos have become relevant to the masses when a *kashrus* "scandal" erupts. Specifically, this refers to situations where it is discovered that the proprietor of a kosher establishment was buying non-kosher meat (or poultry)[1] and selling either the raw meat itself or food prepared with it as kosher. This chapter considers the multiple halachic issues which arise from those unfortunate situations, based on the principles discussed in the previous chapter. We begin our discussion by noting some assumptions:

---

[1] Our focus is on non-kosher meat or poultry which, (as noted below), typically cannot be *batel* due to its being a חתיכה הראויה להתכבד. This is in contrast to other (actual) situations, where the owner used non-kosher cheese (*gevinas akum*), grape juice (*stam yayin*), or flour for *Pesach* (*chametz*), where *bitul* may offer an added basis for leniency.

Assumptions

Our discussion presumes the following facts:

- It is determined that the majority of meat used in the establishment was kosher, and the proprietor was only substituting <u>some</u> of the meat with non-kosher.[2]

- It can be established — by checking the

> **Monsey**
> In *Elul* 5766 people found out that for an extended time, a butcher shop had been selling *neveilah* as kosher. A review of the records of the store, and of the kosher distributor he had supposedly been buying from, showed that more than 50% of the meat in the store was unfortunately not kosher. Accordingly, none of the leniencies associated with כל דפריש were appropriate.

store's records or through other means — that the fraud has been going on for a while, which raises questions about food sold during that time. See the footnote regarding situations where the proprietor was caught with non-kosher meat and claims that this was his first offense, and it is impossible to determine if non-kosher was used previously.[3]

---

[2] This is because any possible leniencies are based on *bitul b'rov* or כל דפריש, and those are only applicable if there was more kosher than non-kosher.

[3] What if the storeowner is caught bringing non-kosher meat into the store, but it is impossible to determine if this was the first time this occurred or if this has been going on for an extended amount of time? *Shach* YD 1:8 says that if the owner had a חזקת כשרות (i.e., was known to be *Shomer Shabbos* and assumed to be scrupulous about observance of *mitzvos*), then it allows us to assume that he never used non-kosher meat until the day that we <u>know</u> that he did. However, *Simlah Chadashah* 2:18 argues that if the storeowner <u>knowingly</u> used non-kosher meat, his חזקת כשרות is destroyed retroactively (i.e., to the time that we have no knowledge of what he was selling). [But *Simlah Chadashah* says that if meat was used on dishes, etc., which are *cheress* and cannot be *kashered*, one may use the dishes as kosher after waiting 24 hours (so that they will be *aino ben yomo* and the prohibition against using them will not be more than a *d'rabannan*)].

Many *Acharonim* takes sides on this disagreement, including *Ketzos HaChoshen* 34:5 (referencing his longer discussion in *Shev Shmaytzah* 3:4), *Chochmas Adam* 2:6, and *Aruch HaShulchan* 1:52 (all of whom agree with *Shach*), and *Pri Megadim* SD 1:8 rules that one should be *machmir* for *Simlah Chadashah* for situations of potential *issur d'oraisah*, but one can be lenient regarding *kashering* if the equipment is *aino ben yomo* and there is a *hefsed merubah*. See considerable discussion on this issue in *Ohr Yisroel* #45 (Year 12 Volume 1 – *Tishrei* 5767).

Within the lenient opinion that the meat from previous days can be assumed to be kosher, what if the storeowner says that some of it (e.g., 25%, or specific packages) is not kosher? Can he be believed? Firstly, see *Shulchan Aruch* YD 2:4 (with commentaries ad loc.) that a person who willingly violates the halacha for financial gain (מומר לתיאבון) has *ne'emanus* in situations where he has no benefit from lying. That seems to describe our situation, where the person had a חזקת כשרות but introduced non-kosher meat to increase his profits and is now reporting on something that he has no benefit from. Secondly,

- There is food whose kosher status cannot be determined, such that it is a *ta'aruvos* and governed by the halachos of רוב, כל דפריש, etc. In other words, we may have specific pieces of meat that we know are kosher or non-kosher,[4] but there are others whose status we cannot determine; it is on this latter group of food that our discussion focuses.

- We will focus on the halachic fallout of the scandal, ignoring that many people would be personally disgusted by the idea of eating food that might be non-kosher. See also *Imrei Dovid*, *Animal Products*, Chapter 23, for a discussion on whether there is טמטום הלב (*"stuffing up" of a person's spiritual heart*) for those who unknowingly ate non-kosher food under such circumstances.

Issues

As noted, we are considering what happens when the proprietor of a store is caught using non-kosher meat or poultry in his store. Consumers are obviously very upset that they may have eaten non-kosher food, and the certifying Rabbi must ponder how it is that he was unaware of what was happening. At the same time, the following very practical *shailos* are relevant:

1. What is the status of raw meat still in the establishment?
2. What is the status of prepared foods still in the establishment?
3. What is the status of raw meat and prepared foods that consumers bought from this establishment and have in their homes?
4. Must consumers *kasher* their ovens, microwaves, dishes, and flatware that were possibly used to heat or cook meat from this establishment?

---

there are many cases where even if a food has a חזקת כשרות, an עד אחד is believed to say that it is not kosher; see *Shulchan Aruch* YD 127:1 (and 127:3) with *Shach* 127:16. [See also *Shach* 127:20 regarding believing a non-Jew to say that meat is not kosher].

[4] For example, they may still be in the original non-kosher packaging, perhaps an experienced butcher can recognize certain pieces as being processed as kosher (e.g., leftover bits of feather, wingtips or tongue tips cut off, other signs of *nikkur* or *melichah*), or can differentiate chickens by their skin color.

Raw meat in the store

What is the status of raw meat still in the establishment?

We saw in Chapter 31 that *Ashkenazim* rule that raw meat is considered a חתיכה הראויה להתכבד [5] and cannot be *batel*.[6] This answers part of the first question: even if the proprietor brought in just one piece of non-kosher meat into the store, it cannot be *batel*, and all meat in the store's main refrigerator or freezer is forbidden.

What about raw chicken that has already been moved to the store's display case and made available for sale to the public? We saw in the previous chapter[7] that when the storeowner takes meat from the main cooler and moves it to the retail display case (or cooks it), that meat is considered "פירש" from the קבוע portion of the *ta'aruvos*. Accordingly, that meat qualifies as כל דפריש מרובא פריש even though it is still in the store where the *ta'aruvos* occurred. This means that, if we determine that the store purchased 90 kosher chickens and 10 non-kosher ones, and they put 20 chickens in the display case, we may assume those 20 chickens are from the majority and are kosher. As noted there, according to *Rosh* only the meat which was put into the display case before the scandal was discovered qualifies for כל דפריש, but one cannot be lenient about meat which separated afterwards.[8]

What happens (in the above case) after 5 days, when all 100 of those chickens have already been put out for retail sale? Does כל דפריש say that every chicken is kosher since it is assumed to come from the majority which

---

[5] In some cases, the meat will also qualify as a דבר שבמנין (for *Ashkenazim*); see Chapter 62.
[6] We also saw in Chapter 31 that if the (raw) meat is cut into small pieces – as is common in some restaurants, particularly those which cook "Chinese" style food – it no longer qualifies as a חתיכה הראויה להתכבד and can be *batel*.
[7] In the section titled "What is considered פירש".
[8] The text assumes that although the storeowner knows that he snuck in non-kosher meat, that is not treated as a case where "the *ta'aruvos* is known", and *Rosh* would agree that one can be lenient until the scandal becomes known to a wider group of people. [In the previous chapter (footnote 12), we cited *Pri Megadim* SD 110:33 who appears to be *machmir* when the קבוע דרבנן is known, but the person who separated the item happens not to know. The current issue is an opposite case, where only one person (i.e., the perpetrator) knows about it and no one else does]. This assumption is logical because (as we saw in the previous chapter) *Rosh* says כל דפריש is effective for as long as people are "permitted" to take from the קבוע, which stops when it becomes known that there is *issur* in the mixture; that occurs when someone other than the perpetrator finds out about the presence of non-kosher meat. Additionally, (a) the assumption underlies the rulings that Rav Belsky and others gave when scandals occurred, and (b) there is a slight support to this notion from *Toras Chattas* 43:1 who uses the term נודע לרבים (*it is widely known*) in the preamble to his citation of *Rosh* (although when he discusses *Rosh* itself he only says נודע התערובות).

were kosher? What about the last 20 chickens? If the previous 80 chickens were kosher (based on כל דפריש), then 10 of these last 20 are kosher and 10 are not, which means there is no longer a majority of kosher chickens in the cooler. Can we still say that any chicken that comes from the cooler is coming from the overall majority that were kosher? In fact, there is a *machlokes* in the *Acharonim* on this issue.[9] Should one be lenient on that question since the entire lack of *bitul* in this case is based on a *d'rabannan* principle?[10] If yes, every piece of raw chicken in the display case can be deemed inherently kosher. If not, only the first 80 pieces will be considered kosher, and the last 20 will not.

Prepared food in the store
What is the status of prepared food still in the establishment?

Things are a bit more complicated if the store <u>cooked</u> the [kosher and non-kosher] meat. As noted, taking the meat from the cooler to cook it means that it qualifies for כל דפריש, and from that perspective the meat [or at least the first 80 pieces] is kosher. However, here we must also contend with the fact that even if the meat is inherently kosher it may have absorbed non-kosher *ta'am* from the pot or oven it was cooked in. This means that if, as in our example, 10% of the store's meat was non-kosher, much more than 10% of the cooked meat in the store is not kosher. This forces us to recalculate whether most of the meat in the store is kosher and we can leniently apply כל דפריש. Making that determination depends on the halachic issue raised above (i.e., the status of the final pieces) and the particulars of the situation.

Among the factors to consider are the following: What percentage of the meat was not kosher? How often do they receive deliveries of fresh meat? Are there multiple skillets, fryers, pans, etc. such that we can apply the principle of סתם כלים אינם בני יומן for each particular cooking implement?[11] How much of the food passes through the deep fryer, and how often do they change the oil in the fryer (because oil used for non-kosher does not become "*aino ben yomo*")?

---

[9] See the different opinions cited in *Badei HaShulchan* 110:67.
[10] In other words, the fact that the non-kosher chicken is not *batel* is due to its being a חתיכה הראויה להתכבד which is a Rabbinic principle. Furthermore, we saw in Chapter 31 that while *Rema* 101:3 treats <u>raw</u> meat or chicken as a חתיכה הראויה להתכבד, *Shulchan Aruch* argues that it is not, and would therefore hold that the chicken was *batel* as soon as it was mixed into the other raw meat in the store.
[11] See Chapter 42.

Kashrus Scandals

> **Manalapan**
>
> There were shortages of chickens in 2022, and the owner of a restaurant in Manalapan, New Jersey, started compensating by sneaking in non-kosher chickens when the *Mashgiach* was distracted. The fact that this was a Chinese-style restaurant was a factor in two unique aspects of this situation: [1] Most meat and chicken was fried, and the oil was rarely changed, and [2] most meat and poultry was cut into small pieces before cooking, which potentially meant that it was no longer a חתיכה הראויה להתכבד (see footnote 6).

For example: A store regularly receives an order of 50 pieces of kosher meat every Sunday and Wednesday morning. One Friday morning, the *Mashgiach* realizes that on the previous Sunday the proprietor snuck 10 pieces of non-kosher meat into the cooler together with his regular order. The store cooks and sells 20 pieces of meat each day. כל דפריש dictates that on any day when there were more kosher than non-kosher pieces of meat in the cooler, the meat used was kosher.

- Accordingly, we can assume that on Sunday and Monday, the meat used was kosher.[12] But on Tuesday morning, there is no longer a majority of kosher meat in the cooler.[13] Therefore, [according to the strict position on the second halachic issue noted above] we must assume that at least half of it was not kosher, which means that the skillet used for cooking is also not kosher.

- As a result, the meat cooked on Wednesday [from the new kosher order] is also not kosher, since it was cooked on a non-kosher skillet. By Thursday, the meat cooked is considered kosher since it is inherently kosher (as it came from the Wednesday order), and the skillet was already *aino ben yomo*[14] from the non-kosher use on Tuesday.[15]

- Thus, when the issue was discovered on Friday morning, we can conclude that meat cooked on Sunday, Monday, and Thursday is

---

[12] On Sunday morning, there were 60 pieces in the cooler of which 50 were kosher and 10 were not. The 20 pieces cooked and sold on Sunday are assumed to have come from the kosher meat, which means that on Monday morning the cooler has 30 pieces of kosher meat and 10 pieces of non-kosher.

[13] On Tuesday morning, there are only 20 pieces of meat left in the cooler, of which 10 are kosher and 10 are not.

[14] In considering when the equipment was *aino ben yomo*, it is worth bearing in mind that kosher establishments are (generally) closed on *Shabbos*, which means that all equipment is *aino ben yomo* each Sunday morning when they reopen.

[15] The text assumes that due to the (a) *sfekos* involved in this situation and (b) the *hefsed* to an entire community which purchased from this purveyor, one need not be concerned for *ChaNaN*; see Chapter 3.

assumed to be kosher, and meat cooked on Tuesday and Wednesday is not. So, if there is a question on which day a given piece of meat was cooked, we can leniently say כל דפריש since there were more "kosher days" than "non-kosher days".

But if the story were a bit different, the results would not be the same. What if the store's typical kosher order was just for 40 pieces of meat and the proprietor snuck in 20 pieces of non-kosher? The majority of the meat is still kosher, but in this case, by Monday morning there is no majority of kosher meat, which means only meat cooked on Sunday and Thursday is kosher, and whatever was prepared on Monday, Tuesday, or Wednesday was not.[16] If so, due to the non-kosher status of the equipment, there were more "non-kosher days" than "kosher days" (even though overall there was more kosher meat than non-kosher) and כל דפריש would not permit cooked meat when we do not know on which day it was cooked.

> **NOTE**
>
> Earlier we noted a *machlokes* regarding applying כל דפריש to the "last" items separated from the *ta'aruvos*. If one adopts the lenient approach to that issue, then all the meat cooked in the store is assumed to have been kosher and the equipment's status was never affected.[17]

---

[16] Briefly, on Sunday morning there were 40 pieces of kosher and 20 pieces of kosher, so the 20 pieces sold were all kosher; on Monday there were 20 pieces of kosher and 20 of non-kosher, so the 20 pieces sold were half kosher and half non-kosher; on Tuesday there were 10 pieces of kosher and 10 pieces of non-kosher and they were all sold; on Wednesday and Thursday they had all kosher meat, but on Wednesday the skillet was non-kosher from the cooking done on Tuesday.

[17] We know that there was non-kosher meat in the store. If so, is it appropriate to "decide" that all the meat cooked was kosher and the equipment never became non-kosher? *Shulchan Aruch* and *Rema* 109:1-2 discuss a similar question regarding a *ta'aruvos* which qualified for *bitul b'rov* (as a יבש ביבש): can one person eat all the pieces of meat (knowing that one is not kosher)? Can all the pieces be cooked together in one pot? See there that in practice we generally are strict regarding these issues since it is certain that the person is consuming the non-kosher or its *ta'am*. But what about cooking the different pieces of meat in the *ta'aruvos* in separate pots, where there is no specific pot that surely had the *issur* in it? *Shach* 109:12 is strict if the cooking happened before people became aware of the issue (קודם ידיעת התערובת), but many others are lenient (see *Badei HaShulchan* 109:47). Our case is similar to "separate" pots, because the different pieces of meat were cooked on separate days that span more than 24 hours (which means that *b'lios* absorbed on the first day are "gone", i.e., *aino ben yomo*, when some of the subsequent cooking occurs). That might lead to the conclusion that according to *Shach* one should be strict in our case.

However, even according to *Shach*, many assume that his strict opinion regarding cooking that happened before ידיעת התערובת is limited to cases of *bitul b'rov* (as יבש ביבש), but in cases – like ours – of כל דפריש, one can be lenient even without ידיעת התערובת; see *Badei HaShulchan* (*Biurim*) 110:5 ד"ה ד"ה כל and ולא on pages 145 and 146, respectively. The text follows this approach. Therefore, if כל דפריש allows us to assume all the meat was kosher (as per the lenient approach to the issue raised in the earlier text), and the meat was cooked on different days, we can say that the equipment "never" became non-kosher (even though we know that at some point the non-kosher meat was cooked there).

Kashrus Scandals

In many cases, the details necessary to address these questions are not readily available when the scandal is uncovered. The investigative methods used to determine the relevant facts (see the footnote)[18] require tedious research and extended amounts of time and will typically not happen fast enough for consumers who want "instant" direction on whether the food they've bought may be eaten.

Food taken home

What is the status of raw meat and prepared foods that consumers bought from this establishment and have in their homes?

The answer to this question is essentially identical to the previous two,[19] as follows: People who bought raw meat from the store had no intention of trying to separate it from the group, and therefore *Rashba* would say that it qualifies for כל דפריש. But according to *Rosh*, since this is a case of קבוע דרבנן, only meat which was purchased – or put into the retail display case, as noted earlier – before the scandal was discovered is permitted based on כל דפריש, but anything separated from the group after that point is forbidden.

> **Los Angeles**
>
> This is exactly what Rav Belsky ruled when this type of situation occurred in Los Angeles before *Pesach* 2013. At 3:00 PM on a given day the Rabbis in the community became aware that a storeowner had been bringing non-kosher meat into his kosher store for some time, and Rav Belsky ruled that meat purchased before 3:00 of that day is permitted but anything bought afterwards is forbidden.

---

[18] Some methods of investigating the extent of a scandal – which might be performed by the certifying Rabbi, a private investigator, and/or a forensic accountant – include:
- Checking paperwork/receipts and conferring with kosher suppliers/distributors to see if orders have been consistent or have dropped off (indicating that meat was coming from other/non-kosher sources).
- Compare sales with purchases to see if the amount of kosher meat purchased can satisfy all the food sold.
- See how prices at this store compare with the competition. If this store's prices are always significantly lower, that may indicate their use of cheaper non-kosher supplies.
- Interview the store's customers, *Mashgiach*, and employees, to see if/when they noticed any changes in taste, quality, or practices.
- Check all available video from the store's closed-circuit cameras, doorbell videos, etc.
- Where possible, review the store's accounting records and credit card bills for purchases at non-kosher outlets.

[19] In the previous questions we were required to accept that the meat or cooked food qualifies for כל דפריש even though it is still in the store, since it was put into the retail display case or taken for cooking. In the current cases, where the food was taken home, it is more obviously an example of כל דפריש, since the food was removed from the store.

If the case was one where the store or caterer was cooking food for the public, the status of food that people purchased is exactly as noted above regarding cooked food found in the store. Namely, we must (a) consider the halachic question of whether the "final" pieces are forbidden, and [assuming we take a strict stand on that] (b) determine whether the days when the meat <u>and</u> equipment were "kosher" outnumber the days when it was not.

Kashering

Must consumers kasher their ovens, microwaves, dishes, and flatware that were possibly used to heat or cook meat from this establishment?

For many people, the issues raised until this point are academic, either because they have already eaten the food they bought from the store, or they find it repulsive to even consider eating food that came from a store caught perpetrating such a fraud. Accordingly, the most common question that people face is whether they have to *kasher* the utensils which they used to heat or serve food from the store.

In this regard, we can divide the issue into several parts.

If the food which this person bought is halachically considered "kosher" – as per the details and situations noted earlier in this chapter – then clearly the utensils do not require *kashering*. Simply, if the food is kosher, it cannot possibly have affected the kosher status of the dishes, oven, etc. with which it came into contact.

If the food is not considered kosher, then the issue is further split into two parts. The first group includes items like dishes, flatware, etc., where the person knows that they used <u>some</u> of the dishes with this food but cannot be certain about any specific dish. We saw in Chapter 36 that in such cases, the potential non-kosher dishes, etc., are *batel b'rov* in the other dishes, and one is often not required to *kasher* any of the dishes, especially those made of *cheress* or other materials which cannot be *kashered* (although one might be required to wait until they are *aino ben yomo* before using them).

The second group includes devices like an oven or microwave where the person knows for sure that they were used with the food bought from the store. The person has just one oven or microwave, so if they cooked raw meat from this store, it was in this oven, and if they reheated prepared food they bought from the store, it was in this microwave. Since, as noted, we are discussing a case where the person must assume the food that he purchased was not kosher, the oven or microwave should be *kashered* before it is used for kosher. If that presents a particular difficulty (or as relates to the glass plate in the microwave which cannot be *kashered*), see the footnote for reasons to consider allowing their use without *kashering*.[20]

---

[20] In evaluating this question, a Rabbi will bear in mind the following issues which often apply. Most of these issues were discussed in this chapter and/or the previous one. While there was basis for being *machmir* on each individually, the Rabbi may feel it is appropriate to be lenient in cases which involved more than one of these issues, and it is also a *sha'as hadchak*. The issues are as follows:

- *Rema* is of the opinion that raw meat can be a חתיכה הראויה להתכבד, but *Shulchan Aruch* disagrees.
- *Shulchan Aruch* follows *Rashba* that meat which separates from the group (without intention), qualifies as כל דפריש, but *Taz* and *Shach* accept *Rosh* that this is only true if it separated before anyone knew about the תערובות.
- *Pri Megadim* is unsure whether *Rosh* would be lenient if one person (i.e., the person buying the food) did not know about the תערובות, even if other people did.
- Some are of the opinion that כל דפריש permits <u>all</u> the items that separated from the group, including the "last" ones, which plays a role in deciding if "most" of the food was not kosher.
- *Shulchan Aruch* (OC 451:26) says that glass does not absorb any *ta'am*, and even *Rema*, who disagrees, is of the opinion that in certain cases of *b'dieved* one can be lenient (see *Mishnah Berurah* 451:155).
- It is worth bearing in mind that (a) the lack of *bitul b'rov* for a חתיכה הראויה להתכבד, and (b) the prohibition to use utensils which are *aino ben yomo* from non-kosher use, are both Rabbinic halachos.

Chapter 65

נתגלגל

שולחן ערוך סימן ק"י סעיף ט

ספק טרפה שנתערב באחרות כולן אסורות עד שיהא בהיתר כדי לבטל האיסור אם הוא מדברים המתבטלים, שכיון שספק הראשון היה בגופו אין להתירו מספק ספיקא.

הגה: ויש אומרים הטעם דאסור הואיל והספק הוא איסור מדאורייתא ולא נוכל לומר עוד ספק שאין כאן איסור רק שנתערב באחרים, לא מקרי ספק ספיקא ואסור, אבל אם היו ב' ספיקות אם היה כאן איסור כלל ונודעו ב' הספיקות ביחד מתירים ספק ספיקא בכל מקום אפילו באיסור דאורייתא וגופו של איסור ואפילו היה לו חזקת איסור, כגון עוף שבחזקת איסור עומד ונשבר או נשמט גפו ספק מחיים או לאחר שחיטה, ואם תמצא לומר מחיים שמא לא נקבה הריאה, יש להתיר מכח ספק ספיקא, אף על פי שיש לברר על ידי בדיקת הריאה אין לחוש. ועיין לעיל סימן נ"ג.

In the current halacha,[1] *Shulchan Aruch* considers *bitul* and *sfek sfekah* if a *safek teraifah* got mixed into kosher meat. In passing, *Shulchan Aruch* notes that this discussion presupposes that this is a type of meat which is suitable for *bitul*, but if it is not – such as if it is a חתיכה הראויה להתכבד – then the issue is moot, and the mixture is clearly forbidden. Why is that so? In previous chapters we saw that this idea that certain items cannot be *batel* (e.g., חתיכה הראויה להתכבד) is a Rabbinic concept. If so, *mid'oraisah* the mixture is surely permitted, and that means that the question we face is not more than a potential *issur d'rabannan*. If so, the principle of ספק דרבנן להקל should allow us to assume that the *safek teraifah* is actually not a *teraifah* altogether?

Shach[2] says that we see from here that when an issue begins as a *d'oraisah safek* [such as here, where the *safek* is whether the animal is a *teraifah*], but then becomes "downgraded" to a *safek d'rabannan* [such as here, where the *issur* would be *batel* if not for the *d'rabannan* concept of חתיכה

---

[1] *Shulchan Aruch* 110:9.
[2] *Shach, Kuntress Hasefeikos* #19 (printed at the end of *Shach* YD 110).

[הראויה להתכבד], we do not apply the principle of ספק דרבנן להקל. Rather, we say that this is a *safek d'oraisah* which was נתגלגל (literally, "rolled over") into an *issur d'rabannan*, and it is treated with the strictness of the original *safek d'oraisah*.

However, *Shach* notes that there appears to be a contradiction to this idea from *Shulchan Aruch* 111:3-4. There it discusses a case where a person has two pots of meat, one of *heter* and one of *issur*, and two pieces of meat – again one of *heter* and one of *issur* – and one piece of meat fell into each pot, but no one knows which piece fell into which pot. If the situation is such that even if the *issur* had fallen into the pot of *heter* it would be *batel b'rov mid'oraisah*, and only not *batel mid'rabannan* (since for that we require *bitul b'shishim*), we may assume (be "תולה") that the *heter* meat fell into the pot of *heter*, and the *issur* fell into the *issur*. That leniency – of being "תולה" – only applies when dealing with an *issur d'rabannan*, so why is it that in this case – where the *issur* under discussion is *assur mid'oraisah* – one may be תולה? This indicates that although the underlying *issur* is a *d'oraisah*, at this point the entire question is just one of a *d'rabannan* (since, even if the *issur* fell into the kosher pot it is *batel b'rov* on the *d'oraisah* level) so we give it the leniencies associated with *issurim d'rabannan*. In other words, this halacha implies that there is no strictness of נתגלגל, and one can be lenient if the final/current issue is a mere *d'rabannan*.

Shach offers one resolution to this apparent contradiction, and other *Acharonim* suggest alternate answers. The different aspects of this question are discussed in *Imrei Dovid*, Alcoholic Beverages, Chapter 22 (Part 2), where it is applied to the following question: A liquid medicine contains glycerin, and it is unknown whether the glycerin is from non-kosher animal fat or kosher vegetable oil. May one dilute the liquid medicine in water to the point that the glycerin is *batel b'shishim*? Is that forbidden since glycerin is a potential *issur d'oraisah*? Or is it permitted since the prohibition to dilute the medicine (i.e.,אין מבטלין איסור לכתחלה) is Rabbinic in nature, allowing the person to rely on ספק דרבנן להקל (and from that perspective assume the glycerin was kosher)? Is this a case where נתגלגל requires us to be strict or allows us to be lenient? These issues are discussed in *Imrei Dovid*, ibid.

Chapter 66

Papain

שולחן ערוך סימן ק"י סעיף ט

ספק טרפה שנתערב באחרות כולן אסורות עד שיהא בהיתר כדי לבטל האיסור אם הוא מדברים המתבטלים, שכיון שספק הראשון היה בגופו אין להתירו מספק ספיקא.

הגה: ויש אומרים הטעם דאסור הואיל והספק הוא איסור מדאורייתא ולא נוכל לומר עוד ספק שאין כאן איסור רק שנתערב באחרים, לא מקרי ספק ספיקא ואסור, אבל אם היו ב' ספיקות אם היה כאן איסור כלל ונודעו ב' הספיקות ביחד מתירים ספק ספיקא בכל מקום אפילו באיסור דאורייתא וגופו של איסור ואפילו היה לו חזקת איסור, כגון עוף שבחזקת איסור עומד ונשבר או נשמט גפו ספק מחיים או לאחר שחיטה, ואם תמצא לומר מחיים שמא לא נקבה הריאה, יש להתיר מכח ספק ספיקא, אף על פי שיש לברר על ידי בדיקת הריאה אין לחוש. ועיין לעיל סימן נ"ז.

This halacha[1] discusses *safek teraifah* which was mixed into other foods, and whether *sfek sfekah* should be applicable, since there are two *sfekos* – *safek* if it is a *teraifah, and safek* if the piece in my hands is the questionable piece or just one of those which is surely permitted. In turn, this question is the opening for *Shach* and others to present extensive discussion of the rules and principles with which *sfek sfekah* operates. That corpus of halacha is beyond the scope of this work. However, the entire halacha is based on the underlying assumption that a *safek issur* – such as *safek teraifah* – is forbidden, and that is based on the maxim that *safek d'oraisah l'chumrah*.

This chapter will discuss one very notable exception to that concept[2] – ספק ערלה בחוץ לארץ – and specifically how it potentially applies to the kosher

---

[1] *Shulchan Aruch* 110:9.
[2] Two other examples are ספק טומאה ברשות הרבים מותר (*Gemara, Pesachim* 19b) and (on a *d'oraisah* level) ספק ממזר מותר (see *Rambam, Hil. Issurei Bi'ah*, 15:21).

status of papain, an enzyme made from papaya.[3] To understand the issue and the exception, we begin with some background on modern papaya farming methods, and the halachos of *arlah*.

Papaya

Papaya plants grow very quickly and produce fruit within a year, after which they will continue to produce fruit for a few more years. However, since the tree produces less fruit each year, by the time the tree is three years old, it is producing so little fruit that typically it is cut down and replaced with a fresh tree. That appear to present a very clear halachic issue, because fruits are forbidden as *arlah* if they grow during the first three years of a tree's life,[4] and that halacha applies even to items which grow in *chutz la'aretz*.[5] If papaya trees are regularly cut down before they are three years old, that would mean all papaya is *arlah*!

> At this point in our discussion, we will assume that papaya is halachically classified as a fruit (rather than a vegetable) and is therefore subject to the prohibition of *arlah*. However, we will see towards the end of this chapter that this is not a foregone conclusion.

This issue is actually not so meaningful for papaya itself, based on a combination of two factors. Firstly, not all papayas are *arlah* since (a) some trees are kept for somewhat more than 3 years, and (b) in some cases, the "3-year" *arlah* count takes less than 36 months (see the footnote).[6] In fact, in *Eretz Yisroel* where they track this issue, they find that 20% of papaya is

---

[3] Significant elements of the structure and content of this chapter are based on the excellent article on this topic by Rabbi Gavriel Price (OU) in *The Daf HaKashrus* 18:3 (December 2009); the author thanks Rabbi Price for sharing his research.
[4] *Shulchan Aruch* YD 294:1.
[5] *Shulchan Aruch* 294:8.
[6] There are two options for how the three years of *arlah* are calculated, based on which part of the (Jewish) calendar they were planted (see *Shulchan Aruch* 294:4-5):
  [Option A] If the tree was planted between *Rosh Hashanah* and the 15th of *Av*, Year 1 ends on the next *Rosh Hashanah*, Year 2 ends on *Rosh Hashanah* of the following calendar year, and Year 3 ends on the 15th of *Shevat* of the year after that. Thus, if a tree was planted on *Rosh Chodesh Av* 5783, Year 1 ends on *Rosh Hashanah* 5784, Year 2 ends on *Rosh Hashanah* 5785, and Year 3 ends on *Tu B'shvat* 5786. In this case, the total *arlah* period is only about 2.5 years. But if the tree was planted on *Rosh Chodesh Cheshvan* 5783, Year 3 of *arlah* would also end on *Tu B'shvat* 5786, and the *arlah* period would be about 3.25 years.
  [Option B] If the tree was planted between the 15th of *Av* and *Rosh Hashanah*, Year 1 ends at *Rosh Hashanah* of the next calendar year (i.e., more than 12 months after planting), Year 2 ends on *Rosh Hashanah* of the following calendar year, and Year 3 ends on *Rosh Hashanah* of the year after that. For example, a tree was planted on *Rosh Chodesh Elul* 5783: year 1 ends on *Rosh Hashanah* 5785, year 2 ends on *Rosh Hashanah* 5786, and year 3 ends on *Rosh Hashanah* 5787. In this case, the total *arlah* period is about 3 years and 1 month.

not *arlah*.[7] Secondly, there is a significant halachic difference between *safek arlah* (i.e., cases where one is unsure if a given fruit is *arlah*) for fruit grown in *Eretz Yisroel* as compared to *chutz la'aretz*. If fruit grew in *Eretz Yisroel* and one is unsure if it is *arlah*, they must be *machmir* and not eat it, just like with other *safek d'oraisah*. However, if the same *safek* arose with fruit that grew in *chutz la'aretz*, the fruit is permitted, even though *arlah* in *chutz la'aretz* is also *assur mid'oraisah*.[8] This is because the *issur* in *chutz la'aretz* was taught through a *halacha l'Moshe m'Sinai*, and that transmission included a special leniency that *safek d'oraisah l'chumrah* does not apply in this case.[9] Thus, one may eat papaya which grew in *chutz*

---

[7] Dr. Moshe Zaks collects information on *arlah* and the charts he creates are printed in the הליכות עולם journal of the בית מדרש להלכה בהתיישבות (www.bhl.org.il). For the past several years it has shown that 80% of papaya grown in *Eretz Yisroel* is *arlah*.

[8] *Shulchan Aruch* 294:9-10.

As a result of this *halacha*, most consumers in *chutz la'aretz* rarely consider the halachos of *arlah* since they may eat just about any fruit in the market, even if they do not know whether it is *arlah*. However, the halacha is relevant for a person who has his own fruit-bearing trees, because he may know with certainty that a given fruit is from a tree which is less than three years old. However, even in that case, it is only forbidden to knowingly eat fruit from that tree, but if the fruit was picked and he is unsure whether it came from the "old" or "new" tree, he may eat it (in *chutz la'aretz*) (*Shulchan Aruch* ibid).

[9] The simple reading of *Gemara, Kiddushin* 39a, is that the principle of *safek d'oraisah l'chumrah* also applies to a *halacha l'Moshe m'Sinai*, and *arlah* in *chutz la'aretz* is a special exception to that rule. This point is specifically made by *Beis Yosef* (294:9), and it is also relatively clear that this is the position of *Prishah* 294:20, *Taz* 294:13 and *Shach* 294:19. *Beis Yosef* says this to counter the apparent implication in *Tur* that the *Gemara* is teaching that *safek d'oraisah l'chumrah* does not apply to any *halacha l'Moshe m'Sinai*. *Beis Yosef* finds this position untenable and goes so far as to suggest that there might be a typographical error in *Tur*. [*Prishah* and *Taz* suggest alternative explanations of *Tur* which also assumes *Tur* did not mean that *safek* is permitted for all *halacha l'Moshe m'Sinai*].

In contrast, *Pri Megadim* (beginning of the פתיחה כוללת) cites many – including the way *Rambam* is understood by *Ramban* (*Sefer Hamitzvos, Shoresh Sheini*, page 27a) (who personally disagrees with *Rambam*) – who say that *safek d'oraisah l'chumrah* only applies to a standard *issur* that is written in the *Torah*, but not to one whose source is a *halacha l'Moshe m'Sinai*. [*Pri Megadim* himself (YD 110:5 in the מחודשים) rules that even in this case *safek* is *l'chumrah*]. *Nodah B'yehudah* YD 2:46 takes a more nuanced approach, writing that *Rambam* and *Rash* (in their explanations of *Mishnah, Mikvaos* 3:7) say that when a *halacha l'Moshe m'Sinai* creates a "new" halacha, one can be lenient in cases of *safek*. But if the *halacha l'Moshe m'Sinai* merely provides some details (e.g., the *shiur*) of an existing *mitzvah* which is written in the *Torah*, then the standard rule of *safek d'oraisah l'chumrah* applies.

[According to *Nodah B'yehudah*, *Rambam* might understand the question and answer in the *Gemara* ibid. regarding *safek arlah* in *chutz la'aretz* as depending on whether this *halacha l'Moshe m'Sinai* is merely adding a detail to the *Torah's mitzvah* of *arlah* in *Eretz Yisroel* (in which case *safek* is *l'chumrah*) or creating a new/separate halacha (in which case one can be lenient). The question assumes they are one *mitzvah*, while the answer says כך נאמר, that they are separate. This conceptual question of the status of *arlah* in *chutz la'aretz* will be discussed in the "Peel" section of the upcoming text. There, we will see *Rambam's* position is that it is a separate *mitzvah*, which would be consistent with the *Gemara's* conclusion as per (this explanation within how *Nodah B'yehudah* explains) this opinion of *Rambam*. There we will also see that *Shulchan Aruch* disagrees with *Rambam*, and that position would be consistent with *Beis Yosef* cited above].

la'aretz because some papaya is not *arlah*, and the mere possibility that any given fruit is one of those permitted ones, is enough to permit it.[10]

Papain

However, if we consider how papain is collected, we will see that this line of reasoning will not suffice to permit it. We have already seen that papaya trees are uprooted every three years, and new shoots are planted in their place. Farmers rotate this process, so that at any time, some of the trees are newly planted, and others are 1, 2, or 3 years old. As the papayas ripen, the farmers gently scrape or scratch the fruits so that the papain will ooze out of the peel without ruining the fruit itself. A small amount of papain is obtained from each fruit (and each fruit can be tapped a few times before it ripens), and all the papain from the field is mixed together and brought to a central location for further processing.

This brings us to another halacha regarding *arlah*. Although, *safek arlah* is permitted (in *chutz la'aretz*), if *arlah* is mixed into other foods, it makes those foods forbidden unless the *arlah* is *batel*. [If the mixture is *min b'mino*, the *arlah* must be *batel* in 200 times its volume, and if it is *aino mino*, then standard *bitul b'shishim* suffices].[11] In other words, if someone is unsure if a given papaya is *arlah*, they can be lenient and eat it, but when papain from *arlah* and non-*arlah* are mixed together, the overall mixture is forbidden.[12] Thus, the permissibility of *safek arlah* does not seem to be enough to allow papain.

Peel

Thus far, we have assumed that if a papaya is *arlah*, then papain is also *arlah*. This is based on the halacha that the prohibition includes all parts of the fruit, including the peels and pits (but not the leaves, sap, or other

---

[10] See *Rav Pealim* OC 2:30 who makes this point.
[11] *Shach* 98:27 and *Gr"a* 98:31.
[12] The text presents the issue as one of *ta'aruvos*: we know that some/much of the papain is *arlah* and it is not *batel* in the non-*arlah* papain. Alternatively, one can explain it as based on *rov*: since most/*rov* of the papain is from trees that are less than 3 years old, the entire lot is deemed *arlah*. [Nonetheless, if a person was to have just one fruit, the leniency of *safek arlah* in *chutz la'aretz* would permit him to eat the fruit].

parts of the tree).[13] Therefore, even though papain is extracted from the peel,[14] it is subject to this *issur*.

However, *Tzlach*[15] suggests that this detail of *arlah* – that peels are also forbidden – only applies to fruits which grow in *Eretz Yisroel* and not to *arlah* in *chutz la'aretz*. *Derech Emunah*[16] suggests, based on an understanding proposed by Rav Chaim Soloveitchik,[17] that this is grounded in the approach of *Rambam*, that *arlah* in *Eretz Yisroel* and *arlah* in *chutz la'aretz* are two separate halachos. Those details which the *Torah* specifies for *arlah* in *Eretz Yisroel* do not necessarily apply in *chutz la'aretz*. One example of this principle is the *chumrah* that inedible peels are forbidden, which does not apply in *chutz la'aretz*. If so, even if a given papaya is *arlah*, the papain extracted from its peel is not forbidden.

While this detail presents a basis for leniency, it is clear that not all *Poskim* agree with this approach, as follows: Rav Chaim bases his concept on *Rambam*,[18] who rules that *netah revai* (a *ma'aser sheini*-like status of fruit grown the year after *arlah* finishes) does not apply in *chutz la'aretz*. Rav Chaim understands that this is because the *Torah* only speaks about the *netah revai* "extension" of *arlah* as relates to *arlah* of *Eretz Yisroel*, and there is no reason to apply it to the "separate" type of *arlah* in *chutz la'aretz*. *Rambam* himself notes that some *Geonim* partially disagree with this application (*netah revai*), and Rav Chaim says that this is because they disagree with *Rambam's* approach that *arlah* in *chutz la'aretz* is a separate halacha from *arlah* in *Eretz Yisroel*.

If we look at *Shulchan Aruch*,[19] the primary opinion cited is that *netah revai* applies fully in *chutz la'aretz*, with *Rambam* only listed as an alternate

---

[13] *Shulchan Aruch* 294:1-2.
[14] Papain was originally discovered by observing the natives using papaya leaves to preserve food, but the way it is extracted commercially is from the fruit. As noted in the text, leaves are not subject to the prohibition of *arlah*, which means that if companies would begin extracting papain from the leaves (a possibility being researched), the principle that *safek arlah* in *chutz la'aretz* is permitted would allow the use of all papain as long as one did not specifically know that it was extracted from the fruit.
[15] *Tzlach, Berachos* 36b.
[16] *Derech Emunah* (*Be'or HaHalacha*), *Hil. Ma'aser Sheini* 9:13 s.v. *assurin*.
[17] *Chidushei Rav Chaim HaLevi al HaRambam, Hil. Ma'acholos Assuros* 10:15. The general concept can also be seen in *Tzlach* ibid.
[18] *Rambam, Hil. Ma'acholos Assuros* 10:15.
[19] *Shulchan Aruch* 294:7.

opinion (ויש מי שאומר), and *Rema* cites the *Geonim*.[20] Thus, *Shulchan Aruch* and *Rema* appear to take the position that *arlah* in *chutz la'aretz* is merely a variation of *arlah* in *Eretz Yisroel* (rather than a separate halacha). It therefore follows that peels of *arlah* fruit in *chutz la'aretz* should also be forbidden, just as they are in *Eretz Yisroel*. This is borne out in *Shulchan Aruch* who rules (*Yoreh Deah* 294:1-2) that peels are included in the *issur* of *arlah*, and in subsequent halachos (294:3, 7-10 &17) he discusses *arlah* in *chutz la'aretz* and how it differs from *Eretz Yisroel* and does not say that peels are treated any differently in *chutz la'aretz*. Thus, we can conclude that *Shulchan Aruch* holds that the peel of an *arlah* fruit – or the papain extracted from an *arlah* papaya – is also included in the prohibition of *arlah*, even in *chutz la'aretz*.[21]

Although *Shulchan Aruch* and *Rema* are strict on this matter, it might still be appropriate to be lenient, based on the principle[22] that as relates to *arlah* in *chutz la'aretz*, one can always follow a legitimate lenient opinion (כל המיקל בארץ הלכה כמותו בחוץ לארץ). If so, although we cannot permit papain in *chutz la'aretz* based on the idea that *safek arlah* is always permitted in *chutz la'aretz*, we potentially can do so based on this other lenient principle that applies to *arlah* in *chutz la'aretz*.

Papaya Revisited

Our entire discussion follows the assumption that papaya is a fruit which is subject to the *issur* of *arlah*. This is logical, since papaya meets the criteria given by the *Gemara*[23] and *Tosefta*[24] for determining which produce is classified as a fruit (and obligated in *arlah*) as opposed to a vegetable (which is not).

However, several later *Poskim* suggested alternate criteria for identifying a fruit/tree, according to which, papaya is not halachically considered a fruit at all. [Most of those *Poskim* were not discussing papaya, but rather other

---

[20] *Gr"a* 294:28 favors the *Geonim/Rema*, and *Shach* 294:17 rules that due to the disagreement one should be *podeh* (transfer the *kedushah*) the possible *kedushah* from all *netah revai* (in *chutz la'aretz*) onto money.

[21] See footnote 9.

[22] *Gemara, Berachos* 36a. [*Tzlach* himself notes this principle as relates to this application].

[23] *Gemara, Berachos* 40a-b says that the defining criterion of a tree is that after harvesting the produce, new fruits will grow in the coming season without need for replanting.

[24] *Tosefta, Kilayim* 3:15, cited in *Rambam, Hil. Kilayim* 5:20, and both are noted by *Radvaz* 3:531/966 as relates to *arlah*. *Tosefta* says the criterion is that the leaves of trees do not come from the trunk but rather from the branches, while the leaves of a non-tree will even come from the primary trunk.

foods where similar issues apply; see more on this below]. Among those proposed criteria are that a plant which (a) produces edible crops during its first year of planting,[25] or (b) whose crops are better in the first year than in later years,[26] is so different from a typical tree, that it is not considered a "tree", and its produce is halachically classified as a vegetable.[27] Papaya fulfills both of these criteria, so that these *Poskim* would say that it is not a "fruit" and not subject to the *issur* of *arlah* at all, even if we know it grew within the first three years after planting.

Other *Poskim* disagree with these alternate criteria. Nevertheless, it is generally accepted[28] that, as relates to papain from *chutz la'aretz*, one can follow the lenient approach based on the aforementioned principle of כל המיקל בארץ הלכה כמותו בחוץ לארץ. Earlier we saw this principle applied to permit papain specifically, and we now see that it can potentially permit all papaya in *chutz la'aretz*.

Eggplant plus

Until now we have discussed papaya, which is commercially never grown for more than three years, thereby raising a question that its fruit should always be *arlah*. That issue was based, in part, on the assumption that the two ways to identify a "tree" is based on the criteria given by the *Gemara* (plant lasts from year to year) and *Tosefta* (leaves do not grow from the trunk). However, we noted that later *Poskim* offer two alternate ways of identifying a tree; since papaya does not fulfill those criteria, it is not a "fruit/tree" and is therefore excused from *arlah*. The two alternate criteria were:

A. Year 1 .... The trees do not produce edible crops in the first year after planting.

B. Degradation ..... Produce of the tree is better in later years than in the early years.

---

[25] *Radvaz* ibid. (end). *Chazon Ish*, *Arlah* 12:3, and *Shevet HaLevi* 6:165, reject this position.
[26] *Birkei Yosef* to *Shulchan Aruch* YD 294:3.
[27] These *Poskim* do not offer sources for the criteria they are suggesting. Rather, they are a blend of personal logic and a justification for the common practice in their time (including by eminent *Poskim*) to eat eggplant despite its apparent *arlah* concerns.
[28] Rav Schwartz wrote a *teshuvah* permitting papaya (and his logic extends to papain), and Rav Belsky and Rav Schachter are also reported to have permitted it. This appears to be the generally accepted ruling at the national *hashgachos*. [*Shevet HaLevi* 6:165 says that personally he rules that papaya is forbidden (although it is not clear if this is limited to *Eretz Yisroel*) but does not protest those who rely on the lenient opinions. *Yechaveh Da'as* 4:52 permits it even in *Eretz Yisroel*].

Papaya produces fruit during the first year, and the subsequent crops are worse than that first year's fruit. Therefore, both approaches would say that papaya is not a fruit. The *Poskim* who suggested those criteria were not discussing papaya but were rather taking positions on the permissibility of eggplant.

In most parts of the United States, eggplant does not survive the cold of winter and must be replanted each year. If so, it seems obvious that eggplant is not a "tree" since it does not meet the *Gemara's* criterion of a tree/fruit. The reason so many *Poskim* discussed eggplant is because it originated in the tropical climates of South Asia, where the weather is warm enough for the plant to last through the winter. Thus, from their perspective it appears to be a tree, but it never produces fruit for 3 years, hence the question that it seems to always be *arlah*. In addition to the two alternate criteria noted above, others suggest the following ways of identifying a tree:

C. Hollow trunk .... Trees have solid trunks, and if the trunk is hollow (like a reed), that is a sign that this is not a tree.[29]

D. 4 years .... The *Torah* does not forbid *arlah* unless the tree will produce fruit <u>after</u> the years of *arlah* end (when the fruit would be permitted).[30]

E. 5 years .... The *Torah* says[31] that in the 5th year – after *arlah* and *revai* end – the produce will be available for consumption, and this teaches that if the plant will stop producing fruit before the 5th year, the restrictions of *arlah* and *revai* do not apply.[32]

---

[29] *Responsa Halachos Ketanos* 1:83, cited and accepted by *Rav Pealim* OC 2:30. [*Halachos Ketanos* was a *Sephardic Gadol* who lived in the 1600s]. *Shevet HaLevi* 6:165 (discussing papaya) suggests proofs against this suggestion and therefore disagrees with it.

[30] *Sha'arei Tzedek* (by the author of *Chochmas Adam*), *Sha'arei Mishpitei Ha'aretz* (*Chochmas Adam* 6:18 and *Binas Adam* 6:2), (noting that *Radvaz* rejected it). *Tzitz Eliezer* 2:15 argues that we are not authorized to derive halachos by interpreting *pesukim* in this manner.

[31] *Vayikra* 19:25.

[32] *Chazon Ish*, *Arlah* 12:3. He further suggests that when the *Gemara* says that a non-tree is identified by having a trunk that does not "last" (אין הגזע מתקיים), that does not mean that the trunk dies out during the winter (as most understand it), but rather that it does not last long enough to produce fruit which is free of all restrictions (i.e., to the 5th year). Thus, this opinion has the unique feature of claiming to be based on the *Gemara*, as opposed to the others which are independent logical ideas without significant sources.

All these ideas were proposed as extra ways of identifying trees and non-trees using features not mentioned in the *Gemara* or *Tosefta*. Each is suggested by one or more *Poskim*, and just about every one of them is also rejected by others (some of which are noted in the footnotes). Nonetheless, as noted earlier, since *safek arlah* is permitted in *chutz la'aretz*, we can be lenient if even one legitimate *Posek* accepts a given line of reasoning.

We have seen that these lines of reasoning can also potentially justify eating papaya (and papain), by positing that papaya is not a "fruit", just as eggplant is not. Similarly, these ideas are used to explain why one may eat raspberries[33] and the type of pepper used to make tabasco sauce.[34]

---

[33] The raspberry plant can live for as much as 10 years, but the stems/canes that grow above the ground each live for only 2 years. We rule that "the plant survives the winter" (i.e., the *Gemara's* criterion for a tree) refers specifically to the parts which are <u>above ground</u>, and if so, it follows that the fact that the roots and crown live for 10 years is inconsequential. Instead, we look at the canes and they survive the winter (so this is a "tree") but never last for 3 years (so all fruit should be *arlah*). [Although one could argue that since, overall, there will be canes above ground for 10 years, this is a "10-year" plant/tree, and we should not view each cane separately and conclude that each cane is a "2-year" tree].

Those plants that only produce fruit in the spring (spring-bearing), will have just one crop per cane, and that will be in the cane's second year of growth. Raspberries which are fall-bearing, have fruit within a few months after the cane grows, and they can then grow another crop in the spring that follows. Thus, both types qualify for reason "B" (degradation), "D" (4 years), and "E" (5 years) and the latter type also qualifies for reason "A" (year 1). [The author is unsure if the stems are hollow (reason "C")]. *Maharsham* 1:196 discusses raspberries and permits them based on reason "B". He also considers a lenient approach, based on a proof from *Yerushalmi*, *Arlah* 1:1, that bushes are inherently not considered "trees", even if they have all other signs of a tree.

[34] See the article by Rav Yosef Ephrati in *Halichos Sadeh*, Volume 100, regarding the *capsicum frutescens* peppers. It includes several varieties including tabasco pepper (used to make tabasco sauce), Hawaiian pepper, and certain other ones including the ones used to make *schug* (a *Sephardic* hot dip). These (unusual) peppers are considered perennials, since they continue to thrive during the winter (meeting the *Gemara's* criterion for a tree/fruit) but do not survive more than 2 years (thereby raising the *arlah* question). They begin producing fruit/peppers a few months after they are planted. As with many of the other foods noted in the text, they appear to meet all (or most) of the *Acharonim's* 5 possible ways to classify a plant as a non-tree.

Some tentative research has been done into whether the issues raised in this chapter also apply to passion fruit. [The *arlah* charts (see footnote 7) say that 40% of passion fruit is *arlah*]. On the one hand, the purple passion fruit lives for much more than 3 years (rendering each fruit permitted as *safek arlah*), but it is not clear (a) if the yellow passion fruit trees last more than 3 years, (b) if any trees could theoretically last more than 3 years, but are not commercially viable after the 3rd year and are cut down, (c) if any yellow or purple passion fruit grow in the tree's first year after planting, (d) if all juice is made from yellow passion fruit, or whether purple ones are also used for that purpose, and (e) whether the *ta'aruvos* issue noted regarding papain (i.e., juice of *arlah* mixed with juice of non-*arlah* which is not permitted without *bitul* in 200 times the *arlah's* volume), is relevant to this juice. This issue requires further research.

Epilogue

ל"ג בעומר תשפ"ד

As this 17-year project to create the אמרי דוד series comes to an end, the following words, which *Rambam* wrote at the conclusion of his *Pirush HaMishnayos*, accurately capture my feelings:

בריך רחמנא דסייען

כבר השלמנו חבור זה כפי שייעדנו, והנני מבקשו יתעלה ומתחנן לפניו שיצילני משגיאות. ומי שימצא בו מקום פקפוק או שנראה לו בפירוש הלכה מן ההלכות באור טוב ממה שבארתי יעיר על כך וידינני לזכות, כי מה שהסתלטי על עצמי בזה אינו מעט ולא בצועו קל אצל בעל צדק וחוש הבחנה טוב. ובפרט בהיות לבי טרוד לעתים קרובות בפגעי הזמן ומה שגזר ה' עלינו מן הגלות והנדוד בעולם מקצה השמים ועד קצה השמים, ואולי כבר קבלנו שכר דבר זה גלות מכפרת עון. יודע הוא יתעלה כי יש הלכות מהם שכתבתי פירושן במסעותי בדרכים, ומהם ענינים רשמתים בהיותי על גבי האניות בים הגדול, ודי במצב זה, נוסף על היותי מעיין במדעים אחרים. ולא תיארתי את המצב אלא כדי להסביר התנצלותי במה שעלול להראות למבקר שידקדק בו, ואין ראוי להאשימו על הקורתו, אלא יש לו שכר מאת ה' על כך, ואהוב הוא עלי כי היא מלאכת ה'. ומה שתיארתי ממצבי במשך זמן חבור פירוש זה הוא שגרם שנשתהיתי בו זמן רב.

אני משה בר' מימון הדיין בר' יוסף החכם בר' יצחק הדיין בר' יוסף הדיין בר' עובדיהו הדיין בר' שלמה הרב בר' עובדיהו הדיין זכר קדושים לברכה. התחלתי לחבר פירוש זה ואני בן שלש ועשרים שנה והשלמתי אותו במצרים ואני בן שלשים שנה שהיא שנת אלף וארבע מאות ותשע ושבעים לשטרות.

ברוך הנותן ליעף כח ולאין אונים עצמה ירבה

This is also an opportunity to thank:

- אבי, שהביאני לעולם הזה ומלמד אותי חכמה שמביא אותי לחיי העולם הבא
- My mother who raised and cares for me כאשר ישא האמן את הינק and who invested hundreds of hours editing all volumes of this series
- My father-in-law ע"ה and mother-in-law תחי', who transmitted their dedication to *Torah* values to us, their children, and many others

- The *Poskim* שומרי משמרת הכשרות from whom I learned, and particularly Rav Belsky זצ"ל, Rav Schachter שליט"א, Rav Schwartz זצ"ל, and Rav Reiss שליט"א, from whom I have/had the most direct contact and whose rulings are well documented in this series
- The administration and staff of cRc Kosher where I am blessed to work, and who were the original audience for the thoughts contained in these volumes
- My wife, who את חיל אשת כי עמי שער כל יודע, and who has supported and encouraged my learning and writing during all of life's ups and downs

May *Hashem* bless each of you with
דורות ישרים מבורך ובנים עוסקים בתורה הקדושה ובמצוות

A final thought from *Chayei Adam's* postscript to his *sefer*, explaining a phrase in מזמור לתודה:

"הוא עשנו ולא אנחנו" והקרי הוא לו בוא"ו
כי בעולם הזה כאשר רואה אדם שמצליח
הוא תולה בעצמו ואומר כחי ועוצם ידי עשה לי את החיל הזה
אבל לעתיד לבא יכירו הכל כי הוא עשנו, לשון תיקון
כי הכל נתקן ממנו יתברך ולא אנחנו עשינו שום דבר

INDEX

Chapters where specific topics and issues are discussed

Topic	Chapter
10% rule	4
12 months	41
6 Hours, waiting after tasting or chewing	18
6 hours, waiting due to דוחקא דסכינא	15
6 hours, waiting for "DE"	11
60:1 or 100:1?	27
6-18 minutes, for fast *kovush*	48
960:1 for *bitul*	30
Absorbed *ta'am*, transfer	7
Absorption of *ta'am*, fish and meat	12
Absorption, in vs. out	10
Absorption, welds vs. screws	10
Ach'shvei	19
Ain kavonoso l'vatel	28
Ain kavonoso l'vatel, and coatings	43
Ain mevatlin issur l'chatchila, see *bitul issur l'chatchila*	
Aino ben yomo vs. *pagum*	29
Aino ben yomo	41
Aino ben yomo, reinvigorated by *davar charif*	16
Aino ben yomo, and *bitul* of *keilim*	36
Aino ben yomo, and pot covers	8
Aino ben yomo, and *yesh lo matirim*	36
Aino ben yomo, kashering if always	43
Aino ben yomo, using utensil and *bitul issur l'chatchila*	28
Aino ben yomo, with Nat bar Nat	11
Aino mino, also see *min b'mino*	
Aino mino, and tasting	18
Aino mino, by taste (טעמא) or name (שמא)	21, 33
Air Up water bottle	60
Alcohol, distilled, and *chametz* after Pesach	21
Alimentum	38
Always *aino ben yomo*, need to *kasher*	43
Amines, as a *davar hapogem*	4
Amylase, as *ma'amid*	1
Animal hides	27
Appliances, and coatings	43
Arlah	66
Arlah, and *chazusah*	35
Arlah, and *yesh lo matirim*	36
Arlah, *safek*	66
Aroma, as compared to taste and mouthfeel	39
Asafetida (חילתית)	14
Asui l'hishtamesh b'shefah	29
Asui l'hishtamesh b'shefah, and *bitul issur l'chatchila*	28, 29
Asui l'hishtamesh b'shefah, and *ChaNaN*	3
Asui l'hishtamesh b'shefah, and coatings	43
Average person, and tasting	18
Avidah lit'amah	25
Avidah lit'amah, which absorbed standard *ta'am*	26
Avidah lit'amah, which is only *assur mid'rabannan*	26
Avodah zara (תקרובת), and *bitul*	62
B'lios, and *yavesh b'yavesh*	61
B'lios, in vs. out	10
B'lios, meat and fish	12
B'lios, passing through eggshell	25
B'lios, without heat	47
Barley malt, see malt	
Barley, *yoshon* in a *chodosh* facility	33
Barrel, *bitul* calculations	20

Topic	Chapter
Basar b'chalav, creation in a drainpipe	13
Basar b'chalav, and *ChaNaN*	3
Bee legs	39
Beryah	30
Beryah, crushing to allow *bitul*	28
Beryah, which is inherently disgusting	46
Bishul akum, kashering afterwards	29
Bishul akum, which was a *ma'amid*	1
Bitrex, as a *davar hapogem*	4
Bitul b'rov	37, 61
Bitul b'rov, and non-foods	19, 43
Bitul b'rov, and חמץ שעבר עליו הפסח	21
Bitul b'shishah, stam yayin	4
Bitul b'shishim, or 100:1 ratio	27
Bitul in 960	30
Bitul issur l'chatchilah	28
Bitul issur l'chatchilah, and *aino ben yomo*	40
Bitul issur l'chatchilah, avoiding *issur* without *bitul*	13
Bitul issur l'chatchilah, *chametz* before *Pesach*	12
Bitul issur l'chatchilah, for meat and fish	12
Bitul issur l'chatchilah, milk into bread	28
Bitul issur l'chatchilah, milk into water	12, 28
Bitul issur l'chatchilah, rennet for cheesemaking	28
Bitul issur l'chatchilah, while washing dishes	13
Bitul issur l'chatchilah, safek issur	28
Bitul, and *tevillas keilim*	36
Bitul, calculations	20
Bitul, meat and fish	12
Bitul, of *keilim*	36
Bitul, of *sefer Torah*	62
Bitul, of מלח הבלוע מדם	26
Black olives, and *Pesach*	35
Blenders, and *zeh v'zeh gorem*	2
Blends, part ראויה להתכבד and part not	31
Boiler condensate, draining or flushing	4
Boiler condensate, tasting	19
Bone char	27

Topic	Chapter
Bone products	27
Bourbon from a Jewish owned company	21
Bourbon, and *chametz* after *Pesach*	21
Bracha acharonah, for a *beryah*	30
Bread, dairy	17
Breakfast cereal, with malt	33
Brewer's yeast, as a *ma'amid*	1
Bugs are *nosein ta'am lifgam*	46
Cake and crackers, dairy bread	17
Calcium	27
Calculating *aino ben yomo*	41
Calculating *arlah* years	66
Calculating *bitul*	20
Capsicum Frutescens peppers, and *arlah*	66
Carmine, and *chazusah*	35
Carmine, *kashering* after use	1
Carmine, *kashering* at manufacturer	38
Cartilage	27
Cask, *bitul* calculations	20
Cast iron pans, pre-seasoned	43
Castoreum	26
Catalyst, as a *ma'amid*	1
Caustic, as a *davar hapogem*	4
Cereal, with malt	33
Certification of marijuana	60
Certification of *mitzvah* items	45
Chalav stam, and *ChaNaN*	3
Challah, and *yesh lo matirim*	36
Chametz after *Pesach* (and bourbon)	21
Chametz dishes mixed into *Pesach* dishes	36
Chametz she'avar alav haPesach	1
Chametz, airborne flour in factory	28
Chametz, and *aino ben yomo*	40
Chametz, and *ChaNaN*	3
Chametz, and *chozer v'niur*	61
Chametz, and *issur mashehu*	34
Chametz, and *kli sheini*	50
Chametz, and *nifsal mei'achila*	4
Chametz, and *nosein ta'am lifgam*	37
Chametz, and *yesh lo matirim*	33
Chametz, cracked or wet wheat kernel	34
Chametz, was a *ma'amid*	1
ChaNaN	3
ChaNaN, and calculating *aino ben yomo*	40

Topic	Chapter
ChaNaN, and אפשר לסוחטו	55
ChaNaN, with לינת לילה	3
Charif, see *Davar charif*	
Chatichah har'uyah l'hiskabed	31
Chatichah har'uyah l'hiskabed, crushing to allow *bitul*	28
Chazusah	35
Cheese mold	54
Cheese wires, *kashering*	15
Cheese, use of non-kosher rennet	28
Cheese, with non-kosher *ma'amid*	1
Chewing, and waiting 6 hours	18
Chewing, and דוחקא דסכינא	15
Chezkas kashrus, and scandals	64
Chiltis	14
Chodosh malt, in *yoshon* flour	33
Chodosh, and ספק ספיקא	33
Chodosh, *bitul* of residual flour and barley before *yoshon*	33
Cholent, *bishul* on bones	27
Chozer v'niur, and *chametz*	61
Chumros, and *ChaNaN*	3
Chutz la'aretz, and *arlah*	66
Chutz la'aretz, and *netah revai*	66
Cigtrus	60
Civet	26
Coatings	43
Coffee creamer	3
Coffee, raw beans absorbed aroma from wine barrels	60
Coffee, roaster also used for decaffeinated coffee (*Pesach*)	7
Coils (steam) in jacket	4, 7
Cold mixtures, and *ChaNaN*	3
Coloring agents	35
Comparing fish fillets	32
Complete, definition as relates to *beryah*	30
Concentrates, and *avidah lit'amah*	26
Concentrates, *bitul* calculations	20
Condensate return	4
Condensate return, tasting	19
Cooling tunnel	50
Cottage cheese, made with rennet	1
Creamer	3
Cricket powder	46
Cut fruit and vegetables, non-kosher store	15, 16

Topic	Chapter
D'oraisah which became a *d'rabannan*	65
Dairy bread	17
Danger	12
Danger, meat and fish	12
Davar charif	14
Davar charif, and *aino ben yomo*	40
Davar charif, and *Nat bar Nat*	11
Davar charif, מחליא ליה לשבח	16
Davar chashuv	62
Davar gush	51
Davar hama'amid	1
Davar hama'amid, and emulsifiers	2
Davar hapogem	4
Davar hapogem, see also *pegimah* and individual chemicals/candidates	
Davar shebiminyan	62
Davar sheyesh lo matirim, see *yesh lo matirim*	
"DE" Foods	11, 61
Decaffeinated coffee	7
Defanos mikariros	50
Dental work, and *duchkah d'sakinah*	15
Deodorizing	40
Depth, and *kovush*	48
Dish sanitizing machine	13
Dishes, *bitul*	36
Dishes, washing together	13
Dishwasher, commercial, shared for meat and dairy	13
Dishwasher, commercial, *kashering*	13
Dishwasher, double drawer	13
Dishwasher, home, shared for meat and dairy	13
Dishwasher, home, *kashering*	13
Distance that *ta'am* transfers	10
Distilled alcohol, and *chametz* after *Pesach*	21
Double drawer dishwasher	13
Double *kashering*	3
Double *mashehu*	33
Double oven	6
Double walled heat exchanger	4, 7
Draining condensate	4
Dripping, is it *irui kli rishon*	9
Drums, as a *davar shebiminyan*	62
Dryer, freeze	5
Duchkah d'sakinah	15
Duchkah d'sakinah	15

Topic	Chapter
e-Cigarette juice	6, 19
Efshar l'sochto	55
Egg, with chick inside	56
Eggplant, and *arlah*	66
Eggplant, and *arlah*	66
Eggs, as a *davar shebiminyan*	62
Eggs, purchasing on *Pesach*	2
Eggshell, *b'lios* passing through	25
Emulsifier, and *ma'amid*	1
Emulsifier, in fruit coatings	43
Emulsifier, *zeh v'zeh gorem*	2
English muffins, and dairy bread	17
Enocianina, and *chazusah*	35
Enriched rice on *Pesach* for *Sephardim*	24
Enzymes for sugar and olives, and *ma'amid*	1
Equipment, and *ChaNaN*	3
Erev Pesach, see *Pesach*	
Estimations of *bitul* ratio	20
Excretions	55
Expertise, lack of, and tasting	18
Factories, and *davar charif*	16
Factories, and *stam keilim ainum b'nei yoman*	42
Fast day, tasting	18
Fatty acids, and flavors	26
Faucet, *kashering*	6
Faucet, water coming out is *irui kli rishon*	13
Fermentation products, for *Pesach* USA vs. Europe	26
Fermentation	55
Ferrous gluconate, and *chametz*	35
Fillets, comparing fish to identify kosher ones	32
Fire burns small amounts of *issur*	5
Fish and meat	12
Fish forks	12
Fish oil	12
Fish, and *duchkah d'sakinah*	15
Fish, comparing fillets to identify kosher ones	32
Fish, from a non-kosher fish store	15
Fish, injected with fish protein	24
Fish, skin tags	32
Flavors, and *avidah lit'amah*	26
Flavors, *zeh v'zeh gorem*	2, 26
Flour, *yoshon* in a *chodosh* facility	33

Topic	Chapter
Flushing condensate	4
Flushing equipment, to remove *chodosh*	33
Foil pans, coatings	43
Foods, and מחליא ליה לשבח	16
Formulas for calculating *bitul*	20
Freezer dryer	5
French toasts, and dairy bread	17
Fruit vs. vegetable, and *arlah*	66
Fruits and vegetables, from a non-kosher store	15, 16
Fruits, coatings	43
Furfural, from oats, for *Pesach*	26
Fusel oil, wine	26
Gelatin, does it have *ta'am*	39
Gelatin, from hard bones	27
Gelatin, in yogurt stabilizer blend	3
Gerairah	15
Gid hanasheh, does it have *ta'am*	39
Glass, absorption of *ta'am*	4
Glucosamine	27
Glucose isomerase, as a *ma'amid*	1
Glucose, for *Pesach*, USA vs. Europe	26
Glycerin, in e-cigarettes	6
Glycerin, in hookah	6
Glycerin, in liquid medicine	3, 19
Glycerin, in toothpaste and mouthwash	19, 43
Glycerin, likelihood it is non-kosher	19
Grasshoppers	46
Grates, see stovetop grates	
Grease, on a knife	15
Grinding, and דוחקא דסכינא	15
Hadachah	15
Hag'alah, and *bitul issur l'chatchilah*	40
Halacha L'Moshe m'Sinai, and *safek d'oraisah l'chumrah*	66
Handle of pot	10
Hard bones vs. soft bones	27
Heat exchanger, double walled	4, 7
Heat on one part of the utensil	10
Heat sealer	52
Heat vs. temperature	49
Heating media	6
Heating oil, and *pegimah*	4
Herring, as *davar charif*	14
Heter vs. *Issur*	3, 11, 13, 18, 25
Hides, of animals	27
Hood over stovetop	6, 8

Topic	Chapter
Hookah	6
Hopelessly lost	24
Horns	27
Immobilized enzymes, and *ma'amid*	1
Induction cooktop	7
Inedible excretions	55
Inedible items, certification	45
Inedible	37
Inedible, and coatings	43
Inedible, but provides other non-taste benefit	38
Inherently forbidden, and *avidah lit'amah*	26
Inherently forbidden, and *davar shebiminyan*	62
Inherently forbidden, and *beryah*	30
Inherently forbidden, and *chatichah har'uyah l'hiskabed*	31
Inherently forbidden, and *ma'amid*	1
Insect eggs, as *beryos*	30
Insects, burning to allow *bitul*	28
Insects, hopelessly lost in vegetable	24
Insects, pureeing infested vegetables	28
Instant Pot, shared for fish and meat	12
Irui kli rishon	50
Irui kli rishon, and נפסק הקילוח	13
Irui kli rishon, dripping	9
Irui kli rishon, in a sink, dishwasher, or dish sanitizer	13
Irui kli rishon, pot still on the fire	13
Issur d'rabbanan, and *ChaNaN*	3
Issur d'rabbanan, and חזותא	35
Issur mashehu, limits	33
Issur mashehu, *safek*	33, 34
Issur mashehu, תרי משהו	33
Issur, safek, kashering after	56
Issur, safek, tasting	19
Issur, which can be removed from the *ta'aroves*	24
Jacketed kettles	4
Jewish owned bourbon company	21
Juice, and scale insects	24
Juice, vaping	19
K'dei klipah	15
K'dei netilah	15
Kashering, for *asui l'hishtamesh b'shefah*	29
Kashering, when unknown if *ben yomo*	42

Topic	Chapter
Kashering, after a *davar gush*	51
Kashering, after a *kashrus* scandal	64
Kashering, after *bishul akum*	29
Kashering, after dairy bread	17
Kashering, after *kovush*	48
Kashering, after *safek issur*	56
Kashering, after whisky use	40
Kashering, after דפנות מקררות	50
Kashering, and *bitul issur l'chatchilah*	40
Kashering, and *bitul* of *keilim*	36
Kashering, and *ChaNaN*	3
Kashering, as part of pot production	43
Kashering, carmine manufacturer	38
Kashering, dishwasher (home or commercial)	13
Kashering, faucet	6
Kashering, freeze dryer	5
Kashering, *issur* was not *batel* but was not *nosein ta'am*	1
Kashering, needed after 12 months	41
Kashering, tunnel pasteurizer	50
Kashering, twice	3
Kashering, via *ne'itzah*	15
Kashering, vinegar factory	50
Kashrus scandals	64
Keilim, bitul	36
Keurig	11
Kitnios shenishtaneh, and *bitul issur l'chatchilah*	28
Kitnios, and *avidah lit'amah*	26
Kitnios, and *ChaNaN*	3
Kitnios, *batel b'rov*	26
Kitnios, enriched rice for *Sephardim*	24
Kitnios, infant rice cereal	34
Kitnios, which was a *ma'amid*	1
Kli rishon and *kli sheini*	50
Kli sheini, and *davar charif*	15, 50
Kli sheini, and *duchkah d'sakinah*	15
Kli sheini, on meat before *melichah*	9
Knife nowadays	15
Knife sharpening	15
Knife, *b'lios*	15
Knife, cleaning	15
Knife, unknown status, and *davar charif*	16
Knife, used for *chametz* and then *Pesach* food	34
Koji fermentation	55
Kol d'parish	63

Topic	Chapter
Kol kavuah	63
Kovush	48
Kovush, *ta'am* transferring	10
Lach b'lach vs. *yavesh b'yavesh*	55
Lach b'lach vs. *yavesh b'yavesh*, *bitul* requirements	61
Lach b'lach, and אפשר לסוחטו	55
Large oven	57
L-cysteine	3, 27
Leek, as *davar charif*	14
Lemons (cut), from non-Jews	16, 61
Lemons, as *davar charif*	14
Libun kal for a *ben yomo*	5
Linas laylah, with *ChaNaN*	3
Liquid medicine, and glycerin	19
Liquid medicine, diluting	3
Liquid, definition	48
Liver, tasting to see if there was a gall bladder	19
Los Angeles *kashrus* scandal	64
Lubricants	43
Ma'amid, see *davar hama'amid*	
Malt, and *chametz*	33
Malt, as a *ma'amid*	21
Malt, *chodosh*, in *yoshon* flour	33
Manalapan *kashrus* scandal	64
Marijuana certification	60
Maris ayin, and *bitul issur l'chatchilah*	28
Marshmallows	12
Mashehu, see *issur mashehu*	
Mead fermented with brewer's yeast	1
Meat and fish	12
Meat and milk on same stovetop	58
Meat is *lifgam* into oil	40
Meat, and *davar shebiminyan*	62
Meat, and *duchkah d'sakinah*	15
Meat, raw, and חתיכה הראויה להתכבד	31
Meat, without *melichah*, *bitul*	33
Mechalyah leh lishvach	16
Medicine, coatings	43
Medicine, liquid, and glycerin	19
Medicine, liquid, diluting	3
Medicine, tablets with stearates	24
Melach habaluah m'dam	54
Melichah, hot water beforehand	9
Melichah, meat without it, being *batel*	33
Microorganism, status	55

Topic	Chapter
Microwave, and *zei'ah*	6
Microwave, glass door	53
Microwave, status as a *kli rishon*	50
Milk from cows that ate *chametz*	55
Milk powder, *bitul* calculation	20
Milk, purchasing on *Pesach*	2
Min b'mino vs. *aino mino*	39
Min b'mino vs. *aino mino*, *bitul* requirements	61
Min b'mino, and tasting	18
Min b'mino, and *yesh lo matirim*	33
Min b'mino, and סלוק את מינו	22
Min b'mino, by taste (טעמא) or name (שמא)	21, 33
Min b'mino, cases where טעם כעיקר applies vs. ones where it doesn't	21
Min b'mino, see also *aino mino*	
Mitzvah items	45
Mixture where *issur* is hopelessly lost	24
Monoglycerides	2
Monsey *kashrus* scandal	64
Mouthfeel	39
Mouthwash	19
Movement, and *kovush*	48
Muktzeh, and *davar shebiminyan*	62
Nails	27
Nat bar nat	11, 13
Nat bar nat, washing dishes	13
Ne'itzah	15
Netah revai in *chutz la'aretz*	66
Neutralizing amines, as a *davar hapogem*	4
Nifsal mei'achila vs. *sheloh k'derech achilah*	4
Nisgalgel	13, 65
Nitzuk chibur	53
No *ta'am* at all	39
Non-foods, *bitul issur l'chatchilah*	28
Non-foods, *bitul*	19, 43
Non-foods, certification	45
Non-Jew, concern he'll switch food	58
Non-Jewish manufacturer, creating *bitul*	28
Non-kosher store, buying fish, fruits, and vegetables	15, 16
Nosein ta'am lifgam which provides other non-taste benefit	38
Nosein ta'am lifgam	37, 38

Topic	Chapter
Nosein ta'am lifgam, and *zeh v'zeh gorem*	2
Nosein ta'am lifgam, purposely added in	46
Nosein ta'am lifgam, bugs	46
Nosein ta'am lifgam, determination	46
Not *lishvach* and not *lifgam*	39
Nutramigen	38
Observable phenomena	4
Oil (heating), and *pegimah*	4
Oil (olive), transported in non-kosher barrels	4
Oil, meat is *lifgam* into it	40
Oleh al shulchan melachim vs. *chatichah har'uyah l'hiskabed*	31
Olives, black, and *Pesach*	35
Olives, enzymes as *ma'amid*	1
Onion, as *davar charif*	14
Orange juice, and scale insects	24
Oven, and coatings	43
Oven, and *zei'ah*	6
Oven, large vs. small	57
Oven, shared for meat and dairy	6
Ovum, mixed into liquid eggs	22
Oyster shells	27
Pagum vs. *aino ben yomo*	29
Pans, coatings	43
Papain, and *arlah*	66
Papaya, and *arlah*	66
Paper, and sizing agents	43
Passion fruit/juice, and *arlah*	66
Pearled barley, see barley	
Peel of fruit, and *arlah*	66
Pegimah candidates	4
Pegimah, and *asui l'hishtamesh b'shefah*	29
Pegimah, see also *davar hapogem*	
Pegimah, tasting boiler condensate	19
Pegimah, washing dishes	13
Pesach production, tasting for *ta'am* of *chametz*	18
Pesach, airborne flour in factory	28
Pesach, and *ChaNaN*	3
Pesach, and coated fruits and vegetables	43
Pesach, and *kol d'parish*	63
Pesach, and pot covers	8
Pesach, and *reichah*	57
Pesach, and *yavesh b'yavesh*	61

Topic	Chapter
Pesach, and *zeh v'zeh gorem*	2
Pesach, *bitul* before vs. during	2
Pesach, black olives	35
Pesach, dental appliances	15
Pesach, enriched rice for *Sephardim*	24
Pesach, furfural from oats	26
Pesach, glucose, USA vs. Europe	26
Pesach, infant rice cereal	34
Pesach, *kitnios* is *batel b'rov*	26
Pesach, Koji fermentation	55
Pesach, milk from cows that ate *chametz*	55
Pesach, one sink for *chametz* and *Pesach* dishes	13
Pesach, relying on *stam keilim ainum b'nei yoman*	42
Pesach, חמץ שעבר עליו הפסח (and bourbon)	21
Pickles, as *davar charif*	14
Pine oil, as a *davar hapogem*	4
Pizza dough, and dairy bread	17
Plastic, and lubricants	43
Plate underneath food cut with דוחקא דסכינא	15
Pogem, see *davar hapogem* and *pegimah*	
Polysorbates	2
Polystyrene	43
Pot cover	8
Pot handle	10
Pot, identifying the type	20
Pot, ratio of content to walls	20
Pots and pans, coatings	43
Pouring oil or spices into hot pot	53
Pre-seasoned cast iron pans	43
Pressing, and דוחקא דסכינא	15
Propylene glycol, and *pegimah*	4
Pureeing infested vegetables	28
Radish, as *davar charif*	14
Raspberries, and *arlah*	66
Raw meat, חתיכה הראויה להתכבד and	31
Reichah	57
Reinvigoration of *aino ben yomo ta'am*	16
Removable *issur*	24
Rennet, in cottage cheese	1
Rennet, *ma'amid* for curd and whey	1
Retort, steam heated	6

Topic	Chapter
Reversibility, and *nifsal mei'achila*	4
Rice cereal, infant, for *Pesach*	34
Rice on *Pesach* for *Sephardim*	24
Rodent	44
Rum, fermented with *chametz*	1
Rust, and *asui l'hishtamesh b'shefah*	29
Safek arlah	66
Safek d'oraisah l'chumrah, and *Halacha l'Moshe m'Sinai*	66
Safek issur mashehu	33, 34
Safek issur, and *bitul issur l'chatchilah*	28
Safek issur, and *ChaNaN*	3
Safek issur, *kashering* after	56
Safek issur, tasting	19
Safek, and *sfek sfekah*	33
Safek, based on lack of wisdom	23
Sakanah	12
Salek es mino, see סלק את מינו	
Salt added to food on *Shabbos*	2
Salting	54
Sanitizing machine	13
Saturated with heat	50
Scale insects, and orange juice	24
Scandals (*kashrus*)	64
Scotch aged in sherry casks	2
Screws, absorption of *ta'am*	10
Sealer (with heat)	52
Seasoning on pans	43
Sefer Torah, *bitul*	62
Separation, meat and fish	12
Sephardim, tasting for *Ashkenazim*	18
Sfek sfekah, and *chodosh*	33
Sfek sfekah, and *safek*	33
Sfek sfekah, and *yesh lo matirim*	33
Shabbos, and *davar gush*	51
Shabbos, *bishul* of bones in *cholent*	27
Shabbos, salt added to food	2
Shark fin, does it have *ta'am*	39
Sharpening of knives	15
Shatnez, and *bitul*	62
Shellac, has no *ta'am*	39
Sherry casks, and *zeh v'zeh gorem*	2
Shrink tunnel	52
Sink, shared for meat and dairy	13
Skin tags	32
Small oven	57
Soap, and *pegimah*	13
Soft bones vs. hard bones	27
Solid object, and *kli rishon*	51

Topic	Chapter
Specific gravity	20
Specific heat capacity	49
Speed that *ta'am* transfers	10
Spice grinding, and *duchkah d'sakinah*	15
Spices, for meat and dairy	6
Spoiling vs. bitter additives	4
Stabilizer blend (powder), and *ChaNaN*	3
Stabilizer, and *ma'amid*	1
Stam keilim are not *ben yomo*	42
Stam yayin, and *ChaNaN*	3
Stam yayin, *bitul b'shishah*	4
Steam coils in jacket	4, 7
Steam system	4
Steam system, tasting boiler condensate	19
Steam system, and *ChaNaN*	3
Steam table, shared for meat and dairy	11
Steam vacuuming	9
Stearates, do they have *ta'am*	39
Stearates, on medicinal tablets	24
Stir hot pot with cold spoon	10
Store (non-kosher), buying fish, fruits, and vegetables	15, 16
Stovetop grates, shared for different uses	7
Stovetop, and *zei'ah*	6
Stovetop, cooking meat and milk side by side	58
Stovetop, shared for kosher and non-kosher	5, 58
Stovetop, shared for meat and dairy	5, 58
Styrofoam cups	43
Substrate	55
Sugar, enzymes as *ma'amid*	1
Sugar, made with bone char	27
Surface propagations	55
Swallow vs. tasting with the tongue	18
Ta'am kalush	4, 26
Ta'am lifgam, see *nosein ta'am lifgam*	
Ta'am transferring	49, 50
Ta'am travelling and transferring	10
Ta'am, foods which have none	39
Ta'anis, tasting	18
Tabasco peppers/sauce, and *arlah*	66
Tank, *bitul* calculations	20

Topic	Chapter
Taste the *issur* in mixture vs. *issur* just affects taste of mixture	26
Taste, as compared to aroma and mouthfeel	39
Taste, measured by average people	38
Tasting a *ta'aroves*	18
Tasting vs. swallowing	18
Tasting, and *ach'shvei*	19
Tasting, boiler condensate	19
Tasting, foods with bad taste	19
Tasting, for *ta'am* of *chametz*	18
Tasting, *issur*	19
Tasting, on a fast day	18
Tasting, *safek issur*	19
Tasting, steam system condensate	4
Tasting, waiting 6 hours after	18
Tata'ah gavar	52
Temperature of *yad soledes bo*	49
Temperature vs. heat	49
Terumah, and *yesh lo matirim*	36
Tevel, and *yesh lo matirim*	36
Tevillas keilim, and *bitul*	36
Tevillas keilim, for utensil with metal *ma'amid*	1
Thermal conductivity	49
Timing, and *kovush*	48
Tofu, does it have *ta'am*	39
Toothpaste	19, 43
Totes, as a *davar shebiminyan*	62
Transfer of *ta'am*	10, 49, 50
Transfer of *ta'am*, into glass	4
Transfer of *ta'am*, through metal	4
Translation of vegetable names	14
Trei mashehu, and *chodosh*	33
Tumbler	52
Tunnel pasteurizer	50
Two *mashehu*	33
USA vs. Europe, glucose for *Pesach*	26
Utensils, *bitul*	36
Vacuum, steam	9
Vape juice	6, 19
Vapor	6
Vapor, and *ta'am*	4
Vapors	60
Vegetable names	14
Vegetable vs. fruit, and *arlah*	66
Vegetables and fruits, from a non-kosher store	15, 16
Vegetables, coatings	43

Topic	Chapter
Vegetables, pureeing infested ones	28
Vinegar, as a *davar charif*	14, 16
Vinegar, *kashering* a factory	50
Vitamin premix in formula	3
Vitamins, in rice, for *Sephardim* on *Pesach*	24
Volume vs. weight (*bitul*)	20
Waiting 12 months	41
Washing dishes	13
Water loops	4
Wax coatings	43
Weak *ta'am*	4, 26
Weight vs. volume (*bitul*)	20
Weight, and *davar shebiminyan*	62
Welds, absorption of *ta'am*	10
Whey from cheese with non-kosher *ma'amid*	1
Whisky, and *aino ben yomo*	40
Whisky, as *davar charif*	14, 16
Wine barrel, *bitul* calculations	20
Wine barrels, and coffee beans	60
Wine fusel oil	26
Wine, and *aino ben yomo*	40
Wine, with non-kosher mother of vinegar	1
Worcestershire sauce	12
Worm in radish	16
Yad soledes bo	49
Yavesh b'yavesh	61
Yavesh b'yavesh, and *issur mashehu*	34
Yeast, as a *ma'amid*	1
Yedias hata'aruvos, only the perpetrator knows	64
Yedias HaTa'aruvos, and *ChaNaN*	3
Yesh lo matirim	33
Yesh lo matirim, examples	36
Yoshon, and ספק ספיקא	33
Yoshon, barley pearling on *chodosh* equipment	33
Yoshon, flour milling on *chodosh* equipment	33
Yoshon, flour with *chodosh* malt	33
Yotzeh from non-kosher	55
Zeh v'zeh gorem	2, 26
Zei'ah	6
כלי לכלי vs. אוכל לאוכל	7
אחשביה, see *Ach'shvei*	
אין בו טעם כלל	39

Topic	Chapter	Topic	Chapter
אין הבלוע יוצא מחתיכה בלא רוטב	7	יבש ביבש, see *yavesh b'yavesh*	
אין כוונתו לבטל	28	ידיעת התערובת, see *Yedias HaTa'aruvos*	
אין מבטלין איסור לכתחלה, see *Bitul issur l'chatchilah*		יוצא מן הטמא	55
		יש בזה כלי לחמץ	2
אינו בן יומו, see *aino ben yomo*		יש לו מתירין, see *yesh lo matirim*	
אינו מינו, see *aino mino*		יש שבח עצים בפת	55
איסור משהו, see *issur mashehu*		כדי נטילה	15
אם יחלק אין שמו עליו	30	כדי קליפה	15
אסור מתחלת ברייתו	30	כל דפריש מרובא פריש, see *kol d'parish*	
אפשר להסירו	24	כל קבוע כמחצה על מחצה, see *kol kavuah*	
אפשר לסוחטו	55	כלי העשוי להשתמש בשפע, see *asui l'hishtamesh b'shefah*	
אש שורף דבר מועט	5		
בריה, see *beryah*		כעין תורא	17
גזירה אינו בן יומו אטו בן יומו, see *aino ben yomo*		כריסו של תינוק נכוות בו, see *yad soledes bo*	
		לינת לילה, with *ChaNaN*	3
גידולים	55	מחליא ליה לשבח	16
גרירה	15	מילתא דעבידא לטעמא, see *avidah lit'amah*	
דבר גוש, see *davar gush*		מין במינו, see *Min b'mino*	
דבר המעמיד, see *Davar hama'amid*		מין בשאינו מינו, see *aino mino*, and see also *min b'mino*	
דבר חריף, see *Davar charif*			
דבר חשוב	62	מכוער הדבר	28
דבר שבמנין, see *davar shebiminyan*		מלח הבלוע מדם	25, 54
דבר שיש לו מתירין, see *yesh lo matirim*		מליח כרותח	54
דוחקא דסכינא	15	מלקות for eating a *beryah*	30
דפנות מקררות	50	מעמיד, see *Davar hama'amid*	
הבל הקדירה	57	מפליט ומבליע כאחד	9
הגדיל האיסור מדתו	38	מרדה	59
הדחה	15	נ"ט בר נ"ט, see *Nat bar nat*	
השביח ולבסוף פוגם	38	נותן טעם לפגם, see *nosein ta'am lifgam*	
זה וזה גורם, see *zeh v'zeh gorem*		ניצוק חיבור	53
זיעה	6	עירב בו דבר מר vs. נסרח גוף האיסור	4
זיעה בעלמא	6	נעיצה	15
זרוע בשלה	27	שלא כדרך אכילה vs. נפסל מאכילה	4
חביות גדולות	62	נפסק הקילוח, definition	13
חזותא, see *chazusah*		נפשו של אדם קצה מהם	46
חזקת כשרות, and *kashrus* scandals	64	נתבקעו	34
חילתית	14	נתגלגל, see *Nisgalgel*	
חלב דבני ריינוס, and *ChaNaN*	3	סופו להתפשט	3
חם מקצתו חם כולו	10	סלק את מינו ואת שאינו מינו רבה עליו ומבטלו	22
חמירא סכנתא מאיסורא	12	סלק את מינו, and *chodosh*	33
חמץ שעבר עליו הפסח, see *chametz she'avar alav haPesach*		ספק חסרון חכמה	23
		ספק ספיקא, see *sfek sfekah*	
חתיכה הראויה להתכבד, see *chatichah har'uyah l'hiskabed*		סתם כלים אינם בני יומן, see *stam keilim* are not *ben yomo*	
חתיכה נעשית נבילה	3	עבידא לטעמא, see *avidah lit'amah*	
טיפת חלב	4, 10	עכבר	44
טעימת ישראל, see *tasting*			
טעימת קפילא, see *tasting*			
טעם קלוש	4, 26		

Topic	Chapter
עשוי להשתמש בשפע, see *asui l'hishtamesh b'shefah*	
פירשא	55
קבוע דאורייתא	63
קבוע דרבנן	63
ריחא, see *reichah*	
שינוי, and *kol d'parish*	63

Topic	Chapter
שיתננו על האש וירתיח, see *kovush*	
שפשוף	15
תקרובת עבודה זרה, and *bitul*	62
תרי משהו, and *chodosh*	33
תשמישו תדיר, see *stam keilim ainum b'nei yoman*	
תתאה גבר	52

Made in the USA
Las Vegas, NV
07 October 2024

b610a831-753e-41be-8e23-bd7d0de25c67R01